S0-CDQ-290

the Unofficial Guide™ to Dealing with the IRS

Robert G. Nath

Macmillan • USA

Macmillan General Reference
A Simon & Schuster Macmillan Company
1633 Broadway
New York, New York 10019-6785

Copyright © 1999 by Robert G. Nath

All rights reserved, including the right of reproduction in whole or in part in any form.

This publication contains the opinions and ideas of its author[s] and is designed to provide useful advice to the reader on the subject matter covered. Any references to any products or services do not constitute or imply an endorsement or recommendation. The advice presented in this publication is not intended for use by any particular person and does not constitute the rendering of legal or accounting advice. The publisher and the author[s] specifically disclaim any responsibility for any liability, loss or risk (financial, personal or otherwise) which may be claimed or incurred as a consequence, directly or indirectly, of the use and/or application of any of the contents of this publication.

Certain terms mentioned in this book which are known or claimed to be trademarks or service marks have been capitalized.

Alpha Books and Macmillan General Reference do not attest to the validity, accuracy, or completeness of this information. Use of a term in this book should not be regarded as affecting the validity of any trademark or service mark.

Macmillan is a registered trademark of Macmillan, Inc.

ISBN: 0-02-862683-4

Manufactured in the United States of America

10 9 8 7 6 5 4 3 2 1

First edition

This book is dedicated to my wife, Judy, for her patience, her editorial skills, and her managerial skill in juggling the demands of our three children. Judy's invaluable editorial suggestions, refinement, eye for detail, and humor helped to make this book complete.

This book is also dedicated to my three children, Jennifer, Cheryl, and Daniel. Their enthusiastic hugs and the end of the day always gave me the extra energy I needed to burn the midnight oil.

and

To my father, Jack H. Nath, and to the memory of my mother, Claire S. Nath, who were always there when I needed them.

Acknowledgments

Many helped in many ways to bring this book into print. My colleagues James H. Jeffries III, Esq., and Eric L. Chase, Esq., contributed valuable insights and suggestions to the text, Former revenue officer Deluvina Valdez reviewed many of the chapters and contributed valuable suggestions. R. Sue Williams, Patty Feury and Liz Simmons typed (and retyped) the manuscript. I also received the encouragement of my partners, Dexter S. Odin, Esq., and James B. Pittleman, Esq., and editorial suggestions as well from them, my partner John Dedon, my sister Barbara Gold, my brother Ronald Nath. my father Jack H. Nath, my brother-in-law Ronald Sussman, and my in-laws June and Jules Sussman. I also thank my agents Perry Knowlton and Andrew Pope of Curtis Brown Ltd. and John Jones, Debra Englander and Richard Staron at Macmillan for their efforts to bring this book to the public.

Contents

The *Unofficial Guide* Reader's Bill of Rights

We Give You More Than the Official Line

Welcome to the *Unofficial Guide* series of Lifestyles titles—books that deliver critical, unbiased information that other books can't or won't reveal—*the inside scoop*. Our goal is to provide you with the *most accessible, useful* information and advice possible. The recommendations we offer in these pages are not influenced by the corporate line of any organization or industry; we give you the hard facts, whether those institutions like them or not. If something is ill-advised or will cause a loss of time and/or money, we'll give you ample warning. And if it is a worthwhile option, we'll let you know that, too.

Armed and Ready

Our hand-picked authors confidently and critically report on a wide range of topics that matter to smart readers like you. Our authors are passionate about their subjects, but have distanced themselves enough from them to help you be armed and protected, and help you make educated decisions as you go through your process. It is our intent that, from having read this book, you will avoid the pitfalls everyone else falls into and get it right the first time.

Don't be fooled by cheap imitations; this is the genuine article *Unofficial Guide* series from Macmillan Publishing. You may be familiar with our proven track record of the travel *Unofficial Guides*, which have more than three million copies in print. Each year, thousands of travelers—new and old— are armed with a brand new, fully updated edition of the flagship *Unofficial Guide to Walt Disney World*, by Bob Sehlinger. It is our intention here to provide you with the same level of objective authority that Mr. Sehlinger does in his brainchild.

The Unofficial Panel of Experts

Every work in the Lifestyle *Unofficial Guides* is intensively inspected by a team of top professionals in their fields. These experts review the manuscript for factual accuracy, comprehensiveness, and an insider's determination as to whether the manuscript fulfills the credo in this Reader's Bill of Rights. In other words, our Panel ensures that you are, in fact, getting "the inside scoop."

Our Pledge

The authors, the editorial staff, and the Unofficial Panel of Experts assembled for *Unofficial Guides* are determined to lay out the most valuable alternatives available for our readers. This dictum means that our writers must be explicit, prescriptive, and above all, direct. We strive to be thorough and complete, but our goal is not necessarily to have the "most" or "all" of the information on a topic; this is not, after all, an encyclopedia. Our objective is to help you narrow down your options to the best of what is available, unbiased by affiliation with any industry or organization.

In each *Unofficial Guide* we give you:

- Comprehensive coverage of necessary and vital information
- Authoritative, rigidly fact-checked data
- The most up-to-date insights into trends
- Savvy, sophisticated writing that's also readable
- Sensible, applicable facts and secrets that only an insider knows

Special Features

Every book in our series offers the following six special sidebars in the margins that are devised to help you get things done cheaply, efficiently, and smartly.

1. "Timesaver"—tips and shortcuts that save you time.
2. "Moneysaver"—tips and shortcuts that save you money.
3. "Watch Out!"—more serious cautions and warnings.
4. "Bright Idea"—general tips and shortcuts to help you find an easier or smarter way to do something.
5. "Quote"—statements from real people that are intended to be prescriptive and valuable to you.
6. "Unofficially…"—an insider's fact or anecdote.

We also recognize your need to have quick information at your fingertips, and have thus provided the following comprehensive sections at the back of the book:

1. **Glossary:** Definitions of complicated terminology and jargon.

2. **Resource Guide:** Lists of relevant agenices, associations, institutions, Web sites, etc.

3. **Recommended Reading List:** Suggested titles that can help you get more in-depth information on related topics.

4. **Important Documents:** "Official" pieces of information you need to refer to, such as government forms.

5. **Index.**

Letters, Comments, and Questions from Readers

We strive to continually improve the *Unofficial* series, and input from our readers is a valuable way for us to do that.

Many of those who have used the *Unofficial Guide* travel books write to the authors to ask questions, make comments, or share their own discoveries and lessons. For Lifestyle *Unofficial Guides*, we would also appreciate all such correspondence, both positive and critical, and we will make best efforts to incorporate readers' feedback and comments in revised editions of this work.

How to write to us:

Unofficial Guides
Macmillan Lifestyle Guides
Macmillan Publishing
1633 Broadway
New York, NY 10019
Attention: Readers' Comments

The *Unofficial Guide* Panel of Experts

The *Unofficial Guide* editorial team recognizes that you've purchased this book with the expectation of getting the most authoritative, carefully inspected information currently available. Toward that end, on each and every title in this series, we have selected a minimum of two "official" experts comprising the "Unofficial Panel" who painstakingly review the manuscripts to ensure: factual accuracy of all data; inclusion of the most up-to-date and relevant information; and that, from an insider's perspective, the authors have armed you with all the necessary facts you need—but the institutions don't want you to know.

For *The Unofficial Guide to Dealing with the IRS,* we are proud to introduce the following panel of experts:

> **Thomas Locicero** Mr. LoCicero, B.A., M.S., CPA, is a self-employed Certified Public Accountant with 30 years experience in tax, accounting, and management advisory matters. Mr. LoCicero is a tenured associate professor at

St. John's University teaching accounting and investment courses. His prior experience includes 13 years with the IRS as Revenue Agent, Group Manager, and Branch Manager in the examination division and 6 years with international accounting firms as Senior Tax Manager.

Mr. LoCicero was a contributing editor to "Passive Activity Loss Rules," published by Warren, Gorham, and Lamont (1989). Mr. LoCicero's particular area of expertise is tax consultation to attorneys and accountants in Brooklyn; tax preparation for corporate, partnership, and individual clients; and representation before federal, state, and city tax authorities.

Deluvina Valdez   Deluvina Valdez is an enrolled agent who runs her own tax consulting business in Colorado Springs, Colo. She represents individuals and businesses nationwide in collection matters before the IRS, specializing in offers-in-compromise with an offer acceptance rate of over 90% Valdez began working with the IRS in Denver in 1980, graduated magna cum laude from New Mexico Highlands University in 1982, then accepted a permanent position as a Renenue Officer in the Collections Division. Her collection background is extensive, including experience with levies, liens, seizures, bankruptcies, trust fund penalties, redemptions, and all other collection matters. Valdez left the Service in 1991, and spent several years with the Justice Department in Washington, D.C. before starting her own business, the Tax Collection Consultants. She can be reached at her e-mail address: TCC@kktv.com.

Introduction

"The Congress shall have power to lay and collect taxes..."

—U.S. Constitution, Article I, Section 8, Clause 1

"The Congress shall have power to lay and collect taxes on incomes, from whatever source derived, without apportionment among the several States, and without regard to any census or enumeration."

—U.S. Constitution, 16th Amendment

From these simple words and humble origins has sprung the one government agency that touches nearly everyone—the Internal Revenue Service. It's also one of the most complex of agencies. That complexity, coupled with the IRS's potent enforcement powers, sometimes generates confusion, fear, and misunderstanding.

As our government's need for money increases every year, this agency is blessed or cursed by Congress with the task of policing a 3,000-page tax code that intrudes ever more into daily life. Well-meaning efforts by reformers, as in the recent flat-tax and Taxpayer Bill of Rights debates, rarely slow a system that always seems to outlast its harshest and most frequent critics. For most of us, the encroachment of the IRS is like background noise, annoying but somehow tolerable. The tax collector's outstretched hand captures part of our paychecks. We file tax returns once a year. We answer the IRS's occasional questions.

For others, the IRS can be a nightmare that never ends. Every year, the IRS:

- Collects more than $1.7 trillion in taxes and fees;
- Conducts more than 1 million audits;
- Tries to find 5 million to 10 million people who have not filed tax returns;
- Penalizes other millions who did;
- Tries to collect more than $200 billion from over 10 million other tax delinquents; and
- Issues 3 million liens and levies in that effort.

The IRS is a silent partner in many divorces and marriages. It polices millions of businesses, large and small. It can levy on wages, ruin your credit, get your records by force if necessary, seize assets, and even sell your home. In cases of evasion or fraud, these tax police can throw you in jail.

But even as the IRS becomes more powerful, Congress asks it to do more, not less. The IRS now enforces more than 150 civil penalties, collects child-support payments, and polices our vast private pension system. It keeps your tax refund when you owe some other debt to the government. It regulates charities and performs myriad other tasks.

Every few years, citizens and their representatives raise a hue and cry about the system's supposed unfairness. The latest effort, the flat-tax debate, followed closely on the heels of other reform proposals such as a consumption tax and value-added tax. So far, all these "abolish the IRS" movements have died a quick death. Like it or not, the tax system is here to stay. We might as well learn to deal with it.

But clearly *some* reform is afoot, even if slowly. For the last six years, the IRS has advertised a new way of doing business. To the agency, or at least to its headquarters in Washington, D.C., this "revolution" is as sweeping as any in its history. It represents a change in attitude, style, and method that will affect every one of us. Some of these ways live up to their promise. As to others, there is more promise than results.

In the past, hearing the letters "IRS" always produced a measure of respect or a stab of fear. This is the agency that sent Al Capone to jail when no one else could. This is the agency that seizes your salary, puts a lien on your home, and disallows your deductions. But it is also the agency that loses paper, mishandles your return, makes you wait years for refunds, and gives you bad tax advice. In the past, the IRS made only modest efforts to correct its "tough guy" image. The IRS was an enforcement agency; it wanted us to know that.

Things began to change about six years ago. The tax system started to break down. The IRS was being crushed under mountains of paper. It was losing returns, misfiling documents, and mistreating tax-payers. Horror stories began to surface. Congress held the usual hearings and the media publicized the worst stories. Moreover, the agency had to admit that some of those stories were true.

What has changed? The "new" IRS wants us to see it as a business, not a bully. Some of its new "businesslike" ways will translate into real dollars, true savings, and refreshing changes in the way we deal with the agency every day. But other changes will make life harsher for some people.

The first part of the agency's change was to join (or catch up with) the electronic age. The IRS has embarked on a ten-year program to modernize the entire tax system. Some parts of the program are already in place and functioning, and are a welcome change.

For example, millions can now file their returns electronically, resulting in quicker refunds. When you move around the country, the IRS has more and better information, more quickly available "on-line" in your new location. Correspondence with the agency is getting easier, though it still has a long way to go. Another good side of the electronic revolution is that our paperwork burden will abate. From electronic filing, to "one-stop reporting" of wages and wage information, to cutting down on letter-writing blizzards between taxpayers and the agency in favor of telephone calls—all of this will eventually make a big difference, though it has only just begun.

But the electronic age in taxes also means that Uncle Sam will watch you more accurately and close-ly. The government will know where you live and when you move, so hiding will be more difficult. The

IRS is always exchanging information about your taxes with state governments and is becoming more efficient all the time. So even if the agency can't track you, your new state of residence can, and it will send electrons to the IRS telling where you are.

For nonfilers—that is, people who have dropped out of the tax system—the chances have gone way up that the IRS will now find you and get you back in the system. For the rest who do file, audits will become more scientific. Using sophisticated computer programs, the agency will eventually "know" whether your business is likely to produce more taxes—and then go after those taxes. Its computers will "sense" where the dollars are and where the cash is hidden.

The second big change is in the way the IRS collects taxes. The welcome mat is now out for the millions who owe money to the IRS. Six years ago, the agency decided to write off its uncollectible accounts and get what it could from the rest. To settle over $100 billion of accounts receivable, the IRS liberalized the offer-in-compromise program, under which the IRS will settle for less than the full amount owed. And, true to promise, the IRS now accepts about half of all offers made, up from less than 20 percent only four years ago.

But watch out for the teeth behind the sweet talk. If you ducked the system for years and have now been persuaded that the IRS will be a "nice guy" about your old taxes, be careful. Once you are back in the system, they know where you are, and if your offer is not accepted, you're now a new customer.

There is also real change for people who can't qualify for an offer but have to pay all they owe. The liberalized installment agreement program means that about 97 percent of delinquent taxpayers will qualify to pay over time. Again, this is both carrot and stick. Most people eventually default on their agreements to pay taxes over time. For them it is back to square one—full collection by force.

Finally, the IRS wants to entice 5 to 10 million tax system dropouts to come in from the cold. These are people who have not filed federal income tax returns in one or more years. Sometimes the default can be six years, ten years, or longer. To get these people back into the system, the IRS promises some leniency if they come in voluntarily. Those who do, however, can look forward to dealing with local IRS tax collectors if they owe money on those returns— and most do. All in all, the new IRS will be more efficient, with all that "efficiency" implies. Efficiency may mean more prosecutions, sharper audits, and better collections. But everyday tax life may become somewhat simpler. Efficiency will ease many every-day burdens, reduce paperwork, speed refunds, and result in fewer errors.

This book is intended to navigate through the most common, most important issues people encounter with the IRS. Many times you simply need to get along with the agency. At other times the IRS becomes a series of traps with frustration all along the way.

Despite the frightening complexity of the tax code, enforced by the one-sided powers the IRS enjoys, there is no need to fear this agency or need-lessly lose a tax battle with it. All you have to do is understand the system and its people and take advantage of the many rights at your command.

This guide gives you a battle plan when you go to war with the IRS over collection of taxes. The IRS may have the death rays, but you have star shields and even a few weapons of your own. Understanding how to use them can save you thousands of dollars and oceans of tears. The guide also levels the field in that much-dreaded aspect of tax life—the tax audit. This part encourages you to face audits head-on, and to appeal unfavorable audit results to get a better deal. Another section explains when and how you can fight the IRS in court—and possibly win. Other chapters explore the many ways in which the IRS is part of our everyday lives—from filing returns, to not filing returns, to organizing records, even to many ways of getting money back from the IRS.

In most chapters you will find case examples. Most are drawn from actual reported court decisions, with the names and places changed, and the facts condensed.

Meet The IRS

▪ The imbalance of power▪ Where the
disparity came from▪ The IRS pyramid▪ How
the IRS learns about you▪ How the IRS
assesses a tax▪ How long can they keep at it?

PART I

How the IRS Operates

Most of us realize, at least vaguely, that the IRS has extraordinary powers to collect the taxes people owe. And those who face an IRS audit or collection problem face these powers head-on. The agency's full arsenal displays a range of powers people ordinarily think should not be given to the government, or at least not in a single agency. But the agency's powers have all been granted by your legislature and mine, the U.S. Congress, and the federal courts have consistently upheld these powers as legal and constitutional. While the IRS usually exercises most of its authority with great forbearance, sometimes bordering on reluctance, its powers are available in any case. In this chapter you will learn about the IRS's organization, its vast powers, how it learns all about you, and how it comes to send and collect a tax bill.

The IRS's draconian powers

In starkest form, the IRS has the power to:

- Invade your business and seize its equipment and other assets;

- Seize your personal bank accounts without court order;

- Make legally-binding tax assessments, and enforce them, without court order;

- Seize other assets, such as your retirement accounts, insurance policies, even your home;

- Sell them to the highest bidder without your consent;

- Send information about you to the states, Congress, the president, the Department of Justice, and other government agencies, without your consent;

- Adjust your tax accounts, shifting payments among tax years, without your prior knowledge or consent;

- Propose new taxes, impose penalties and interest, and make you sue to contest them;

- Sue you for back taxes, foreclose on property, and even set aside transfers and conveyances to others;

- Get virtually anyone to talk to Service agents about your taxes and financial affairs, and obtain most documents that bear on those financial affairs;

- Terminate your tax year and issue an instantaneous assessment, in cases of fraud and evasion, or where collection is in jeopardy. If you show an inclination to flee, the agency can even obtain a civil writ of arrest.

> **"**
> [Taxes are] the lifeblood of government...and their prompt and certain availability an imperious need.
> — *Bull v. United States*, 295 U.S. 247 (1935)
> **"**

Against all of these powers, you have few weapons:

- You can't sue the IRS for an injunction to stop it from assessing or collecting taxes;

- You can't sue the IRS to stop it from gathering information, or from revealing that information about you to other agents, other government agencies, even to customers, clients, and friends;

- You can't sue the IRS at all without the consent of Congress, a consent given in only a few (about ten) types of tax cases.

Once again, every one of these IRS powers, and your corresponding legal incapacity to fight them, have been ruled constitutional in case after case. Because of this severe mismatch, if the IRS did not exercise its powers with restraint, in all likelihood Congress would swiftly take the powers away.

The most recent and clearest example of this is the IRS Reform and Restructuring Act of 1998. Among many other things, this new law may severely restrict the IRS's authority to collect taxes, by subjecting its actions to multiple levels of review.

Where it all came from

After the states ratified the Constitution in 1789, Congress created only four cabinet agencies, among them the Department of the Treasury. Throughout most of its history, the Treasury Department simply collected customs duties, administered the sale of public lands, and managed the federal debt, budgets, and other financial matters. Income and employment tax collection were not even on the Treasury's original list of chores—there *were* no such taxes.

Watch Out!
With limited exceptions, you can't stop the IRS from seizing your bank accounts or other assets, or from selling them without your consent and sometimes without your knowledge.

Unofficially...
In terms of how
much money it
collects, the IRS
is about as effi-
cient now as it
was three
decades ago. In
1967, it cost the
IRS 45 cents to
collect $100 of
taxes. In 1996,
that cost was 49
cents per
$100 of taxes
collected.

Congress enacted the first income tax during the Civil War, as one of a series of special war measures. Accordingly, on July 1, 1862, Congress created the Bureau of Internal Revenue, the IRS's predecessor, to oversee tax collection. This first income tax was repealed, however, immediately after the end of the war. Another income tax lasted for a brief period, from 1870 to 1872. Twenty years elapsed before Congress enacted the next income tax, in 1894, and the Supreme Court ultimately declared that tax unconstitutional.

The modern taxing system began only in 1913, when Congress passed and the states ratified the 16th Amendment to the Constitution, which gave the federal government the authority to assess and collect income taxes. Even then, however, taxes were not assessed on most citizens: only the rich and famous paid taxes. And it was only in 1950, a mere forty-eight years ago, that Congress brought the modern Internal Revenue Service into being.

What a difference these years make! The agency now has over 110,000 employees serving a national office, four regions, thirty-three districts (subsets of regions), ten service centers, a data center, and a computer center.

The Agency orchestrates a tax system that rakes in more than $1.7 trillion every year, processes more than 2 billion pieces of paper, polices more than 200 million tax returns of seven main varieties, generates 150 million pieces of correspondence, and performs a host of other functions. The agency has more than 27,000 revenue agents and other tax return auditors, 17,000 revenue officers and other tax collectors, and five thousand special agents—the ones who investigate tax crimes.

The IRS pyramid

The IRS has always been organized in a pyramid, though that may change in 1999.

1. The highest layer is the **National Office,** which consists of the commissioner and a staff. This office bears responsibility for the overall administration of the Internal Revenue Service. Its various assistant commissioners formulate broad policy based on national trends in audits, collection, data gathering, freedom of information, criminal investigation, and other areas of national interest.

2. The next layer consists of four **regional offices.** Each has its own regional commissioners, regional inspectors, regional counsel, and other functions. These offices generally coordinate all of the districts within their jurisdiction and report to the national office.

3. The next layer, **district offices and service centers,** do the real work of the Internal Revenue Service. Each one of 33 districts is headed by a District Director who is chiefly responsible for implementing national policy. District Directors have wide authority to set procedures within their districts, authority they do not hesitate to exercise.

IRS functions

Each of the three levels of the IRS pyramid is also organized into three major functions: examination, collection, and criminal investigation. (There are also Taxpayer Service and Taxpayer Advocate functions.)

Unofficially...
The idea behind
the IRS reorgani-
zation seems to
be functional.
Most individual
taxpayers have
common prob-
lems that should
be administered
within a single
unit. Similarly,
the other units
would have spe-
cialized expertise
for the entities
under their
jurisdiction.

The Examination Division audits tax returns. It employs revenue agents and tax auditors. The Collection Division, staffed by revenue officer groups, collects the taxes. The Criminal Investigation Division, using special agents, investigates tax crimes. The Office of Taxpayer Advocate is a section that is supposed to take your side when you are choking on IRS red tape. There is also a Taxpayer Service function that attempts to resolve administrative problems within each district.

In almost every case, these revenue agents, tax auditors, revenue officers, special agents, taxpayer service representatives, and problem resolution officers do the real work of collecting taxes, auditing returns, and performing related duties. These are the officers you will face when you have an audit, collection, criminal, or other tax problem.

A shake-up in 1999?

The new Commissioner of Internal Revenue, Charles Rossotti, has promised a shake-up of the agency, including a total restructuring of the way it is organized. The goal behind this restructuring is to modernize the IRS and implement five guiding principles:

- Understand and solve problems from the taxpayer's point of view;
- Expect management to be accountable;
- Use balanced measures of performance;
- Foster open, honest communications;
- Insist on total integrity.

To accomplish these goals and modernize the IRS, the national office and regional office structure would be replaced by four management functions, each with autonomous responsibility in its own area.

These four groups are the management of:

- Individual taxpayers with wage and investment income
- Small businesses and self-employed taxpayers
- Large business taxpayers
- Employee plans/exempt organizations and state and local governments.

These new functional units will not be in effect until at least the year 1999.

You can't hide from the IRS

In almost every IRS investigation, of whatever type—audit, collection, or criminal investigation—the agency needs to know more about you, your family, your finances, and your tax return. Agents use three classes of sources:

- you
- public records
- third-party records and sources

You

The IRS gathers most of its information voluntarily, simply by asking you questions. For example, a revenue agent might call or visit you and ask, "What is your justification for deducting medical expenses on Schedule A of your tax return?" A revenue officer might ask, "Where do you keep your bank accounts, stocks, and bonds?" Frequently, agents also make their requests in a more formal way, such as by an Information Document Request or a letter.

Public records

The second main source of information is public records. Years ago, the well-known actor Peter Sellers starred in the movie Being There. Mr. Sellers played Chauncy Gardener, a childlike housekeeper

Bright Idea
In most cases, it's wise to volunteer the information the IRS requests from you. The IRS can obtain it anyway, and things usually go easier if you cooperate.

who had spent his entire life tending one house. Through a series of errors, Chauncy becomes an adviser to the President of the United States. In the course of checking into Chauncy's background, investigators discover that Chauncy has absolutely no history—no tax returns, no military history, no purchase and sale of assets—nothing.

There are no Chauncy Gardeners in America. Almost everyone leaves tracks that become public records. It could be buying a home, filing a court case, getting a government check, earning interest on a bank account, or inheriting property. The IRS has access to public records just like anyone else, and its agents comb through these records all the time, using all of these sources of information.

> **66**
> [The IRS] can investigate merely on suspicion that the law is being violated, or even just because it wants assurance that it is not.
> —*United States v. Powell*, 379 U.S. 48 (1964)
> **99**

Third-party records and sources

The third source of information is third parties. These could be banks, brokers, mortgage lenders, or insurance companies. Customers, clients, friends, relatives, and employees are also sources.

The law gives IRS agents of every job description the widest possible authority to "inquire after and concerning" anyone who may be liable to pay an internal revenue tax. To enforce this authority, the IRS has subpoena power.

The IRS's version of this administrative subpoena is called a summons, used when someone does not voluntarily testify or supply data. The agency resorts to this summons power thousands of times a year. In almost every case, it gets the information, records, and testimony it wants. In fact, you and the third parties the agency summons can be held in civil contempt of court for refusing to obey a summons. Technically, it's also a crime to disobey a summons, though this crime is rarely prosecuted.

The Service's summons power is far-reaching. It extends to any "books, records, papers, or other data which may be relevant" to your tax liability or its collection. That language, straight from the tax code, was deliberately chosen to be all-encompassing. It means the IRS can get any corporate record, deed, bank account, or accountants' records, certain lawyers' records (where the attorney-client privilege does not apply), and almost anything with a number on it.

The IRS has used this summons power to seize all types of paper records, notes, telephone records, computer tapes, and even guns. Very few defenses exist against the IRS summons. If you are the summoned person, you can plead the Fifth Amendment, but that is seldom an effective legal defense and leads the agent to assume you are hiding something. You may invoke other privileges such as the attorney-client or doctor-patient privilege, but these are narrowly defined and easily breached. Beyond these defenses, the IRS can legally force you or a third party to produce virtually any record or document, and to testify about it.

The tax collection officers

The IRS uses tax collection officers at three different levels.

The notice level

First, there is the notice level. If you file a return that shows a balance due or your return is audited and you owe more tax, you will get a series of up to five notices. Each is of increasing urgency, instructing you in no uncertain terms to pay. The notice cycles vary from a few weeks to twenty-five weeks, depending on whether you've had past defaults,

Watch Out!
Many people have heard of the new "accountant's privilege," part of the 1998 tax reform act. Don't rely on this. While it may protect you in some cases, tax facts are generally not privileged, and if you are about to confess a true tax crime, your CPA will rush you off to a lawyer anyway.

what type of tax is involved, and other factors. Since 1997, anyone who owes taxes for a back year also gets an annual statement of the amount still due. You will never see the collection officers who issue these notices; they're all generated by computer, automatically, and in the millions, from various service centers and the national computer center in Martinsburg, West Virginia. The IRS collects billions of dollars simply by sending these past-due notices.

ACS

If the notice system fails, your case will be transferred to the Automated Collection System (ACS). Basically it's a computerized, paperless accounts receivable system. All delinquent accounts, business or personal, appear on the ACS computer screens. ACS has call sites all around the country. The collection officers in ACS will call you, your employer, friends, third parties, and anyone else they can think of to get full payment of the taxes. They will also negotiate with you for installment agreements. Failing that, they will generate notices of levy on your wages, bank accounts, and other assets, and file notices of federal tax lien. Again, the IRS collects billions of dollars this way.

The "field"

If the ACS fails to collect the tax in full, or if the case is complicated, ACS will send the case "to the field." This means that your case goes to a living, breathing revenue officer in one of the districts around the country.

Revenue officers have many jobs, but their foremost task is to collect the most money they can in the shortest possible time. They are thoroughly trained in collection techniques, including how to locate you and your assets, how to interview you, and when to take strong action. They know how and when to seize assets, when not to, and when to negotiate with you. Still, they are terribly overworked. Revenue officers may have between 40 and 100 cases to pursue at the same time. And the moment they close one case, another takes its place.

Cases are assigned to revenue officers according to the priority of the case. If you owe $500 for one year, that will receive low priority. If you owe $100,000 for five years, that might be a high-priority case.

Revenue officers also investigate nonfilers, that is, people who have not filed one or more tax returns that are now overdue. Chapter 7 discusses the nonfiler in more detail. If you are a nonfiler, revenue officers might persuade you to file the delinquent return, make one for you, or refer the case for criminal investigation.

Revenue officers all go out into the field to collect the taxes. They have ample authority to investigate your personal and business affairs. To that end, they may ask you to complete financial statements, narrative statements about your business, and other documents. They can investigate your business to decide whether your workers are employees rather than independent contractors, making your business liable for the payroll taxes attributable to these workers. In the case of a business that has defaulted on its payroll taxes, they will investigate whether you are personally liable for a portion of those taxes. (See Chapter 6.)

To collect your back taxes, these revenue officers have the authority to seize any property you or your business owns. The process is easy. They simply send a notice of levy, affix a notice of seizure to the prop-

Unofficially...
Revenue officers are primarily motivated not by retribution but by money—they want to collect as much as they can in as short a time as possible.

Bright Idea
Pay close attention to the 1998 tax reform act. It has potentially put a big dent in the authority of revenue officers to seize and sell assets. (Chapter 4 discusses this in more detail.) These new procedures will not stop the IRS completely, but can usually slow it down.

erty, or haul it away. They also have the authority to sell noncash assets and apply the money to your back taxes.

It's these powers that make the tax collection system a force to be reckoned with. When you make an offer in compromise, request an installment agreement, or seek relief from a tax lien, you are required to deal with revenue officers. When you have not filed a tax return, revenue officers can recommend that you be prosecuted, or, if not, they can file a return for you, and then file a notice of tax lien to "protect the revenue."

The tax auditors

Revenue agents and tax auditors of the examination division audit income and other tax returns of businesses and individuals. Like revenue officers, these agents have the summons power. They can also propose more taxes, penalties, and interest. You are usually stuck with their figures unless you can persuade a higher office in the IRS or a court to change them. And in all of these dealings, the burden of proof is usually on you.

The criminal investigators

Special agents of the criminal investigation division investigate eleven main types of tax crimes and related offenses—about thirty tax and nontax crimes in all. Tax evasion, false statements, and failure to file a return are the most common. Special agents also have the summons power, and never hesitate to use it when they meet resistance. Special agents conduct raids, seize records and monies, trace assets, and arrest people who try to interfere with any other agent of the IRS.

The Office of the Taxpayer Advocate

The newly named Office of Taxpayer Advocate has branches in every IRS district to help you when you run into a bureaucratic brick wall. They are like ombudsmen, slashing through the red tape, taking your side in cases of extreme hardship, and performing many other useful, pro-taxpayer functions. Chapter 14 discusses what they do and how they help.

These are the categories of people you will usually meet when you have an IRS problem. They know their jobs and are fully aware of their power and authority. So if you want to be on an equal footing with them, you, too, need to know your rights and powers and use them wisely.

How the IRS assesses a tax

The end result of an audit is a tax bill, which is also the beginning of a collection case. Since most confrontations with the IRS are about money, that tax bill becomes critically important. Understanding that tax bill is the first step to dealing effectively with it. Sometimes these bills seem to strike out of the blue. Other times you'll see them coming but are unable to duck. Or the amounts can be a total surprise. Many people have difficulty comprehending these bills.

The plain vanilla bill

The most common type of bill is the one you get if you don't pay the tax due with your return (called a "balance due" return). When you send your return to one of the seven regional service centers, someone opens the envelope, unfolds the return, and scans it manually or by machine into a computer. The agent enters your name, other identifying data, and key income and deduction items. Electronically filed returns are "entered" automatically.

Timesaver
The 1998 tax reform act strongly encourages the IRS to get people to file electronically. In fact, electronic filing is a true blessing if done right. It greatly reduces errors, speeds your refund, and, in general, makes it less likely that the IRS will bother you about small mistakes.

The agent punches the numbers into a huge data bank called the master file, on which everyone has an account. More than 140 million accounts track individuals; 40 million accounts track businesses in the business master file. Your master file contains a running balance of all your transactions, credit or debit, year by year. Master file records go back a minimum of ten years. So, when you send in a return, your own individual master file account will register "return filed and liability assessed."

The IRS codes this and other transactions with one of about 400 different three-digit codes, such as "150" for filing a return or "670" for a later payment. Then the computer records the amount you pay with the return and a code indicating "payment with return." It will already have noted how much withholding is credited to your account. If you have paid everything, the balance in that year's "module" will be zero. If you have overpaid, the computer generates a refund check. An underpayment generates a notice of tax due. All of this is done automatically and electronically. Because the IRS keeps track of more than 200 million tax returns, it could not be done any other way.

Incidentally, the Service is constantly changing the number and frequency of the notices it sends. Recent legislation, in 1997 and 1998, also requires the IRS to send additional notices of tax due, and to make the notices clear, plain, and *non-technical*.

If you owe a balance, you'll normally get up to five notices over as many as twenty-five weeks (sometimes fewer). The first will be a *Request for Tax Payment*. The second, third, and fourth are more insistent. The fifth, sent by certified mail, is a *Notice of Intent to Levy* or Final Notice. That legally required notice means the IRS can start seizing your assets thirty days after it is sent. And the agency means business. When the thirty days have run out, the next thing you know, your bank account has been seized or your wages levied.

If there's an error in the IRS notices, call its toll-free number to alert the computer that you believe the bill is incorrect, so the IRS won't seize your property. Your follow-up evidence normally completes the correction process. Always make note of the person(s) to whom you speak and when.

This balance-due notice is the most basic type of bill. There are some variations on it. If you have a credit or refund on file from a previous year, the IRS will absorb that first, then bill you for the rest or generate a refund. Another variation occurs when a business loses money. The law allows the business to carry that loss back for three tax years. But the IRS will not do this automatically. You must file a special form to carry back your losses three years, a step that already begins to slow down the computer.

Paying even the basic, plain vanilla tax bill can be complex. What if you have moved? Millions of people do every year. There's no way the IRS can keep track of every move. Besides, it is up to *you* to tell the Service where you have moved.

If you don't let them know, calls, notices, and levies may go unanswered, and you will be hard-pressed to undo them. Even if you never receive the notices, the IRS has complied with the law by notifying you (at the last address it knows) before seizing assets.

These balance-due notices also show accrued interest and penalties. The first notice may tell you how the penalties and interest are calculated, but

Bright Idea
It's crucial to check the accuracy of payment-due notices as soon as you get them. If they're wrong, call and write to the IRS to make corrections or notify the system of an error. The notice contains clear, well-written instructions on how to do this. Don't wait for that last notice.

Timesaver
Use Form 8822 to notify the IRS of your move. If you file a tax return from a new residence, the IRS computers log in your new address. But they do not routinely or quickly check back to prior years, and there are many mistakes. You are always better off being proactive.

later notices just tack "accruals" onto the last balance. You can learn the breakdown of tax, penalty, and interest by asking for a transcript of your account from any IRS office or calling the nationwide toll-free number, (800) 829-1040.

Remember also the magic of daily compounding. Interest on your tax bill is compounded daily on everything: the tax, the penalties, and the interest. You are in fact being charged interest on interest, and it's all perfectly legal. Daily compounding raises the effective IRS interest rate by more than 1 percent (to more than 9 percent currently). If you throw in the typical penalties, you're often paying an effective interest rate of more than 20 percent.

Everyone knows that the IRS receives billions of documents every year. Its computers now match your W-2 forms to your income tax return. The computers also match dozens of other types of reports. These might include Forms 1099 for interest, dividends, and miscellaneous income, and many others. The IRS even matches information from state governments.

If there is a mismatch between one of those forms and your return, the IRS will send you a notice. Even more scary is the case where the IRS finds you have received income, but it does not detect a filed return. That makes you a "nonfiler," discussed in Chapter 7. This "matching" bill works in the same way as any other. Either you pay it, or the IRS will assess it and attempt to collect.

The audit bill

The second most common type of bill is the one you get following an IRS audit. If you and the agent agree on the audit results, you sign an agreement form and the agency sends you a bill four to six weeks later. These are relatively straightforward, at least if you have understood the audit itself. The bill will usually recite the tax, penalties, and accrued interest to some date near the expected date of payment. Interestingly, these audit-related bills often do not find their way to the master file.

Applying your tax payments—the "voluntary payment" rule

Many times you will get a bill that seems to have no rational connection to what you think you owe. (The only consistent feature is that the bill exceeds what you think you owe.) This can happen because the IRS has applied your payments to some other tax bill, or to interest and penalty first, before applying it to taxes as you intended. Like any other creditor, the IRS applies payments in its own best interest. The IRS manual tells the technicians to apply the money to the oldest liability, first to tax, then to penalties, and last to interest.

To avoid this problem, you may "designate" your payment, a simple procedure to tell the IRS where you want the money applied. The agency must honor your request as long as the payment is voluntary, hence the name "voluntary payment" rule. In this context, *voluntary* means

1. You are paying outside bankruptcy.

2. The IRS has not levied the money you are paying.

Designating your payments can often save you big bucks. Let's say you owe taxes for 1990 and 1995. You intend to file bankruptcy in 1996 to discharge the taxes from 1990 (see Chapter 13, "The Bankruptcy Alternative"). You send in the payment,

Bright Idea
Designating a payment is simple. In the memo portion of the check, write, for example, "Apply to tax year 1996, tax only, Form 1040, SSN: 123-45-6789." It also helps to send a cover letter with the same instructions. Just be sure your designation is crystal clear.

instructing the IRS to apply it to 1995, the tax for which is not dischargeable if you file for bankruptcy in 1996. Undesignated, your payment would have been applied to the 1990 tax, leaving the full liability for 1995 unpaid even after you discharge 1990's remaining taxes in bankruptcy.

A variation of the voluntary payment rule is the designation on Form 1040 itself. People who over-pay their taxes during the year can check a box to apply the resulting refund to the next year's taxes. But if you owe a back tax, the IRS's computers will ignore this and instead offset your overpayment against any other tax you owe regardless of the voluntary payment rule. So far, the courts have sustained the IRS on this issue.

Nonfiler assessments

IRS studies estimate that between 5 million and 10 million people have not filed one or more tax returns. That's an astounding number for a system that supposedly depends on voluntary compliance, but it rings true with actual experience. While non-filers come in from the cold all the time, each year's filing deadline creates new ones or extends the delinquency of others. It is not unusual to see cases where people have not filed for three to six years; ten to fifteen years is not unknown.

When the IRS catches a nonfiler, it can:

- prosecute;
- assess and collect;
- both prosecute and assess and collect.

The agency mostly just wants people to file and pay, so usually it won't prosecute. Instead, the agent opens a case file for you for each year of nonfiling.

Then, if you don't file quickly on your own, the agent makes a "Substitute for Return" rather than a true return. She starts with a blank Form 1040 or 1040A for the year involved. She fills in your name, address, and Social Security number, then opens an account in the individual master file for that tax year. The agent then "audits" the blank return. Gross income will consist of anything the agent can find that you received. Usually the income figures come from bank accounts, W-2 and 1099 forms, or any other source of income.

How about deductions? When the IRS is preparing a substitute form, it will only give you one exemption—yourself. It will also give you a standard deduction, but no itemized deductions, even if it knows you have some. In other words, the IRS makes all assumptions against you and in its favor, then generates a proposed tax bill from the result. You have the right to contest that bill, but you must go to court to do so (or request audit reconsideration; see Chapter 8 and below). If you don't contest the bill—and most people don't—the computer generates the tax assessment and the IRS comes after you to collect.

Despite the apparent arbitrariness of such a bill, you can still fight it. To do so, file a true return, request reconsideration of your bill, and make arrangements to pay the true tax.

The unknown "assessment from hell"

Sometimes, the IRS sends a bill no mortal can decipher. The dates are wrong and the amounts are wrong. It gives little clue as to what the IRS is really upset about. Such bills are quite rare, but if you do receive one, you must take action *immediately*. Spend

Moneysaver
If you file a true
return after the
IRS has prepared
a substitute
return, you will
probably not be
excused from
penalties. But at
least your tax
bill will be lower
than the one the
agent generated,
because the IRS's
return will make
all assumptions
against you.

no time thinking about it or questioning whether you might have owed some tax in a past life. Immediately call the nationwide 800 number, (800) 829-1040, identify yourself, and ask what the bill is all about. Get as much information as you can. If this information allows you to figure out why the IRS sent the bill, you can either accept the charge or challenge it. But if you still can't figure it out, take the next step and call the Office of Taxpayer Advocate. They're on your side in cases like this, and they help willingly.

The goal with this or any other tax bill is to determine whether you in fact owe all of the tax, penalties, and interest for which you have been billed. If you don't, you'll need to assemble any evidence you have and send it to the IRS for reconsideration. If you do owe what you've been billed, the IRS will force you to make arrangements to pay it.

How long can they chase you?

The basic rule is: the Service can audit you for three years, and collect for ten years more. See Chapter 8 for further discussion of the statutes of limitations pertaining to audits.

The ordinary collection statute is ten years from the date the IRS "assesses" the tax, that is, sends your bill; prior to 1989, the deadline was six years. Note the big difference between *assessment* and *collection.* Let's say the IRS assesses your tax on the deadline three years after you file your return. The collection period starts then and lasts ten years from that date. So you may be living with this IRS problem for thirteen years.

It can be even longer if the period of limitations for assessment or collection is extended. For instance, if you file an offer in compromise, the statute of limitations on collection is extended for the time the offer is pending, plus one year. So you may decide not to file an offer if you are already close to the deadline. The ten-year collection statute is also suspended any time you or your assets are in the custody of a court, plus six months. This includes bankruptcy or receivership. So filing for bankruptcy stops the tax collection period until the bankruptcy is over, plus six months. This is the trade-off the law exacts for keeping the IRS at bay under the bankruptcy laws.

You also extend the collection period when you file an emergency Application for a Taxpayer Assistance Order (Form 911). (See Chapter 14.) The extension is the price you pay for quick intervention to avoid a harsh collection result. If you contest an IRS levy or an IRS lien, as now allowed under the 1998 tax reform act, again the statute of limitations on collections is suspended.

Remaining outside the United States for a continuous period of six months also suspends the collection period. It starts running again when you return to the United States. Many times taxpayers extend the collection period by written agreement, called a *waiver* (Form 900). The Service asks for this waiver for many installment agreements that would otherwise lapse at the ten-year deadline. Finally, the government can also take legal action to extend the ten-year period by suing you in federal district court to reduce the tax assessment to a judgment (Chapter 16). If the government wins, the tax lien is extended for more years, depending on your state's law governing such judgments.

Watch Out!
If you don't file a return at all, there is no statute of limitations governing how long the IRS can audit you.

Just the facts

- Always respect the IRS's powers, but don't be overawed by them. Understand the audit and collection process.

- Question every bill that does not seem right, and demand back-up and calculations.

- Meet all deadlines for submitting more information, or advise the IRS when you cannot.

- Seek help from a professional or the Office of Taxpayer Advocate in an emergency.

GET THE SCOOP ON...
- The IRS "menus" for audits and collection
- You do have defenses
- Do you need a tax professional?
- The care and feeding of your tax professional

Chapter 2

Why You Have Problems with the IRS

Americans have always had a love-hate affair with taxes. They hate paying them, but generally love having the federal government the taxes pay for.

But the link between what you pay and what you get for your tax money is diffuse, not direct. Paying taxes is not like buying a suit or ordering dinner at a restaurant. If you do those things and don't like the results, you can complain, maybe get a refund, and take your business elsewhere. With taxes, its different. Don't like the defense budget? Too bad, as many people found out when they excluded some tax payments to protest the Vietnam War. Outraged over the $900 hammers the government could buy off the shelf for $3? You can write your congressperson, but you can't legally stop paying taxes.

So this built-in resentment against the IRS and paying taxes stems from the fact that taxes are not voluntary but are mandatory, and people can't clearly see the direct benefit of the hard-earned dol-

Watch Out!
The tax rules—
both substantive
and procedural—
are sadistically
complex. And
they change just
about every year,
thanks to the
same U.S. Con-
gress that
requires you to
know them all.

lars they pay. Few pay taxes joyfully or willingly, in part because they don't directly control their tax dollars in any meaningful way.

On a more practical level, this clash of interests makes for problems with the IRS over two issues:

1. Do you owe them money?

2. If you owe it, can you pay it all?

For the vast majority of us, the answer to both questions is "yes." Most of us owe some money to the IRS. We pay it in part through the withholding system; we calculate the remaining debt when we fill out and file our tax returns. Our problems with the IRS arise when either of these questions is answered "no," but the IRS says "yes."

And the problems persist because:

■ The IRS usually interprets the tax laws in its own favor, resulting in more taxes on audit than we expected to pay when preparing our returns.

■ The IRS collects taxes with a bias, resulting in coercion and, on rare occasions, oppressive tactics. The IRS always has the iron fist inside the velvet glove.

■ Preparing a tax return is a nightmare even under the best of circumstances, and people are always distracted from this task by everyday events in their lives. This applies both to assembling records for an audit and to storing them for several years.

All of these issues result in problems big and small for many Americans. Some people come into the crosshairs of the IRS; others who avoid that bullet get headaches from the sheer effort involved in staying out of sight. To paraphrase Winston Churchill, our tax system is the very worst ever invented—except for every other one.

Menu choices big and small

The tax system has been described as at once coercive and cooperative: coercive because the IRS can throw you in jail for tax evasion and seize assets without your consent; cooperative because if even a small percentage of taxpayers (estimated around 10 to 20 percent) were to refuse to cooperate openly, the system would quickly come crashing down.

For the reasons noted above, a large number—but relatively small percent—of Americans have problems with the IRS. The rest simply try to keep a low profile.

Yet despite this ultimate coercion, Americans do have choices. Imagine yourself going out to eat. The waiter brings a menu; you select an appetizer, main course, and later a dessert. The waiter may regretfully say, "Sorry. That menu choice is not available. Please choose another." With any luck, the choices are to your liking and you leave satisfied.

Dealing with the Examination or Collection Division of the Internal Revenue Service is something like dining out (though nowhere near as tasty or satisfying). It's often a pleasant surprise to discover how wide an array of choices the law and IRS procedures allow for managing your back-tax bill or tax audit.

It's simply not the case that you must always pay in full, and immediately, or go to debtor's prison. The tax audit and collection "menus" contain powerful choices that apply to almost every tax debt, business or personal. You can choose one "course," then another, or a combination. You can even start with one and then switch to another later.

Sadly, many people resign themselves to no menu at all; they believe that whatever the IRS says

Unofficially...
Even more choices are available for back-tax payment following passage of the 1998 tax reform act in July 1998. Throughout this *Unofficial Guide*, you will find many of the new, taxpayer-friendly provisions.

goes. Not so. Knowing the full range of choices, and how and when to make them, can give you true power in an otherwise one-sided contest.

That's the good news. The bad news is that the IRS also has its own menu of choices it wants to impose on you. Agents of the IRS can make one or more choices, or select them in combination. (Or the IRS "chef" may inform you that some courses are not available.)

Naturally, your selections may be radically different from the choices the IRS makes. The key to survival is to understand your options from the start, make your choices wisely, and look into the IRS's priorities and prepare to deal with them. True enough, the IRS has great power to back up the choices on its menu, but with some exceptions the Service restrains the use of its own power.

Your audit "menu"

Let's see what's on the menu today.

1. **Contest the audit right away.** You can't choose whether you're audited, only the tactics to use if you are. You can cave in to the agent's proposed new taxes or fight the audit at that level. You'd be surprised how often agents will make favorable adjustments or decisions, though clearly they usually side with their employer.

2. **Fight, then appeal.** Even if you've contested the audit and lost, you still have powerful procedural rights within the IRS. First, you can appeal. (Chapter 10 discusses this in detail.) At least in theory, the Office of Appeals is a neutral IRS office whose job description reads: "Settle this case if you can." In most cases, that's exactly what happens.

3. **Go to court**. You don't have to give up even if you "lose" on appeal. You can fight the IRS in court even without paying the tax. (See Chapter 15). You can pay the tax and fight in a different court (Chapter 16). In both courts, the judges are even more "neutral" than the IRS appeals officers. They call things as they see them. When taxpayers lose in these courts, it's often a function of bias in the law itself against taxpayers and in favor of the IRS, or a failure of proof by the taxpayer, who almost always has the initial burden in these cases.

You can also mix and match your audit menu choices. You can tell the IRS you want to go directly to court from the audit level. You can settle some issues and take the others to court. You can give up some issues, trade others, and so forth. This flexibility within the audit system gives you plenty of opportunity to make your case. But in the end, when you've made your choices, if you end up with a tax bill, your "collection menu" comes in to play.

The collection "menu"
The collection menu has even more choices.

Pay in full within thirty days
Some people who owe a back-tax debt can quickly pay in full: sell a stock or bond; borrow money; raid the mattress. Sometimes they may liquidate a nest egg, such as a retirement account they've been nurturing for many years. When the IRS catches them, they may reason, "Okay, you got me; it's worth any price to get you off my back." The stimulus of a single call or letter is often enough to spur the writing of a check or the rapid sale of an asset to pay in full. In fact, the IRS motivates millions to pay billions simply by asking for the money.

Watch Out!
The choices on the collection menu cover only whether, how, and how soon you pay, rather than whether you owe the tax in the first place.

Moneysaver
People are often
surprised that
bankruptcy can
ease your tax
pain at all. But
it's true. Always
consider bank-
ruptcy—even if
just a tip of the
hat—if you have
a big tax bill you
can't pay.

Pay in full, over time

If you can't pay in full right away, the installment agreement comes in handy (see Chapter 12). To be sure, the accrued interest and penalties make for financial torture, but at least you'll be able to see the end. While installment agreements can last an extremely long time, the IRS normally looks for full payment within thirty-six months or fewer. If you agree to stay within that time limit, you'll have lots of room to negotiate the details.

Pay part now, pay part over time

Suppose after liquidating some assets such as a stock, bond, or IRA, or borrow $5,000 from a rich uncle, you still can't pay the tax in full. The Service might allow you, or even force you, to pay the rest by installments.

Sometimes, if you need time to pay, you can *force* the IRS to accept this menu choice. The most important way is through a bankruptcy such as a Chapter 11 or Chapter 13 reorganization. (These names derive from chapters of the Bankruptcy Code.) In these bankruptcies, you essentially ask the bankruptcy court to approve a long-term install-ment agreement, sometimes up to five years. The IRS will often agree to your plan, or have little real-istic choice but to go along. Still, bankruptcy is strong medicine, because it ruins your credit and has other negative effects as well. (Chapter 13 of this book details the how and why of tax bankruptcies.)

Pay in part, write off the rest

Does the IRS ever actually write off a debt? Yes, through the offer in compromise program. (See Chapter 11.) Convincing the Service to accept an offer can be difficult, especially if you try to do it yourself without professional help. But if you succeed, you normally end up paying only a fraction of what you owe. The national average is about ten to thirteen cents on the dollar for accepted offers. This means the IRS gives up nearly 90 percent of the money on claims it compromises. Sounds great, so why not choose this menu option right away? Usually, because the IRS thinks that you can pay more than you will offer, or that you can pay in full now or over time. After all, its job is to try to collect to the max—quickly! Still, think about whether you may be eligible for an offer in compromise.

Pay nothing

The expression "you can't get blood from a turnip" applies in the world of IRS collections, too. In fact, the IRS classifies so many taxpayer delinquencies as "currently not collectible" it even has a separate form and verb for it (Form 53, as in "Let's fifty-three this case"). The IRS shelves these accounts for six months, a year, or more. The Service can in theory revisit your account, but it often does not. Whether "currently not collectible" status is desirable is another story, however. The federal tax lien stays in place. The tax debt can last for up to ten years, sometimes longer. And you are also subject to periodic reviews to see whether you are still as poor as before.

Reduce the amount you owe

Sometimes you can actually reduce the amount of tax you owe. An example is "audit reconsideration" (see Chapter 8). Even if your case is in "collection" status, you ask the IRS to reconsider it either because it is wrong or because the agency failed to consider some evidence. Another type of case

Bright Idea
Beginning in
1998, by law the
IRS must now
explain its inter-
est and penalty
computations in
clear, simple
language.

involves people who have failed to file federal income tax returns, so-called "nonfilers," for whom the IRS is authorized to make returns and assessments. Such people can always request audit reconsideration if they file true original returns.

You may also challenge the IRS's computations. True, the assessment is *usually* correct, but not always. Has the IRS correctly computed penalties and interest? Has it applied all of your payments? Has it applied them to the right tax periods? You are entitled to an accounting from the IRS simply by requesting it.

Any agent can pull your transcripts to check these items. If you don't understand some of the entries, ask for an explanation. If the agent can't explain an entry you believe is incorrect, that fact alone may be grounds to ask the agent to do more research or to postpone the payment of the tax until the discrepancy is resolved.

Finally, you can resort to bankruptcy to reduce your taxes. It's a widespread and tragic myth that you can never eliminate taxes in bankruptcy. In fact, you can. Income taxes are potentially dischargeable in bankruptcy. Even employment taxes, while not generally dischargeable, can sometimes be negotiated downward once a bankruptcy is filed. Still, filing for bankruptcy is a major step that should never be taken lightly. A host of nontax considerations should be in play.

Call the boss

You can appeal any collection agent's decision to at least one or two levels. Call the agent and state "I would like to speak to your supervisor. Please give me his/her name, title, and telephone number." If two levels of appeal do not work, sometimes you can launch a flanking attack by appealing to the Office of Taxpayer Advocate. Chapter 14 discusses this topic in detail.

Sue

Usually a last resort, suing the government over taxes can reduce your taxes or delay the day of reckoning. It can be downright thrilling if you win, and you'll be ecstatic if you also win attorneys' fees. Chapters 15 and 16 discuss the types of lawsuits available to contest taxes, when they are permitted, and the chances of success.

The IRS's "menu"

So far we have discussed *your* choices. Of course, the IRS has its *own* menu, with choices all its own. Here are some of the entrees:

Pay all—now!

First and foremost, the Service wants you to pay in full, right now, on the spot and immediately! In fact, most people can and do pay, even without being challenged. Were that not so, the shortfall of revenue would make the government collapse like a punctured tire. The IRS is hugely successful in persuading many taxpayers to pay in full "voluntarily," even if they owe one or more years of back taxes.

Pay in full now, involuntarily

Next on the IRS menu is the iron fist inside the velvet glove. The agency has vast enforcement powers by which its agents can seize and sell assets. Few of your assets can elude its grasp. The IRS wants people to pay voluntarily, but does not hesitate to use its enforcement powers in millions of cases.

Unofficially... More than 1 million people file for bankruptcy each year. This statistic gives some idea of how popular bankruptcy is, but no one knows how many people are unaware of their right to reduce or eliminate taxes through bankruptcy.

Unofficially...
These days, the tide for offers in compromise is "in." A new Commissioner, committed to taxpayer service, took office in 1998. Also, Congress bashed the IRS so much in 1998 hearings that the agency is at least temporarily more friendly.

Pay in full—soon

The Service can and will give you extensions of time to pay, within reason (*its* reason). As a rule of thumb, three to four months (usually fewer) is about as long as you will get to pay in full without making some other arrangement like an installment agreement. Installment agreements of up to three years are common. Often they last longer.

Pay part now and the rest later

The Service usually asks you to pay as much as you can now, such as by selling assets, borrowing against them, or borrowing from friends and relatives. Then it asks you to pay the rest over time through an installment agreement.

Pay all later

This is the installment agreement. It's on your menu, too, but it's way down on the fed's list (it may be high or low on your own list). The Service dislikes installment agreements, though a workable one that is paid in full yields the IRS a "profit"—the penalties. Installment agreements stretch out payment to the government and prolong the taxpayer's pain—neither is a result the IRS normally enjoys. Moreover, by recent count 80 percent of installment agreement payers defaulted before final payment. Why? People lost their jobs, expenses increased, or the installment amount was set too high to begin with. Still, the IRS approves about 2.6 million such agreements per year; despite the high failure rate, these agreements raise billions of dollars.

Pay part now, write off the rest

This is the *offer in compromise*. Officially, the IRS encourages agents to explore offers in compromise, especially if the taxpayer brings up the subject. Officially, too, the offer is a useful collection tool, that is, an acceptable way for a revenue officer to resolve a case. But in the real world, the tide shifts for and against offers. When the revenue officer considers an offer, it's sometimes because she is convinced there is little else she can do.

Pay nothing now or later

This applies to "currently not collectible" accounts. The Service recognizes reality: some people simply cannot pay their past-due tax bills—not now, maybe never. Unlike some businesses, the IRS will not write off the uncollectible bill, at least not until the statute of limitations on collection expires (normally after ten years). Instead, it will shelve the case as "currently not collectible" but may revisit the case in the future.

Sue the taxpayer

The IRS usually views lawsuits to collect taxes as a last resort. Still, it does not hesitate to use this option in many cases. Chapter 16 explains when and how.

Dueling menus and rules of the restaurant

Your goal is to select menu choices that are best for you and make them digestible to the IRS. This can often be done with a minimum of hassle and pain. Other times a struggle is inevitable. This book guides you on the best way to convince the IRS that your choices of appetizer, entree, and dessert are acceptable. You can start by learning the rules of the restaurant.

1. **Read IRS Publication 594**, "Understanding the Collection Process." It's a terrific publication—well-written and even-handed. It provides an

Timesaver
Always deal with
your audit or tax
bill promptly and
meet all dead-
lines. As much as
you may want to
forget about your
audit or bill, the
IRS will not.
Generally speak-
ing, the faster
you respond and
the more busi-
nesslike you are,
the better the
outcome will be.

excellent summary of your rights in the collection process. Those rights include the opportunity to reconsider your tax bill, make an offer, propose an installment agreement, engage a representative, and receive fair and courteous treatment.

2. **Insist on courtesy and confidentiality.** You have a right to fair, professional, and courteous treatment. If you don't get it, call the agent's boss. And, in turn, extend this same courtesy to the agents with whom you deal.

3. **Use the Problem Resolution Program.** If you run into major roadblocks or snafus, often the Problem Resolution Office (renamed in 1998 the Office of Taxpayer Advocate) can help. Appendix B contains a list of Problem Resolution Office numbers and addresses. Also consult Chapter 14 before running to the PROs.

4. **Understand your tax bill.** The IRS usually calculates your tax balance correctly. But sometimes it makes mistakes. Ask to see the agency's calculations, but don't use this as an excuse not to pay or otherwise address the back-tax bill.

5. **Put it in writing!** Document any significant statements, decisions, or evidence in writing. Send it to the IRS address listed on your tax bill or collection notice. *Without exception*, keep a copy of whatever you send.

Helping you get through it all

Do you need a tax lawyer or other tax professional to help you survive all of this? There's an old expression, "He who acts as his own lawyer has a fool for a client." This motto holds doubly true in tax matters.

The tax laws, regulations, and the IRS's internal procedures abound with detail after thorny detail, deadline after hidden deadline. Every day, people who "go it alone" miss these deadlines, requirements, and rules, undercutting or destroying their own cases. They don't realize they are committing legal suicide, and when they do, it's often too late for a tax professional to step in and rescue the situation. You don't *always* need a tax professional; indeed, many taxpayers handle their own matters successfully. But your chances of getting the best result are greatly increased if you either know what you're doing or hire someone who does.

You might need a tax professional if...

The following are some common situations where you might need a tax professional:

- **Criminal investigations.** In some IRS matters, you unequivocally need a tax professional. The best example is the criminal investigation. The moment you find out you are the subject of a criminal investigation, STOP! Call a tax lawyer immediately. This seems like common sense, but the IRS counts on taxpayers *not* to do this. When its criminal investigators, the special agents, come knocking at your door, they want one thing: to interview you or, in some cases, to seize your records under a search warrant. If your case is criminal, the agency already believes you have committed a tax crime; they now just want you to confess the essential facts under questioning. Consenting is equivalent to signing your own guilty plea. And, unfortunately, feeling intimidated, many taxpayers cave, spending two to ten hours with a special agent cataloging their crimes (though often they don't think of it as a confession).

Bright Idea
The IRS might not explicitly tell you they have opened a criminal investigation, so be alert to the signs. One sure sign is inquiries of your friends and neighbors. Another is an agent who knocks on your door, identifying himself as a "special agent of the Criminal Investigation Division" of the IRS.

After such an interview, your lawyer's role is reduced to arguing about the length of your sentence.

You have an absolute right to seek legal advice when the special agents—or any other agents for that matter—come calling. They understand this right and will not press the point if you insist on getting legal advice. No one can imprison you for seeking legal advice, but the IRS can and will prosecute you after you consent to an interview in which you "make their day."

■ **Bankruptcy.** Filing for bankruptcy should be done with the assistance of an attorney, preferably one who knows the tax aspects of bankruptcy. Some attorneys otherwise well-versed in the bankruptcy laws and the practices of their local bankruptcy courts lack expertise in tax matters, including bankruptcy tax matters. Since the reason you're going to them is to get relief from or manage your tax problem, be sure your bankruptcy lawyer has tax expertise as well.

■ **Civil suits.** If the government sues you or you want to sue the government, find a lawyer experienced in tax litigation. This would be true whether you are contesting a statutory Notice of Deficiency in the United States Tax Court (see Chapter 15) or your case proceeds in a federal district court (see Chapter 16). It's not absolutely essential for this lawyer to be versed in tax matters and procedures, but it certainly helps. Many otherwise fine litigators feel uncomfortable handling tax cases. Besides, tax litigators are not hard to find; each year the Department of Justice and the Internal Revenue Service graduate dozens into private practice.

Other civil matters

Aside from the cases mentioned above, it's not always obvious what type of tax professional you need, or even that you need one at all. To decide, think about some tax-related tasks and questions. Tax professionals are asked to provide a multitude of services. Among these are the following:

- **Preparing a tax return.** This is the most common service accountants, enrolled agents, and some tax lawyers offer. Surprisingly, anyone can be a paid tax preparer: you don't need a college degree, nor do you have to pass any test. The only requirements are that you prepare the return and be paid for it. Millions of people rely on paid preparers. If you're unsure of your work, you don't have the time, or you procrastinate (and who doesn't, from time to time?), find a qualified, well-trained tax preparer.

- **Offering tax advice on a pending transaction.** Thinking about selling a business? Selling a house and reinvesting the proceeds? Collecting disability payments or damages from lawsuits? Divorcing and dividing the assets? The tax impact of these and hundreds of other questions is not always certain. You may need professional advice about their tax implications.

- **Getting information from the IRS**. You may need to obtain a copy of your tax return from a past year, or a transcript of your account. A tax professional can help you cut through the red tape to get this information more rapidly.

- **Handling other disputes.** You may get into a fight with the IRS over someone else's taxes—an employee, a customer, or a client. Lien priority contests between the IRS and builders,

Moneysaver
You might be able to handle a simple correspondence or office audit by yourself, without hiring a tax professional. Of course, if you have been cheating on your taxes, this would be an excellent time to consult an experienced criminal tax attorney!

merchants, and financiers are extremely common. A professional's help is often critical in such a case.

- **Handling the IRS audit.** Do you need a tax professional to help you survive an audit? The answer depends on the type of audit, the amount of money at risk, and other factors. Consider engaging a tax professional for a full-scale field audit or a Taxpayer Compliance Measurement Program audit.

- **Addressing an error on a past tax return.** How should you handle a mistake on a prior return, such as overstating a deduction or failing to report income? Do nothing? Amend your returns? A tax professional's help may come in handy in making your decision.

The list of issues and questions with which a tax professional can assist you goes on and on. These are only some of the most common.

If you are still considering handling the matter yourself, consider two more questions.

First, how comfortable do you feel handling this matter by yourself? Answers range from "completely at ease" to "scared to death." And a little knowledge can be dangerous. Some tax rules are so obscure few people know they exist, and these arcane rules can destroy you. So check with an expert, if only to verify your own judgment as to whether you can handle the matter. People who are nervous about their tax issues, whether from fear of the IRS or insecurity about their own knowledge of the tax laws, often exercise clouded judgment, a fatal error in the tax business.

Second, is your regular tax representative—accountant, enrolled agent, or tax attorney—qualified to and comfortable with handling *your* matter? Not all tax professionals can handle every type of tax case. For example, some lawyers feel uncomfortable preparing returns; accountants may decline to handle a complex audit in cases where evidence is hard to assemble. You'll usually know your representative's comfort level from the start. If not, it's certainly fair to ask. Tax professionals have an informal referral network, so if yours does not feel up to the task, she usually has people to call for help. Sometimes the help may be a simple "Let me run this one by you." Other times the professional may recommend transferring your case. But you, the client, should never hesitate to pick up the phone and call your own tax professional to ask if she can handle *your* case.

Who are the tax professionals?

There are five main types of tax professionals who can represent you before the Internal Revenue Service.

- **Tax attorneys.** These are lawyers who have made tax their specialty. Almost all are graduates of law schools, and all have taken and passed the bar exam of at least one state. The law license alone entitles them to practice before the Internal Revenue Service in tax matters. Many such tax attorneys are former IRS or Justice Department (Tax Division) attorneys, and so have detailed knowledge of the workings of the IRS.

Unofficially...
Believe it or not, a few states allow people to take the bar exam and obtain a law license even without having gone to law school. California is one example.

- **Certified public accountants.** CPAs have studied accounting in school and have passed a rigorous CPA examination given by each state's society of CPAs. Certified public accountants are trained in all aspects of financial and tax accounting, as well as in tax return preparation. They often represent their clients before the Internal Revenue Service.

- **Noncertified accountants.** Like CPAs, noncertified accountants have long and rigorous training in all aspects of accounting and tax return preparation. They differ from CPAs only in that, for one reason or another, they have not taken (or passed) all parts of the CPA exam.

- **Enrolled agents.** Enrolled agents are non-lawyers, non-accountants who have passed a tough IRS examination on all aspects of tax law and tax administration, qualifying them to practice before the Internal Revenue Service. Though you don't have to be a lawyer or an accountant to take the Enrolled Agent examination, many enrolled agents do have an accounting or legal training.

- **Enrolled actuaries.** Like enrolled agents, enrolled actuaries have passed an IRS examination. Their field of expertise is limited to actuarial matters. This refers to the mathematical computations underlying retirement plans, pension plans, and deferred compensation plans. It also encompasses estates and trusts and other topics where sophisticated mathematics (actuarial calculations) must be made and defended.

Although their specific areas of expertise vary, most tax professionals are called upon to perform a number of similar tasks.

1. One of the most common is **handling tax audits and tax collection.** The professional will need to meet with you or at least confer by phone, analyze your case, and perform any necessary legal research. She must gather the facts and advise you of your rights and choices under the law, IRS regulations, the Internal Revenue Manual, and the vast array of unwritten IRS procedures that permeate the tax audit and collection culture. Sometimes she may call a revenue agent or revenue officer one or more times, write to him to argue your position in the audit, or defend you against collection actions. She will need to document your position legally and factually.

2. A second common task is the **protest**. The tax professional who files a formal protest (see Chapter 10) first needs to meet with you, analyze the facts and the law, and develop any more facts required to prove your case. He may follow this protest with more research, fact gathering, and finally a meeting with an appeals officer at which he argues your case. Then he may follow this meeting with more work. Finally, when the IRS has offered a proposed settlement, he will counsel you on whether to accept it or to litigate the matter.

3. A third task is **litigation**. A tax litigator is usually (but not always) engaged when all else fails and a case must be tried in court. The litigator has many tasks, the most important being meeting

Bright Idea
Sometimes it takes two, three, or more calls before you find the right person to handle your case, but the effort will be repaid. Ask other lawyers where they would go with a tax problem, including their own.

with you and your CPA or other tax professional; interviewing you and gathering facts; performing legal research; interviewing witnesses; preparing for trial; and trying or settling the case. The tax litigator must respond to the IRS's requests for pre-trial discovery, including depositions, and prepare to try the case. She will also need to discuss settlement with you and the IRS and, depending upon the outcome of the case, file or defend an appeal.

Finding a tax professional

The best way to locate a competent tax professional is by recommendation. Ask around. If you have a regular family or business lawyer, ask her. Inquire of the accountant or an enrolled agent who regularly does your work whether he feels comfortable representing you, or indeed whether you need representation at all. If he is not comfortable, maybe he can suggest someone to call.

Some tax professionals advertise in accounting journals, legal periodicals, sometimes the newspaper, the Yellow Pages, over the airwaves, and of course the Internet. Some tax representatives will even seek you out, such as by checking public records at county courthouses for filed notices of federal tax lien or IRS or state court judgments for taxes. Then they send advertisements or canvassing letters suggesting that you might need their services. Bar associations also maintain lawyer referral services and lists. Some tax advocacy groups also maintain lists of recommended professionals.

Regardless of how you come upon a tax professional, the critical issue is whether she can handle the matter at a cost you can bear. Moreover, in most cases, your tax representative cannot guarantee the outcome. After all, you are dealing with the IRS or a court, which has wide discretion whether to grant you relief.

Choosing an ethical professional

All tax professionals are subject to a strict code of ethics and practice. The formal name of this code is Circular 230, published by the IRS. Among other things, this code requires tax professionals to be truthful with the IRS, not to misrepresent the facts, and to be prompt in meeting deadlines. It also requires practitioners to submit records or information to the IRS promptly upon request and not to interfere or attempt to interfere with the IRS's efforts to gather information.

Practitioners must also exercise "due diligence" in preparing papers for the IRS and in ensuring that whatever they say or write to the IRS is correct. Finally, practitioners must not engage in any "incompetent or disreputable" conduct. And, of course, lawyers, accountants, enrolled agents, and all others must avoid conflicts of interest among their clients.

Lawyers, accountants, and enrolled agents are also subject to other codes of ethics, including those of state bar associations, ethical codes of state CPA or enrolled agent societies, and their own, hopefully well-developed, sense of right and wrong. None of these codes, however, require tax professionals to take positions against your interest. In fact, most specifically require the tax professional to represent your interests "zealously," as long as the professional remains within the bounds of the law.

Watch Out!
Always be alert to any unethical practice a tax professional suggests. Ask, "Is what you're suggesting within the bounds of your ethical codes?" If you get an equivocal answer, look elsewhere.

Choosing a tax professional

Bright Idea
Lawyers and CPAs have a new (though narrow and easily breached) communications privilege with prospective clients. This means that in some circumstances the IRS cannot compel them to disclose the content of what you and they discuss. So be candid with them. What you don't say will come back to bite your hand.

When choosing a tax professional, search in stages. First, once you have someone in mind, give her a call. Explain your problem in as much detail as you can, and answer any questions the tax professional asks.

Whatever your particular circumstances, always ask the following questions, either by phone or when you first meet the representative face to face:

1. **"Do you need more facts to understand exactly what my problem is?"** A good tax professional will spot all the issues, check deadlines and statutes of limitation, ask a dozen other questions you hadn't thought to ask, and spot dangers of which you may be only vaguely aware. Remember: There can be a big difference between answering your specific tax question and solving your overall tax problem. Hire the professional who will solve your problem.

2. **"Do you know much more than taxes?"** The best tax professionals know the Internal Revenue Code at a minimum. But they are also knowledgeable in commercial transactions, financing, loans, real estate, divorce, and bankruptcy, among other legal areas. This additional expertise is essential to you; the IRS's rights and yours often involve these areas of the law. Your tax professional can't suggest bankruptcy unless she knows whether bankruptcy will discharge the taxes or enable you to propose a viable plan of reorganization.

3. **"How much and what kind of experience do you have?"** No tax professional should take offense if you ask about his experience. Does he only represent people in court? Handle only audits?

Collection matters? How long has the professional been in practice? Ask what percentage of the professional's time is devoted to dealing with the IRS. Find out whether he knows the agents in the local office, and for how long. Don't be afraid to ask whether he enjoys a good reputation with them. You can be sure that every professional who has had a case or two in the local IRS office has some reputation. You need to know whether it's good or bad.

4. **"What basic game plan do you have in mind for my situation?"** Be prepared with the facts when you interview the professional. Above all, gather the paperwork—yours and the IRS's. The professional can save *hours* simply by reviewing the papers. A thorough tax professional will identify your goals and craft a plan to achieve them even if there are detours along the way.

   For instance, if you come in with a tax audit problem, you should be advised of the possible outcomes at each stage: the revenue agent's level, an appeal within the IRS, and possibly Tax Court. If you come in owing $100,000 in taxes, the professional should guide you on what to expect at each stage, and what the best and worst outcomes might be. Of course, not all possible outcomes are knowable at the first meeting; new legal and factual questions are not only common—they are inevitable. But the overall goals can usually be spelled out early on. In short, at the end of this meeting, expect to know at least generally where you are going and how you are to get there. In many cases you'll come out with a realistic, step-by-step game plan, including the strengths and weaknesses of your situation.

Moneysaver
Don't faint when you hear a lawyer's hourly rate. A lawyer who charges a high hourly rate is not necessarily "too expensive." She might be able to accomplish in two hours what a lower-priced lawyer could not accomplish in ten.

5. **"Have I understood what the professional is talking about?"** Make sure you understand your professional, both in general and in many of the details. If you do not, ask yourself whether that professional is right for you. The tax law can be frighteningly complex, of course, but it's not Sanskrit. A good tax professional can explain it to anyone. Albert Einstein once explained the theory of relativity to nonscientists in a short book entitled *Relativity.* Therefore, a tax professional should be able to explain your IRS rights and options to you. More important than any specific questions you might ask, always bear in mind that the tax professional will become your legal confidant and your moral confessor. Be sure that you enjoy complete comfort with the relationship, or look elsewhere.

The Cost

Most tax professionals charge by the hour; some on a contingency; some a combination. (Criminal cases cannot ethically be charged on a contingent fee basis.) While hourly rates are important, don't be put off by sticker shock. It's actually more important to know how much the engagement *as a whole* will cost, from start to finish and at each stage. Ask yourself whether you are getting value for your money. Is the expected recovery worth the cost? Remember that tax professionals usually cannot guarantee the outcome of an IRS fight, so you may be faced with spending without the absolute assurance of a good result.

Fees vary widely among various types of tax professionals. Lawyers charge anywhere from $50 to $500 per hour, depending upon their experience, their firm's practices, and their location, among other factors.

Accountants and enrolled agents often charge lower hourly rates than do attorneys, but, again, the range can vary considerably. There's no hard-and-fast rule, but accountants and enrolled agents' fees often range from $50 to $300 per hour and higher. These fee structures may sound high, but if you handle the matter yourself, you may only need a little guidance or hand-holding; this is not expensive, even at high hourly rates. In the end, it's all a cost-benefit analysis: What are you spending and what can you expect to get in return?

With these principles as your guide, choosing a tax professional with satisfying results will be easier. And above all, don't delay. The absolute worst course is to stick your head in the sand. Fighting the IRS effectively takes time. Moreover, if you delay, you will surely miss a number of deadlines.

Relating to the professional

An incredible amount of trust is taken for granted whenever you hire a tax professional to help with an IRS problem. Often it's a person whom you don't know or have just met. Sometimes the professional comes recommended by someone you trust, other times not. You are about to hand this person a lot of *your* money and responsibility for your financial life. Always remember that the trust factor should be used for your benefit.

In some ways the tax professional involved in a difficult collection or audit matter is like a father confessor. You can and should tell that person anything and everything that might conceivably bear on your tax problem; let the professional sort out the relevant from the unimportant. The professional needs to know *you*—your personality, your toler-

ance for controversy and difficulty, and many other
things—before he or she can guide you successfully
through the IRS maze. Relate to him as a human
being as well. After all, he's heard many stories. You
may think yours is unique, and perhaps it is. But
your lawyer, accountant, or enrolled agent has heard
dozens of similar ones. The professional you hire is
and should be a friend as well as an adviser. Viewing
him in this way can almost always be to your benefit.
You'll give more of yourself and get more in return
by way of a good result.

Just the facts

- Your problems with the IRS always involve two
  ultimate questions: "Do you owe?" and "Can you
  pay?"

- The tax system gives you ample room for good
  choices in handling any audit or collection matter. Know those choices and act on them wisely.

- Find out early if you need professional tax help.

- If so, choose carefully—then follow your professional's advice and guidance.

IRS Weapons to Collect Overdue Accounts

PART II

GET THE SCOOP ON...
■How the lien arises ■ What the lien
attaches to ■ Overcoming and releasing
the lien ■ Discharging property from the
lien ■ Suing the IRS over lien releases

The Federal Tax Lien

Chapter 3

The federal tax lien is a legal charge or encumbrance on a taxpayer's property—such as your house or car—to secure the eventual payment of the tax debt. You can think of the tax lien as a legal ball and chain that attaches to each piece of property you own. The more you owe, the heavier the ball and chain.

As we will see, the federal tax lien usually does not cause problems until the IRS files public notice of it. Once filed, however, this notice can cause embarrassment, damage your credit, and even hamper your efforts to sell property. The IRS is fully aware of this impact—indeed, they count on it. Agents know that tax lien filing is a big club, and they carry it around and use it from time to time. If the tax you owe is large enough, and if you pay slowly enough, the IRS will almost always file a "Notice of Federal Tax Lien" to "protect the revenue." Translation: The agency will file the notice to make sure you do not sell property out from under its claim.

Unofficially...
In fiscal year
1996 the IRS
filed 750,000
Notices of Feder-
al Tax Lien; in
1995, 799,000.

Once the IRS files notice of the lien, there is usually little you can do with your properties unless you get the IRS's input and consent. Later in this chapter, we'll examine how to deal effectively with the federal tax lien even after notice of it has been filed.

How the lien arises

When you file a tax return of any kind—income, employment, estate, or other—the IRS enters the tax you report as an assessment on its computer system, called the *Master File.* The same is true when the IRS assesses a tax after an audit, or makes an assessment without your knowledge or consent. The IRS keeps track of Individual Master Files by Social Security number, and Business Master Files by Employer Identification number.

This "assessment" is simply the official recording of your tax liability on the IRS's computers, signed by a designated officer. At the point of signing, you officially have a tax assessment. The computer also tracks any payments you make. Since most people pay their taxes in advance (with payroll deductions) or, at the latest, when they send in their returns, the self-assessment on the return is considered fully paid the moment the return is recorded on the master file.

Tens of millions of people, however, file returns with a balance due. These are usually income, employment, or estate tax returns. Of course, the IRS immediately assesses the taxes on these "balance due" returns and sends notice to the filer, demanding payment.

If the taxpayer does not send payment within ten days, the federal tax lien automatically goes into effect. At this point, you don't actually see that the lien has arisen, since notice of it is neither sent to you directly nor filed publicly. It's a secret lien, known only to the IRS and the taxpayer (who is presumed to know that the lien is in place). The lien lasts until it is paid or becomes unenforceable because the statute of limitations has passed.

If you do not pay after ten days, the IRS begins sending a series of ever more threatening demands for payment. Individuals typically suffer through five notices, while businesses sometimes receive only two. At this point, the IRS really gets rough. Agents call; they threaten to file a notice of lien, seize your assets, or levy your wages. You can avoid these painful results by paying in full or by agreeing to an acceptably short installment. If you do not, the IRS files a Notice of Federal Tax Lien.

This notice is a one-page form filed with the land records of your city or county; some state laws require that it be filed in another office—for example, the Office of the Secretary of State in your state. The notice includes name and address, the tax periods involved, the type of tax involved (by form number), and the amounts owed.

What the lien encumbers

The federal tax lien is not a laser-guided smart bomb, zeroing in on a precise piece of property. It's more like nerve gas, contaminating everything in its path.

By law, it attaches to everything you own: all of your right, title, and interest in every piece of property, anywhere in the world. This surprising feature of the tax lien makes it different from every other creditor's rights to your property. Sometimes a tax-

Watch Out!
The 1998 tax reform act now requires the IRS to verify the balance due, and that the lien filing is appropriate, considering the taxpayer's circumstances and the value of the equity in the property. But of course, it is still the IRS who decides what is "appropriate."

Bright Idea
Make a lien search when you are thinking of buying certain types of property. In buying a home, this is routine. For business buyers, this should be routine as well, though it is often overlooked.

payer will say "The IRS has put a lien on my house." Yes, on his house, and on everything else the taxpayer owns—automatically. Your mortgage and other non-IRS liens attach to specific pieces of property; the federal tax lien is universal. Many a sad businessperson has discovered this fact after buying the assets of a failing business. She thought she got a bargain, only to find that the federal tax lien followed the assets right into her hands.

Here are some important examples of the federal tax lien's reach. It encumbers:

■ Real property, including every home you own, wherever located. To make the lien enforceable against third-party claims, however, the IRS has to file public notice of the lien in the city, county, or state office where the property is located. If it does not, the tax lien will not attach to that property when it is sold.

■ Money you might have on deposit in escrow with a court, a real estate agent, or elsewhere.

■ Your bank account, brokerage account, insurance policies, and other near-cash property. It also attaches to lawsuits or claims you may have against other people, licenses (such as liquor licenses), certain property you transfer in a divorce, property you transfer to third parties, stolen property held by the police, partnership interests, and interests held in trust.

■ The vested portion of your retirement plans, such as a pension plan or IRA, and your vested share of a profit-sharing plan. The IRS may not be able to get at this money right away (if you can't), but it's still valuable property, and, as such, the lien attaches to it.

Example: a business

James and Joseph went into business together as "Jim's Boutique." Joseph was the silent partner who supplied start-up money. Everything went well until they failed to pay some payroll taxes. The IRS filed a notice of lien and levied on the partnership's bank account. The partners went straight to court, screaming that the money belonged to them individually. "You're right, guys, that's not the partnership's money," said the court. "It belongs to James and his silent partner, Joseph." But this makes no difference: the lien still attaches to the bank account, because the partners were personally liable for the debts of their partnership. Therefore, the IRS could levy their personal assets.

Example: marriage

Jordan and his wife, Jodie, were happily married for many years. Their financial life was not as blissful. Jodie had recently filed a claim for disability compensation with the Social Security Administration, then unfortunately passed away soon thereafter. The couple, who filed joint returns, owed $13,000 in back taxes, and the IRS had filed a Notice of Federal Tax Lien. Jordan was otherwise destitute. Social Security granted Jodie's claim and issued a check for $14,000, payable to Jordan and Jodie. The money was exempt from all normal creditors' claims. Twenty days later, however, the IRS levied on the $14,000, claiming the funds were subject to the federal tax lien.

So here's the picture: Jordan's wife had died, Jordan was destitute, and the IRS successfully claimed Jodie's disability money. By law, the IRS tax lien, unlike the claims of ordinary claimants, attached to "after acquired" property, including Jodie's disability windfall.

Timesaver
Your lien search will go much more quickly in our information age. Records are increasingly available in electronic form. In some states you can even use the Internet to check court records for liens. You can also have a search done by paralegals or staff at title companies.

Example: lawsuit

Chad was merrily driving along a Kentucky road one day when a monster eighteen-wheeler came out of nowhere and plowed into him. The inevitable lawsuit followed. The trucking company set up a settlement fund for Chad. That's the good news. The bad news is that at the time Chad owed federal taxes, and a lien had arisen. Who got the money? The IRS, of course.

The IRS lien does not always prevail

Examples like those above litter the casebooks. Time after time, the government has enforced the federal tax lien against all types of property, including alimony payments, accounts receivable, loans, condemnation awards, military pensions, reserve accounts, trust accounts, and just about anything else that has value reducible to cash.

Still, despite its pervasiveness, the lien filing does not steamroll everything in its path. The IRS respects the "first in time, first in right" principle. So, for instance, a properly recorded first mortgage on your home takes precedence over the federal tax lien.

The same is true for personal property subject to a prior lien. So the lien filing poses no problem for your lender, who almost always records its interest first.

If you sell property before the tax lien is recorded, that lien does not attach to the property, because it is no longer yours when the lien notice is filed. This important principle is really common sense: If you have sold, transferred, or made a gift of property at the time the tax lien arises, there's nothing to which the lien can attach. If however you conveyed it in an effort to evade the government, that's fraud. The long arm of the IRS can then reach the property in the hands of your transferee.

Superpriorities

As noted above, when you are considering buying properties such as businesses and homes, you should check to be sure that no lien attaches to the property, because the IRS lien will follow the property into your hands. Despite the power of the tax lien, however, you don't always have to worry about it even if it is filed. In several types of property sales, the lien simply does not attach to the asset you are buying or selling no matter when the lien is filed. The rationale in each of these cases is that commerce would grind to a halt if every buyer had to conduct a lien search before buying property from a seller. These cases include the following.

1. **Securities.** When you buy and sell stocks, bonds, notes, and so forth, you don't have to worry about the seller's tax debts. Without this legal exception, financial markets would clog quickly.

2. **Motor vehicles.** This exception protects the buyers of new and used vehicles from the tax lien, unless they in fact know that the tax lien exists.

3. **Retail property.** No one checks to see whether the Big Pricebreak Store has a tax lien on file before they buy a television or refrigerator, and no one should have to. But if you buy the store's inventory in bulk, or if you buy to help someone evade or hinder the collection of taxes, then the tax lien attaches to whatever you buy.

4. A **casual sale** such as a garage or yard sale. In such cases, the property has to be sold for less than $250 and the buyer must not actually know there is a lien on file.

Unofficially...
Additional super-priorities protect repairpeople, mechanics' liens, some attorneys' liens, and some commercial and real estate financing. Also protected are some insurance, endowment, and annuity contracts. Finally, banks that give passbook loans are also protected.

That's the bad news. Because of the lien's power, you are always better off convincing the IRS not to file a notice of lien. But if you own realty, or if you owe more than $10,000, the IRS will almost always do so.

Overcoming the federal tax lien

Still, don't lose hope. Working to discharge property from the lien is the solution to selling the property. The tax lien causes people two major heartburns:

- It ruins your credit.
- It sabotages the sale of your property.

If you want to refinance or sell property, any title search will reveal the lien. Many mortgages contain "no lien" clauses, which will trigger technical default if you allow a lien to be recorded, even if you have never missed a payment. The same is true for many security interests in personal property.

Credit rating

The IRS does not contact credit reporting agencies about the filing of a lien. As a result, lien filing or not, your credit rating usually remains intact until you try to borrow more money or the credit reporting agency has some other reason to check your debts. Although credit rating companies store millions of data files, they usually record only what is reported to them. They do not sit down each month and say "Okay, this month let's investigate 10,000 people to see if tax liens have been filed against them." They normally check only when one of their clients, like a mortgage or title company, asks them to check, or when someone sends them credit information. Only then will they discover the notice of lien. Even then, they may not always check every place the lien has been filed.

Still, if your goal is to borrow more money, or to sell or refinance an asset, it does not matter whether the credit reporting agency finds out about the lien. You are required by law to disclose your tax debt on any financial statement you prepare in connection with the application.

A drag on selling property

The second biggest complaint people make about the federal tax lien is that it undermines their ability to sell their property. When lenders discover you have a federal tax lien on file, they will minimally get slightly nervous, and at times will run far and fast.

One thing the IRS could not do (until 1996) to solve this problem was to "unfile" the notice of lien. Regardless of whether the notice was filed appropriately or not, once a notice was filed, it became part of one's permanent record, although certain things could be done to avert its worst effects. Many people complained about this practice. So in 1996, as part of the Taxpayer Bill of Rights, Congress gave the IRS the authority to withdraw a Notice of Federal Tax Lien.

The agency can withdraw the notice if the filing was premature or against agency procedures, or if you entered an installment agreement. It can withdraw to "facilitate the collection" of the taxes or promote the best interests of you and the government. Of course, the discretion is left mostly to the IRS, so you should not expect wholesale withdrawals of liens; the IRS views the filing of a notice of lien as one of its most powerful weapons. Still, this new possibility exists, and you should not hesitate to ask for it, particularly in the case of property sales.

Moneysaver
When applying for a loan, call the IRS at (800) 829-1040 to get a current IRS transcript of the balance due on your tax lien. Since the IRS does not regularly update tax liens in the land records, your old one may fail to reflect payments. Your lender, however, will want this evidence of the current balance due.

Bright Idea
If the IRS refuses to withdraw the lien notice, you can possibly sue. The law now allows several agency-level and court challenges for "unauthorized" collection actions and failures to "release" a federal tax lien. These theoretical possibilities are virtually untested in real life, however.

Even if a notice is filed and not withdrawn, however, you should not give up on trying to sell your property. The law gives you some flexibility to get around this lien.

Releasing the lien in full

Outright release of the filed notice of lien is extremely rare. You can ask for such a release, however—indeed, the IRS must grant it—if any one of the following conditions applies:

1. You don't owe taxes at all, but the IRS erroneously files a notice of lien in your name;

2. You give a bond to secure payment of the taxes;

3. You pay the full liability (including penalties and interest);

4. The statute of limitations on collection expires.

In the first case, you must notify the IRS of its error, and it must issue a certificate of release stating that the lien filing was erroneous.

The second option is so rarely used that most revenue officers don't even know where to send you to buy a tax payment bond acceptable to the IRS. The reason for this is simple: in most cases, if people could afford to buy these bonds, they could afford to pay the tax.

The third and fourth possibilities, full payment and expiration of the statute of limitations, are more realistic. Some people outlast the tax collector, usually a ten-year wait from the first assessment. If you haven't signed an extension of time for collection or taken some action that extends it by law (such as filing for bankruptcy or making an offer in compromise), you can ask for a certificate of release of the federal tax lien once it expires.

If you think the ten years have passed, call your local IRS office or the toll-free number (800) 829-1040 and ask for a "literal transcript" of your account to be sent to you. Ask the IRS technician whether the liens in your name have expired.

A transcript will tell you how old the assessment is. Once you are sure the assessment is more than ten years old and has not been extended, write the district director (the chief IRS official in your IRS district) and ask for a certificate of release to be filed. The IRS is normally prompt about filing these releases. If it delays, you can appeal the delay within the IRS and even sue for damages if the delay is too long. Chapter 16 discusses whether and when you can sue the government for its failure to release a notice of lien.

The third way to get a release is to pay the liability. Obviously, this is not an option for most people. If they could have paid, they would already have done so.

But people's financial circumstances change. People borrow money, come into an inheritance, or earn more money and might decide they want to pay the taxes.

For example, Sudden Sam had a federal tax lien going back to 1977; the lien had been extended into 1994 for various reasons. The IRS was threatening to sell his property. After all that time, he had made some money and bought valuable property. Now he was in a position to borrow against the property and liquidate some retirement accounts to fully pay the liability. In that way, he protected the value of his major properties against the discount that would have resulted from a forced tax sale.

Watch Out!
Discussing your liens with the technician carries some danger: the agent might wake up and refer your case for more collection. But that danger is usually small. Still, if you want to play it safe, ask solely for a transcript.

Bright Idea
You are considered to have "paid in full" if the IRS accepts an offer in compromise and you have paid the offer amount. An accepted offer "settles" the old debt for a lesser sum, which you then pay. Thousands of people do this every year. See Chapter 11 for full details.

Unfortunately, it often happens that by the time people decide to pay, the original tax bill has ballooned with mega-penalties and interest.

Discharging specific property from the lien

Even if you cannot secure a release of lien, there are still plenty of ways to sell your property out from under it. Property may be discharged from the tax lien if:

1. The IRS is paid in full.

2. The IRS is paid the value of the taxpayer's interest in the property.

3. The tax lien is worthless.

4. A bond is posted.

5. Certain other property is still subject to the lien.

The IRS is paid in full

Let's say you want to sell a crane you have been using in your construction business for five years. The crane is worth $100,000. You've paid down the debt on it to $20,000, but you owe the IRS $50,000. If the IRS seized and auctioned the crane, it might get $60,000. After the IRS paid the $20,000 debt, $40,000 would be left for the government. You would still owe $10,000 in taxes. But in the open market, you could get $100,000, fully paying the IRS and the old debt, and leaving you with $30,000 to lease a new crane.

If you can get the revenue officer to agree, the two of you can sign a contract to allow you to sell the property free and clear of the lien. The revenue officer issues a certificate that "discharges" the crane from the federal tax lien so the buyer can have it free and clear. The proceeds of sale are then put in a special fund subject to the lien, usually at a bank.

Then that money is divided, with $20,000 going to the first lienholder, $50,000 to the IRS, and $30,000 to you.

The IRS receives the taxpayer's interest in the property

A variation of this scenario is even more common. You find a buyer for the crane, call the revenue officer, and schedule a settlement. The revenue officer attends, bringing a certificate discharging the crane from the federal tax lien in exchange for a certified check for $50,000.

The same technique works in real estate sales. In fact, if you want to sell a house, a building, or land, and a federal tax lien is on file against you as the owner, you can't sell unless you give the IRS its share of the equity at settlement. The process is the same: Put the property up for sale, get your best price, and insert a line for the IRS at the settlement table. It does not even have to be for the full amount you owe. As long as the IRS gets all your equity (after paying the superior liens), it will be happy.

For example, suppose Tim owes the government $70,000 in taxes. His house is worth $110,000. The first mortgage is $40,000. He sells the house, and, after commissions, the amount available for distribution is $100,000. The settlement agent pays $40,000 to the First Mortgage Bank and $60,000 to the IRS. Even though Tim will still owe $10,000 in taxes, the revenue officer will come to the settlement armed with a certificate of discharge of property from the federal tax lien.

Why is the IRS willing to give you this freedom? Quite simply, by releasing the property, the Service gets every last dime out of it. If it didn't let the sale proceed, it would get nothing. So it's in the agency's interest to issue the release, and it normally does.

Moneysaver
In discharge applications, try to get your expenses of sale, attorneys' fees, and so forth paid ahead of the IRS. To do that, list each expense clearly on your application. If the priority of an expense is in doubt, ask your professional advisor.

The tax lien is worthless

In the above example, suppose the first mortgage was $150,000, not $40,000. That scenario happened depressingly often in the 1980s, when the value of people's homes went through the roof and they merrily borrowed—also through the roof—against that value. Then the recession set in, plunging values through the floor. In such a case, the IRS's lien is valueless because the first mortgage exceeds the market value. There's no equity in the sale for the IRS, so the agent might as well let it go. The agent will therefore issue the release.

Another discharge alternative

Another way to get a discharge of property is extremely rare. The government can, at its discretion (that is: if it wants to), discharge one piece of property if all the other property you own is worth at least twice the unpaid taxes plus all other liens on that property.

For example, suppose you own two pieces of land, the first worth $10,000, the second worth $100,000. There is a $5,000 mortgage on the second piece. You owe $10,000 in taxes. The IRS can discharge the first piece of property from the tax lien so you can sell it because it has plenty of equity in the second piece. Specifically, the second piece of land is worth $100,000, but two times the other debts on it, including the tax debt, comes to only $30,000 (two times $5,000 plus $10,000). Will the Service release the first piece? Maybe not. After all, the release is discretionary; it goes against a revenue officer's training and experience to release your valuable property without getting something for it. But the law does allow this remedy.

To put these property discharges in motion, send for Publication 783, Certificate of Discharge of Property from Federal Tax Lien. This publication tells you what you'll need. Make the application for the discharge by letter. In general, you need to include a description of the property, how you will be divested of your ownership, and who the buyer and seller are. Also include information on the tax liens, the amount of federal taxes owed, costs of sale, value of the property, and the holders of prior liens. You will also have to certify that you are selling the whole property, or at least all of your interest in it.

Subordinating the lien

In some cases, you can ask the IRS to subordinate its lien to some other claim. The Service will normally subordinate if it can make more money in the long run. As an example, let's say a builder owes taxes. He is in the middle of a construction project that will net a big profit. But the bank won't release the money necessary for completion because the revenue officer has filed a notice of lien. Here, the IRS can subordinate its lien to the bank's fresh capital in the hope that by doing so, the builder will make a healthy profit from his work and have more money to pay to the Service.

To get this subordination, ask or write the revenue officer, providing the information specified in Publication 784 (Application for Certificate of Subordination of Federal Tax Lien). The revenue officer will consider the application, and, if she agrees, sign a certificate of subordination, which is filed in the same office as the lien notice.

Unofficially...
The 1998 tax reform act created a new right for third-party owners of property, against which property a tax lien has been filed, to obtain a release as a matter of right. It involves posting a bond or making a deposit, refundable after investigation reveals that the taxpayer had no rights in the property.

Withdrawing a notice of lien

The 1996 Taxpayer Bill of Rights allows the IRS to withdraw the notice of lien. Why would it do so? One reason would be if it expects that the withdrawal will "facilitate the collection" of the taxes. Let's say you want to sell some property to which the lien has attached. You request the IRS to withdraw the notice of lien. It will be in the IRS's interest to do so if the agency will be included at the settlement table. Probably, this will work as follows. You negotiate the deal and arrange for the settlement. At the settlement table, the settlement agent draws a check to the IRS, in exchange for which the IRS will supply a formal withdrawal of lien. The settlement agent will then file the lien withdrawal in the land records, so that clear title to the property may be transferred.

The lien may also be withdrawn if the filing was premature or in violation of the IRS's procedures; the taxpayer has entered into an installment agreement to pay the liability in full, or withdrawing the notice will otherwise be in the best interest of the taxpayer and the IRS.

Be a true American—sue!

Now you can also the IRS. The IRS Restructuring and Reform Act of 1998 grants you a right to appeal a past lien filing by hearing before an "impartial" IRS officer. That translates to the Office of Appeals, the same office that considers appeals from income tax audits.

If you appeal, the hearing office *must* consider:
- whether the law or administrative procedures were followed,
- spousal defenses,

- the appropriateness of collection actions,

- most important, "collection alternatives." These include substituting other assets, an installment agreement, an offer in compromise, or posting a bond.

The new law does not say when the hearing office must decide, but presumably there will be regulations on this. If you lose your appeal at this level, you can go to court—United States Tax Court or federal district court, depending on which court has jurisdiction over the type of tax involved.

All of these fine-sounding procedures do not apply in the special case where the IRS has made an official finding that collection of the tax is in jeopardy, or where the IRS has levied on a state to collect a refund. Also, while the IRS must give you notice of the lien filing, the new law contains no legal requirement that you actually receive it!

The new law does not state what the court can do if it concludes the IRS was wrong. A separate law allows courts to fashion wide-ranging remedies in cases pertaining to the IRS, so we'll have to wait for the first cases to learn how this law plays out in the real world.

"Persuading" a stubborn agent to release a lien

Sometimes, even if you are on the side of truth, justice, and the American way, a hostile or stubborn agent just doesn't "get it." When logic fails, go to the boss, the "Group Manager." Then go to *his* boss, the "Branch Chief." If you are not successful you can keep going to higher levels, but it's usually futile. Instead, look to the new law, the IRS Restructuring and Reform Act of 1998.

Watch Out!
The withdrawal does not release the lien. It merely withdraws public notice of the lien. The underlying lien remains in place, though now third parties may gain a priority over the IRS.

Watch Out!
The deadlines for
a hearing are
short. The agent
must give you
notice within
five days of the
lien filing. You
then have only
thirty days from
the day after
notice to request
a hearing.

Failure to release a federal tax lien is actionable in court under two statutes. One Code provision makes the IRS liable for certain "unauthorized" collection actions. This *may* be read to include any time an agent negligently, recklessly, or intentionally disregards any provision of the Internal Revenue Code, or any regulation.

You can also consider the beefed-up request for a Taxpayer Assistance Order if the IRS refuses to release the lien. (See Chapter 14 for details.) Also, you can take some satisfaction from the knowledge that a really nasty agent may now be fired if he or she refuses to issue release for retaliatory or harassing purposes.

Just the facts

- Always try to convince an IRS agent not to file a notice of federal tax lien in the first place.
- Consider appealing the agent's filing of the lien notice—a new right granted under the 1998 Act.
- Retain or get copies of all tax liens filed against you, as well as of other, non-tax, liens.
- To release the lien, arrange for a payment plan for an offer in compromise.
- Failing such a release, you may still sell property by asking for a discharge of the property from the lien.

GET THE SCOOP ON...
The enormous power of the IRS levy ▪ What can
the levy capture? ▪ What's beyond its reach? ▪
Beating the levy without beating yourself ▪
How the IRS sells property it seizes

IRS Levies

I magine that you buy a television or a new suit on credit. When you fail to make a payment, the seller has the power to quickly seize your bank account or paycheck or even force the sale of your house. Imagine also that the seller needs no court order, hearing, judge, or jury to do this. That would be a truly frightening situation. Yet, in its starkest form, that's precisely the power the Internal Revenue Service has to seize your property when you fail to pay your taxes. In practice, the IRS almost never uses this seizure power in such an arbitrary fashion, but the authority is solidly entrenched in the law.

The levy is simply the act of seizing your property to pay a back tax. It should not be confused with its collection cousin, the federal tax lien. When you fail to pay a tax for which the IRS has billed you, a lien, that is, a legal charge on property, occurs by law automatically. That lien is secret at first—no one knows about it except you and the IRS. Only when the IRS files notice of the lien in the local courthouse or land records does the public "know" that you owe taxes and that the IRS has a lien on your property to secure payment. This notice of lien is not a levy; it seizes nothing. It merely encumbers your property.

The levy is the actual seizure. In fact, the IRS does not even have to file a notice of lien before seizing your property. Legally all it must do is bill you for the taxes, demand payment, and wait thirty days.

Choose your poison: varieties of the levy

The IRS levy comes in three main varieties.

- The **wage levy** captures most of your paycheck, the commissions you've earned, and just about any other compensation due to you.

- The **nonwage levy** is a one-time seizure of specific property, such as your home, car, real estate, bank account, or insurance policy.

- The **jeopardy** or **termination levy,** which is rarely used, is a hurried-up version of the nonwage levy. Reserved mostly for gambling, drug, and money-laundering cases, the jeopardy or termination levy is almost instantaneous. In fact, sometimes IRS officials will authorize revenue officers by telephone to make these levies.

If the IRS's levy power sounds ominous to you, it should. Many people have challenged this power in court; few have succeeded. In case after case over the past sixty years, the U.S. Supreme Court and dozens of lower courts have rejected challenges to the IRS's levy power, ruling that this power to seize property without a court order or judgment is completely constitutional, indeed necessary to the proper functioning of government. Examples abound.

Lose your bail, back to jail

Abelard had a bad habit of violating tax laws and accumulating back-tax bills. In fact, he owed the government $925,000. As luck would have it, he violated his state's criminal laws as well and was arrested and thrown in jail. Heloise, his good friend, came to his rescue by lending him $5,000 for bail money. The IRS found out about it and immediately levied on the clerk of the court for the bail money. "They can't do that," screamed Heloise and Abelard's lawyer (who also claimed the money for his legal fees). "Yes, they can," said the court. According to the court, once Heloise loaned the money to Abelard, it became his, and the court bailiff held it only in trust. So the IRS got it.

In no particular hurry

This levy power stands a world apart from a private creditor's rights to collect money. Normal creditors are subject to dozens of state and federal laws that regulate and restrict their right to dun you by telephone, write you nasty letters, and otherwise take steps to collect their money. Not so the IRS (though, starting in 1998, it too must obey a version of the Fair Debt Collection Practices Act). Ordinary creditors must also go to court to get a judgment if all else fails. If they want to seize your wages or your property in others' hands, they must first give the judgment to a sheriff to be served on your debtor. Not so the IRS. You can usually file for bankruptcy to foil most creditors, but bankruptcy often merely slows down the IRS. In short, there's very little shelter from this nuclear bomb of collection once it is dropped.

Unofficially...
In 1996, the IRS issued over 3 million levies and made 10,000 additional property seizures. The total yield from these and all other bills was $29 billion.

Watch Out!
Don't make the mistake of thinking of the IRS as an ordinary creditor. In numerous ways discussed in this chapter, its power is less restricted and its ability to seize your assets vastly greater.

Not team players

Andrew certainly had his problems with the U.S. government. One arm of the Department of Justice filed a multi-million-dollar claim against him and sued him for it. That division threatened to seize his assets, so Andrew agreed to escrow some money, awaiting the outcome of the suit. In the meantime, the IRS filed a notice of lien against Andrew and levied on the account. It levied again three years later, and again the following year. Andrew threatened the bank that held the escrow. The Justice Department threatened Andrew, and the IRS threatened everyone. Naturally, a lawsuit followed. The bank ran to federal court, asking for protection.

Who won? The IRS, of course. What about the agreement between the Justice Department and Andrew to keep the money in escrow? "That was another division," said the judge. "That agreement is not binding on the Tax Division. Besides, the agreement doesn't say that the money must be held, only that the division would use its 'best internal efforts' to make sure no other government agency levies on the funds." So, the IRS won the money.

No saving for a rainy day

Theodore bought an annuity contract from the Big Umbrella Life Insurance Company. He dutifully made contributions totaling more than $13,000. Four years into the contract, the IRS made an assessment against Theodore totaling $55,000. Then the IRS levied on the insurance company. "No way," said the insurance company. "The annuity is not in our possession or custody." The court disagreed. The insurance company had to cut a check to the IRS for the cash withdrawal value of the annuity. Congress intended that the IRS should be able to reach "every interest in property a taxpayer might have," said the court. The right to withdraw the cash value is itself a valuable property right, so the IRS could reach it by levy.

Before the IRS levies

The 1998 tax reform act imposed some important new restrictions on the IRS's levy powers. Moreover, because the levy is so powerful, the IRS has voluntarily limited its use of it. As a result, you almost always get plenty of warning before a levy hits—sort of like an oncoming freight train. For example, you get a bill from the IRS if you file your tax return with a balance due, or if you owe more tax after an audit, or if you fight the IRS in tax court and lose. All of these bills are called *assessments*, and they tell you to pay, or else. The "or else" implicitly includes the threat of a levy.

As noted earlier, the IRS normally sends up to five notices of tax due to individuals, and as few as two to businesses. Each new notice is more urgent than the one before. The last notice, called the *Intent to Levy*, arrives by certified mail. Thirty days after the Final Notice, the IRS is legally free to seize any property it can find. (Before the IRS levies, the case must also be reviewed. The IRS must reverify the taxpayer's information, recheck the balance due and the value of the property, and affirm that the levy or seizure is "appropriate" given the taxpayer's value of the property and circumstances.)

You won't necessarily know

Cosnider the following example. The IRS matches a Form 1099 with a man's return and finds an error resulting in underpayment. The Service sends a bill for the taxes due, but this is two years after the man

Bright Idea
Although the IRS's notification procedures were in place even before they became law in 1998, the Congressional hearings on the bill brought to light cases where the IRS went overboard in its zeal to seize. If the IRS has violated these new laws by failing to conduct a proper review in your case, you can sue in court.

and his wife filed their return and moved, as millions of Americans do every year. Because of that move, the IRS didn't know where they lived, and the notice was not forwarded. Notice after notice went unclaimed, including the Final Notice of Intent to Levy. Finally the IRS locates the man's whereabouts and levies his wages. His boss fires him. (Such firing is illegal under federal law, but it happens in the real world.)

"You mean the IRS can levy even if we never *receive* that Final Notice?" the man asked his lawyer. "That's right. The Service only has to send it to the last known address."

An extreme example? Yes, but it does happen. In most cases, however, people are not completely unaware that they owe taxes. They get the notices—at least some of them—but they stick their heads in the sand. In fact, the IRS sometimes issues so many notices that people feel intimidated by the sheer volume of paper. So they stack the envelopes in the corner, hoping the paper will grow legs and walk away. They might go so far as to reject certified mail, figuring that it must be bad news from the Internal Revenue Service and hoping it will fade like morning fog if they simply ignore it. No matter. The IRS freight train continues to chug inexorably toward them, gaining speed with each new notice.

IRS levy policy and practice

As noted above, because the levy is so powerful, the Service's policy is to use it sparingly. In fact, the 1998 tax reform act, and even the IRS's own Internal Revenue Manual, require this restraint. So as an institution, the IRS is not primarily interested in seizing your wages, car, or other property, at least at first. What the IRS really wants is your attention and a commitment to face your tax problem and deal with it.

"Dealing" with a tax debt means crafting a payment solution such as filing an offer in compromise, making an installment agreement, or borrowing money. So think of the levy as an abrupt wake-up call. Having obtained your attention, the Service will typically release most levies if you begin to cooperate. (But they may take one paycheck or a bank account, so don't count on total mercy.) Surprising as this sounds, in the real world it holds true, and confirms the IRS's policy not to use the levy power unless it sees no other choice.

All is not lost when the IRS levies

You also have certain rights when the IRS levies. For example, you may request expedited review if the IRS seizes personal property that you need for your business. You also have the right to request that property be sold within sixty days. Note that these "rights" do not automatically grant you the relief you seek. They are generally at the discretion of the IRS. You also have the right to a preseizure review using the Collection Appeals Process or the new pre-levy appeal procedures described below. If the IRS wants to seize your home, it now must go to court to obtain a court order. And before the Service seizes business assets, the District Director must personally review the agent's proposed action.

People who are deemed "uncollectible" now also have a right to get a levy release. Many people who owe taxes can't afford to pay anything—their pay only covers basics. So the IRS declares them "currently not collectible." In the past, some agents levied on their wages anyway. Now these "uncollectibles" have a legal right to a levy release.

Watch Out!
Even after the 1998 tax reform act, you can still be subject to levy even if you never receive notice of any debt to the IRS. But the act does say exactly how the IRS must give notice—in person, left at your home or business, or sent by certified mail to your last known address.

Moneysaver
You have the right to a release of any levy if the equity in your property is not enough to warrant its sale. For example, a home worth $100,000, with a debt of $90,000, has no equity for IRS purposes. The IRS discounts the market value because it knows a forced sale will not realize full market value.

The IRS's internal policy, and the law also require the release of the levy under certain other conditions. For example, if your tax is paid or it expires, the levy must be released. If you enter an installment agreement, or if releasing the levy will facilitate tax collection, it may be released. Also, according to the 1998 tax reform act, if the levy is creating an undue economic hardship, it must be released. This last condition, in fact, is the one most often relied on to obtain a release of a levy.

Avoiding or releasing the levy

What can you do when the revenue officer's threat to levy seems real, or if she has in fact already levied?

Before the levy is issued, by far the most important tactic is: *Communicate!* Never let a notice go unanswered. Write and call the IRS every time it notifies you or every time it asks for information. Stay in touch with the revenue officer or the Automated Collection System representative. Ask that no seizure action take place. Consider getting help from a tax professional, and ask for time from the IRS if you need it.

Also consider appealing the proposed seizure, either to the Problem Resolution Office or to the revenue officer's group manager, and from there to the Office of Appeals.

Under the 1998 tax reform act, the IRS must give you thirty days' notice and advise you of certain rights *before* it can levy. The most important of these is the right to a hearing before a neutral, independent hearing officer. That means the Office of Appeals. You get one notice for each tax period at issue.

The notice must tell you several things, all in clear, nontechnical terms:

- The amount of unpaid tax
- Your right to a hearing within the thirty days
- The IRS's proposed action (to seize and sell assets)
- The law relating to levies and sale of property
- IRS procedures governing levies and sales
- The appeals available to you
- The alternatives you have that would prevent a levy, such as an installment agreement
- The law and procedures relating to redemption of property and release of liens

The hearing is covered in the law by the "Right to Fair Hearing," and by this Congress surely means business. In the past, "appeals" to higher levels within the IRS, while sometimes successful, often were futile. Even the Taxpayer Assistance Order provisions were only a partial remedy in most cases. Now, the law allows you to stop that levy by actions you can take—you no longer have to beg and plead with IRS appeals officers who are often as enforcement-minded as the agent you're dealing with.

The hearing must be conducted by an officer with "no prior involvement" in your case. The appeals officer will consider many issues, including:

- Whether all law and procedures were followed
- Whether the levy is the "appropriate" thing to do
- Spousal defenses, such as the "innocent spouse" (see Chapter 8)
- Collection alternatives, such as posting a bond, substituting other assets, and making an installment agreement or an offer in compromise

Bright Idea
Be sure to familiarize yourself with the new, important rights created by the 1998 tax reform act for anyone threatened by a levy. These rights represent the first time that you can mount one, and in some cases, two, independent challenges to any levy.

Unofficially...
Whenever you're negotiating with the IRS, the less hostile and the more businesslike and cooperative you are, the better things will usually go.

The new law specifically requires the appeals officer to determine whether the proposed collection action balances the need for efficient collection with your legitimate concern that collection action be no more "intrusive than necessary." Never before have such broad administrative rights been available to ordinary citizens *before* a levy is served. What's more, while your appeal is pending, the IRS may not seize your property.

If you lose at the Office of Appeals, now, for the first time, you can go to court! The United States Tax Court and the federal district courts are newly authorized to review the IRS's decision. The levy is still suspended, however, only in cases where you are contesting the underlying merits of the tax, that is, contesting that you owe the tax in whole or in part. These rights also don't apply in jeopardy assessment cases, in criminal cases, and in cases where the IRS has levied on a state to collect a state tax refund.

If you don't exercise these rights, you must deal with the agent. If the IRS has just levied on your bank account, your car, or your business property, you obviously will have to take immediate action. The most extreme form of action is to file an emergency bankruptcy petition. Such a petition will usually result in the release of tangible property and real property, but not cash or cash equivalents.

Still, filing for bankruptcy ought to be a last resort, never done lightly or without careful consideration. Other alternatives are far less extreme. For instance, you may call the revenue officer and ask for release of the levy. Of course, if the revenue officer is willing to do this at all, there will be conditions. These may include entering into an installment agreement, providing updated financial information, or doing anything else the revenue officer deems appropriate.

If the levy is creating a true hardship, you may seek a Taxpayer Assistance Order (see Chapter 14) or simply go up the chain of command through the group manager, branch chief, and chief of collection in your district. It's all a matter of negotiation.

What can the levy capture?

Almost nothing is beyond the reach of the levy. Bank accounts, wages, commissions, accounts receivable, stocks, bonds, the cash value of insurance policies, jewelry, and even homes can be seized and sold by the IRS. The law excepts only eleven narrow categories of property from the levy power. The exceptions, discussed in more detail below, include books, tools of your trade, and some parts of your salary, among other things. Everything else is fair game.

Of course, the IRS goes for the easy targets first: bank accounts, cars, stocks, bonds, and wages. Its second set of targets are items such as insurance policies and accounts receivable. Third, the agency really hits home: it can seize your retirement accounts and your home (with some restrictions).

Bank accounts

These assets are easy marks. The Service sends a one-page form entitled *Notice of Levy* to your bank. From the instant the levy is received, by law the collected balance in your account is frozen.

Then the bank waits twenty-one days, after which it sends that frozen balance to the IRS. (Of course, the bank also deducts the usual processing fees!) The twenty-one-day grace period was added by the 1988 Taxpayer Bill of Rights as a window for you to work things out with the IRS. But you're certainly

Watch Out!
The "collected balance" is not your checkbook balance but the balance you have at the bank. This means that unpaid checks will bounce once a levy hits the bank.

bargaining from a position of weakness. Many revenue officers, knowing they have the money, will simply refuse to release the first bank levy.

The IRS uses names and Social Security numbers to find and identify bank accounts. A levy to the First Patriotic Red-Blooded American Bank contains your name, Social Security Number, and a description of the tax due according to the IRS. It also contains a demand to pay the account balance.

What if you have a joint account and you are not the owner, or you own only part of the funds? Examples would include a bank account in trust or a joint account where a nondelinquent taxpayer like a child or spouse puts in some of the money. If so, the IRS has no right to those funds. But quite often the account does not designate someone else as owner. So convincing the IRS to release this levy is roughly equivalent to pulling teeth from an alligator's mouth.

If it's in your name, or bears your Social Security number, the IRS will try to take it—on the legal presumption that it must be all yours because you have the right to withdraw it all. The burden is on you to prove that someone else owns the funds in the account in whole or in part. In principle, that's done by showing who deposited the money, but this can be difficult. In fact, it was IRS seizures of joint accounts in parent-child names that prompted Congress to expand the freeze period to twenty-one days from the original ten.

The IRS knows where you bank from many sources: your last several tax returns, a Form 1099 the bank may have filed for you, a Collection Information Statement you gave to the IRS the previous year, or simply good detective work on the agent's part in the computer system. Revenue officers will sometimes let loose a flurry of levies, at random (brokers, employers, or any other third-party payer) just to see what targets they hit. Often they strike gold.

In the meantime, since your account funds have been frozen, your checks will begin to bounce. Each bounced check results in another modest bank charge, which can quickly add up, as well as the damage to your reputation in the eyes of your payees. So those twenty-one days are precious time in which to beg the IRS to release the levy. The price is usually an interim agreement to begin paying the taxes in installments. (See Chapter 12.)

Wages and salaries

A wage levy is "continuous," meaning the IRS has to levy only once to get your wages, salaries, or commissions week after week, month after month. It differs from one-time levies, which seize only the property in the possessor's hands the moment the levy hits.

The wage levy is probably the IRS's most effective attention-getter. It instantly focuses the thinking of all but a few reluctant taxpayers. Out of every $100 of wages, the IRS's take is typically $70 to $90. The exact amount depends on the number of exemptions you have claimed on your W-4. The IRS has a formula for this calculation that is set out in the levy notice to your employer.

Not many people can live on the paltry sum a wage levy leaves, so you need to act instantly when that happens. In many cases, the IRS will release a wage levy after you ask. However, the agent may insist on taking one paycheck and require full financial disclosure and an installment agreement.

Moneysaver
The case of IRS seizure of joint accounts is the ideal case to invoke the new appeal rights to contest the levy before it is made. You'll have a full opportunity before a neutral officer, and possibly a court, to make the case that the amount is owed by a non-taxpayer.

Watch Out!
The "continuous"
IRS levy also
reaches certain
"specified pay-
ments" that are
not wages, such
as some unem-
ployment and
workers' compen-
sation benefits.
Starting in 1998,
levies on these
must be specifi-
cally approved by
an IRS official.

To get the release, call the toll-free number on the levy form itself and explain the situation. State the obvious: you need your wages to live on; you won't be able to pay the rent or mortgage, or feed or clothe your family if your wages are seized.

Of course, only make these statements if they are true, but in the case of a wage levy, they almost certainly will be true. Also tell the agent that you intend to pay attention now and work out your collection problem.

You have several choices. You can sell assets or borrow money; this is not usually a realistic option if the case has gone so far as to require a levy. You can "deal with" the tax collection problem by filing for bankruptcy, which will in fact require the IRS to release the levy as to future wages (but not as to funds seized or frozen before you file). Bankruptcy is not always a permanent solution, though in many cases it can be. (See Chapter 13.)

You can also ask the IRS to stop collecting completely because you can't pay anything.

The Service shelves "currently not collectible" accounts for six months, one year, or longer. From time to time, however, it reviews your case to see if you are doing better. In the meantime, an agent will file at least one Notice of Federal Tax Lien, protecting the IRS's position against the claims of competing creditors and preventing the sale of your home or other property (including property you acquire after the lien is filed). This gives you some immediate relief from the levy.

"Currently not collectible" status is like cancer in remission: it doesn't cure the problem, and the symptoms could reappear at any time.

Finally, you can suggest that you will never be able to pay your taxes in full, but you may be able to pay 10 percent, 20 percent, or some other fraction. This condition calls for filing an offer in compromise, a deal in which the Service permanently forgives some part of the taxes as long as you pay the rest. See Chapter 11 for a discussion of *offers in compromise.*

Those are your choices. Select one, or a combination, and propose it, if you're to have any chance of the Service releasing the levy.

Retirement accounts

That nest egg you were incubating for retirement is definitely not exempt from IRS levy. This fact surprises many people, because the law bars ordinary creditors from seizing retirement accounts. In fact, if you file for bankruptcy, retirement monies are exempt from the claims of your ordinary creditors—but the IRS is no ordinary creditor. It has seized retirement accounts.

In one well-known case, the IRS levied the entire IRA of a retired judge! Seizing a retirement account is a last resort; the agency will usually exhaust almost every other source of collection. So if you can arrange an installment agreement or an offer in compromise, the IRS may leave your retirement account intact.

But when a retirement account is seized, there's triple trouble:

1. You lose the whole thing;
2. You'll trigger the income taxes due because of that withdrawal;
3. You'll owe a penalty for estimated taxes.

Unofficially...
Being unable to pay at all is so common that the IRS even has a form for it, Form 53. When you use Form 53, the Service concludes that your account is "currently not collectible."

Moneysaver
The IRS can legally get only what you can get. The Service "steps into your shoes," as lawyers like to say. If you can't tap your retirement account now, the IRS can't levy on it. So be sure you know the rules of your retirement plan, and use them to defend against an intended levy!

So while the IRS has paid all or part of your old liability with the IRA, it has also created a fresh new one for the tax year in which the seizure occurs.

Insurance policies

The IRS can seize the cash surrender value of any whole life policies you own or any other type of policy that has cash value in it, such as universal life or a retirement annuity. Term life policies, which have no cash value, are of no interest to the IRS. The IRS seizes the equity in the policy by sending the levy to the insurance company. By law, the carrier is then required to send a check for the cash value, less loans, fees, or penalties.

Your home

The IRS seizes homes, cars, and other big-ticket items by physically slapping a preprinted sticker, called a *Notice of Seizure*, on the property. Things the IRS can haul away, it will. In fact, the IRS seizes so many cars and trucks that the local collection office often has standing arrangements with towing companies and storage lots. Physically putting that sticker on a car, home, or other property is an act that legally seizes the property for the IRS. That means it's a felony to sell, remove, or damage it.

Agents record all seizures in a central notebook and then schedule the properties for sale. Any time the IRS seizes assets on private property, it needs either your consent or a court order. This rule stems from the Fourth Amendment's restriction on unreasonable searches and seizures. The IRS's warrant to enter business or personal premises is called a *Writ of Entry*. A taxpayer who refuses to consent to entry only delays the inevitable by a few days or weeks.

The revenue officer obtains the writ by asking the U.S. Attorney's Office to go to court, usually a formality. Normally you won't even know that the agent has asked for this Writ of Entry. The U.S. Attorneys can obtain it without your knowledge or consent, and you would have no legal standing to contest its issuance even if you knew it was being sought from a judge. The same probably holds true for the new (1998) requirement to obtain a court order before seizing a personal residence.

Community property

Nine states are "community property" states: Arizona, California, Idaho, Louisiana, Nevada, New Mexico, Texas, Washington, and Wisconsin (which has a form of community property). Figuring out what the IRS can reach in a community property state is difficult; each of these states has its own peculiar twists and turns on the community property laws. And since the IRS's liens and levies can reach only what you, the taxpayer, own under the law of your state, the issues become quite muddled and complex.

Still, people who live in these states should note a few general principles about community property and how the IRS's rights might apply in those states. In general, and subject to your particular state's law, community property is property that comes into a marriage. Separate property is property each spouse has before marriage, or which is acquired by gift or inheritance. Community and separate property generally retain their character, but people who commingle separate property can, in effect, make it community property. "Transmutation" agreements can also convert separate property to community property.

Watch Out!
Driving your car away with the seizure notice on it, or removing the notice, is a quick and easy way to get yourself arrested. Revenue officers watch for this, and won't hesitate to call the Criminal Investigation Division to haul you away.

Unofficially...
The IRS is often careful about enforcing its claims in community property states. The agents are cautioned to ask for a legal opinion on what is liable for the tax debts and what is not.

As a general rule, community property is liable for the debts of either spouse or both spouses. That means the IRS can levy on one spouse's income for the other spouse's tax debt. This has created havoc for spouses in many cases. If you are faced with such a threat where only one spouse owes taxes, several options are available. First, you and your spouse may keep completely separate property accounts, including separate bank accounts. Remember that this works only for property that is not "community property." Also, where a state allows you to "transmute" community property into separate property, this can often give you protection against the IRS.

Exemptions from levy

By law, the following types of property are exempt from levy. But don't get your hopes up; even if your property fits one of these categories, exempting it usually won't feed the children.

- Workers' compensation payments are exempt, including any amounts payable to dependents.

- Wages, salary, and other income are exempt, but only a small fraction figured according to a formula. The formula is linked to the standard deduction and personal exemptions, prorated on a weekly basis. Figure only 10 percent to 30 percent of your net paycheck will remain yours.

- Clothes and schoolbooks are exempt, but only to the extent "necessary" for you or members of your family. In practice, the IRS rarely levies on clothing or schoolbooks. (It might if you had an expensive fur coat.)

- Homes. If the amount you owe is less than $5,000, the IRS can't seize your home at all. The same applies to any other realty you own except rental property. Also, in larger cases the IRS can't seize your home or business assets without a court order or specific approval by an IRS official.

■ Fuel, provisions, furniture, and personal effects (up to $6,250) in your home, arms for personal use, and livestock and poultry are exempt. So your guns, chickens, cows, and firewood are exempt from IRS levy. Even so, the exemption limit is $2,500 in value.

■ Unemployment benefits, including amounts for dependent care, are exempt from levy, but again, that's not much. Since disability benefits are not unemployment compensation, they can be seized.

■ Annuities or pensions payable under the Railroad Retirement Act and the Railroad Unemployment Insurance Act, special payments to Medal of Honor winners, and annuities for Armed Forces members are exempt. Again, the amounts are not large. Social Security benefits? Government pensions? These can be seized. It happens all the time.

■ Judgments for the support of minor children are exempt up to the amount of salary, wages, or other income necessary to comply with the court order for support. And, they are exempt only if the judgment was entered before the levy was issued. You bear the burden of showing how much is necessary to comply with the court order, and the Service does not have to release the money until shown that the money will in fact be used to support the child.

Unofficially... Books and tools of a trade, business, or profession up to $3,125 in value are exempt from levy. For some, this could mean a car, and some tools, so they can continue in business. In the real world, agents rarely like to seize these items; it kills the goose that lays the golden egg.

Watch Out!
For levies that
ACS, not an
agent, issues,
the pre-levy right
to a hearing
does not
begin until Janu-
ary 1, 2000.

- Welfare and Job Training Partnership Act payments and books and tools necessary for the taxpayer's trade, business, or profession are also exempt.

- Finally, your home is exempt from seizure, except where the local district director personally approves the sale.

The Automated Collection System

Most wage and nonwage levies originate in the IRS's Automated Collection System (ACS). ACS is the Service's mighty reserve army, activated after a Service Center's computer nudges you to pay and you don't.

In fact, most problems that occur with the IRS's collection arm result from the taxpayer's failure to heed warnings from ACS notices or to cooperate in giving information to the IRS. Most levies are not "out of the blue." You get plenty of opportunity to work things out. In fact, the sooner you respond to any of these notices, the better off you usually will be.

As its name implies, the Automated Collection System collects automatically by machine-generating levies and notices of lien. ACS also has a staff of real people. They work in large rooms at seven regional Service Centers around the country, calling taxpayers to convince them to pay, or receiving their calls.

The ACS people work in teams. They have a number of interrelated goals. First, they will demand full payment of the tax. At the same time, they want to interview you to determine if you can pay, and how much. This interview will also establish sources on which they can levy in the future. They will set deadlines for paying or filing returns, and they will warn you that collection action will follow swiftly if you fail to meet any of these deadlines.

If your case is complex, they will research it for you. All day, ACS employees talk to taxpayers like you who call trying to get a break or make a deal on their taxes. When you call, the agent is trained to note in the computer everything you say, including your promises to file an offer in compromise, make installment payments, or take other action. When you call back again, you will usually get another agent, but that agent will have the institutional memory at her fingertips.

In most cases, a mere contact by the Automated Collection System is enough to wake you up about your past taxes. So even though you have received multiple notices from the Service Center and a Notice of Intent to Levy, you still have some credibility if you respond quickly and forthrightly to the ACS representative. To be sure, that representative will pump you for information, exposing your financial neck. But you really have no choice, and, in any event, an attitude of cooperation is the only way you can hope to avoid levies and possibly avoid notices of federal tax lien.

Calling the Automated Collection System can sometimes be a terribly frustrating experience. The agents are trained to collect taxes and to be tough. They are usually lied to numerous times between breakfast and lunch. And they've heard enough sob stories to keep Ann Landers supplied for years.

When you call, remember a few rules:

- Have all your information ready. This includes complete financial data on your assets and liabilities, income, and expenses. The agents will usually ask for all of this, plus addresses, phone numbers, and so on, even before you discuss how you're planning to deal with the back taxes.

Unofficially...
Sometimes, liens are unavoidable. The cutoff point is usually taxes of $5,000 or more. Where the tax is between $2,000 and $5,000, and an installment agreement is for more than twelve months, a lien must also be filed. ACS will warn you that notices of lien are routinely picked up by credit bureaus.

Timesaver
Get Form 433-F
before you call
the IRS. Down-
load it from the
Internet
(www.irs.ustreas.
gov) or get it
from another ser-
vice. Go over
each line item
before you call;
the agent will
ask about each
of these anyway,
and your
preparation adds
credibility.

■ Be friendly and businesslike with the agent.

■ Always tell the truth.

■ Explain exactly the hardship the levy is causing and why you need relief from it. The agents already know the levy is painful, but you may have to explain the details.

■ Propose a realistic, sensible plan of action to resolve the delinquent taxes. To do this, prepare *in advance* all your monthly income and expense figures. ACS will usually take these over the phone. Use the checklist in Chapter 11 as a guide.

■ Your attitude, and that of the ACS agent, is crucial. Expect no breaks if you antagonize the agent. But if you are cordial, cooperative, and meet your deadlines, you may win over the agent and distinguish yourself from others who do not. And be sure that the tax bill you are discussing is correct. The IRS usually gets it right, but not always. Check the bill. Is it for the right tax period? Are penalties and interest properly calculated? It never hurts to be sure. Finally, if you don't like the result you get with ACS, appeal to the agent's supervisor. Then appeal again if you must. You can also appeal to the Office of Taxpayer Advocate if you believe that the installment agreement ACS insists on is too burdensome. Chapter 14 discusses this in more detail.

The ACS agents will then set deadlines depending on what the next step is, such as thirty days to submit a financial statement, or, if the amount you owe is small, ten to thirty days to submit a signed installment agreement. If you cannot meet the deadline, call before the deadline expires to get an exten-

sion or to tell the agent you cannot meet the deadline, and why.

Despite the IRS's resort to a levy, you do in fact
have credibility when you call the Automated Collection System to request relief. But you lose it fast if
you miss even one deadline. And remember, the IRS
has most of the power; you have little.

Normally, the agent will release a levy if you face
your collection problem squarely and propose an
acceptable solution.

Selling seized property

The Service conducts no "sale" when it seizes your
wages, tax refunds, bank accounts, cash value of
insurance policies, and other cash assets. It simply
takes the money and pays your tax bill. But other
property, such as homes, stocks, bonds, and cars
must be converted to cash. Here's how they do it.

The IRS gives formal notice (usually one to two
pages) of the seizure to you, the owner of real property, or to the possessor of personal property. That
notice, required by law, must recite the taxes owed
and describe the property seized. The notice gives
you the chance to work things out with the IRS, or,
if not, to attend the sale and bid for the property.
Notices of seizure and everything else having to do
with property sales are strictly construed against the
IRS. If the assigned agent makes a mistake and real-
izes it, he will usually back off and redo the process,
knowing that he can't give clear title if any minor
detail is wrong.

After sending or delivering the *Notice of Seizure*,
the revenue officer makes sure that the title to the
property is in the taxpayer's name. The revenue
officer wants to be sure that the property is really

Bright Idea
You need to
ensure that the
levy release gets
to your employer
in time for your
next paycheck.
Otherwise,
you may lose
that, too.

Unofficially...
Beginning no
later than 2000,
the agency
must adopt a
"uniform asset
disposal system."
Congress enacted
this requirement
to bring some
regularity to IRS
auctions. Now
the IRS must
determine the
minimum bid for
property and
can't sell below
that minimum.

yours and that the prior liens or mortgages are taken into account. After all, the IRS wants cash. If the mortgage or lien exceeds the value of the property, there will be no cash for the IRS, so selling it makes no sense. Selling property that has no equity for the IRS is also a violation of the IRS manual.

Beginning in 1998, agents are formally required to analyze the value of the property and the tax debt before they sell it, to make sure the sale is truly merited.

Next, the revenue officer prepares a *Notice of Sale* on an IRS form. The agent normally issues this notice within thirty days after the Notice of Seizure, mailing a copy to all lienholders and to you, the taxpayer. Then he publishes the Notice of Sale in the local newspaper or posts it at the post office nearest the property. The revenue officer will also typically post the notice on or outside the property to be sold, such as on a business property or a home. The notice sets the conditions of sale, such as the date and time.

The sale must occur between ten and forty days after the notice. But agents often postpone these sales. The most common reasons are that they don't think they'll get enough money from them or the taxpayers involved are finally working on the collection problem.

Sometimes the IRS hires an auctioneer to sell property. This happens often with cars, particularly if there are many to sell.

But the IRS is perfectly capable of holding its own auction, either by "sealed bid" or public auction. In public auction, the revenue officer stands up, calls the bidding to order, recites a statement of his authority, and opens the bidding at a minimum amount. Then, as in any auction, he tries to get the highest price and declares the property sold to the highest bidder. In a sealed bid sale, people submit sealed bids in advance. The revenue officer opens them at the appointed time and place and declares the winner.

The IRS calculates a "minimum bid" for all property it sells. Essentially, the minimum bid is the least someone would have to pay to get title to the property. For example, let's say a home is worth $100,000, and the first mortgage is $40,000. An IRS formula reduces the $100,000 fair market value of the home to account for the forced sale condition of the auction. While this formula varies, a typical discount would fix the forced sale value at $68,000. The minimum bid would then be $28,000, the forced sale value of $68,000 minus the mortgage of $40,000. So a successful bidder could get a $100,000 property for $28,000, subject to the first mortgage of $40,000. What about the $32,000 of "value" that was somehow "eliminated" by the IRS's formula? The taxpayer can protest long and hard, but that value is lost.

The IRS can sell property that two people own together, even if only one of the owners owes taxes. The nondelinquent owner is paid his share. That doesn't normally happen with homes, which are usually owned as "tenants by the entirety" by a husband and wife in states that recognize this form of ownership. The IRS cannot seize and sell such a home where only one spouse owes taxes, nor can it get a court order to sell the home unless both spouses owe taxes or agree to the sale. Tenancy by the entirety is one of the few safe havens against a forced sale of property.

Redemption of property

In theory, you can reclaim your property even if the IRS has seized it. If it's real property such as a home, you have 180 days to "redeem" the property after sale by paying the amount the purchaser paid, plus interest at 20 percent per year. It's a tough rule, but many taxpayers have used it. Watch out, though: the law says 180 days, not six months.

What about personal property? That cannot be redeemed once it has been sold.

Just the facts

- Pay attention to levies and pre-levy notices. The levy exists to get your attention, and failing that, to take your property for back taxes.

- The IRS uses the levy sparingly.

- Quickly develop an overall plan of action to solve your tax collection problem if you are hit with a levy.

- Tell the truth to the IRS. Agents are human beings, too. They listen and pay attention to life stories, especially after levies are issued.

- Consider getting the help of a tax professional to handle a levy or your collection problem in general.

- Consider using the powerful new (1998) rights to fight levies: the pre-levy hearing and the court challenge.

GET THE SCOOP ON...
How the IRS looks at and asserts a penalty ▪
The "pain" of each penalty ▪ Fighting a penalty
▪ How to make your penalty appeal

Penalties

Chapter 5

Over the past decade, Congress has asked the IRS to preside over a virtual explosion in categories of tax penalties—more than 150 and counting. Sometimes it seems there is a penalty for everything, whether you are right or wrong, whether you look left or right, up or down.

In this chapter, we'll explore the nine most common penalties. We'll see how they arise, how you can fight them, when they can be abated, and how you can appeal if you don't get satisfaction the first time. It might be helpful to glance at the summary chart in Appendix E to get an idea of how these common penalties arise and may be handled.

How the IRS looks at penalties

As an institution, the IRS has the overall goal of imposing and administering penalties fairly. Ever since the penalty program was revised in 1992, agents are supposed to treat similarly situated taxpayers alike, allow them an opportunity to be heard, and act in a fair and impartial manner. Whether this translates into real understanding at the agent's

Unofficially...
In 1996, the Service assessed nearly 34 million penalties for $13 billion. It abated only 3 million of these penalties, about $7 billion worth.

level is another matter entirely. Results vary widely around the country. The imposition of most of these penalties depends greatly on the agent's discretion, or on the judgment of an appeals officer when the agent sustains the penalty.

For this reason, you cannot count on the general "feel-good" objectives of the Internal Revenue Manual. To avoid or overturn these penalties, you must have at your command facts and proof showing "reasonable cause" or meeting a similar standard. Still, the IRS approach must be consistent, accurate, impartial, and correct, with adequate opportunity for you to be heard. In fact, if you present anything resembling reasonable cause to the agent, he is required to advise you of the reasonable cause provisions even if you don't already know that they exist.

For all of these penalties, your reasonable cause or other explanation will be examined quite closely. The IRS will ask many questions, including the following (all drawn from the Internal Revenue Manual):

- Does your reason really address the penalty imposed?

- Do the dates and explanations you offer clearly correspond to the events on which the penalties are based?

- Is this the first time the penalty has been imposed, or are you a repeat offender?

- What is the length of time between the reasonable cause events and your attempt to repair the problem?

- Did you take too long and fail to try to correct the problem?

- Were the events that caused your noncompliance truly beyond your control, or could you have anticipated them?

Asserting or assessing the penalties

The IRS can assess or assert a penalty in many different ways. It depends on the type of penalty and, in part, on how you trigger the penalty.

- Late filing penalty. Sending a late return to an IRS Service Center automatically attracts the 5-percent-per-month late-filing penalty if the return reflects a balance due. But you can still suffer this penalty later, even if the return calls for a refund. Let's say the IRS, auditing a late return for which you were expecting a refund, assesses taxes that exceed what you'd already paid. Suddenly, your return becomes a balance due return, subject to the late-filing penalty.

- The same holds true for the late-payment penalty and the estimated-tax penalty.

- The negligence, substantial understatement, and fraud penalties are normally assessed as a result of an audit, rather than arising automatically at the IRS Service Center where you file your return. That's because a real, live person must look at your facts and affirmatively determine that you acted negligently, committed civil fraud, or substantially understated your taxes.

- The bad-check penalty is simple; the IRS assesses it anytime you bounce a tax check.

- The penalty for failure to deposit payroll taxes starts at 2 percent on the first day and escalates to 10 percent depending on how late you are and how often the IRS has to nudge you by formal notices.

Watch Out!
Always file. If you don't file, the IRS might prepare a "Substitute for Return," estimating how much tax you owe by making all assumptions about exemptions and so forth in the IRS's favor. Suddenly you'll receive a nasty penalty even though you may have paid all the taxes you really owe.

Unofficially...
In 1994, the IRS
imposed the
late-filing penal-
ty more than 5
million times.

■ Finally, the IRS imposes the Trust Fund Recovery Penalty on corporate officers and employees who were responsible for their company's failure to pay withholding taxes. This special penalty is a world unto itself. Chapter 6 discusses it in detail.

These penalties are designed to hurt!

For each category of penalty proposed or assessed by the IRS, different rules apply and different fines or interest rates apply.

Late-filing penalty

The late-filing penalty is extremely high—5 percent per month (or any part of a month) for each month a return is late, to a maximum of 25 percent. The stiffness of this penalty shows that the IRS is serious about having returns filed on time, even when the filer cannot pay in full immediately.

To avoid this penalty, you can apply for an extension to file, but this may not solve all your problems. The first extension, to August 15, is usually automatic. The second, to October 15, is discretionary, but usually granted if you have anything resembling a good reason. Both extensions may be disallowed if you have not paid enough taxes with the extension form. The courts consistently uphold the IRS on this point.

Late-payment penalty

The IRS assessed this little cousin of the late-filing penalty more than 17 million times in 1994. It's imposed automatically by computer when you send a return without full payment. This penalty is 0.5 percent per month, up to 25 percent of the amount you owe. It increases to 1 percent per month after the IRS sends you a "final notice" that your payment is overdue.

The IRS must not simultaneously impose the late-filing and the late-payment penalties, so if you filed more than five months late, you get a free ride on the late-payment penalty for those five months. That's the good news. The bad news is that the maximum for both penalties, put together, is 47.5 percent of the tax due. And that does not include interest, which accrues in the penalty as well as the tax.

Estimated-tax penalty

The estimated tax penalty is the third penalty relating to return filing. This penalty normally arises when you have income that is not subject to withholding, such as interest or dividends, but you haven't paid enough tax on it during the year. As with other penalties, it is asserted by the IRS automatically when you file your return. For this penalty, the IRS even provides a worksheet you can send with your return showing the amount of the penalty.

Accuracy-related penalty

The next group of penalties relate to the accuracy of your return. These penalties range from 20 percent to 75 percent, so, in theory, a taxpayer who really messes up by filing late, paying late, and filing an inaccurate return can rack up penalties from 77 percent to 132 percent of the tax due, plus interest. It doesn't often happen, but, surprisingly, the law allows such a result.

For example, Speedy Sam filed his 1991 federal income tax return three years late. The tax due was $10,000. He had no reasonable cause for this delinquency so the IRS assessed the maximum late-filing penalty (25 percent) and a late-payment penalty (22.5 percent). Then Revenue Agent Ronnie Rushmore audited the return, finding that Sam had committed civil fraud. (Sam had left out income from a stock sale on purpose, that is, with intent to evade the tax laws.) So another $5,000 in tax was asserted, plus a 75 percent civil fraud penalty on this item. If the whole return was fraudulent, the penalties could have totaled 132.5 percent of the tax due.

Negligence. The negligence component of the accuracy penalty can be asserted following an audit. In the real world, some revenue agents propose it routinely. The penalty is 20 percent of the additional tax due. It applies when the IRS concludes you have negligently disregarded tax rules and regulations.

Watch Out!
Some revenue agents think that any time they catch a mistake you make, you must have intentionally disregarded the rules.

Substantial understatement. In place of the negligence penalty, the agent can propose the "substantial understatement" penalty, also 20 percent of the additional tax due. The details of imposing this penalty are complex, but as a rule of thumb, if you owe $5,000 more tax after an audit, the revenue agent can invoke this penalty.

Civil fraud. The civil fraud penalty is imposed when the revenue agent concludes you have intentionally evaded the tax laws. This is the big one, 75 percent of the amount of tax due to fraud. It is routinely asserted after any criminal conviction for evasion. Civil fraud differs from criminal fraud in that it has a lower burden of proof: criminal fraud requires proof beyond a reasonable doubt; civil fraud requires only "clear and convincing" proof. In the words of the IRS manual, the IRS must prove that you materially misrepresented facts, you knew of their falsity, and you intended the IRS to rely on them and act as if they were the truth.

For evidence, the IRS will generally look for "badges of fraud." These might include specific items you understated, fictitious or improper deductions, or false entries or double sets of books. Other badges are destroyed records, false or inconsistent statements, transfers of assets, and consistent underreporting of taxable income over many years. Anything you say or do that looks dishonest, misleading, or evasive could be a badge of fraud. And remember, if the agent finds enough of these badges of fraud, he or she must suspend the investigation and refer the case to the Criminal Investigation Division (CID).

While you wait to hear whether the CID will take your case, you will live in suspended animation, never knowing whether you face jail time. But even if you are "relieved" by the case remaining civil, you could suffer the 75 percent fraud penalty on the underreported tax.

Fraudulent failure to file. People who fail to file returns can't incur the civil fraud penalty—they haven't filed a fraudulent return in the first place. So Congress invented the "fraudulent failure to file" penalty, also up to a whopping 75 percent of the tax due.

For example, Daniel and Diane lived in Spokane, Washington. They made a living through bookmaking (no, not the bibliophile version). Unfortunately for them, this was illegal. The police paid them a surprise house call. Among the things discovered in the raid were wagering records such as "pay and collect" sheets, other bet sheets, cash, bookmaking books, and other gambling paraphernalia. There was also a phone bank that attracted the interest of the police and eleven audio cassette tapes that made for interesting listening. All of this led to raids on several safe deposit boxes plus the seizure of $50,000 in currency. Daniel and Diane were of course convicted of gambling under state law. But their problems didn't stop there. They had not filed federal income tax returns when the raids took place. The IRS added the fraudulent failure to file penalty and the court sustained it.

The same "badges of fraud" that signal tax evasion also point to this new penalty. These include:

- Failing to file returns
- Engaging in an illegal occupation
- Concealing assets
- Failing to cooperate with the tax authorities
- Dealing in cash
- Failing to make estimated payments
- Keeping inadequate records
- Understating income

Although the penalties discussed above are the most common penalties normally encountered, there are more than 100 others. These are more rare, or apply to other types of taxpayers such as return preparers, banks, mortgage companies, and other reporting institutions.

Fighting these penalties on the front lines

Fortunately, the tax laws and IRS procedures give you many ways to fight these penalties, at least eight in most cases. That's the good news. The bad news is that all eight ways are uphill.

1. Preemption. This is the first principle in fighting a penalty. Convince the IRS not to propose the penalty in the first place. In the case of the

late-filing, late-payment, and estimated-tax penalties, send your return to the IRS Service Center with a written request to "nonassess" these penalties due to reasonable cause. You can do the same thing by walking into a local IRS office, speaking to the taxpayer service representative, filing your returns with her, and requesting nonassertion of these penalties.

2. The second path is to let the IRS assess the penalties, then file your "request for abatement." You may also request nonassertion to any revenue officer on an assessed penalty (but not if your return is still in audit).

3. A third way is to claim reasonable cause (or other grounds for nonassertion) during an audit if the penalties are proposed for the first time at that stage. With negligence, substantial understatement, and fraud, the revenue agent's level is normally the place to start. You may also appeal to the revenue agent's boss, the group manager. But the chances of a reversal at this level are somewhere between "slim" and "none."

4. Fourth, you can wait for the Collection Division to begin collecting the assessment, and then request abatement due to reasonable cause.

5. Fifth, you can pay the penalties and file a claim for refund, asserting reasonable cause in your claim or in a later lawsuit for refund of the penalties.

6. Sixth, you can make an offer in compromise (see Chapter 11) on the grounds that you don't owe the penalty because you have reasonable cause. This type of offer is known as an offer based on "doubt as to liability."

Bright Idea
Prepare your case to fight penalties in advance, and attach a complete statement of reasonable cause to the return. That way, you show you understand the problem and have addressed it forthrightly.

Unofficially...
The Trust Fund
Recovery Penalty
is often contest-
ed in federal
court suits. See
Chapter 6 for
more details.

7. Seventh, you can file for bankruptcy. A bankruptcy can often discharge a penalty that is
   more than three years old. But the technicalities
   of this rule are complex. In fact, it is unwise ever
   to file bankruptcy without sound legal advice,
   especially if you are filing to discharge a tax
   penalty. You need to proceed with caution, and
   after full consideration. Chapter 13 discusses
   how to manage taxes and penalties in bankruptcy.

8. Finally, you may fight any of these penalties in
   court. When the IRS assesses them after an
   audit, you may go to United States Tax Court
   first, that is, without having to pay the penalty.
   (See Chapter 15.) If you prefer, you can pay the
   tax and penalty, then file a claim for refund. If
   the claim is denied or six months pass without
   action, you can file suit in federal district court
   or the United States Court of Federal Claims to
   contest the penalty. Chapter 16 discusses these
   procedures in more detail.

With all of these paths to choose from, how do
you make a choice? Generally, it's best to fight the
penalties at the earliest stage and the lowest level.
This could be when you first file your return if it's a
balance due return, or at the audit stage if that's
where the penalty is first asserted. Generally, the
later you launch your claim for abatement or
nonassertion, the less likely the IRS will be to listen.
Besides, in the tax business, its usually better to
know bad news as quickly as possible. It helps in
your tax and business planning.

Appealing denial of penalty abatement

All of these paths converge when you appeal. You may appeal the denial of your abatement claim after most of these stages. The appeal goes to the Office of Appeals, the same office that considers income tax appeals following an audit and, since 1998, many appeals on tax collection issues. Appeals officers have full authority to abate or compromise penalties, wherever the appeal comes from within the system.

If you are denied at audit, or at the Service Center when you file a return, you will usually receive a polite denial letter explaining your rights to appeal. The IRS must also furnish a statement explaining how the penalty was computed. The IRS normally allows thirty days to file a protest. Then, the Revenue Agent or Taxpayer Service Representative packages your file and ships it to the Office of Appeals. The appeals officer reviews the case, contacts you, asks for more information if you have it, and schedules either a phone call or an in-person conference to review your appeal.

Now let's say the appeals officer denies your request for abatement of the penalty. Are you out of luck? Of course not. You can still fight some penalties in court. The Tax Court has jurisdiction if you haven't paid the penalties. The U.S. district courts or U.S. Court of Federal Claims can hear the case if you have.

Proving your case

You, not the IRS, have the burden of proving your case to abate these penalties, except for fraudulent failure to file and civil fraud. To avoid the late-filing,

Bright Idea
Appeal IRS penalties. There is usually no reason not to do so. And, as this section shows, you have many chances to contest these penalties—at least three and sometimes four or five, depending on how often you appeal within the court system.

late-payment, estimated-tax, and bad-check penalties, you must show "reasonable cause," or something conceptually similar. The casebooks and professional literature are littered with thousands of cases interpreting what these two little words mean. It all boils down to this: If you have a pretty good excuse, the mistake wasn't your fault, you tried to prevent it, and you corrected it as best you could, that's reasonable cause.

Even then, however, you don't always win. Remember that thousands of taxpayers who thought their cases were airtight have gone to court and lost. Even those who eventually won only wound up in court in the first place because the IRS initially rejected their statements of reasonable cause.

The Internal Revenue Manual spells out what the agency considers reasonable cause. All winning arguments in penalty excusal cases are variations of these. Here are the eleven "official" reasonable causes.

Death, serious illness, or unavoidable absence

A death, serious illness, or unavoidable absence of you or a member of your immediate family may be reasonable cause. Of all the official excuses, this is probably the most common. "Serious illness" appears to be epidemic among nonfilers, that is, people who are so late with their returns that they haven't filed at all. The Service's own studies of nonfilers have shown that a pattern of nonfiling often results from a serious physical or mental illness. It could be a bitter divorce; a business disaster; mental illness; drug, alcohol, mental, physical, or sexual abuse; or other personal tragedy lasting for years at a time. Combinations of two or more of these disasters are common.

If the tale of personal woe is serious and credible, the IRS often grants the request for abatement. In many cases, a mental illness, drug abuse, or alcoholism has prevented an otherwise diligent taxpayer to fail in filing and payment obligations. (Don't, however, try the excuse one man used: "tax-return-phobia." His phobia was real, but imagine the consequences if this diagnosis had been accepted as an excuse by the court. Of course, it was not.)

In some cases, if you can prove serious mental or physical illness, such as severe depression and paralysis, you should be relieved of the penalty.

The key here is to convince the IRS that your claim is not frivolous. The nature of the particular syndrome, such as alcoholism, depression, or abuse, often stretches back many years, so the more you elaborate on how the illness got started and how it culminated in your late filing or late payment, the more likely an IRS employee will be inclined to believe you and find you have shown reasonable cause.

A full statement of reasonable cause can sometimes run to ten single-spaced, typewritten pages, with a half an inch or more of medical, social, or psychiatric documentation. To request abatement of these penalties due to illness, write the IRS a letter, include Form 2751, and tell the full story. Include the dates and nature of your illness or absence, show how the illness or absence prevented compliance, and note whether other things you did in life, such as running your business, also suffered as a result. This will help convince the IRS that you are not engaging in special pleading.

It is impossible to overstate how important good documentation is for this type of reasonable cause. The IRS treats your statement of reasonable cause very seriously.

Watch Out!
Don't let fear of disclosure keep you from using personal crises as a reason to have a penalty abated. IRS agents diligently guard the privacy of the information you submit. And, as painful as it may be to recount the details, a compelling story often causes the IRS to give you the benefit of the doubt.

Fire, casualty, natural disaster, or other disturbance

Believe it or not, some people succeed in abating penalties by claiming, "There was a flood in my basement," or "A fire burned my records." Of course, it's one thing to say and another to prove. You have to show how and why. Address whether you could have gotten your tax return or payment together by other means. Again, documentation always helps. Enclose fire, police, or insurance reports, if available, and attach any other supportive documentation. Notarized statements from disinterested third persons are always credible and helpful. Pictures also are worth a thousand words.

Unable to obtain necessary records

When your records are missing, the "reasonableness" of your cause depends on whether you exercised "ordinary business care and prudence," even though your records disappeared. In your request for abatement, specify the nature of the records, why they were unavailable, how you tried to fix the situation, whether you called the Service about the missing information, and why you couldn't use estimates and still comply.

For example, Sal was divorced from his wife Mona. She moved out and took all records of income and expense pertaining to Sal's profession. He went to court to get the records back, but failed. He met with the IRS before the due date, told them he was at his wit's end trying to get his records, and signed an extension until July 15 to file the return. Before that deadline, he went again to the IRS and told them he still couldn't get all of his records together. So the IRS told him to do the best he could, which he did. Naturally, the IRS penalized him. But the court rejected this penalty. He had done all he could to reconstruct his records, and even asked for professional help, so his conduct should not be penalized.

Lack of funds

Not many people succeed by saying "I can't pay," but if you have a good reason, it's worth a try. An inability to pay despite your best efforts or due to circumstances beyond your control might be reasonable cause for late payment. For example, if you were about to pay a tax bill but someone stole or embezzled the money you had set aside, that might be reasonable cause if you had no way of preventing or foreseeing it. If undue hardship, bankruptcy, or insolvency might have resulted if you paid the taxes on time, you might have reasonable cause. An example might be a sudden, totally unexpected bill, or a sudden downturn in business.

The following happened in a case involving a company building ships for the Navy. The Navy and the builder had the usual fights over performance of the contract, but nothing horrible happened until the Navy stopped progress payments. Eventually, the taxpayer-contractor could pay only certain subcontractors and suppliers, and as a result failed to deposit payroll taxes. The Navy then terminated the contract, owing the company more than $165,000. "Reasonable cause," said the court. The company did the best it could, and it had a right to rely on the Navy's promise to pay. It was the government's own fault that the contractor couldn't pay its taxes.

Ignorance of the law

This one is especially tough. We've all heard that "ignorance of the law is no excuse," a principle that

Moneysaver
You might qualify to have your penalty abated if there has been a recent change in the tax law pertinent to your case, and information about the change is unavailable to people generally. This is one of the few cases where "ignorance of the law" is a valid excuse.

applies doubly when it comes to taxes. Still, there's a tiny bit of wiggle room in this principle. The IRS's manual says that ignorance of the law, combined with other facts and circumstances such as limited education or lack of previous tax-penalty experience, may support reasonable cause. For instance, where you confront a difficult or complex tax issue and the Service doesn't give you guidance, the IRS may concede that reasonable people might differ as to how to treat the issue.

Making a mistake or being forgetful

Again, this is not usually a valid excuse, but some court cases have held that a subordinate's error was excusable. An example might be if you tell your trusty assistant, "Now, Dr. Watson, I want you to take this tax return and immediately go to the post office to mail it." When Dr. Watson fails to mail the return because he forgot and stuck it in the drawer, that might be reasonable cause. Of course, if Dr. Watson had a reputation for forgetting things, the IRS would conclude that you could have anticipated his behavior, and you'd be out of luck.

Even if your trusted employee makes the mistakes, however, this may not be reasonable cause, as one physicians' group found out. The longtime, trusted secretary was supposed to make tax deposits and file returns, but did not. The courts ruled that the doctors could not delegate this ministerial responsibility to someone else, then avoid responsibility for that employee's failure.

Relying on the advice of a competent tax adviser

If your accountant or lawyer made a mistake in advising you, you shouldn't be blamed for it. Of course, you have to prove that an adviser you selected made the mistake. Also required is proof the adviser was otherwise competent, and that you gave complete information and cooperation. If your accountant says you don't have to file on April 15 and don't even need an extension, that might not be reasonable cause, because everyone, specialist or not, is expected to know that April 15 is the ordinary deadline for filing taxes. But if she informed you that a $100,000 court award was not taxable, and it really was taxable, that might be reasonable cause, because this is a gray area of the law and not everyone can be expected to know the precise rules.

Erroneous oral advice from the IRS

Where the IRS gives you bad advice, you would expect to have reasonable cause, and indeed that is so. But, again, you must jump through hoops. You must show you gave the IRS accurate and complete information, and that you exercised ordinary business care and prudence when you relied on the advice. Because this relates to oral advice, proving these elements is difficult, but even your detailed handwritten notes of your conversations with the IRS may suffice.

To appreciate how difficult it is to prove the "erroneous oral advice" scenario, consider the case of a law firm that failed to file employment tax returns for most of two years. Naturally, this minor omission attracted the IRS's attention. Marilyn, a revenue officer, got the case, and the firm asked for her help. She helped fill out the returns, and the firm sent in payment of more than $100,000, which, on Marilyn's advice, they regarded as full payment. "Not so", said the IRS's computers, and, so a large penalty was assessed. Could the law firm get out of it? No. Marilyn was mistaken, but her mistake was

Bright Idea
To help support your claim of erroneous oral advice from the IRS, keep a written record of what office you called, the person to whom you spoke, and the date the IRS gave you the advice.

Unofficially...
In the real world,
the IRS is fairly
liberal about
abating penalties
when its own
employees gave
incorrect advice
in writing.
It tends to give
the taxpayer the
benefit of
the doubt.

the fault of the company: she had access only to the tax information shown on the IRS computer, and some of this information was erroneous because the firm had filed an incorrect return in the past.

Erroneous written advice from the IRS

The same idea is at work in this case as in the previous one, but your proof is a little easier here. In fact, there's even a law requiring the IRS to abate any penalty attributable to its own erroneous written advice. But that advice must refer to your specific written request. Also, as above, you must have given the IRS complete and accurate information about your situation, and you have to have relied on the advice.

Failure to deposit due to lack of coupons

Employers deposit payroll taxes using a coupon, Form 8109. If you don't have or run out of these coupons, you may have reasonable cause for failure to deposit, but you need to show you used ordinary business care and prudence. This includes requesting the coupon books five to six weeks in advance but not receiving them in time. Also, federal tax deposit coupons, Forms 8109-B, are available from some IRS offices. Try to demonstrate you didn't have them and couldn't get them in time.

Embezzlement

Employees and officers who embezzle company money are becoming an increasingly common fact of business life. However, blaming a late-filing or late-payment penalty on embezzlers seldom works. Example: For almost thirty years, Hartley worked long and hard in his leather importing business. Then he suffered a heart attack. So his vice president and controller took over. And "take over" they did. They embezzled more than $150,000 and tried to hide their offense by failing to file payroll tax returns. The accountant for the company noticed the problem and sounded the alarm. Hartley returned to find the disaster. Could his company get out of the penalty? "No", said the judge.

Bad-check penalty

This one is difficult but not impossible to have abated. If the bank made a mistake or the IRS made a mistake in handling the check, that's probably reasonable cause. If the check was lost in the mail and you replaced it, stopping payment on the first check, the IRS should abate the bad-check penalty if it later receives your first check and tries to cash it. Also, sometimes a freeze can be placed on your bank account for other reasons, such as another creditor's judgment or the death of a signatory. The Service will usually consider these to be reasonable cause as well, but, again, you have to show you tried to prevent the check being bad or did your best to make it good afterward.

Negligence penalty

When you omit an income item from your return or your deductions are disallowed, you may have acted "negligently." This means you failed to make a reasonable attempt to comply with the revenue laws or failed to exercise ordinary and reasonable care in preparing your tax return. Negligence also includes a failure to keep adequate books and records or to substantiate items of income or deduction properly. Finally, an item on your return is attributable to negligence if it lacks a reasonable basis but falls short of outright fraud.

Watch Out!
To overcome the negligence penalty, the burden of proof is on you to show that you did your best and acted reasonably and prudently in taking the deduction.

In the real world, some revenue agents reason that you must be negligent for every disallowed deduction or extra income. If you had not been negligent, they think, you would not have taken a disallowed deduction, or you would have included the extra item of income. This circular reasoning is not the law, but sometimes you may need to fight long and hard to convince them.

And some actions clearly are negligent. Failing to include an income item (such as bank interest) as to which an information return (such as a Form 1099) has been filed, and taking a deduction or credit that seem too good to be true, are examples. If you are careless or reckless, or if you intentionally disregard IRS rules or regulations, that's negligence.

Check for such things as prior audits where your position was allowed. Prove you examined your return carefully. Show you relied on the advice of an accountant or an attorney, that you reasonably interpreted IRS publications in taking the deduction, or that the law changed. Demonstrate that your position was justified, even if it turned out to be incorrect. In particular, proving an honest misunderstanding of the facts or the law may overcome the negligence penalty.

The rules of the road to avoid the negligence penalty are simple:

1. Take a good-faith position.

2. Stick to it.

3. Make full disclosure to your advisers and the IRS.

"Substantial understatement" penalty

Another component of the accuracy penalty is the "substantial understatement" of taxes. Even if you aren't negligent, the IRS can penalize you 20 percent if the changes to your return result in a "substantial" understatement. You avoid this aspect of the accuracy-related penalty if you disclose the item on the return or you have substantial legal authority for reporting it the way you did.

You may also avert the substantial understatement penalty by finding substantial authority for the position you took on the return. This requires researching the law, including the statutes, regulations, court cases, and other tax authority. Of course, assembling this authority before taking the deduction also satisfies the negligence standard. All these grounds for penalty relief have an additional common element: do everything you can to fix the problem, catch up, or get duplicate records. You can't sit back thinking, "Oh well, I got sick (or I lost my records) so I don't have to file or pay until I get around to it." Show the IRS that you scrambled in every reasonable way to avoid or fix the problem once you learned of it, or to correct it after the failure occurred.

Estimated-tax penalty

To earn relief from the estimated-tax penalty, you must generally show that your failure to pay the right amount of estimated tax was caused by casualty, disaster, or unusual circumstances, and that imposing the penalty would be against equity and good conscience. This is not the same as the "reasonable cause" you may use for other penalties. Even the Internal Revenue Manual itself states that reliance on a competent tax adviser, or erroneous advice from the IRS, would not be enough to waive the estimated tax penalty.

You must show circumstances such as that your records were destroyed by fire, flood, or other natural disaster, you became seriously ill or injured, or

Bright Idea
Every year, the IRS publishes a list of the items (including Schedule A items) that are "adequately disclosed" just by reporting them on the return. As to any other item, consider filing Form 8275 if the item is questionable.

that your estimated-tax payments were offset against past-due child support or other federal debts. There are other waivers available for newly retired or disabled individuals, but, again, these must be shown to include reasonable cause and an absence of willful neglect.

Mechanics of making your abatement request

Try to use official IRS forms, since IRS employees are familiar with them. The supporting documentation for your reasonable cause request need not follow any particular form. Letters, affidavits, or statements will suffice. When you appeal from a denial, you likewise need no particular form; a letter is sufficient. Also, the IRS's denial letters often contain specific instructions on how to frame the appeal letter, whom to send it to, and when.

Above all, don't give up. These penalties might represent your entire profit margin or discretionary budget. They are sometimes quite high, and interest is charged on them. Sometimes you'll have success at the second or third level where the first was a disaster. Take advantage of every chance the law and the IRS give you to contest and protest these penalties.

Just the facts

- IRS penalties apply in a number of situations and are designed to hurt.
- There are several ways to fight an IRS penalty, from convincing the IRS not to assert one in the first place to fighting the IRS in court.
- Each kind of penalty can be appealed using different strategies. Familiarize yourself with the specific characteristics of each.
- When seeking to have a penalty abated, the burden of proof is always on you.

GET THE SCOOP ON...
How a small business gets into big payroll
tax trouble ▪ There ought to be a law! (There
is!) ▪ How the IRS investigates your case ▪
Fighting back against this penalty

The Trust Fund Recovery Penalty

Chapter 6

Statistics show that most of American business is small business, not big business. The entrepreneurial spirit motivates large numbers of people to start their own businesses. No matter what the form, getting those businesses off the ground is often difficult. And, because the tax laws make you, the employer, responsible for withholding taxes, those withheld taxes are sometimes a tempting source of cash for business operations. Hundreds of thousands of business people succumb to that temptation every year, using money that is not their own to pay their bills. A typical case might arise in the following way.

Setting the scene

It had been a banner year for Wonder Widgets, Inc. Sales had finally hit the $1 million mark, an all-time high. The last quarter of the calendar year (October, November, and December) had been exceptionally good, capped by a great Christmas rush. Sure, some

Unofficially...
The income, Social Security, and Medicare taxes withheld from the paycheck are known as the "trust fund" part of the tax. It's considered "in trust" when an employer withholds it from your pay.

of Wonder Widgets' customers were a bit slow to pay, but the money always came in—enough for a great Christmas party and bonuses for Ed Wonder, the president, Ben Bighthard, the controller, and Penny Pencil, the chief bookkeeper.

Early in January, Ed Wonder called a meeting with Bighthard, Pencil, and the sales force, as he did every year. The chief sales representative informed him that they'd just received three big orders from the U.S. government for 30,000 boxes of widgets. To fulfil the order, they'd have to bring on more workers or order new machines, and they'd need more steel and other parts.

Bighthard reminded Wonder that they still carried a lot of debt and had had to pay a 10 percent IRS penalty for late deposit of payroll. But Wonder scoffed at his reluctance and insisted that they could keep operating as they had done.

Unfortunately, January began with a record snowfall and the beginning of a severe recession. Big checks the company was expecting did not come through or bounced. Money was short, but Wonder continued to insist that the employees get paid before payroll taxes and debts to suppliers were paid.

By the end of March, the company owed $10,000 in payroll taxes, and by June, the company fell another $15,000 behind in payroll taxes. Bighthard continued to fill out, sign, and file the payroll tax returns (Form 941) on time.

By September, the company was behind another $10,000, money was tighter than ever, and the recession was biting deeply. Then came the notices. Some IRS computer had awakened to the company's $35,000 tax debt. The first notice came to

Bighthard. It was polite but firm. He called Wonder. "Ed, we just got a notice from the IRS for $35,000. There's a penalty in there as well. What do we do?"

Wonder wondered and pondered. "Pay what you can," he finally said, "but if we can't pay it all, we'll just have to tough it out. I know that the money will be there. Just use the net incoming checks to pay the IRS." "But we promised that money to Soomee Supply, remember? And also to Cold Steel for more parts." "I know," said Wonder. "Just use your own judgment. You and Pencil work it out. You decide who is screaming the loudest, and pay them."

September became October, then November. November rolled into December. On December 15, the knock on the door came. It was an IRS revenue officer, Dan Dollar, there to collect the back taxes. "Did you know, Mr. Wonder," Dollar said in a firm and sincere tone, "that you can be held personally liable for the withheld taxes that you didn't pay to the government? That's what I'm here to investigate."

Wonder cringed. Acid turned his stomach to silly putty. "I guess so," he sighed, "But I really wasn't making any of the payment decisions, at least not lately. I've been out in the field. Ben Bighthard and Penny Pencil were doing all of the decision making and all of the check signing. It's their fault." "Did you know that these taxes were due?" asked Dollar. "Yes, we all did," said Wonder. "We've had the same problem before, and we fixed it! Nobody meant any harm. Lots of money has come in to the company, more than enough to pay the taxes, but there always seemed to be something that was more pressing. But don't worry, we'll catch up."

Watch Out!
A situation like the one described here with the Wonder Widgets, Inc. happens to companies and individuals hundreds of thousands of times each year.

"I know you will try, Mr. Wonder," said the revenue officer. "But in the meantime, I'm here to see who should be made personally liable for these back taxes. It's called the Trust Fund Recovery Penalty. Let's start with—*you*."

Does this scenario sound familiar? Here's how that company payroll tax problem becomes a personal problem, and what you can do about it.

What is this "penalty"?

The Wonder Widgets problem occurs because employers in effect work for Uncle Sam, collecting the IRS's taxes through the withholding system. States with income tax laws (all but two) also impose wage withholding. If most employers didn't obey the withholding laws, our federal and state governments would screech to a halt. And in fact, most employers do comply, doing their best to get their employers the right forms, to withhold the right amount of pay, and to pay that money to the federal and state governments.

By law, employers make three kinds of payments to the IRS after each payday. The check (or electronic transfer) they send covers:

1. The income tax withheld from the employees' paychecks;

2. The Social Security and Medicare tax also withheld;

3. The employer's matching Social Security/ Medicare payment.

The first two items—the withheld portions—are known as the "trust fund" part of the tax. The money doesn't have to be put in a separate bank account, but it's automatically deemed "in trust" from the instant your employer withholds it from your pay. In a perfect world, the money is there.

But the world is far from perfect. What if your employer, like Ed Wonder of Wonder Widgets, just doesn't have the money, or decides to pocket that money? What if he deliberately fails to pay the payroll taxes to the federal and state governments for some other reason? This happens with annoying frequency and for a number of different reasons. The federal and state governments lose billions that way every year.

There ought to be a law!

Actually, there are *several* laws. (There's a law against everything except more laws.) Technically, it's a crime for an employer to fail to pay payroll taxes. The IRS is rarely interested in pursuing criminal sanctions against employers, however; it wants the money. So it uses a special weapon about 50,000 times a year—the Trust Fund Recovery Penalty.

This penalty makes the people who were responsible for the nonpayment personally liable for 100 percent of the money that was withheld but not paid to the IRS, that is, 100 percent of the withheld income and Social Security/Medicare tax. The penalty does not apply to the employer's share of Social Security/Medicare.

For example, suppose the payroll for a two-week pay period totaled $92,500. But the net pay to the employees was only $70,000. The other $22,500 was made up of $15,000 of withheld income tax and $7,500 of withheld Social Security/Medicare. The corporation also owes another $7,500 of Social Security/Medicare. If the employer doesn't pay that $30,000 to the IRS, the people the IRS determines are "responsible" for the nonpayment are each personally liable for the $15,000 and the withheld $7,500 (items 1 and 2), though not for the $7,500 of employer Social Security/Medicare.

Unofficially...
The Trust Fund Recovery Penalty used to be called the "100 percent" penalty, because the penalty equalled 100 percent of the taxes that were withheld but not paid over. It wasn't really a penalty, though; it was just a substitute for the corporation's unpaid tax.

Moneysaver
The cost of paying late is always at least a federal tax deposit penalty, a minimum of 5 percent and a maximum of 15 percent of the amount not paid or deposited, plus interest.

Of course, the corporation is also liable, and the IRS goes after that primary payer first. But the Trust Fund Recovery Penalty makes the responsible persons "guarantee" the trust fund part of the corporation's payment. This penalty is a debt that can follow you for at least ten years, or the rest of your life, whichever comes first. The limited liability you personally enjoy from most corporate debts simply does not apply against this federal law. On top of that, you cannot discharge this penalty by filing for personal bankruptcy, as you can with most personal debts.

Though the debt is enforceable for a long time, many employers either don't realize this or give in anyway to the temptation not to pay the IRS. Most states have laws like the federal one, holding the responsible officers personally liable for state withholding taxes. They also have laws imposing personal liability for many other types of taxes, sometimes including sales tax.

This Trust Fund Recovery Penalty can be a major tragedy for the businessperson. After all, why would any employer not pay these trust fund taxes? For most, like Ed Wonder, it's only because he doesn't have the money. Sure, in some cases the businessperson simply pockets the money and takes a permanent vacation to Tahiti. But those cases are rare. Most business owners want to stay in business and prosper, but when money gets too tight, many take a chance by paying only the squeakest wheels.

Sometimes an employer finds that back taxes keep building up. Their accountants, controllers, bookkeepers, lawyers, or other financial advisers warn them of what they already know, that they must pay those taxes. But the cash never seems to come in the door fast enough, or there are unexpected expenses or economic downturns. To such employers, keeping the doors open is paramount. Since the IRS squeaks only later, though louder, many ever-optimistic businesspeople take a chance by hoping that good times are right around the corner.

What about the employees? They've paid their taxes. Despite their employer's failure to pay that money to the federal government, by law they still get credit on their tax returns.

How the IRS handles these cases

In these payroll tax cases, the IRS is like a hibernating bear. It wakes up late, sometimes years after the first default, but it also wakes up very hungry and aggressive. Often two or three years have gone by; the employer may owe $50,000, $100,000, $200,000, or more. On top of that, penalties and interest have been assessed by the IRS's computers, so the situation often looks close to hopeless.

The longer the default goes on, the easier it is to continue and the harder it is to feel that you can ever catch up.

When the IRS's computers wake up to an employer's default, the Service Centers first print out a series of notices. These notices have lots of information, but they all boil down to this: "Hey, Wonder Widgets, you didn't send us your tax deposits. Do so now, or else." Typically, for every calendar quarter the employer doesn't pay in full, four such notices go out. The first one is polite ("It seems there may be a problem here; please check and pay"), the last a declaration of war ("This is your final notice. Enforcement action may be taken immediately against you"). Some repeat offender businesses and large-dollar cases get only two notices. Others get phone calls, too.

Unofficially...
Charles O. Rossotti, the IRS Commissioner who took office in 1998, has promised a far more proactive approach to payroll tax problems. This means the IRS will try to prevent the default in the first place, or even jump on the default once it is detected, rather than being content to penalize you afterwards,

Bright Idea
The tax reform act of 1998 gives every taxpayer vast new rights to contest IRS levies before they are made. See Chapter 4. Among other rights, you have the right to appeal the intent to issue a levy to the Office of Appeals.

When you get one of these notices, the absolute worst course is to ignore it. The computer remembers (and takes offense) that it sent you the notice and you didn't respond. Once the last notice is issued and thirty days pass, the IRS is legally free to start collecting by any means it can. This can include levying on bank accounts and accounts receivable or even closing down a business where the boss is "pyramiding the payroll taxes."

Sometimes the delinquent accounts are transferred to the Automated Collection System (ACS), the IRS's second-stage collection function. Despite the name, the Automated Collection System employs real people who call you for payment and schedule payment dates or installment agreements. The "automated" part comes into play when ACS automatically files notices of tax lien and issues levies. The IRS collects a great deal of money by these computerized notices from the Service Centers and the ACS (about $20 billion in 1996). But billions still fall through the cracks.

That's when the cavalry, the revenue officers of the Collection Division, charge into action. The computer doesn't give up. It prints out alert notices known as *TDAs*, or *Taxpayer Delinquent Accounts*. One TDA form is printed for each reporting period, in this case, a calendar quarter (January through March, April through June, and so on). The computer, having done its best, now sends the TDA to the local office of the Collection Division. The TDA forms for each quarter arrive at the local Collection Division office, where the case is assigned.

The revenue officer's job is to go out and get the taxes. For the most part, revenue officers are well-educated, well-trained, and tough. They use a range of powers. At one end of the spectrum, they use friendly persuasion. At the other end, they can impose and carry out a corporate "death sentence," physically closing down a business by locking the doors and changing the locks to prevent more tax defaults.

The revenue officer's first step is to call or visit the employer and have a little chat. He does not say, "Hello, I'm Revenue Officer Dan Dollar, and I'm here to help you." He both is and is not. At this first meeting, the revenue officer demands full payment immediately of all the taxes. He also explains how much is due—taxes, penalties, and interest.

Does Ed Wonder immediately turn around and write out a check? Of course not. He doesn't have the money. That's why the company defaulted in the first place. Revenue officers know this, but they are required to make the demand anyway. Then the revenue officer and Ed Wonder discuss how the back taxes can be paid (if they can be paid). Paying over time is possible in some cases.

In cases where a business has defaulted on tax debt in the past, the revenue officer will insist on one absolute, nonnegotiable condition of any deal to pay the back taxes: a company must pay all current and future payroll taxes when they are due, and must demonstrate that compliance to the revenue officer. Otherwise, the revenue officer will close the business. Of course, an entrepreneur like Ed Wonder will agree. What choice does he have? Between business life and death, he'll choose life, even if it turns out to be short. Wonder then gets down to the nitty-gritty: negotiating with the revenue officer for payment of the rest of the back taxes.

Unofficially...
The 1998 tax act imposed some restrictions on the revenue officer's authority to seize business assets. This intention to seize assets must now be personally approved by the District Director. Additionally, the business assets must be evaluated for their collection potential, probably meaning on an item-by-item basis.

Unofficially...
As a rule of
thumb, if a cor-
poration owes
$10,000 in taxes,
about $6,000 to
$7,500 will be
the withheld,
or trust fund,
portion.

The agent goes for your wallet

In the meantime, Revenue Officer Dollar also begins
to investigate the people who might be personally
liable for the nonpayment. He reminds Ed that he
and others in the company can be held personally
liable for the trust fund portion of the payroll taxes.
He tells Ed that even if the corporation can pay, the
IRS is required to investigate others' personal liability for the Trust Fund Recovery Penalty.

In this way, the government can hope to recover
about two-thirds of the unpaid taxes even if other
means fail and the corporation goes under. When
your personal assets are on the line because of this
potential penalty, it tends to get your attention. But
the Trust Fund Recovery Penalty is not automatic or
self-executing. The revenue officer can't just hand
you a bill. He has to investigate thoroughly who
should be assessed, then make a recommendation
based on the facts and the law.

That's all he can do—recommend. That recommendation has to be approved and a bill sent out. As
we'll see, anyone who is considered for the penalty
has the right to appeal before the recommendation
is made final, and the additional right to fight it
afterward in court. The revenue officer's investigation usually lasts several weeks, but can stretch into
months.

Who is a "responsible" person?

The Internal Revenue Code imposes personal
liability for the Trust Fund Recovery Penalty on anyone who

- is a "responsible" person and
- "willfully" causes the corporation not to pay the
  payroll taxes or "willfully" fails to ensure that the
  taxes are paid.

You don't even have to be employed by the corporation to be liable for this penalty. In fact, even other *corporations* have been held liable for this penalty where they took such an active role in the defaulting corporation's financial affairs that they became responsible for the trust fund taxes. But those cases are rare.

These days, as a rule, only the true sources of financial authority inside the corporation will be investigated and held liable. In most cases, the IRS focuses on the officers and directors. So Revenue Officer Dollar will be on the lookout for two issues as to each person he investigates: *responsibility* and *willfulness*.

Responsibility

The *responsible* persons are those who truly control the finances and make the decisions on whom to pay and when. The revenue officer looks for "badges of authority." Signature authority on the checking account is usually a dead giveaway, especially if the revenue officer finds that the signatory also actually signed checks to creditors. In the Wonder Widgets case, clearly Ed Wonder had enough financial authority. What about Bighthard and Pencil? Not at first; but later, when they began to make decisions on their own and signed checks, they became liable.

The revenue officer also looks at the corporate officers, shareholders, and directors. He'll find out who hired and fired employees, a sign of significant authority. Who was responsible for completing the employment tax returns (Form 941)? Who was responsible for signing these returns, for preparing payroll, for cutting the payroll checks? Who negotiated for loans at the bank?

For example, Abel, his two sons, Baker and Char-
lie, and his wife, Delta, all worked together in the
family business, a retail store. While the company
had been formally incorporated for more than
twenty years, the family ran the shop as informally as
their breakfast table. Abel and his sons operated the
store; Delta kept the books. In fact, she had the
authority to sign checks and signed over 10,000 of
them stretching over seven years. Delta was the only
one who had training in financial matters, and she
used that training to work with the bank, the company's accountant, and the IRS. While she called
herself a bookkeeper, in fact she exercised control
and made all the decisions on expenses, including
paying taxes. The company defaulted on $250,000
worth of payroll taxes. Since she could have stopped
this default but didn't, the IRS assessed her for
$194,000, and made it stick in court.

As another example, Robert formed Fixtures,
Inc., to install fixtures in office and commercial
buildings. The next year, he hired his brother Gary
as controller, treasurer, and chief financial officer.
Gary's job was to supervise all accounting, prepare
financial statements, keep up the books, and supervise an outside payroll service. An outside accountant also helped Robert run the business. On top of
this, Robert had signature authority over the checking account.

Three years later, things went downhill. Cash
flow became very tight, and Gary and Robert fought
often over a new computer system that was supposed
to help them. Everyone met in October. The
accountant recommended a delay in paying the payroll taxes for up to six weeks so the company could
save $60,000. "Of course," said the CPA, "there will

be interest, and, at worst, the government can make some personal assessments," but it will give the company breathing room.

That breathing space turned into a gasp and a choke. The payroll taxes went unpaid, and the IRS assessed—you guessed it—Gary. Who won this case? This time, Gary won. True enough, he had the authority to sign checks, but Robert and the CPA actually decided which checks were to be made out. All financial control was in the hands of Robert and the CPA, not Gary. So despite all his apparent authority, he was found not responsible.

To find these and other badges of authority, the revenue officer hunts for and demands to see paper: corporate minutes, stock records, bank records, bank signature cards, and virtually anything else he can find that tells him who had the true authority to direct the payment of creditors. He'll look at contracts and bills, cancelled checks, and receipts.

He will interview as many people as seems appropriate, using an interview form, Form 4180, as a guide. When completed, this form tells the revenue officer virtually everything he needs to know about the financial movers and shakers inside the corporation. This form contains a thorough review of all factors courts have looked to in imposing liability under this penalty.

Willfulness

The revenue officer then turns to the other issue, willfulness. He has to show that a responsible person willfully caused the corporation not to pay, or stood by while other creditors were paid ahead of the IRS. No fraud or evil intent need be proved, only the knowledge the taxes are due at a time when that

Bright Idea
If you are an innocent employee of a company that is falling behind on its payroll tax payments, gather evidence as you go along. This puts control of your tax fate in your own hands rather than depending on the president of the company, who has a vested interest in placing the blame on others.

Watch Out!
Many people so fear the IRS that they immediately give in when the revenue officer proposes to assert the penalty. This is a major mistake. Often an employee was simply following the boss's orders and should not be held liable, at least not for all the taxes. Just because a revenue officer says you are liable doesn't make it so.

person could have paid the IRS. Simple knowledge is enough. In fact, even if you didn't know but *should have* known, that's enough to make you willful.

For example, if you signed a Form 941 payroll tax return showing a balance due, you know taxes are due. If you prepared or saw a financial statement for the company showing taxes due, that's enough. In fact, if the company now in default had even a single payroll tax problem in the past that you knew about, that can be enough to define you as willful. Similarly, in certain situations where you are aware that the company is in financial trouble in other ways, the IRS thinks it is your responsibility to make sure the company is not failing to comply with payroll taxes.

After the revenue officer gathers the evidence, he writes a report as part of a form called Recommendation for *Trust Fund Recovery Penalty Assessment.* True enough, it's only a recommendation; but once the agent "recommends," it's all over but the shouting. The revenue officer sends that form and all the supporting documentation to his boss, the group manager. If the group manager approves, as they almost always do, the revenue officer then calls the responsible persons, asking whether they will agree to the liability.

Remember that the revenue officer, despite his power, cannot actually make you liable or give you a tax bill. All he can do is recommend. You then have rights you can exercise before any bill is issued, and when you exercise those rights, sometimes the penalty is reduced or not imposed.

Now, let's say the revenue officer has called you, and after careful thought you politely say, "No, thank you" to the suggestion that you agree to a $100,000 tax bill. What then?

The revenue officer then writes a formal letter to you in which he says he will recommend the assessment. Again, that is not a bill. It's only a notice to you that he wants to make it official, subject to your right to appeal. That formal letter, now required by law, is known as a sixty-day letter. You have sixty days formally to agree or disagree. If you agree or fail to respond, that ends the matter. Your tax bill will shortly issue, and you will become even better acquainted with the revenue officer as he pursues your personal assets for collection.

If you disagree, you can fight the recommendation by appealing. Should you disagree? Yes, if you truly believe you are not liable for some or all of the default and you have favorable evidence. To stop the revenue officer's recommendation from becoming a legally enforceable bill, respond to the sixty-day letter by appealing with a document called a "protest" whenever there is real doubt that you in fact are liable. It's your right. During that appeal time, no interest accrues on the penalty (nor is it assessed). Appeals can be heard quickly or not, depending on how busy your IRS district is.

Make your appeal more appealing

Let's say you want to appeal. At this point, it is essential to get help from a tax professional experienced with this penalty. Appealing a Trust Fund Recovery Penalty recommendation is complicated. The case law governing who is liable is vast and challenging. You may need only advice. You may need more guidance or reassurance that you're on the right track. Or you may need the tax professional to carry the full burden for you. But whatever your needs, do not appeal on your own. You will almost surely lose. To fight the penalty, send the protest as a letter to the IRS office that proposed the assessment.

Moneysaver
If you have more evidence in your favor, you can send it to the revenue officer. But that's normally a useless exercise. The officer has already made up his mind. Save your evidence for appeal, and argue that "newly discovered evidence" should make a difference in the extent of your liability.

Bright Idea
Appeals officers
know that many
people prepare
and file their
own protests. So
don't worry about
how "legal" the
protest sounds.
Proven facts
always speak
louder than
clever wording,
so just state and
support the facts
and relate them
to the legal
standards as best
you can.

These protests are similar in format to protests in income tax cases. In the protest, acknowledge receipt of the sixty-day letter and state that you are now protesting it. The body of the protest has these six parts:

1. *Name and address.*

2. *Date and symbol of letter.* State the date of the sixty-day letter and the symbols of the letter, normally located in the lower-right or lower-left corner on the first page.

3. *Tax periods involved.* Here state what calendar quarters are proposed in the assessment. You can take these straight from Form 2751, which is an attachment to the sixty-day letter.

4. *Request for appellate conference.* If you want a conference with the office of appeals before a decision is made, say so here. It's almost always in your interest to request a conference.

5. *Findings to which the taxpayer protests.* State the errors you believe the revenue officer made. In Trust Fund Recovery Penalty cases, it is enough to say, "I was not a person responsible for the failure of Wonder Widgets, Inc., to collect, account for, and pay over the withholding and Social Security taxes for the periods stated above." You can also say, if true, that you were either not "responsible" or not "willful."

6. *Statement of facts and argument.* This is the heart of your protest. Here you present all your facts, furnish all the documents you have (providing copies), and make all credible factual and legal arguments to show that you are not responsible at all, or not responsible for all periods, or not willful.

A professional adviser can greatly help. She knows the law and how to gather or present the facts and law in the most effective way. Also, don't worry about whether facts you state would be admissible in court. The rules of courtroom evidence don't apply to appeals cases. Often hearsay and other inadmissible evidence will be considered. Still, everything you say must be true. It's a criminal offense to lie to a federal official, under oath or not, in writing or not. Your concluding paragraph should ask for the result you want. That's usually called *nonassertion* of the penalty, but frame this paragraph exactly in the terms of the relief you seek.

Defenses you may use

People have thought of dozens of defenses to put in protests and in later court cases. Let's take a look at the most important ones.

The "Nuremberg" defense

Maybe you can argue that you, like the defendants at the Nuremberg trials, were "just following orders." From our Wonder Widgets example, Penny Pencil or Ben Bighthard might say, "President Wonder told me what checks to sign, what checks to write, and I just followed orders. Even though I could prepare and sign checks myself, the reality was that only Ed Wonder told me what to do. .In fact, I told him I thought it was wrong not to pay the IRS, but he ordered me around anyway."

That's a common defense bookkeepers and controllers use. It works in most parts of the country if it's true and you prove it. But you bear the burden of proof. Very often the boss will say just the opposite, so try to get other people to back you up, people who have no ax to grind. And put it in writing! Under oath!

Unofficially...
A "designated" or "voluntary" payment is a payment that you designate for a particular liability right on the check itself. For example, you may use the notation "apply to trust fund only" and the particular quarter involved. The IRS is obligated to honor this designation unless the payment is not voluntary.

The "pointing finger" defense

In this defense, Ben Bighthard would point the finger at Ed Wonder and says, "He did it, not me." Ben claims that Wonder was the only person authorized to sign checks, even though Ben was on the bank signature card. Ben also tries to get the backing of others by letters or affidavits. This defense also works for you if you can prove it. If you resigned your corporate office, or went off the company's checking accounts at the bank, show these facts by documents such as new bank signature cards or a corporate resolution demonstrating that you resigned. However, in the real world, corporations often lack such formal documentation.

The "it's been paid" defense

Sometimes all or part of your liability has been paid. The corporation might have paid it by designated payments.

Or some other officer might have paid some part of the liability the IRS now seeks from you. Under IRS policy, you are entitled to credit for those payments. The IRS is also required by law to let you know what efforts it has made to collect from other responsible persons. Insist on that right.

The "your numbers are wrong" defense

Sometimes the IRS makes a mistake in calculating the amount of trust fund taxes. Go back to the corporation's employment tax returns and do the calculations yourself. Make sure any tax deposits the company made during the tax period are allocated to taxes, not to penalties and interest.

The "contribution" defense

If the IRS is coming after you for these taxes, and someone else is also liable, you may sue in federal court to have that person "contribute" his or her share. This right did not exist before 1996, when Congress added it in the 1996 Taxpayer Bill of Rights.

Filing your protest

Once you have assembled your documents and have written your protest, send it to the same office that sent you the sixty-day letter. Missing the sixty-day deadline is fatal to your appeal. The IRS will quickly process the paperwork for an assessment bill. If you can't meet the deadline, ask for an extension. Call the revenue officer assigned to your case as soon as you know you will need more time. Ask for thirty days at a minimum, but for as much time as you realistically need.

Tell the revenue officer why you need more time. He'll usually grant the request, but make you put it in writing. Sometimes he'll grant it grudgingly, sometimes for fewer than thirty days, but he will usually give you enough time. It is one of the great ironies of tax practice that the IRS will grudgingly grant one extension—usually not more than one—and then wait many times the length of that time period to hear your appeal. But that's the way it is.

Now you are ready to assemble your protest. It should have two main parts:

1. A cover letter with all the identifying information that a protest normally requires, as discussed above;

2. As much supporting documentation as you can possibly assemble to show you are not liable for the penalty.

While you're preparing the protest, what's the revenue officer doing? Nothing. He has to wait.

Bright Idea
If the revenue officer won't extend the deadline at all, file a bare-bones protest to preserve your appeal rights. You can supplement it later.

After he gets your protest, he writes a rebuttal. He is forbidden to seize assets or otherwise collect during this sixty-day period (or longer, if extended). He may want to collect, to seize bank accounts or sell your house, but he cannot. The stay of collection is now a statutory right.

What if your corporation is in bankruptcy? There, too, official IRS policy calls for "no collection" as long as the corporation is current in its new payroll taxes and proposes a plan of reorganization that will take care of these taxes. But it's not a hard-and-fast rule. In any case, if the business begins to liquidate assets, or "pyramids" its delinquencies, among other things, the revenue officer can go full speed ahead to recommend the assessment against you.

In the great majority of these proposed assessments, the responsible persons never protest. They throw up their hands and say, "You got me. I'm guilty." And, in most cases, they are. But it's surprising how many times revenue officers propose the Trust Fund Recovery Penalty assessment against persons who are not liable, or who have one or more excellent defenses. Even the 100 percent owner, a president and chief operating officer of a corporation, may still have some defenses, usually relating to the proper amount to be assessed. But most people, feeling bad about the default or, assuming they are absolutely liable, give up without a fight.

In other cases, even if they have a defense, they miss the sixty-day deadline. It's not possible to overstress the importance of meeting that deadline or any extension. If you do, and file a proper protest, the revenue officer will wait until the protest is resolved. You have exercised a right that the IRS grants you, the right to preassessment reconsideration within the IRS.

The appeal

After you file a timely protest, you wait. And wait. And wait. In busy IRS districts, you can wait up to a year to have your protest considered. Some time shortly after you file the protest, you may receive a polite letter from the Office of Appeals, stating simply that it has received your protest, the case is assigned to Ms. Jones, appeals officer, and you will be hearing from Ms. Jones shortly. Then you wait some more. Sometimes the IRS letter will set up an actual appointment, with a date, time, and place, one to four months in the future.

Who are the appeals officers?

The Office of Appeals is an arm of the IRS to which you can appeal the recommendation of the revenue officer without having to go to court. It's the same office that considers appeals from income tax audits and other collection matters. Appeals offices are located in every IRS district.

The IRS set up the Office of Appeals in 1925 to try to keep down the volume of court litigation on tax matters, and it has worked. Appeals officers settle a high percentage of income tax and employment tax cases. In fact, "settlement" is even written into their job description.

In theory, appeals officers are neutral and detached; they are supposed to consider both sides, and try to arrive at a fair settlement. And in fact, they generally do make a good-faith effort to see your side of the case and to consider all your evidence. They are trained to be more objective and detached than the revenue officer. But remember: They get a government paycheck just like the revenue officer who wants to sell your house.

Timesaver
If the IRS sets an appointment time, check your calendar immediately. If you can't meet that date, write or call the appeals officer directly to set up a new appointment. Her number and address are on the letter.

Appeals officers will also candidly tell you that Trust Fund Recovery Penalty cases are tough to settle. Some find it difficult to remain detached. For one thing, the appeals officer has seen a hundred cases come and go, many involving taxpayers who were found to have lied to try to get a better result. Why offer settlement to someone she may suspect of lying, not to mention violating a sacred trust—the obligation to hold employees' monies and pay them over to the government?

Other officers confess they find it hard to settle these cases because all the accused are pointing fingers at each other, even under oath, saying, "He did it, not me." So the appeals officer sometimes throws up her hands and sustains the revenue officer's recommended assessments with the comment "Let them fight it out in court."

In addition to your protest, the appeals officer has the revenue officer's entire case file. That includes everyone else's protests, the interview forms, the revenue officer's written recommendations, and his rebuttal to your protest. The file also contains all of the corporate documents, bank documents, cancelled checks, and other evidence. The size of that big administrative file discourages the appeals officer from settling some cases, because she typically finds so many contradictory accusations and facts. That is also discouraging to you; it means the appeals officer is less likely to reach any settlement at all, or at least one that is good from your point of view. An appeal in a Trust Fund Recovery Penalty case can therefore be very much an uphill battle.

Preparing for your conference

Now you're in the period between the protest and the in-person conference. What can you do? The rule is: Keep moving. Look for more evidence. Find more documents and witnesses. Obtain their statements, preferably under oath, and send them to the appeals officer. If you made a Freedom of Information Act request for the IRS's administrative file, continue to comb through that file for holes in the revenue officer's investigation, helpful facts, or leads to other evidence that can help your case. Relentlessly track down those leads and get them on paper.

Bright Idea
Remain on the lookout for more information to bolster your case. The appeals officer will always take new evidence, up to the date of the conference and even after.

For example, let's say you want to prove that, despite what the president claims, you didn't sign corporate checks to pay bills until six months after you came on the job. Ask for copies of the actual checks from the bank. It is expensive, but the banks have them, often only on microfilm going back a number of years. Then use the checks to prove your point. Suppose you were the secretary/treasurer of the corporation, but the president called all the shots. The bookkeeper has moved to Kodiak, Alaska. But you find and call her. By luck, she kept a copy of the corporation's bylaws. Those bylaws say "the president is in charge of everything." Get the bylaws and send them to the appeals officer.

The idea is to think of any piece of evidence, any fact, any document, that will help prove a negative—that you were not a "responsible" person or that you did not know or should not be expected to have known that the taxes were due.

The conference

Now it's time for the conference. An appeals conference is unlike a court proceeding. The appeals officer does not don a Tyrannosaurus Rex suit for the occasion, but neither does she greet you with a bouquet of flowers. The conference usually takes place in her office. You sit across the desk and proceed to the issues. The discussion can range over the entire history of the corporation, or it may concentrate only on the delinquent periods.

Your task is to use the facts in your protest to convince the appeals officer that you are not liable. Have all of your protest firmly in mind, and be prepared to rebut any contrary evidence. If you have prepared well, there should be no surprises. You'll be especially well-prepared if you made a Freedom of Information Act request for the IRS's administrative files.

Sometimes the appeals officer will have discussed the case with the other proposed responsible persons, a circumstance for which you cannot fully prepare. She'll tell you about those discussions at the conference and ask for your rebuttal. If after the conference you need more time to gather evidence, the appeals officer normally allows it. But if the conference goes well and you don't need more time, the appeals officer will begin to discuss settlement.

As a general rule, appeals officers will rarely suggest a settlement at less than 20 percent of the full amount of the proposed liability (unless it's crystal clear that you're not liable). The 20 percent is considered a "nuisance" settlement. To go lower, they would have to justify in detail why the IRS should not fully concede the case. So if some evidence points to your liability, your best result may be 20 percent of the amount proposed. Appeals officers also have authority to settle if all of the responsible persons get together and agree to chip in an equal amount, or if they pay the full amount, even if somebody pays more than his or her share.

But if everyone denies liability and points the finger elsewhere, often the appeals officer will be unable to craft a settlement and may sustain the full penalty against each responsible person. That doesn't mean the IRS collects three or four times. It will collect only once. But there's no way to predict how it will allot the responsibility: it might collect 100 percent from you, or 50 percent each from two people, or 10 percent from one, 30 percent from another, and so forth. If you are able to settle, the appeals officer writes up the settlement for her boss and sends a copy to you for signature. You sign it, send it back, and await the resulting bill.

Is there life after appeals?

If you try and try but just can't settle, Western civilization does not come to an end. True enough, that's your last chance before a formal bill, the *assessment*, is generated. But it's not your last chance to contest the liability. You can always go to court.

Fighting the Trust Fund Recovery Penalty in court is difficult and expensive. Attorneys in the Tax Division of the Department of Justice, the government's lawyers in these cases, have a long and consistent winning record. Moreover, most of the case law is unfavorable to taxpayers. So before you decide to go to court, consult an attorney experienced in these cases.

There are steps you should take after your appeal is denied before you are able to file suit.

First, to establish the federal court's jurisdiction over your case, pay a portion of the assessment and file a *Claim for Refund* on Form 843 (Claim for Refund). In a Claim for Refund, you pay the tax first and then sue the government in federal district

Moneysaver
Once the assessment becomes formal, it accrues interest until paid or settled. But if you go to court, at least the IRS is prevented by law from collecting against you while the case is pending.

court for a refund of all the tax you have paid. Paying the tax does not mean you agree that you owe it. It simply establishes the federal district court's jurisdiction over the case.

In most cases, people cannot pay the full amount of the assessment, so the law allows you to pay only a small amount for each calendar quarter that you want to place in issue. That amount is equal to the withholding and Social Security/Medicare taxes due for only one employee for each quarter at issue. It could be the lowest paid employee, the highest paid employee, or anyone in between. It can be the same employee for each quarter at issue. If you can't find out how much that amount is, guess. Paying $100 or $200 per quarter will often be enough.

Filing your claims for refund

File one claim for each quarter at issue. Indicate in the "memo" section of your personal check which quarter each check is devoted to. Send your Claim for Refund forms to the regional IRS Service Center by certified or registered mail, return receipt requested. The IRS will process the claim, but since the tax has already been assessed against you, a rejection is inevitable. The rejection letter is your "ticket to court." You have two years to sue, or if the IRS fails to act within six months after you file the claim, you also can sue at that time.

When you file suit, the Department of Justice will counterclaim for the unpaid balance of the assessment. For example, if you sue for a refund of $500 out of a $25,000 assessment, the counterclaim will be for $24,500. The issues in court are identical to those you and the IRS considered before. The judge or a jury will adjudicate who was a responsible per-

THE TEN COMMANDMENTS
OF THE TRUST FUND RECOVERY PENALTY

1. Keep out of harm's way. Don't take responsibility for paying corporate bills if the boss should really have it.

2. Make early requests under the Freedom of Information Act for the IRS's administrative file.

3. Tell the truth—to yourself, to the revenue officer, and to the appeals officer.

4. Meet all deadlines, especially for the protest.

5. Respond to all IRS notices.

6. Keep looking for evidence while you await the appeals conference.

7. Don't fight the penalty alone. Seek professional advice from a tax practitioner experienced in handling Trust Fund Recovery Penalty cases.

8. Be careful what you say to the revenue officer. Anything you say can and will be used against you.

9. Do not fear the revenue officer. Be respectful but not defensive.

10. Stand on your rights. You have them; use them.

Watch Out!
If you pay a portion of the taxes, the government will counterclaim for the remaining balance. So the result could be a federal court judgment against you for the unpaid balance of the assessments.

son and who acted willfully. Witnesses will be called, documents will be introduced into evidence, and the trial will follow the usual pattern of trials in federal district courts.

Some federal courts will complete these trials quickly; others can take years. While you're waiting for your case to be tried, interest accrues on the assessment. If you win, there is no more liability. But if you lose, you have a federal court judgment that can be collected either by the IRS or by the Department of Justice. For more information on collection by these agencies, see Chapter 16.

Just the facts

- Small businesses often default in paying payroll taxes—watch for this danger.

- The IRS seeks payroll taxes first from the corporation, then from its "responsible" persons.

- You have many opportunities to contest the Trust Fund Recovery Penalty within the IRS and in court.

- Pay close attention to your procedural rights and deadlines if the IRS proposes this "penalty" against you.

GET THE SCOOP ON...
• The IRS's "nuke": the jeopardy assessment •
Fighting back • The nonfiler's nightmare • Sending people to jail—the IRS way • Fighting the
criminal tax investigation

Other Big IRS Headaches

Chapter 7

This chapter addresses three of the biggest IRS headaches people can face: jeopardy assessments, nonfiler investigations, and criminal investigations.

Getting "nuked" by a jeopardy assessment

People frequently complain about how grindingly slow the IRS acts. But don't tell that to anyone who has faced a "jeopardy" or "termination" assessment of tax. These assessments are like nuclear weapons delivered by a stealth bomber. The damage is devastating, and you rarely see it coming. To be sure, the IRS doesn't use these weapons very often, mostly reserving them for criminal cases or cases of illegal or unreported income. Still, the Service resorts to jeopardy and termination assessments hundreds of times each year, and won't hesitate to use them in any case where collection appears to be at great risk. So even normal folks must sometimes look over their shoulder when they owe back taxes and try to plan the sale of their assets.

Unofficially...
The IRS process-
es over 200 mil-
lion tax and
information
returns each year
and about 2 bil-
lion pieces of
paper. This
means nearly
everyone leaves
financial tracks
that can be
followed.

What it is

A jeopardy or termination assessment is simply an assessment made very quickly because the IRS determines that collection of the tax is "in jeopardy." Termination assessments are so called because the IRS "terminates" your current tax year immediately, makes the assessment, and proceeds to collect it. Jeopardy assessments are for *past* years where the taxes have not yet been assessed.

In a normal, nonjeopardy case, the Service cannot begin to collect until it has taken these steps:

1. Audited your tax return,

2. Proposed a tax bill,

3. Allowed your appeal rights,

4. Allowed you to go to court, and

5. After the resolution of the court case, assessed the tax and issued a bill.

This ordinary assessment process takes months or years. In a jeopardy case, all the in-between steps are eliminated. It takes only hours. The assessment won't take away your court rights, but, in the meantime, the IRS has seized everything in sight.

Legally, the agency can make a jeopardy assessment if it officially decides that:

■ you are likely to leave the United States soon;

■ you are hiding your assets, transferring them, or otherwise putting them beyond the reach of the government;

■ your financial solvency is in peril.

As you might expect, drug busts often generate jeopardy assessments. Likewise gambling raids where gambling is illegal. Noncitizens who appear ready to flee the country can be the subject of jeopardy assessments, and it would not be surprising if the government jeopardy-assessed people who planned to give up their citizenship to avoid taxes.

The Service determines you are about to flee the country by looking for a number of signs: your citizenship, whether you have a passport, and previous criminal convictions indicating that you might leave. It also checks whether you are liquidating assets, whether some other jurisdiction has warrants out for you, and even whether you have bought airline tickets.

In a jeopardy case that arises from a drug bust, police officers usually find cash and drugs. The experts estimate the purchase value of the drugs, add that to the cash, and advise the IRS. IRS special agents check for filed tax returns. If there are none (and few drug dealers file true returns, if any returns), the agents make a termination or jeopardy assessment by telephone, swoop down, seize the cash, and apply it to the assessed taxes. In short order, the government has $100,000. Theoretically, the suspects could contest the assessment in tax court or federal district court, but the IRS counts on them to be otherwise occupied.

Jeopardy assessments can be for plain folks as well. Let's say you anticipate a huge tax bill and you begin to put property in the names of your children, friends, or relatives, or you transfer property overseas. Nothing prevents the IRS from determining jeopardy exists, and it might well be justified in doing so.

Fighting a jeopardy or termination assessment

You rarely see a jeopardy assessment coming, so it's hard to fight one before it explodes. But afterwards, you have some limited rights. Within five days after

Watch Out!
The IRS knows you are concealing assets when you transfer ownership, use aliases, destroy or conceal records, or use a lot of cash.

Unofficially...
The IRS opened
1.7 million delin-
quent return
investigations in
1996. At the end
of the year, they
had over 2 mil-
lion of these
investigations
open, and that's
only the
nonfilers they
know about.

the IRS makes the assessment, it sends an "informa-tion statement" outlining its reasons. Within thirty days, you can ask for the IRS to review the assess-ment—usually a useless act. Within sixteen days after the request, you can sue the government in federal district court to review the jeopardy assess-ment. The court has jurisdiction to determine whether:

1. The making of the assessmentis reasonable, and

2. The assessed amounts are appropriate.

Almost every case results in a victory for the govern-ment, so they are rarely seen these days.

Where the government's jeopardy assessment springs from a drug or gambling raid, little if any-thing will undo the government's action. But if the government has jumped the gun and unfairly jeop-ardy-assessed anyone else, there are remedies besides the court suit described above. You can always file Form 911, requesting a *Taxpayer Assistance Order*. Chapter 14 describes how to do this.

You can also go up the chain of command, all the way to the District Director of Internal Revenue for your district. That official must personally review the circumstances to approve any jeopardy assess-ment in advance, so he has already said no to you once. But maybe you can persuade the agent that he got the facts wrong or that there are mitigating cir-cumstances. It does not hurt to place phone calls and write letters to him, unless doing so would incriminate you.

Finally, there are more leisurely remedies, such as the normal Tax Court suit filed to contest the gov-ernment's assessment. If the IRS has truly erred and you can prove it, you may be able to recover your money and property.

Why the IRS wants you (the nonfiler)

Jeopardy assessments are sometimes used in connection with "nonfiler" assessments. Every year 5 million to ten million Americans fail to file federal and state income tax returns. Nonfilers come from all occupations and classes. Most are men. The average delinquency period is three years.

Despite the many apocryphal tales of nonfilers who never get caught, few nonfilers escape from the IRS for long. Sooner or later, the IRS is bound to catch up with you. In this computerized age, it is easy for the IRS to scour W-2 forms, credit card records, Social Security listings, and even plain old telephone directories to find anyone who has not filed a tax return.

The Form W-2 from your employer tells the IRS who you are and where you work. Form 1099 tells them who paid you money, where your mortgage is placed, and whether you received barter income. It says where and how much you received in dividends or interest, whether you received a state tax refund, and many other things. Each of these reporting devices can be tracked back to find you. Even if you don't file a tax return for one year, the IRS will look at the last one you did file to try to find you.

But they don't give up if these sources run dry, Do you have credit cards? These are often canvassed by Social Security number. The IRS can also try to locate you through other agencies: the military, the Social Security Administration, the Immigration and Naturalization Service, even the telephone directories. The Service can also use information from credit reporting agencies and consumer reporting agencies. For these reasons, anyone who has not filed a tax return is sitting on a ticking time bomb.

Watch Out!
Your chance at getting an unfavorable government decision reversed always assumes truthful statements to the government. Any false statement to a government official, oral, written, or by demonstrative conduct, is punishable as perjury.

Why people don't file

The reasons for nonfiling range from the absurd to the heartbreaking. Nonfilers clearly have a capacity for denial, taking quick and easy refuge in self-deluding excuses. Some say that filing can wait because they are due a tax refund ("The government owes *me* money"). Even if so, this can't be known with any confidence until a tax return is prepared.

The IRS's surprise for the non-filer

On top of that, the IRS often surprises the nonfiler who thought the government owed him. The agency has the legal authority to file a return for you if you don't file one. On that "Substitute for Return," as we discussed earlier, the IRS makes every possible assumption to increase your taxes. The IRS assumes you have no children and ignores all possible deductions such as mortgage interest, large deductible medical expenses, real estate, and state income taxes.

The result is a Substitute for Return on which the W-2 withholding comes nowhere near the amount necessary to cover the taxes—as calculated by the IRS. To compound the problem, many non-filers are paid as independent contractors, or have other "Form 1099" income on which nothing was withheld. Either way, the tax bill is shockingly large, topped off by a 25 percent late-filing penalty, a late-payment penalty, and interest. Imagine the shock of the nonfiler who believes he is entitled to a refund.

Non-filers can always ask the IRS to reconsider the Substitute for Return, but that takes time and effort. In the meantime, the IRS will spring into action to collect the taxes. Agents will file notices of federal tax lien, levy on your bank accounts, sell your assets, or garnish your wages. You could even lose your job if the IRS contacts your employer and the boss sees your problem as a terminable offense.

Filing for bankruptcy in the hope of discharging the taxes can sometimes work if you meet certain tests. Chapter 13 covers this in detail. But under current law, you cannot discharge income taxes that the IRS bills you on a Substitute for Return. Another excuse people give is: "I didn't have the money to pay." On April 15, that's often quite true, but not an excuse not to file. Others reasons are that they're not legally required to file if they can't pay, a cruel myth.

Years ago, if you filed but didn't pay, the IRS was somewhat slow to act. Even now, the sky does not fall, but instead the IRS issues a series of notices requesting payment of the tax, interest, and penalties shown on the return. The tone of these notices gets progressively more urgent and eventually the IRS collectors move into action.

A delinquent taxpayer has many options to avoid enforced collection, even if he owes money on April 15. But the worst choice is not to file. Among other things, you will automatically be subject to the late-filing penalty (5 percent per month up to 25 percent) for every month or part of a month a return is late. That penalty is easy to avoid—simply file on time—but hard to abate. (Chapter 15 explains this and other penalties, and how to avoid or abate them.) Filing a balance-due return does mean the late-payment penalty will be imposed, but this penalty is a modest 0.5 percent to 1 percent per month. If you file on time, the day of reckoning for the balance due is advanced, but that's preferable to the heavy late-filing penalty.

Bright Idea
Even if you have a refund coming, be sure to file on time. If you wait too long to file for your refund, it may be barred by the statute of limitations. Each year, thousands of people kiss goodbye millions of dollars in this way.

Moneysaver
Always file on
time. It defies
common sense to
risk a 25 percent
late-filing penal-
ty when you can
opt for the 1
percent late-pay-
ment penalty
even if you
can't pay.

Another excuse is: "I'm getting my records together." Variations are: "I never got my W-2," or "I'm waiting for a Form 1099," or "I have all my records; I just haven't organized them, or "The dog ate them." If records truly are missing, you can always file for an extension. But the law says you have a duty to keep your records in sufficient shape that you can file on time. (It's not that hard. Chapter 18 gives you a guide.)

These are only some of the excuses. Dozens of others have been used, limited only by the nonfiler's imagination.

Reasons that work

The law does give credence to good excuses for late filing, that is, "reasonable cause." You are not relieved of the legal duty to file and pay the tax and interest, but you may avoid some penalties. Chapter 13 lists the most common, "IRS approved," reasonable causes.

In the real world, most are rare. The most common is the "serious illness" of the taxpayer or a member of his immediate family. Examples include physical illness and emotional illness, including chemical addiction and recovery, physical abuse, and the stress resulting from death in the family or economic crises. The IRS understands and accepts the plight of some nonfilers, if they are documented them properly and in detail.

For example, a nonfiler suffered through a terrible youthful marriage, a bitter separation, and mental and physical abuse. The other spouse also extorted money over a period of years because of the nonfiler's infidelity. All of this culminated in a bitter divorce. This nonfiler had reasonable cause to abate the late fliling and late payment penalties.

Getting back into the system

On October 1, 1992, and continuing even today, the IRS launched a highly publicized nationwide campaign to entice nonfilers back into the ranks of the taxpaying and return-filing public. Two thousand revenue agents and tax auditors began looking for the nonfilers and tried to bring them back into the system.

In theory, the IRS is searching for everyone who hasn't filed for one or more years. But realistically, the IRS targets only "highly productive" nonfilers, that is, those who owe a lot of taxes.

The IRS's own studies and its internal manual of procedures describe the following callings as most likely to harbor nonfilers and produce the most tax:

- Manufacturing apparel
- Trucking and warehousing
- Wholesale groceries and related products
- Legal services
- Wholesale dry goods and apparel
- Manufacturing and machinery (excluding electrical)
- Mining and quarrying
- General construction
- Retail automotive dealers
- Laundry and dry cleaning
- Automobile repair

The agency's computers augment the effort through computer matching of information reports such as Forms W-2 and 1099 to filed returns. If the computer checks a W-2 or 1099 against your account and finds no return on file, it generates a notice and several follow-up notices if you don't

Unofficially...
The IRS is fishing in affluent neighborhoods, professional groups, and among categories of expense such as mortgage interest, to target returns that will yield the most money. In its first six months of operation, the nonfiler program brought in about 600,000 delinquent returns.

respond to the first. These notices mean you have been discovered. Usually a total failure to respond means your case will be referred to an agent on the task force. The agent or another IRS representative will call, write, or visit—and begin the process of getting you to file, willingly or not.

When the IRS representative catches up with you, he or she will make a judgment as to whether your case should be referred for criminal investigation and possible prosecution. Statistically, few cases become criminal, but you never know if yours will be the unlucky one. To make a criminal case for nonfiling, the agent typically looks for "badges of fraud," that is, illegal sources of income, the hiding of assets, a complete refusal to cooperate, transfers of property, and the like.

High-dollar cases and taxpayers who deal in cash are prime targets for criminal investigation. But everyone, whether prosecuted or not, will then enter the nonfiler system. The assigned revenue officer also will look for a pattern of delinquency over several years, the taxpayer's education level, and other factors.

The revenue officer also considers the amount you owe in deciding whether to refer your case for criminal investigation.

The nonfiler program offers clear benefits if you come forward voluntarily. By official policy, the IRS will not recommend criminal prosecution of a nonfiler who comes forward on his own. Of course, full payment of any tax due will stop the running of interest and penalties. The agency is also more open to working with voluntary confessors on agreements to pay any tax due in installments. It may even forgive some of the tax, penalties, or interest under the offer in compromise program discussed in Chapter 11.

Most nonfilers don't end up owing a hopeless amount, even for very old tax years. In fact, among all tax delinquents (including those who filed on time but simply owe money), fully 97 percent qualify to pay their taxes in installments over a reasonable time, usually six to thirty-six months.

Also, for voluntary confessors, the IRS has said it might look more favorably on "reasonable cause" requests for penalty abatements. But if you have to be dragged, kicking and screaming, into compliance, the IRS will skeptically eye any excuses you may offer. If you have already received a phone call, a letter, or other notice from the IRS, it's not too late to comply voluntarily. But you must respond immediately to be considered a "voluntary" filer.

The downside of not filing

When the IRS catches you, you'll go to jail, pay big penalties, or both. In most cases, the agency doesn't really want a conviction, only a filed and paid return. So it will content itself with making a Substitute for Return and collecting the resulting tax and several big penalties. The agent will, of course, still try to get you to file. He may also issue a summons to you, requiring your appearance and the production of your business and personal books and records. Failure to obey the summons can result in civil or criminal contempt charges, with the usual and customary jail sentences. Finally, the agent can file an actual return for you and sign it himself, though, in most cases, the Substitute for Return is used.

The strongest IRS weapon, criminal prosecution, is the biggest fear of many repeat nonfilers. Nonfiling is a federal misdemeanor (not a felony) punishable by up to one year in prison and/or a fine of up

Watch Out!
Non-filers delude themselves into thinking they won't go to jail even if prosecuted. Wrong! These days, convicted nonfilers will definitely get some "hard time."

Unofficially...
The IRS's new look is firm, no-nonsense, businesslike attempts to get taxpayers back into the system. This new attitude means it will take steps to make it easier for you to pay, file returns, and pay taxes now and in the future. In short, the emphasis is on compliance, not compulsion.

to $25,000 plus prosecution costs for each year that you willfully failed to file. All states that impose income taxes have analogous criminal penalties. Sometimes, if a nonfiler persists for a number of years, the IRS will prosecute the case as "attempted tax evasion," a felony carrying a maximum fine of $100,000, five years in prison, or both (plus prosecution costs), for each year involved. Even a willful failure to pay any tax is, in theory, a criminal offense, though that's rarely prosecuted.

The IRS's approach to prosecution is both carrot and stick. Most years, around April 15, the agency announces a list of about 100 "chosen" individuals who have been or will be indicted for failure to file. In all, the Service prosecutes about 1,000 nonfiling cases each year.

That's small compared to the estimated 5 million to 10 million nonfilers nationwide. So the IRS prefers to prosecute only the most flagrant cases. Adding to the IRS's weapons, in 1989 Congress enacted the "fraudulent failure to file" penalty, equal to 15 percent of the tax due per month, up to a maximum of 75 percent. This penalty applies in cases where there are indications of fraud or attempted evasion, but not quite enough to merit criminal prosecution.

Steps you can take

It's April 15, you're mired in records and paralyzed in nonfiling. Fearing the IRS, you make up your mind to catch up. How should you start? Beyond question, the first step is: Get help. You can't do it yourself. The mild encouragement of a spouse or friend, a few wise words from a tax professional, or assistance from a tax attorney or even from the IRS itself may be enough. But you've procrastinated too long—someone else needs to know about your problem, and ride herd on you until you get the job done.

A five-part filing program like this may ease the way:

1. Prompt and full disclosure to a lawyer or other tax professional

2. Preparation of the returns quickly and accurately—by a lawyer, accountant, enrolled agent, or other professional tax return preparer

3. A plan to pay or settle any taxes the returns show are due

4. If necessary, a full and powerful statement of reasonable cause for nonfiling

5. Luck (but sometimes you can make your own)

Many nonfilers need both a return preparer and an attorney. The preparer's task is to prepare the returns. If necessary, the attorney can review them from a legal perspective and present them effectively to the IRS. A useful rule of thumb is: If three or more years are involved, first see a lawyer experienced in tax matters. Three or more years of nonfiling increases the chances of criminal prosecution, so you may need criminal defense work or legal advice on the civil penalties in addition to accounting help. And remember: the attorney-client privilege shields most discussions you have with an attorney.

Under the 1998 tax act, even nonattorneys have a tax advice privilege, but that narrow shield does not apply in criminal cases. Absent a privilege, the IRS can force these nonlawyer professionals to reveal anything you say to them, and you may be sure what you say can and will be used against you. Therefore, route all discussions through an attor-

Timesaver
Nonfilers with
new-found deter-
mination often
think they can do
it alone. But do
not try this
experiment at
home. Just gath-
er all your
records and
shove them at
the preparer.
Don't even
try to sort them.
If it has a num-
ber on it, take it
to the preparer.

ney, at least until it's clear that the likelihood of prosecution is small and a client privilege unnecessary. But beware: Even if you go first to an attorney, not all communications will be privileged. Your lawyer can advise you on this point.

Your lawyer will also explain in detail the civil and criminal penalties and discuss the likelihood of legal action against you. Criminal prosecution is unlikely if the returns are filed quickly and before the IRS catches you, but civil penalties for late filing and late payment are certain to be imposed if you owe taxes. In addition, the IRS will sometimes suspect fraud and assess additional tax penalties unless you can prove reasonable cause for the nonfiling.

Once this disclosure process is underway, keep it on track. The nonfiler excels at procrastinating; initial good intentions usually fade. Once the nonfiler is into the tax return process, almost invariably he becomes complacent and reassured—the very syndrome that caused the nonfiling in the first place. Delay ensues and sometimes never ends.

After you evaluate the danger of criminal prosecution, the next step is to prepare and file the returns. Those returns must be accurate and totally defensible, but they must also be prepared quickly, especially where your lawyer advises prosecution is likely if the IRS catches you before you file. The preparer should lean toward conservatism, taking all lawful, provable deductions but avoiding those for which there is inadequate proof. Above all else, every penny of gross income must be reported.

Finding all your earnings from the dim, dark past is hard. Here are two great ways.

(1) Have your preparer request "third-party payer" reports from the IRS;

(2) Add up your bank deposits for each year, then subtract transfers. This should match your gross income.

The attorney or preparer will often check behind the client by performing one or more indirect analyses of the correctness of the return and the gross income reported. Even as you prepare the returns, develop a plan to pay or compromise on any back taxes; the IRS will demand payment a few short weeks or months after the returns are filed. If there is no balance due, this is not a problem. But often, and unexpectedly, there is a tax due. Addressing the collection problem up-front helps persuade the IRS that you are sincere and committed. That perception, in turn, may limit civil penalties and ease the pain of payment.

The nonfiler for three or more years should also discuss with an attorney the reasons the returns were not filed. If the penalties are large enough, it may be cost-effective to prepare a detailed affidavit for the IRS explaining the reasons, with any supporting documentation and statements you can find. So make a judgment about how far to go and how much effort and money to spend on a showing of reasonable cause.

What's "reasonable" cause for not filing?

Officially the IRS will accept eight reasons for filing a late return. These are:

- The post office delayed your return;
- You filed the return in the wrong IRS office;
- You relied on erroneous information given to you by an IRS officer or employee;

Watch Out!
The IRS's success rate in prosecuting nonfilers and tax evaders is 98 percent!

Watch Out!
The attorney-client privilege is quite narrow. For example, it will not shield your financial records from compelled production by the IRS. Nor will it protect data shown on a field return or on financial settlements.

- The taxpayer died or was seriously ill, or there was death or serious illness in the immediate family;

- The taxpayer was unavoidably absent;

- The taxpayer's business or business records were destroyed by fire or other casualty;

- The IRS didn't supply the right forms in enough time to file; and

- You tried to get help or information to prepare your return from the IRS, but its representative didn't meet with you.

Of these reasons, the first two, postal delays and filing in the wrong office, are self-explanatory, but you must prove the postal delay. It's easier to prove filing in the wrong IRS office because that office sends the return back to you. (Keep the envelopes!) If the IRS gave you the wrong tax information and you relied on it, that's reasonable cause. Even the IRS makes mistakes. Millions of people call in for advice every year, usually between January 2 and April 15.

But the excuse "I relied on the IRS" is very narrow. The IRS has to have given you advice that you "reasonably" relied on. So if the advice (as heard by you) is totally off-base, you won't have reasonable cause. Also, the information on which the advice was based must have been accurate and adequate. And the burden to prove all of this is on you!

The fourth reason—death or serious illness—is one the IRS and practitioners see often. As noted above, serious illness has to be proved, credibly and completely. It must also cover the periods of nonfiling. Unavoidable absence is also narrowly construed. Very few absences are deemed "unavoidable" for this purpose. Your records were destroyed? Be prepared to prove the date, time, and place; furnish police, fire, or insurance reports; and tell what efforts you made to get copies or recreate them.

Once you are back in the tax-filing and tax-paying system, you may find that you owe no back taxes. You and the IRS simply have a new relationship, and life goes on. But if you owe money, you then have to deal with the Collection Division. It's not as bad as it sounds. In the last five years, the IRS has made paying taxes less painful in many ways. These include forgiving some taxes altogether if the IRS concludes you will never be able to pay them.

The "tax police"—Criminal Investigation Division

The third big headache is that greatly feared animal, the criminal investigation.

What feeling do you get when you receive a letter with the return address, "Internal Revenue Service"? Many law-abiding citizens with healthy superegos think, "Oh my God, I'm going to jail." The fact is, although you need not fear the IRS's Criminal Investigation Division (CID) unless you have committed a tax crime, the fear factor in tax crimes is pervasive. After all, tax fraud, not bootlegging or murder, sent Al Capone to jail. And it is tax fraud that gnaws at otherwise honest people when they "shave" a little on their returns. But, given the infrequency of tax prosecutions, the Criminal Investigation Division of the IRS generates fear far out of proportion to its actual impact.

There is extraordinarily wide variation in the number and kind of people who are prosecuted. Some areas of the country are more prone to tax

Unofficially...
Studies consistently show error rates in IRS advice of around 10 percent.

Moneysaver
Don't forget state returns, which normally follow and parallel the federal returns. The state tax liability can also be large. As a rule of thumb, figure on 10 percent of the federal amount.

evasion than others. The agents may be more or less aggressive in certain areas of the country. The U.S. Attorneys who prosecute these cases may be more interested in one area of the country than another. While it may be desirable to have the criminal tax laws applied uniformly throughout the country, the fact remains that there is wide variation in prosecuting tax crimes.

A 1996 article in the *New York Times* summarized Justice Department data that showed that the statistical chances of being prosecuted for a tax crime in the Roanoke, Virginia, area were fifty-seven times that of the New Mexico area. But that's just the barebones number. The reasons for the variations are many.

Each of the thirty-three IRS districts has at least one CID group. A group consists of eight to thirty special agents. Their job is to investigate suspected criminal violations of the tax laws and related offenses, such as assault on a revenue officer or seizure by the taxpayer of levied property.

Most criminal cases involve the charge of tax evasion, that is, failing to report all income or overstating deductions with specific intent to evade the tax laws. CID also investigates a fair number of nonfiler cases, about 1,000 a year, an occasional failure-to-pay case, and a variety of other tax crimes. Altogether, CID has authority to investigate about thirty tax and nontax crimes.

CID starts a case

Most criminal tax cases arise from routine audits of an individual, corporation, partnership, or exempt organization. At some point during the audit, the revenue agent smells something fishy—a big bank deposit that somehow doesn't square with the tax return, the absence of an expected deposit, an over-stated deduction, a business deduction that is grossly wrong, or the use of many or fictitious corporations. It could be a cash hoard or anything else that seems to be unaccounted for and untaxed.

When the revenue agent spots this, she does not immediately throw the cuffs on. She asks for an explanation. If the explanation does not ring true, she has an "unexplained indication of fraud." At this point, she files Form 2797 ("Referral for Potential Fraud Case"), a brief report that asks CID if it is interested in the case. The agent suspends her audit until CID responds. Special agents do not accept every case; they accept the most promising ones or the ones that have the most potential for publicity. After all, headlines are part of their job of enforcement and compliance.

The winds of case selection blow hot and cold; they also change direction frequently. In the 1970s and 1980s, tax shelters and drug and gambling cases filled CID's plate. The 1990s have seen a shift to money laundering, cash businesses, and traditional tax-evasion cases.

Every new commissioner seems to bring a different policy slant to CID case selection. Generally, though, CID goes for either the most publicity-worthy cases or the ones that will yield the most money or promise the greatest deterrent effect. If the special agent and her group manager agree, they open, or "jacket," the case, and the agent begins the investigation. Often these cases are investigated jointly with the revenue agent, who acts as the special agent's assistant and works the numbers in detail. That cooperation is critical because the special agent must accumulate evidence beyond a reasonable

Unofficially...
The fearsome
reputation of the
IRS is due in
part to the high
profile of some
cases and to the
odds: anyone
investigated by
CID has a 45
percent chance
of actually
going to jail.

doubt that a substantial tax was actually evaded. The revenue agent often has more expertise than the special agent in the accounting aspects of this task.

The second big source of cases is information reports. For example, someone may file a Currency Transaction Report showing more than $10,000 in cash deposited into a bank account. Another source is the confidential informant or tipster, for instance, a fired employee who knew the boss was skimming cash. Other tipsters could be an unhappy wife, husband, or partner, or anyone who has a gripe against an evading taxpayer. CID also often receives information from other law enforcement agencies, such as the Drug Enforcement Agency, the Bureau of Alcohol, Tobacco, and Firearms, the FBI, and local law enforcement agencies. CID will listen to anyone, anytime, and it can pay rewards—up to 10 percent of the taxes recovered.

Investigating the case

Both agents then begin to investigate your case. Even before you ever know they are around, they have looked high and low for information about you, the "subject." The first phase is background. They check everywhere—public records, lien searches, military history, postal covers (a request to the post office to record who sends you mail, and when), national computer banks, newspapers, even electronic data sources. They check the Internet.

The special agent's manual gives them more sources of leads than they could possibly use, but they look at every one they can. The IRS does not engage in court-authorized wiretapping, except for the occasional use of pen registers, which record the numbers of all outgoing calls. These will ordinarily be used only in gambling and other organized crime cases. Very infrequently, CID will resort to search and seizure warrants. Often, however, agents will "piggyback" on other law enforcement warrants if you are the subject of some other agency's attention.

The second phase may well be confidential interviews. They may talk to customers, suppliers, friends, neighbors, and acquaintances. The agents examine your reputation for honesty and look for other personal problems you may have. In the third phase, they appear at your front door, badge and credentials in hand, demanding an interview. This is almost always a surprise if they've done their job well up to that point. It's astounding how many targets will, at that point, invite the agents in, close the door, and confess their tax crimes in a four-hour interview. If the agents successfully do that, in most instances their case is made and the rest is paperwork. It's all over but the sentencing. If not, they have to prove their case out of other evidence.

In this third phase, the agents also launch searches for records where the fact they are searching becomes known to the subject. This would include compulsory summonses to the taxpayer, his business, banks, brokers, accountants, and any other third parties the agents think might have knowledge of the taxpayer's finances or tax transactions.

The fourth stage (sometimes the third) is to formulate a method of proof—how to reconstruct your true tax picture to show where and how you cheated. The final stage is the recommendation for prosecution or nonprosecution. The agents assemble all the data, mark their exhibits, create huge, thoroughly indexed binders of documents, referenced and cross-referenced. These exhibits and the wit-

Watch Out!
Whenever you learn—or even suspect—that you may be targeted by the CID, stop everything! Immediately call a tax lawyer familiar with CID cases and get help!

nesses who will identify them are their case. They forward the case through the group manager. Eventually, it winds up in the hands of the U.S. Attorney's Office for prosecution. There, a case may be further developed by a grand jury investigation.

How CID proves a case

To prove you cheated with criminal intent, the special agent typically selects one of three principal "methods of proof." The first is the *specific item method,* a so-called *direct* method of proof. As the name of this method implies, the agents have found one or more specific items you have omitted from a return or specific deductions you have overstated (the "smoking gun"). They could find these from bank accounts, cancelled checks, or business deductions for personal expenses or from deductions that are wildly overstated. Special agents love specific item cases because they are easy to make. The agents can assume that the rest of your return is right and still get a conviction.

Two other principal methods are indirect methods: the agents prove indirectly that you evaded your taxes. One is the *bank deposits method.* With this method, the agents add all your bank deposits for each year and subtract transfers from one account to another. The difference is presumed by law to be taxable. If you have a net total of $200,000 of bank deposits but you reported only $100,000 on your tax return, you've got some explaining to do. In case after case, the courts have sustained that method of proof as valid and constitutional.

The second indirect method is called the *net worth and expenditures method.* This one is harder to document. With this method, the agents establish your net worth at the beginning of one year and then prove the level to which it grew at the end of one or more additional years. The increases in net worth, plus your other spending, must have come from somewhere. If they arose because you received loans, bequests, or gifts, there is no problem. But if you cannot account for these large increases in net worth and expenditures as nontaxable, the law presumes them to be unreported taxable income. Many a conviction has been obtained by this method.

Defending against the investigation

There are a few things you can do to defend against these investigations. First and foremost, never let the special agents interview you. This first defense is the constitutional privilege against self-incrimination. (However, it is not a defense, in a failure to file case, to plead the Fifth Amendment privilege against self-incrimination.) When they come to the door, state politely but firmly, "I do not wish to be interviewed, and I would like to consult my lawyer." Special agents understand this and will rarely press the point. Then immediately drop what you are doing and call your lawyer. In any criminal investigation, particularly a tax investigation, you will need a criminal defense lawyer well-versed in tax matters. Then follow your lawyer's advice!

Another mistake people make is to begin transferring assets. This shows a guilty mind and achieves nothing. After all, the IRS has full authority to make jeopardy assessments and seize property, even when it's transferred to someone else's name. And it probably constitutes a new, separate crime.

A second defense is the "voluntary disclosure" defense. This applies in almost every case of non-filing. An evader can also sometimes escape prosecution with this defense. It consists of filing original or

Unofficially...
In 1996, 4,000 out of 5,300 CID cases were "fraud" cases. The rest were under the narcotics program. The conviction rate was 73.2 percent for fraud and 87.5 percent for narcotics.

Watch Out!
If agents come to your door, get legal counsel immediately. Tell the agents you want to consult a lawyer. Never, ever, try to explain your way out of this problem. Even if you are as innocent as a newborn lamb, something very serious must have occurred if a Treasury law enforcement agent appears at your door.

amended returns and fully paying the taxes, penalties, and interest before the special agents make their first contact. The Justice Department's policy of nonprosecution in such cases is usually honored.

A third possibility is a grant of immunity. This is more rare, but on occasion taxpayers have negotiated for a grant of "use immunity." This means the Department of Justice will not prosecute you as to documents and information you voluntarily disclose.

Fourth, you may try to attack the agent's method of proof. For example, if the agent finds an extra $50,000 of unexplained bank deposits, explain them by showing that they were a gift, loan, or inheritance (if that is true). Several other defenses may be available, defenses not reserved to tax cases alone. For example, showing that you relied on a lawyer's or accountant's advice to report a deduction or omit an income item might be a defense. But "advice of counsel" must be proved, and you must show that you disclosed all the underlying facts to your professional adviser. This defense is a variation of the "good-faith" defense, in which you argue that for one reason or another, you did not violate a "known" legal duty.

Mental incapacity is also a defense, but that too must be clearly proved. Still, occasionally this defense is successful. As in any criminal investigation, your maneuvering room is usually limited. After all, CID accepts only the investigations it feels have solid conviction potential. If you are to stop this investigation, it's usually at the agent's level or not at all. Even when the agents fail to make a criminal case, they often recommend the civil fraud penalty—75 percent of the understated tax. The lesson is simple: A criminal investigation can have no happy ending except the rare one of no prosecution or an acquittal.

Just the facts

- Anticipate jeopardy assessments, but if you can't, fight them either in court or within the IRS.

- The IRS is serious about tracking down nonfilers; nonfilers can't hide forever.

- Nonfilers should immediately consult tax professionals—attorneys and return preparers—to get back into the system.

- Most nonfiling situations can be successfully resolved, but it takes motivation and hard work.

- If you suspect the IRS is about to open a criminal case, stop everything and talk to a lawyer.

- Don't try to hide your assets; that only makes things worse.

Bright Idea
If you are a non-filer who suspects a criminal investigation may be afoot, you will need to prepare accurate tax returns. Be sure to check (or have your lawyer check) these returns against total bank deposits to ensure you have reported all income.

All About Audits

PART III

GET THE SCOOP ON...

- "Why me?!" ▪ Different kinds of audits
▪ Audit targets and triggers ▪ The Audit Report
and Audit Reconsideration ▪ State tax arising
from a federal audit ▪ The statute of
limitations ▪ The innocent spouse

"Your Tax Return Has Been Selected for Examination"

Chapter 8

One of the most unnerving letters you can receive is the tan envelope with the return address "Internal Revenue Service" and the government stamp ("Penalty for Private Use—$300"). You open the letter carefully, slowly, like a letterbomb. It begins innocently enough: "Dear Taxpayer." Then it hits you: you have lost the audit lottery. You are one of the unlucky 1 percent of individuals or 5 percent of businesses whose tax return will now be examined.

How do people react? There is a range, from "Oh my gosh—get my toothbrush, kiss the kids, I am going to jail," to "Oh no, not again," to "Those so and so's—into the trash you go." Probably the most useful reaction would be, "What's this all about? What type of audit is this?" Why are *you* the lucky one? In most cases, it goes back to the return you filed.

Timesaver
Under the 1998
tax reform act,
the IRS must
include in Publi-
cation 1 (Your
Rights as a Tax-
payer) a general,
nontechnical
statement of the
criteria it uses to
select returns for
audit. This does
not mean, how-
ever, that you'll
get any statistics
or data that will
help you avoid
an audit.

"Hey, what's your DIF?"

The IRS has a scoring system known as *DIF*—short for Discriminant Function System. The IRS "scores" the tax return you file and assigns "points" according to DIF criteria. The details of the DIF scoring system are nearly as secret as our nuclear strike command codes or an aging starlet's birthdate. Few people know all the items on the scorecard, or how many points a return earns for each item. But educated guesses abound, based on the fact that the score sheet is intended to make the IRS money.

So the scoring system likely assigns points for your occupation, the types of income you earn (whether wages or independent contractor income), and your deductions in type and amount. Your tax return may earn DIF points for your being a doctor, and for gross income of $50,000 to $100,000. Even common types of deductions such as mortgage interest or real estate taxes can yield a high score if the amounts you deduct are high. Your return probably also scores high if the IRS has made money from you from past audits (everyone likes repeat business). Higher income individuals such as doctors, a few lawyers, and other professionals probably merit bonus points. Unusual occupations are on the list, as well as occupations that deal in cash, such as jewelers and car, boatyard, or junkyard dealers.

Almost any type of tax loss is also likely to earn DIF scores: casualty losses, business losses, and losses on sales of non–publicly traded stock. Also, it stands to reason that the most commonly used and abused deductions will stand out from the crowd: home office deduction, noncash charitable deductions, travel and entertainment expenses, and legally unallowable deductions.

If your return scores high enough, the computer selects it for a closer look, and it is routed to an office in your area of the country. The IRS has a "classification handbook." Agents use this handbook to classify which DIF-selected returns merit a closer look. The returns selected are then screened according to the importance of the DIF score and the items in question on the return. The IRS will look at the size of the item, its character, and any evidence that you were trying to confuse or mislead the Service in how you reported the item. It will check whether you put it on a schedule that would lead to a lesser tax (for instance, Schedule C versus an itemized deduction) and the relationship between the questioned item and others on the return. This is a judgment call; much depends on the experience of the reviewer.

The IRS recently created a close cousin of DIF known as *DORA*, short for District Office Research and Analysis. This program targets regions of the country, by zip code and specific taxpayer groups, to find areas of noncompliance. It also focuses on specific tax issues. Recent statistics show that the IRS made adjustments (usually in the IRS's favor) in 95 percent of cases it examined under the DORA system. Finally, there is the Coordinated Examination Program (CEP), an in-depth, labor-intensive, multi-agent inquisition once reserved for major corporations but now expanded to about 30,000 companies a year.

These categories cover the great majority of audits. Others get started for a variety of reasons. Maybe you suffered through one audit and the revenue agent thinks the same issues will recur in other tax years. Maybe someone who holds a big-time

Unofficially...
In fiscal 1996, more than 160 million income tax returns were filed. Of these, the IRS audited only slightly more than 1 percent. The mathematical chances of an audit were less than 1 percent if you made between $25,000 and $50,000. If you made more than $100,000, your chances were about 4 percent.

grudge against you has told the IRS about your hidden assets or hidden income (informers can earn rewards of up to 10 percent of the amount the IRS collects). Maybe your corporation has been examined, and as a result the IRS now wants to look at your related personal return.

Whatever the source, whatever the reason, once you get an audit notice, you're stuck with an audit until it is finished.

Not all audits are created equal

The IRS conducts only three basic types of audits:

- the *correspondence audit,*
- the *office audit,* and
- the *field audit.*

The correspondence audit

This type of audit is straightforward and not as painful as you anticipate—something like getting an injection from a big needle in a sensitive part of your anatomy. The IRS finds an apparent error in your return and writes you a letter. In most cases, there is nothing to fear from a correspondence audit. Did you put down the wrong number from your W-2? Forget income from Form 1099 (for nonwage income such as interest and dividends)? The correspondence audit clears this up. Did you take a clearly unallowable deduction? File using the wrong filing status? Make a mistake on your IRA contribution? Claim a questionable refund? Relatively simple questions like these are easily handled by mail. The IRS writes you, notes the issue, and asks for a response.

Heed the deadline or get an extension. If you don't, the tax machine will grind on, sending you a follow-up request, then a "thirty-day letter," and

"
It [DIF] rates the potential for change, based on past IRS experience with similar returns. IRS personnel screen the highest-scoring returns, selecting some for audit and identifying the items on these returns that are most likely to need review.
—Recent IRS fact sheet
"

finally a Notice of Deficiency. If you fail to respond to the Notice of Deficiency, the IRS will assess the error as it sees it. You then have a legally binding bill you usually cannot fight except by paying it first and going to court.

Even a lowly correspondence audit can hide nasty traps. For example, the IRS watches out for alimony compliance, child support refunds that should be paid to another spouse, erroneous refunds, tax credits, and a host of other errors that its computers can detect electronically. Some of these can balloon into big fights between you and the IRS or between ex-spouses. So the rule is, pay attention and respond to these correspondence audits. Since these audits are conducted almost entirely by mail, you won't see an IRS representative. But in a few cases you may speak to one by telephone, and sometimes a phone call helps to clear up the issues. Do not hesitate to call the IRS, even in a correspondence audit, if that phone call will solve the problem.

The office audit

Now suppose your return has a bigger error or contains an issue the computers can't handle. For example, you have unreported income, or you simply scored too high in the IRS's audit lottery. Then your return is selected. Someone in the Service Center where you filed it physically mails such returns with standard cover sheets to the local IRS district office. An officer in that office has to decide which returns to examine, and whether you get an office audit or a field audit and the royal attention of a revenue agent.

Unofficially...
In 1995, more than 50 percent of all audits were "Service Center" audits, typically correspondence audits. Only 25 percent involved a "tax auditor," and another 25 percent involved a revenue agent.

The local office can't audit every return it receives, not even all those it selects for a closer look. Many are therefore "closed on survey." Remember—even the IRS has finite resources, so it must make choices about which audits are most likely to pay off. In many cases, someone looks at the return and decides it lacked sufficient dollar or issue appeal to bother with. As to the rest of the returns, well, they have won/lost the audit lottery.

An examiner assigns some of these returns for *office audit.* This is an audit conducted in the IRS's office. It is usually reserved for issues the selecting officer deems complicated or significant enough to look at, but not heavy-duty enough to merit a full field audit. There are no hard and fast rules for such a decision: it's a judgment call. Usually a Tax Auditor conducts an office audit. She sends you a letter asking for or making an appointment, noting the questionable items and requesting certain records. You gather the records, bring them into the office, and discuss the issues.

Office audits have their own perils. On the income side, tax auditors are trained to spot unreported income by performing indirect checks on the amount of income you reported on your return. They love to dive into cash businesses, and they salivate at the mere mention of "gross receipts." They will ask you many questions: "How did you get your gross receipts number? Have you checked it against other records? Does it square with your checking accounts, personal and business?" They can ask you where you got your money—from gifts, loans, or inheritances? They may ask about your lifestyle. They check your personal return against your main assets and liabilities. If your lifestyle is Jaguar but your income is Volkswagen, you had better be prepared to explain.

Tax auditors also question unusual or very large deductions. Since many taxpayers are poor record keepers, auditors have a field day with many business and personal deductions. In fact, the poorest record keepers are usually people who say or think, "I can keep sloppy records. The IRS can never prove my figures are wrong." Those taxpayers are in for a nasty surprise when they find out that the burden of proof is on them, not the IRS.

So if you have very sloppy records, the IRS will often disallow your deductions for "lack of substantiation," then penalize you for negligence because you kept sloppy records. People who run cash businesses are especially at risk in this type of audit.

The field audit

The *field audit* is the final type of common audit the IRS conducts. This is a full-blown examination of a taxpayer's business and/or personal return. The revenue agents who conduct these audits are often CPAs. Even when they're not, they've had years of training inside or outside the IRS. Revenue agents focus on many of the same issues that an agent in an office audit might address, but they are more thorough. Also, the dollar amounts at stake and the complexity of the issues are usually higher both on the income and the deduction side. Examples might be home office deductions, hobby losses, or complicated business deductions. They might also address capital gains and losses, income from the sale of residences, and pension and retirement issues. Here is a recent list of fourteen of the most commonly audited and appealed issues, on a nationwide basis:

- Gross income

- Trade or business deductions

Watch Out!
You might think that as a result of the widely-reported "reversal of the burden of proof" in the 1998 tax reform act, the IRS now has to prove positively that you've made a mistake in your return. Unfortunately, you still have to carry your burden of proof in order to get a reversal. See Chapter 14.

Unofficially...
In a recent reporting year, the fourteen issues listed here accounted for $56 billion in proposed new taxes, 57 percent of the total of $98 billion involved in all audits. These items also represented 45 percent of the number of cases.

- Deductions for losses
- Bad debts
- Depreciation
- Net operating losses
- Capital expenditures
- Taxability of a corporation on distribution (of assets)
- Taxable year of inclusion (that is, in what year is an item of income properly taxed?)
- Taxable year of deductions
- Last-in, first-out inventories
- Allocation of income and deductions among taxpayers
- Taxes of foreign countries and U.S. possessions
- Definition of gross estate

"Getting to know you" IRS-style

The revenue agent normally selects the site of the audit. Unless the choice is unreasonable in time or place, his choice prevails. Still, if the presence of a revenue agent would harm your business, the agent normally makes alternative arrangements, such as an isolated room or an off-site location. Quite often, the taxpayer's accountant is the buffer between the taxpayer and the auditor, and the accountant can usually work out an acceptable time and place of examination.

How the revenue agent works

Revenue agents work out of groups of six to eight, usually one or two groups in each local office. Their boss is a Group Manager. The Group Manager's boss is a Branch Chief. If you don't like the agent you get, you can't request another. But if you have a communication problem or personality conflict, don't hesitate to call the group manager. You have the right to fair and courteous treatment, and if you are not getting it, like a true American you should complain. In fact, the IRS now routinely trains its agents about what taxpayers have a right to expect from them in an audit.

According to a recent "Fact Sheet," these rights include:

- A right to professional and courteous treatment by IRS employees;

- A right to privacy and confidentiality about tax matters;

- A right to know why the IRS is asking for information, how the IRS will use it, and what will happen if the requested information is not provided;

- A right to representation, by yourself or an authorized representative;

- A right to appeal disagreements, both within the IRS and before the courts.

The revenue agent works steadily and methodically. He often prepares a list of documents he wants to examine, using an IRS form called an *Information Document Request*. IDRs can be two to three pages (in simple audits) and can ask for five, ten, or more items. Agents often freely discuss the issues they are focusing on if you ask them. You can tell a lot about what the agent is thinking just by looking at the documents he wants. Having the records available and in good shape is a good idea.

But records carry their own perils, of course. You, the taxpayer, know where you've buried the bodies: the unreported income, the outrageous

Moneysaver
Keep good
records. As a
rule, taxpayers
who keep sloppy
records wind
up paying
more in taxes.

deductions. The agent does not (at least, not yet). So the agent's questions may range widely. If you have something to hide, discuss that issue ahead of time with a tax professional before responding to the IDR. The revenue agent also has specialists available to him. Examples might be art appraisers and industry specialists. He can request help in any specialized area where he does not feel completely comfortable.

Even taxpayers who have tried to be honest often panic during agent questioning, because their returns contain ordinary, garden-variety mistakes. Still, unless you have truly evaded your taxes and the agent's documentary net threatens to expose your crime, there is no reason to be afraid.

Can the agent really get all those records?

Under current law, the agent's authority to examine records is almost unlimited. As a rule of thumb, the agent is authorized to request any record that is or may be relevant to the examination. (Chapter 1 discusses this authority in more detail.) That agent has the authority to assure himself that the law has not been violated, as well as to find out where it has been violated.

Revenue agents wield other powers, too. They can expand the audit to other years, both before and after the year at issue. Revenue agents can examine any related returns, including especially partnership returns and corporation returns. Those inquiries can open more issues for the corporation, partnership, shareholders, and partners. The agent can refer a case to the Criminal Investigation Division if he suspects fraud. He can propose increases in your taxes and thereby thrust the burden on you to prove him wrong. He can also propose penalties, as to which you again have the burden of proof in most cases. Although these seem like excessively powerful tools, each is fully authorized by law.

What—more audits?

One special type of audit is the *Taxpayer Compliance Measurement Program* (TCMP) audit. In the past, every three years or so, the IRS would select about 50,000 to 150,000 returns for a line-by-line, item-by-item examination. These TCMP audits were like slow torture for taxpayer and auditor alike. In such an audit, you could be asked to verify every item on your return. For example, you would have to bring in birth certificates to verify the existence of children you claimed as exemptions. The agent could demand a copy of your marriage license to verify your "married, filing jointly" status. And the agent could require you to show every mortgage payment, every receipt for a charitable deduction, and every telephone bill for your business.

The IRS used these audits for research purposes to refine the DIF scoring system. These days, the TCMP audits have been shelved because of adverse Congressional reaction. However, don't count on this attitude lasting forever.

The Service can also pester you in many other interesting ways—they are technically not "audits," but they amount to the same thing. A common example is an employment tax investigation. The IRS may claim that the people you employ as independent contractors are really your employees, making you liable for their employment taxes. If your business fails to pay its payroll taxes, you as an officer or director might be personally liable for a portion of these taxes. Or concluding you have committed tax fraud, the agent might refer your case to

Moneysaver
Beginning in early 1999, the IRS may not use financial status or economic reality audits to determine unreported income unless it has a "reasonable indication" that there is a likelihood of such unreported income. This may mean the agent needs an independent source before fishing in this area.

the Criminal Investigation Division. That's in part an audit, too, but it is also a high-level criminal investigation extremely different from a normal audit because the special agent wants to throw you in jail. The IRS is also conducting "lifestyle audits," or "financial status audits."

Agents look at your lifestyle to see whether you live beyond your means. They look at net worth, significant assets, net equity, and business affairs. They search for other assets such as boats and fancy cars. They often perform an analysis called a *cash* T to see whether you are spending more than you are apparently bringing in. Someone who lives well beyond his means can often explain the discrepancy (inheritances, loans, and so on), but in many cases, the lavish or visible lifestyle means the taxpayer has been evading taxes by failing to report all income. So if your spending habits are too lavish, watch out. Such high-profile people tend to become visible targets. Tha following box shows some of the topics that appear in a recent IRS lifestyle audit list.

The questions in the IRS lifestyle audit are just the beginning. The agents have wide discretion, so far uncurbed by courts, to ask questions about your lifestyle.

Requesting audit reconsideration

What if you simply can't get your act together during the audit and the IRS machine grinds out an assessment? You may request "audit reconsideration." It's a great way to have your case reconsidered, even when you've been given an opportunity once or twice already.

You are entitled to audit reconsideration in

Selected IRS "Economic Reality" Questions

1. What real estate do you own and when was it acquired? Monthly rent? Do you manage or do you have a management company?

2. Did you make any improvements to any of your real estate? What was done, how much was it, and how was it paid for?

3. How many autos do you own? What are they? What is the payment?

4. Do you own any large asset (over $10,000) besides auto and real estate? What is it, where is it kept? Is it paid for? If not, what is the payment?

5. Did you sell any assets? If so, what, to whom, and for how much?

6. Do you ever take cash advances from credit cards or lines of credit? How much and how often?

7. What cash did you have on hand in the audited year, personally or for business, not in a bank—at your home, in a safe-deposit box, or hidden somewhere?

8. What is the largest amount of cash you had at any one time in the audited year?

9. Did you deposit all paychecks into the bank? What account?

10. Do you have a safe deposit box? Where? What is in it?

11. Were you involved in any cash transactions of $10,000 or more?

12. Employee business expenses: What meals are being deducted? Provide appointment calendar receipts, business purpose, and business relationship for all expenses.

Unofficially...
You must respond to agents' lifestyle audit questions unless you invoke the privilege against self-incrimination, or the attorney-client, physician-patient, spousal, or some other applicable evidentiary privilege.

many cases. For instance, you can ask the Examination Division to reconsider your case if you have new information suggesting the IRS's assessment is excessive. Reconsideration may be available if the IRS made a computational error, you didn't get notice of the proposed adjustment in time, or you simply didn't have enough time to substantiate your position. Ask for reconsideration if you didn't receive the IRS's audit report or the follow-up statutory Notice of Deficiency. Finally, if you have one or more unfiled returns, you can automatically get audit reconsideration by filing true original returns. The Service has broad discretion to reconsider and abate any assessment that is too high (or increase one that is too low) even after an audit has been closed.

The mechanics of your request are simple. Address a letter to the local Service Center, the Collection Division, or even the local Office of Taxpayer Advocate. State that you are requesting audit reconsideration. An amended return with a cover letter will suffice. In your letter or amended return, note the issues you are questioning and the grounds for abatement or adjustment. Attach a copy of the tax return in question and the IRS's audit report, if it is available. Also enclose all documentation you can find to support your position.

The IRS has a long list of required information, depending upon what issue you select. For example, if you ask for an additional exemption for a dependent, the Service wants to see items such as school, medical, or other records to determine residence, a record of income, or a copy of the birth certificate. The IRS publishes "substantiation requirements" for many other items, such as retirement accounts, alimony payments, medical and dental expenses, auto expenses, and entertainment. The request is routed to the local Service Center. If it is accepted, the Service Center sends it to your local IRS office, where your friendly revenue agent or tax auditor reopens your case. Then you're back in the IRS audit loop.

What's on the horizon?

The IRS is always looking for new and different ways to audit the American public. Over the past few years, it has invented something called the *Market Segment Specialization Program (MSSP)*, a fancy name for audits of entire industries at one time.

So far, the Service has identified more than ninety-eight industries or issues for this special audit status. These include law firms, accounting practices, bed-and-breakfasts, the construction industry, and many others. Then the agency devises an entire audit strategy that applies to every audit it conducts in each of these groups. These guides tend to be long, complex, and detailed.

To go along with MSSP guides, the IRS is training industry specialists in the Audit Specialization Program. The typical revenue agent is a generalist; she'll take whatever case is assigned, from verifying your mortgage interest to measuring unreported income. Industry specialists concentrate on one type of business, such as restaurants, auto dealerships, or landscape services. They know these industries inside and out. They know how much business you should be doing, what your expenses are likely to be, and where the holes in your records usually are.

Bright Idea
The MSSP guidelines are available on the IRS's web site, www.irs.ustreas.gov. They show exactly what the agent will be looking for, and so are extremely valuable if they apply to your industry or business. They give record keeping tips and so are, in a sense, checklists to better business practices.

The Service is also testing the *Automated Issue Identification System*. This system uses computerized artificial intelligence to spot possible audit issues on your tax returns. It can also classify returns for examination. For example, suppose that you run a bed-and-breakfast. Your costs are 10 percent higher than normal for your size and location, according to the IRS computer. You might have run afoul of the IRS's Automated Issue Identification System. It's not Big Brother, but it begins to come close. Finally, the IRS is neck-deep in the age of computerization. It has computer audit specialists, particularly useful for big cases and big taxpayers. Naturally, the goal of all of this is maximum dollars and compliance.

What can the agent do to you?

When the agent finishes his audit, what happens? Actually, nothing. Strictly speaking, the agent can only *recommend* some action, really a choice of four possibilities:

- **No change.** The agent found no errors, or only minor ones not worth pursuing. He writes a *No Change Report*, and sends you a letter advising you that the examination resulted in no change to your return.

- **Agreed case.** The agent found errors and proposed more taxes (or a refund), possibly penalties. (Interest is added automatically by law.) You agree with all the changes or choose not fight them. The agent writes a *Revenue Agent's Report* and asks you to sign it. By signing you agree to the immediate assessment of the taxes. You soon get a bill from the IRS for the extra taxes, penalties, and interest.

- **Unagreed case.** You and the agent could not resolve any of the issues. He reports the entire audit as "unagreed." He sends this Revenue Agent's Report to you or your tax representative. It has a cover sheet and a summary page reciting exactly what items the agent is increasing or decreasing, and by how much. The report explains each item. The summary sheet sets out how much tax the agent proposes. Often it has a calculation of penalties and sometimes of interest.

- **Partially agreed case.** You agree with the agent on some issues, but not all. This hybrid case is split. The agent prepares a partial agreement form, and describes the remaining issues as unagreed.

Moneysaver
Before 1996, the IRS could abate interest only for "ministerial errors." Now you can also request interest abatement for "managerial" errors. For example, the IRS assesses a tax without ever giving notice of the proposed tax liability.

If all or part of the audit is not agreed upon, the agent will send you a thirty-day letter. This formal letter advises you of the proposed changes and gives you thirty days to agree or disagree. If you don't agree, you may want to appeal. Nothing in the law grants you the right to an appeal within the IRS, but the agency found a long time ago that internal appeals often settle cases. In fact, it has an entire branch devoted to these appeals, the Office of Appeals.

People often ask whether the agent has the authority to settle an issue that is in conflict over the facts or law. Usually, he does not. His job is to call an issue one way or another, not to settle an issue based on litigating hazards. Appeals officers, however, do have this authority. If you write the IRS that you want to appeal within the thirty-day deadline, the agency will not assess the tax. Instead, it sends the case to the Office of Appeals. Chapter 10 explains how appeals should be handled.

Bright Idea
If the Notice of
Deficiency is
wrong but you
simply missed
the ninety-day
deadline, you can
still file a claim
for refund.
See Chapters
16 and 17.

What if you do nothing? Remember one of the rules of IRS survival:

DOING NOTHING USUALLY HURTS YOU.

In this case, the IRS sends you a formal letter called a *Notice of Deficiency*. Unlike the thirty-day letter, this Notice of Deficiency is required by law before the IRS can assess a tax. The notice is a formal proposal that you owe more taxes. It gives you ninety days (not three months) to file suit in the United States Tax Court to contest the notice. (See Chapter 15.) Filing suit in the Tax Court stops the IRS from assessing the tax it had proposed, at least until the case is resolved. But if you miss the ninety-day deadline by a day, an hour, or even a minute, the IRS makes the assessment against you several weeks later and sends a bill.

At that point, there is little you can do but pay the bill. The court case, an agreed assessment, or an unagreed assessment ends the audit process that started when your return was "selected for examination."

Your state tax is not far behind

By ambush and attrition, state governments are slowly recapturing the powers they had ceded to the federal government. As this trend accelerates, the states need ever more money to run their programs. They also need stronger enforcement mechanisms to ensure they reap the fields of green within their borders. Everyone who owes a federal tax should consider whether he will end up owing a state tax as well. (It's usually a "given" that you will.) States are no longer paper tigers when it comes to tax enforcement. They also gain strength every day.

State-federal cooperation has been a feature of our federal system since the first days of the republic. The states and federal government continue to cooperate very closely when it comes to taxes. One thing they share is information—lots of it. The IRS and many (in some areas, all) state governments have signed a series of protocols, called *Information Sharing Agreements,* of which the public is largely unaware. The first type of sharing agreement is for tax information. The exchange goes both ways. The IRS tells states what you earn and states tell the IRS what you have reported to them. They also share refund information, and, of course, states are required to send you an IRS Form 1099 when you get a state tax refund.

The states and the IRS also share employment and sales tax information. The reporting cycle is every eighteen months to three years. For example, the federal government wants to know how much your business is reporting to the state for sales tax purposes so it can check this against the amount you reported on your federal return. Cheating usually shows up when you report more gross sales on your state sales tax returns than gross income on your federal income tax return.

The states and the IRS also share employment information. They exchange data on your employees, so you can't tell the state you have "employees" while you call them "independent contractors" for federal tax withholding purposes.

Most prominently, the IRS shares the results of income tax audits with your state's department of taxation. State laws require that you amend your state income tax return if you owe more after a federal audit. The same laws also suspend the statute of limitations on assessment if you owe more state taxes as a result of a federal audit. So, even though more than three years have passed, the state can still assess more state tax as a result of your federal audit.

Watch Out!
The IRS's Refund
Offset Program
collects debts to
federal agencies,
such as overdue
child support,
tax liabilities,
even future
IRS taxes. But
beginning with
refunds payable
after December
31, 1999, the
IRS has
enhanced powers
to collect
these refunds.

Often, the states have computer programs to generate a bill to you whether or not you file an amended state tax return after your federal audit. Some states also cooperate with the IRS to investigate or audit you, the taxpayer. For instance, suppose a state investigates your business to see whether your workers are employees or independent contractors. The choice makes a big difference in your state unemployment tax. It makes an even bigger difference to the withholding and Social Security taxes you must pay to the IRS. The state will share the results of this investigation with the IRS. As electronic filing and computerization of federal and state tax records become more common, we'll be seeing much more of joint audits and joint collection.

Nonfilers need to be especially alert to state-federal cooperation. The nonfiler who owes taxes to the federal government almost always owes state taxes as well. The state taxes may be only 1 percent to 10 percent of the federal total, but they are still important. So the nonfiler should file state tax returns when he files delinquent federal tax returns.

All states with tax laws have vigorous enforcement provisions as well. These laws include criminal penalties for violating state tax statutes of all varieties—income, employment, sales, and so on. Moreover, states are enforcing these statutes more diligently and regularly than at any time in the past. Their methods include arresting people for failing to pay taxes, prosecuting for evasion or nonfiling, closing delinquent businesses, and similar strong medicine. The criminal investigation divisions of the states and the IRS also share information after they complete their investigations. States have civil seizure powers comparable to those of the IRS, including levying on wages and seizing bank accounts. Tax refunds are also a prime target. Each year, states seize $20 million to $30 million in state tax refunds and send them to the IRS.

The states have asked the IRS to return the favor with federal refunds, though so far it has not. Still, the IRS does collect child-support payments from tax refunds. It sends those monies to the states that have signed up for this program.

On the happier side, states are working ever more closely with the IRS to make your tax life simpler. For example, there is a big push to make it possible to file both federal and state returns at one time and in one place, electronically. This idea has been tested since 1990. Eventually, it will become standard practice.

States also have authority to compromise a tax you owe. The leniency or strictness of these programs runs the gamut from reasonable to impossible, but the authority is there. Call your state tax department for information. (Often the states don't publicize their compromise authority, for fear that people will flood them with requests and stop trying to pay their current and past-due taxes.) The key to survival is to anticipate the state tax liability. Check whether it can be reduced or compromised and then address the state tax problem before it surprises you.

Unofficially...
The number of electronically filed federal returns jumped from 7.5 million in 1991 to almost 15 million in 1996.

Time is (not) on your side—statutes of limitation

Anyone who has ever missed a deadline—and that's most of us—knows you can lose opportunities you would otherwise have exercised. That principle holds true ten times over in tax matters, where real legal rights and real dollars are at stake. Statutes of limitation in tax cases destroy millions of tax claims each year, on the taxpayer's side and the government's. In most cases, there is nothing you can do about a missed deadline. The law is that hard-and-fast. It's therefore useful to guide you through the most common deadlines and their extenders, and give a few hints on how to avoid missing them.

The most common statutes of limitation the IRS must obey are those dealing with the assessment and collection of taxes. Filing your federal income tax return triggers the well-known "three-year rule." The IRS has three years to assess more taxes, whether by audit or other adjustment on its computer system. But audits often last beyond the three years. Some do not even start until two years into the limitations period. So the IRS often asks for extensions. Give careful thought to each request. The downside of refusing is that the IRS will simply stop its audit and immediately assess the tax or send you a Notice of Deficiency. That action will force you to go to Tax Court to prevent a proposed assessment from becoming a formal bill. The IRS rarely misses these deadlines. So you are usually better off agreeing to the extension. In most cases, it is your only good choice.

If you file an amended tax return within sixty days before the three years runs out, the IRS legally gets more time to audit—an additional sixty days after receiving the amended return. For instance, if you file an amended return on the last day within the three-year period, the new deadline would be sixty-one days later.

The basic three-year rule on assessments is subject to many exceptions. Two are mentioned above:

(1) you extend by agreement and (2) the IRS issues a formal Notice of Deficiency proposing more taxes. That Notice of Deficiency is not a bill; it is only a formal proposal. Issuing that notice suspends the period of limitations on assessment until ninety days runs or you file a petition within the ninety days and the Tax Court resolves your case. Two other exceptions to the three-year rule are as follows:

- **The six-year rule.** The IRS has six years to assess a tax if you omitted 25 percent of gross income from a tax return. This rule protects the Service in high-dollar cases. It also alerts the Service to be very thorough about other tax years in which you may have omitted income.

- **The "forever" rule**. Some taxes are forever, that is, subject to no statute of limitations. Such is the case with civil tax fraud. Tax fraud consists of filing a false return with intent to evade the tax, or willfully attempting to evade the tax. (Criminal tax fraud must be prosecuted within six years from the date the crime was committed—usually the date the fraudulent return was signed.) There is also no statute of limitations on assessment where you do not file a return at all.

A special case: the "innocent spouse"

One audit issue is of special importance: the issue of the "innocent spouse." Consider the following example. Emily and Ernest were married in 1940. Emily had only a high-school education. Ernest handled all of the family's finances. Emily took care of the house, using the couple's joint checking account to pay for groceries, utilities, and the mortgage. Emily also raised two daughters. The couple filed joint federal income tax returns. Meanwhile,

Bright Idea
When you receive a request for extension from the IRS, try to limit the extension, possibly to one tax year, or to certain issues the IRS has already examined. Try to avoid giving an open-ended extension. Read the extension language carefully. And ask the agent to explain its fine print.

Ernest and his brother formed a partnership to open a store. He never discussed the store's business with Emily. To prepare the couple's joint tax return, Emily gave their reliable accountant a list of household expenses, then simply signed on the dotted line.

Things went well for years; then Ernest passed away. The IRS audited the couple's joint returns and assessed more than $40,000 in taxes. Without Ernest, Emily found herself alone: solely and completely liable for all of these taxes. They did not live lavishly; there were no expensive fur coats, luxury yachts, trips to Bermuda, or private schools. Emily always did as Ernest asked, keeping faith with her husband and his professional accountant-advisers. Yet, because she signed the joint returns, she was held liable for all of the tax, even though she had no involvement in the operations of the business.

Congress felt there ought to be some remedy for situations like this, so in 1969 it passed the "innocent spouse" statute, a part of the Internal Revenue Code. If you meet the criteria, you get complete absolution from all tax, penalties, and interest that you would otherwise by responsible for by signing a joint return.

Although many people every year take advantage of the innocent spouse law, meeting its tests is difficult even after the 1998 changes, so you are almost always better off having professional help to prove this issue.

When you may claim to be innocent

You may raise the innocent spouse defense almost any time in the tax process, but the issue usually arises during an audit. For example, the agent finds a hidden bank account, or one spouse is arrested for drugs or gambling. A corporation's president is charged with extra income because the corporation paid personal expenses, or one spouse is responsible for an unallowable deduction. These events and myriad others could result in an increase in taxes. Then the "innocent" spouse claims, "I had no idea my husband [or wife] had all this extra income [or had taken unallowable deductions]."

This defense also can arise during a divorce. In the divorce decree, the husband (or wife) commits to pay the taxes for past years when the couple filed a joint return. The IRS audits those returns, or finds some other reason to propose more taxes. The wife (or husband) can claim innocent spouse status at that time. Finally, we also see the issue in garden-variety collection situations. Here, the IRS is trying to collect on past-due taxes from joint returns. Often one spouse will raise the innocent spouse defense. Note that the innocent spouse defense is not available as to taxes actually reported on a return, only to increases the IRS proposes.

Five tests for proving you are innocent

Proving innocent spouse status is arduous even under the best of circumstances, and sometimes a spouse is not eligible no matter how unfair the overall situation is. Let's explore how a spouse can establish innocence. The proof has five elements, some easy, some difficult.

Filing a joint return

First, you must have filed a joint return for the tax year involved. This item seems simple enough— either you signed or you didn't. But sometimes a wife denies the genuineness of her signature on the

Moneysaver
The IRS Reform and Restructuring Act of 1998 made substantial changes to the innocent spouse provisions. In particular, it allows qualifying spouses to "split" the liability, so that they pay taxes only on the income attributable to them, not their spouses' income as well.

Unofficially...
Under pre-1998 law, the understatement of tax had to be "substantial," and the items had to be "grossly" erroneous. Many taxpayers could not overcome these hurdles. The 1998 tax reform act eliminated them, making the innocent spouse more widely available, especially to lower-income spouses.

return. Then the fight starts. The husband claims she in fact signed, or that he signed her name with her permission. Even where one spouse doesn't sign the return at all, the IRS sometimes argues that the facts show the spouse intended to file a joint return. If so, by law it's a joint return.

Understatement of tax

The second requirement is that there be an understatement of tax attributable to erroneous items of one spouse. Watch the details: there must be an understatement of tax on the return. This means that you are stuck with anything you reported on the return as the true tax. You may be innocent, if at all, only as to extra taxes the IRS proposes.

For example, Jack and Jill were married for ten years. When Jill signed their joint returns, Jack said, "Don't worry, dear, I'll pay the taxes." He always promised he would, and the IRS never knocked on the door. When they divorced in 1995, Jack promised again to pay all taxes due on past returns, $50,000 in total. The divorce became final. Jack moved to Kodiak, Alaska, and Jill was left in the IRS's target zone, struggling as a single mother to support three children, all under the age of five.

Innocent spouse? No! Maybe Jill can get relief in other ways, such as urging that collection would be a hardship. Chapters 11 and 12 discuss these options. But she is not an innocent spouse under the law. She signed all the returns, and there was no understatement of tax. The return stated exactly how much tax was owed. It simply was not paid.

Ignorance of the understatement

The third legal requirement is that the spouse must not have known, nor had reason to know, of the understatement of tax. This rule does not mean you can sign the return in blank or not read it all. You can't hide your head in the sand and expect to get tax relief. Instead, the requirement is to show you acted with "reasonable prudence."

For example, if you reviewed the return but relied on your husband, wife, CPA, or lawyer to prepare it correctly, that would be reasonable prudence. But if you put your left hand over your eyes and scribbled your signature with your right, that's not reasonable.

It's also not reasonable prudence if you ignore obvious warning signs that something is wrong or too good to be true. A spouse who lives in a million-dollar home knowing her husband earns $20,000 a year cannot be "innocent." Maybe a spouse's suspicious behavior could put you on notice; maybe your lifestyle is way above your earnings. Possibly there are unusual or inconsistent warning signs, such as long, unexplained absences from home, lavish gifts, erratic behavior, or sudden changes in lifestyle or net worth. The agent and the IRS will seize on any of these to show you should have known that there was something wrong with the tax return you signed.

Fairness

The fourth requirement is that, under all the circumstances, it would be inequitable to hold you liable for the understated taxes. "Inequitable" generally means "unfair." This is a catchall requirement that limits relief to the truly needy. The rich and famous of the world do not usually qualify. If life was hard when you signed the return, but life is great now, the theory goes, there's no unfairness in holding you responsible for past taxes. Still, the law makes an explicit exception for "normal support."

Moneysaver
If you can't argue for complete relief, argue for partial relief. For example, suppose that a husband told his wife he omitted $100,000 of income, but the real omission was $1,000,000. His wife may make the innocent spouse claim with respect to $900,000 of income.

So, if your spouse supports you with food, clothing, and shelter within normal amounts, not lavishly or extravagantly, the government cannot claim you failed the "inequitable" test by that fact alone.

For example, one recent case shows how far this argument will stretch. Lucy and Larry were married. Larry started a business raising and selling radishes. He was so successful that he built a house on ten acres, complete with swimming pool, tennis court, clubhouse, and airplane landing strip. Thirty years later, Lucy and Larry divorced. She got $225,000 each year as guaranteed income, plus the house, clubhouse, swimming pool, and tennis court (apparently, Larry kept the landing strip).

Two years later, the couple remarried each other. For three years, Larry gave his wife $15,000 per month, plus two Mercedes Benz and trips in the airplane. Naturally, they had a getaway in Florida during the winter growing season. However, the winds of love blow hot and cold. They divorced a second time, this time permanently. As a parting gift, Lucy got $4.28 million as alimony. Of course, the IRS then came into the picture, proposing massive taxes on the couple's jointly filed returns. Lucy said, "I am an innocent spouse." The IRS said, "You've got to be kidding. Just look at your lavish lifestyle, including your $15,000-a-month allowance, new cars, European vacations, race horses, a full-time maid and gardener, two homes, and a clubhouse, swimming pool, and tennis court. You must have known that Larry was underreporting his taxes, and besides, it's certainly not unfair to hold you liable."

Believe it or not, the court sided with Lucy. "One person's luxury may be another's necessity," said the court. She was rich before the returns were filed, she was rich during the years in question, and she was rich afterward. Nothing in her lifestyle would have put her on notice that anything had changed.

The two-year deadline

The fifth requirement is that you make an "election" to invoke innocent spouse status within two years after the IRS begins to collect against you. This one is easy to fulfill but also easy to forget. And missing the two-year window is fatal to your claim.

Filing the claim of innocence

Despite occasional wins like Lucy's case, in the real world agents are extremely reluctant to believe your claims of innocence, or even to credit sworn testimony to that effect.

Often, you must prepare to go to court to prove innocent spouse status. But courts are often skeptical about granting relief, and the cases are inconsistent from courts of appeal around the country. Your case must be excellent to prevail. The best way to prove you're an innocent spouse to the IRS or a court is to assemble a catalog of evidence and present it to the IRS or to a court if necessary. Follow these steps as closely as possible.

Prepare the affidavit

First, prepare your own affidavit. Tell your life story, focusing especially on the years of trouble with your spouse. Common to these cases are long, sad stories of spouse abuse, psychological and physical domination, alcoholism, drug abuse, and other dysfunctional behavior. Wives who are abused and dominated by their husbands can often be innocent spouses. It is common sense that if one spouse dominates the relationship, he or she can take charge of the taxes, and the return comes out wrong without the other spouse's knowledge or consent.

Unofficially...
Even if you fail the innocent spouse tests, and can't make an election under the 1998 law to have separate liability, the new law allows the IRS to grant relief from liability by taking into account all the facts and circumstances and finding that it is inequitable to hold you liable.

It's also very common for innocent spouse cases to arise out of family businesses. One spouse (usually the husband) runs the business with an iron hand. The other spouse minds the home and children, participates in community activity, and has minimal involvement in the business. Then, when the IRS proposes more tax, the wife claims innocence because the husband ran the business and refused to keep her informed of income or tax-related matters. It's common to hear, "My husband ran the business. He refused to let me participate in it. I trusted him to file the returns, and we had the accountant to help get it right. When I asked him about the return, he would just say to sign and not ask any questions." While sometimes this can be merely a convenient excuse, quite often it is the truth.

Your "life history" affidavit should be long and detailed. Include everything. Show how the other spouse's personality, bad habits, or ways of doing business meant that you could not know that the taxes were understated. Demonstrate the unfairness of holding you liable for the other spouse's errors.

Assemble third-party testimony and objective evidence

Second, begin to assemble third-party witness statements. Evidence from people with no ax to grind on your issue is always credible with the IRS and the courts. If your three best friends knew of your spouse's alcoholism, drug abuse, or domineering nature, have them write affidavits. Bankers may have known of his secretive business habits. Counselors and friends can testify about the personalities and financial habits they observed.

In addition to witness statements, gather objective evidence. This would include bank statements, notices, business records, and anything else on paper that supports your case.

Get help and be persistent

Third, get help. Find a friend or ask a professional whether your case is good and how it can be improved. Then follow up. Ask the revenue agent or tax auditor for as much time as you need to put the evidence together. Cite helpful court cases. These are available in the professional literature, but you may need some help finding them.

Whatever happens, don't give up. Statistically, you will lose your claim at the agent's level. You may then appeal to the Office of Appeals or go to court. If the case comes up after the assessments have been made, consider requesting audit reconsideration. Finally, ask the Office of Taxpayer Advocate for help. Make your innocent spouse case to that office if you never had sufficient opportunity to prove your case to the agent. Even if that Office does not sustain the claim, it may refer your case back to the examination division for reaudit. The officer may decide that your case is so worthy, and enforced collection would be so unfair, that it will stop the Collection Division anyway under the "hardship" rules. Chapter 14 discusses how the Office of Taxpayer Advocate comes to your rescue in cases of clear hardship.

Recent developments

There is to be a new form for claiming innocent spouse relief, but as of press date, it is not yet officially available. So assemble and organize your evidence in any way that makes sense. You may choose

Bright Idea
Don't be discouraged from searching for records and affidavits to support your case. You will be amazed at how much support you can find once you start to look with the innocent spouse squarely in mind.

separate exhibits with exhibit numbers, or simply bundle it all together. Write a cover letter to the agent setting forth all the facts and asking for innocent spouse relief. Be sure to keep a copy, which you will surely need.

The 1996 Taxpayer Bill of Rights also helps a bit on the collection side. Let's say you can't prove innocent spouse status, or you've settled your innocent spouse claim somewhere in the middle. You therefore still owe taxes, but, in the meantime, what has the IRS been doing to collect against your ex-spouse? Now, an agent must tell you whether she has tried to collect, the general nature of her efforts, and how much has been collected. These facts may put some pressure on the agency to spread the burden of these joint taxes.

The tax reform act of 1998 also enacted a very important innocent spouse relief provision for divorced or separated spouses. It is important because it does not depend on the IRS; *you* can invoke it on your own. Under this new law, you may elect to be taxed separately from your spouse if you were no longer married or were legally separated, or you are not living in the same household as the other joint return filer during the past twelve months. You can make this election up to two years after the date the IRS begins collection activity, so there is plenty of time to act. But if you had *actual* knowledge of the items giving rise to the tax deficiency, you are not eligible. Moreover, if you and your spouse engaged in a fraudulent scheme to transfer assets, this election does not apply. If you make this election, your tax liability is generally figured on a "married filing separately" basis, although there are a number of fine details and exceptions to this rule.

Just the facts

- Read your audit rights and be familiar with them.

- Be businesslike, cooperative, and truthful with the IRS agent.

- Prepare well for your audit by reviewing your return and the documents requested.

- Always fight for whatever deductions you believe are legitimate.

- Consider amending your state tax returns if you pay more to the IRS.

- If you are an innocent spouse, be aware of the 1998 law that makes relief easier or allows you to elect separate tax liability treatment.

GET THE SCOOP ON...
- Making your return "audit-proof"
- The importance of keeping good records
- Organizing your tax records
- Preparing for a painless tax season

Chapter 9

Avoiding an Audit

Would you like to ensure that the IRS never selects your return for audit? Who wouldn't? In fact, there is only one surefire way: Don't file one at all. This, however, is not an option for most. The next best thing is to file one with average gross income (subject to withholding), average deductions or standard deductions, no partnerships, no fancy shelters, and no tax losses. Even returns like that have some chance of audit, but the mathematical odds are slim.

At the opposite extreme, would you like to ensure that your return is in fact selected? Take big tax losses, operate a business in cash, and keep sloppy records. Don't report income you earn from third-party payers who report it to the IRS, and take unusual or extremely large deductions.

Ideally, we would avoid this extreme, but unfortunately, there are limits to how much control we have over the look of our returns. Much of our economic life finds its way to a tax return; all income and deductions must be reported, and reported

Moneysaver
You can get average deduction statistics from the IRS's web site, www.irs.ustreas.gov or by calling (202) 622-4000, the IRS's Public Affairs Office in Washington, D.C. Some local offices may also have these statistics.

truthfully, no matter what the numbers may be. If those facts mean you have a higher chance of audit, there is usually little you can do.

Ways to avoid an audit

Still, even though there is no magic formula to make a return audit-proof, there is some room for maneuvering. Here are several techniques.

Keep deductions within the averages

Each year, the IRS publishes the average deductions people claim for each major category on Schedule A of the individual tax return: mortgage interest, charitable contributions, state and local taxes, medical expenses, and miscellaneous deductions. You probably won't earn many audit selection score points if your deductions are within these averages. True enough, you spend what you spend, and if you are entitled to the deduction, you should take it. Moreover, you risk the charge of filing a false return if you omit a valid deduction for the purpose of evasion. A missed deduction also costs you money. Still, you can legally time some deductions, with the collateral effect of bringing them within the averages.

For example, sometimes you can delay payment of a state income tax until January 1 of a new year, or accelerate the payment to the current year. You might decide, for cash flow or timing reasons, to prepay some interest on a mortgage, defer paying some interest, pay down principal to obtain a lower rate, or refinance to obtain an adjustable rate mortgage with its lower interest payments in the first year. You may decide to accelerate or delay medical expense payments, or do the same with charitable contributions and miscellaneous expenses. Bear in mind that all of these timing strategies may cost you money; a deduction delayed to a later tax year means you pay more tax this year (though less in a later year).

Report all third-party payer income

Report all W-2 wages and Form 1099 income, no matter how small, on page 1 of the return or Schedule B, respectively. Report income from every third-party payer: your bank, employer, union, state tax department (for an income tax refund), and a host of others. One way to check whether you have actually received all 1099 forms is to go through your bank account at the end of the year. Identify all deposits as wages, dividends, interest, rebates or refunds, and insurance reimbursements. Then decide whether each is required to be reported as gross income.

Use the right forms

The IRS loves forms. It has hundreds from which to choose each year. New ones are devised all the time. Using the wrong form often results in at least a notice inquiry. The notice inquiry asks about your income or deduction item. If you put it on the wrong form, normally you need only put it on the right form or send an explanation, and that is the end of the matter. But sometimes using the wrong form triggers the interest of an agent.

For example, Schedule F is used by farmers. You may get audit selection points if you use this schedule. If you suffered a loss, perhaps the agent may conclude that your farming activity was only a "hobby," causing disallowance of the loss.

Schedule C also attracts the IRS's interest. Sole proprietorships that are typically cash-intensive probably earn more audit selection points. So the

Bright Idea
Don't get carried away with your fear of being audited. In any given year, you have only one chance in a hundred of being audited, and most audits are routine correspondence audits.

choice of how to characterize and name your business is important. But the name must be accurate. Using a misleading name to avoid audit scrutiny could be a criminal false statement: if you run a pawnshop, you can't call it a bank!

Operate a noncash business

Since cash-based businesses are inherently subject to error or abuse, they invariably attract more than the usual IRS attention. To avoid trouble, use checks, credit cards, bank deposits, and anything else that generates a true record of your income and expenses. After all, in a tax audit, you, not the IRS, have the burden of proof. Some cash businesses try to have it both ways. They keep meticulous records reporting some of their cash, but other cash slips mysteriously through their fingers and into someone's wallet. The IRS has ways of finding this, including using industry averages, net worth examinations, and undercover techniques in criminal investigations. So reporting less than the average for businesses of your type may well trigger an audit.

For example, if dry cleaners usually report gross income of $500,000 per year and yours reports $250,000 in a high-volume area, this may be an audit trigger. In any case, it may cause an agent to look more closely if your return is selected for some other reason. The same can happen for other reasons, for instance, if you claim too much by way of deductions or cost of goods in a cash business.

Use only employees, not independent contractors

For years, the IRS has fought a running battle with many industries over the tax classification of subcontracted workers. Are they employees, making the owner ultimately liable for their payroll taxes? Or are they independent contractors, responsible for their own income and self-employment taxes? From an audit selection standpoint, it's probably safer to classify your workers as employees, despite the extra burden of withholding and filing larger payroll tax returns. Still, for competitive reasons, or paper-work-burden reasons, your business might continue to use subcontract labor. This issue might trigger the IRS's attention if you have a large deduction for "subcontract labor" or a similar category of expense.

Don't use a proprietorship

Choosing a corporate, limited liability entity, or partnership form of doing business, instead of a proprietorship, may lessen your chances of being selected for audit. Proprietors tend to be more lax in their record keeping and more cash-intensive, and have other practices that might attract the interest of the IRS. Incorporating or using a partnership will double your paperwork and reporting requirements, but the net amount of tax should generally be the same unless you use a "C" corporation and make a huge profit. Even then, tax planning can cut down or eliminate the double taxation that this form of corporate life normally entails.

Watch cosmetics and arithmetic

Common sense steps include:

■ File on time,

■ Check your income and deductions, and

■ Check your arithmetic.

A clean, neat return is a return that avoids at least one extra pair of eyes.

Unofficially...
If you feel strongly that your workers are independent con-tractors and eco-nomically it makes sense to treat them this way, you now have a new right to go to the U.S. Tax Court to challenge the IRS's determina-tion that your workers are really your employees.

Timesaver
It is total folly
these days for
any business to
operate without
a high-quality
computer system.
This is good
business prac-
tice, enabling
you to keep bet-
ter tabs on your
income and
receipts, and it
certainly adds
credibility to any
examination by
the IRS or any
other agency.

Avoid unusual deductions or exclusions from income

Millions of people claim unusual deductions or unusually large deductions. For example, some might try to deduct the cost of a small in-ground swimming pool as a medical necessity (shown by doctors' statements). Such a deduction is extremely unusual and is quite likely to be challenged. An unusually large deduction might be one for mort-gage interest twice or three times the national aver-age. Other examples of unusual deductions the IRS loves to hate are home office deductions, hobby loss-es, casualty losses, and business operating losses.

In a sense, these are not "unusual"—millions of people take them every year. But agents tend to see these types of deductions as subject to abuse, so they examine them carefully and often. Exclusions from income also catch the IRS's eyes. You might receive money during the year that is not reportable gross income. Examples would be loans, gifts, inheri-tance, or awards from some lawsuits.

In all these cases, the decision you face is whether to claim the deduction or omit the income, and whether to disclose your choice. If the IRS finds that you have filed incorrectly, its most common sanction is to penalize you for negligence or for sub-stantially understating your tax liability.

Check your lifestyle

Truly rich people who flaunt their wealth need not worry. But if you seem to be living beyond your means and an agent suspects you are overspending your income, you may be subjected to an IRS "lifestyle" audit. The basic idea is that you had to get the extra money from somewhere. If the agent looks long and hard, you may not be able to show where you obtained your evident riches. This alone can bring you under the IRS's audit microscope.

Hire a pro

Using a professional return preparer does not, by itself, reduce your audit selection score, but it can help in a number of ways. First, the professional may spot a troublesome deduction or omission of income that could have triggered an audit. Since the professional also does this for a living, common mistakes on the return are less likely. If for no other reason, a second pair of eyes that are not your own (or Aunt Alice's) can objectively review the tax return for errors and trouble spots.

Many businesses use professional return preparers as a matter of routine. They also make frequent use of payroll services to pay payroll taxes and prepare payroll tax returns. Both of these techniques are well-advised. While quality among commercial payroll services varies, the competent ones can be a godsend to a busy executive. Payroll tax compliance, a soft spot in many businesses, is often the first place the IRS looks. Once it looks there, it has a license to look elsewhere. So using a payroll service can often avoid that first inquiry from a curious agent.

Keep your evidence

Audits don't always accelerate from zero to 100 in less than thirty seconds. An agent may question only one or two items on a return, be satisfied you have your evidence lined up and ready to go, and end the audit at that. By contrast, nothing tweaks an agent's curiosity more than evasive answers, sloppy records, or inconsistent and unpersuasive evidence. So, if you are tempted to take an unusual deduction, keep all of your records and evidence together, ready to go in case they're needed.

Tax audits are a fact of life and always will be, even if for only a small percentage of taxpayers. So the goal of minimizing your chances of audit should

Moneysaver
If you have income you believe you are not required to report, you can immunize yourself against certain penalties by disclosing the item on Form 8275, attached to your return. You'll have to decide, however, whether filing this form increases your chances of an audit. (The IRS claims it does not, but many don't believe this.)

not lead to extreme conservatism on your tax returns. Even the IRS encourages you to take every deduction to which you are entitled. While you don't want the nagging threat of an audit to rule your life, taking care to keep records and prepare your return carefully can minimize the chances of your becoming personally acquainted with an IRS revenue agent.

"They don't eat much"

Record keeping, for business or tax purposes, is almost a world unto itself. People have all kinds of ideas on what records they must keep, and for how long. Surprising as it may seem, with a few narrow exceptions that do not apply to most people, there is absolutely no legal requirement to keep any specific types of tax records. Of course, you will certainly want to. The IRS encourages accurate record keeping, and good records are essential to know how you're doing financially. But the only "law" is to keep records the tax regulations require. And, strictly speaking, for most people those regulations require only that you keep records that are "sufficient to establish the amount of gross income, deductions, credits" for your tax returns. Translation: Keep whatever records you need to support your tax return. (At the end of this chapter is a handy guide showing suggested record-retention periods.)

Of course, what good would a tax rule be without exceptions? Some specific requirements apply to farmers, certain types of wage earners, corporations that use computerized records extensively, and exempt organizations (mostly charities). Also, if you've been a poor record keeper in the past, the IRS can specify in writing that you have to keep checks, receipts, or other specific types of records.

Even when the tax regulations are more specific, such as the requirement to keep books of account, they are also vague in some ways, stating only that the books of account must be kept accurately but in no particular form. Your books just have to be organized well enough to enable an IRS agent to examine them and make sense of them.

And, of course, the burden of proof in tax examinations and most tax cases in court is on you, the taxpayer. So although the regulations don't say you must keep specific records, it is wise to do so.

The importance of keeping good records

Many businesspeople look on record keeping as a necessary evil, a chore to be avoided or delegated. Thousands adopt the attitude, "I must be making money, just look at my sales" right before their ship sinks. If businesspeople who thumb their noses at record keeping realized how critical good records are, they would treat them with great importance. After all, you can't possibly know with accuracy whether you are making money, and how much, unless you know your income, receipts, payables, and receivables. This point cannot be overemphasized: You need "down to the penny" records primarily to run your business right. Secondarily, they help enormously at tax time.

For example, in one case, Marshall, owner of a small business, was in a cash crunch at the end of the year. It seemed impossible; sales had doubled and expenses had certainly not come anywhere near doubling. His bookkeeper had recently left, so one Monday he decided to take a look at her work. By Friday, he needed $150,000 to meet payroll, tax payments, and other expenses. The bank balance

Unofficially...
The vagueness of IRS record-keeping rules is understandable. The IRS cannot possibly keep up on all the types of records that people generate. And a regulation that spelled out exactly what records to keep would be self-defeating—so quickly outdated it would be impossible to administer.

was $5,000. He looked at the bookkeeper's accounts receivable files. To his horror, the bookkeeper had failed through ignorance or oversight to bill $200,000 of work. Some was never billed, some was marked as "paid" when it was not; other files were too confusing to understand. Marshall painstakingly reconstructed every file, called his customers, and saved the day. But it cost him countless hours of agony, some tax penalties, and plenty of interest on undeposited receipts.

Besides the advantage of being able to track whether your business is making money, there are several other good reasons to keep good business records:

■ It avoids costly penalties and allows you to take normal business discounts vendors often allow for quick payment. You can also avoid late-payment penalties, interest charges, and IRS charges for late payment of payroll taxes. Other tax penalties also can be avoided. This kind of control is impossible without good record keeping.

■ In the 1990s and beyond, your business must be lean and mean. No one has extra money to throw around at unnecessary expenses. A wasted dollar comes from *your* bottom line. You can't have an accurate picture of expenses— where to cut or where to add—without accurate and timely records. It is no exaggeration to say that for many businesses the difference between profit and loss is the control over expenses and income that comes with good record keeping.

■ Lenders are impressed with accurate long-range (over three years) record keeping. It shows a mastery of your business; it implies accuracy; it instills confidence. In fact, institutional lenders such as investment bankers and commercial banks will demand not only good records, but also audited records. Your CPA cannot start to audit your records unless you give her an accurate set and a system for keeping records that works into the future.

■ Good record keeping builds credibility in every area of your business. It shows you are on top of things. Customers and vendors have more confidence in everything else you say about your business.

■ If you want to sell your business, multi-year, accurate financial statements are a must. It's hard to play catch-up after five or six years of neglect. Many buyers want audited financial statements, or at least ones that are "reviewed" by a certified public accountant.

■ Going public is the dream of many business people: You become instantly rich and retire to the beach of your choice. But you have no hope of taking a company public without audited financial statements, which means they must be well organized and accurate from the start.

What records, and for how long?

In the absence of detailed requirements, be guided by common sense and good judgment. Here are some guidelines for the most common types of records that people create and use.

In general

A good rule of thumb is to keep any tax-related paper a minimum of four years. These records would include proof of Schedule A items: medical expenses, taxes, interest, contributions, and miscellaneous deductions including unreimbursed employee expenses.

Timesaver
The IRS strongly supports the electronic storage of records. In 1997, it issued Revenue Procedure 97-22, a guide on maintaining electronically-imaged hardcopied documents to a disk, and transferring computerized books to a disk. Obtain this guide at your local IRS office or IRS web site.

For example, if you claimed deductions on your individual return, keep the receipts, cancelled checks, check registers, and so on, for at least four years. A deduction taken on January 1, 1996, is normally not reported to the IRS until April 15, 1997. The IRS then has at least three years to audit the return and assess more taxes.

But people who trash their records at 12:01 a.m. on April 16 three years after they file their return take an unwise, needless tax risk. Many events, some totally unexpected, can extend the normal three-year period of limitations, and then you are stuck—unable to meet your burden of proof—if the IRS audits your return.

What are these events? It may sound strange, but, from time to time, strictly by accident, the IRS loses tax returns. The IRS sends a polite letter: "We don't have any record of your return." After picking yourself up off the floor, you write back, "What do you mean? I sent it in!" The IRS responds: "Prove it." Since you didn't send the return by certified mail, return receipt requested, you can't prove you filed it. But, you have a copy! It's even dated, and it bears your signature. "Not enough," says the IRS. "Re-sign and redate the copy, and send it in." So you send in a copy of the return you *did* file, signed and dated anew. The IRS audits that return and proposes more taxes. There you are, more than three years after you filed your original return—without records.

Another example: You trash your records at the three-year mark, confident to a moral certainty that the return is totally correct. But you forgot about some income you earned because you never got a Form 1099. That extra income was more than 25 percent of your gross income. The law says if you omitted 25 percent of your income, the IRS has six years, not three, to audit your return. If the IRS accuses you of civil fraud, there's no statute of limitations on assessment at all! It may assess a new tax at any time.

Your home

Keep records on your home, such as purchase documents and improvement records, until four years after you sell it, or until you die, whichever comes first. Be able to prove what you paid for the home, purchase expenses, improvement costs, and any other adjustments to your cost basis. Many people never really "sell" their home for tax purposes. If you're lucky, you'll buy two, three, or more homes during your lifetime. For "rollover" sales, each time you sell a home and roll over the paper profit (the "gain"), you report that transaction on your tax return even though you don't pay tax. Your heirs later inherit the home at its market value. Under changes effective in 1997, some of the profit on the sale of a residence is excluded from tax.

In either case, home records are important. Some people can't qualify for full deferral when they roll over the gain from one sale. Some taxpayers sell other real estate such as investment property. Still others go through a divorce and divide the marital properties, including the home. Here it's crucial to keep all records relating to your purchase, as well as records for any additional money you put in over time.

Stocks, bonds, and other investments

Keep records on various investments until four years after you sell them. When you sell these assets, you report the profit or loss on your next tax return.

Moneysaver
If you own investment property such as real estate, keep records of capital improvements (big-ticket items or repairs that can't be deducted right away). These add to your basis, decreasing your profit and therefore your tax when you sell. They also serve as a record of your basis for depreciation.

Profit or loss is the sales price minus the cost, so you need to know the cost of the property, known in the trade as "basis." You also need to report when you bought and sold the stock, the expenses of sale, and whether it is a capital asset. Let's say you bought 100 shares of Consolidated Widgets, Inc., in 1970. You sell them in 1990. You report that sale on April 15, 1991, and pay tax on the profit. If the IRS ever questions what you paid for the stock, you'll need your twenty-year-old records to prove the basis. Then add four years to April 15, 1991, to get to April 15, 1995.

That's a total of twenty-five years of record keeping, which might seem overwhelming. But records don't eat much, so storing them costs little.

Business records

The technical requirements for keeping records on travel and transportation expenses, entertainment, meals, gifts, and lodging are so extensive that they virtually defy description. Despite the volume of rules, however, we're all required to follow them. How long should you keep records? Again, the rule of thumb is four years at a minimum, because the statute of limitations on business audits is generally three years after the return is filed. This rule applies whether you report your business profits on an individual return (Schedule C) or whether you are a shareholder in a small corporation and receive dividends from that corporation.

Tax returns

Keep your tax returns forever. True enough, their usefulness may diminish after four or more years, but you'd be surprised how many unanticipated needs you will have for old tax returns. And, the day after you toss them is the day you'll discover you need them. Surprisingly, you can't even count on the IRS to find an old return for you. The agency keeps these returns for only about six years.

Gifts

Keep records of gifts you receive for as long as you hold the gift, plus four years. When you sell the gift, you many need to prove the giver's basis (or cost), as well as the market value and any gift tax the giver paid on it.

Organizing your records during the year

By far the biggest problem tax practitioners face when dealing with the IRS is the failure of clients to act like pack rats. If people would only save paper, they would save millions in taxes and professional fees. Life would be easier for the audited taxpayer, and, believe it or not, the IRS would also be happier, or more inclined to give you a break on your audit or collection problem. A few simple rules will help in most situations.

Rule 1: Save paper

Unfortunately, people throw away valuable documents every day—receipts, checks, notices, bills, you name it. Billions of dollars of tax-saving evidence winds up in landfills or incinerators, much of it impossible to reconstruct. And even when you can reconstruct it, it's expensive, time-consuming, and frustrating. So, why not just keep the records in the first place? It's easy, and you need not be especially organized to keep your records in good enough shape that preparing for tax season or an audit is a breeze.

Many people use the "shoebox" approach. They throw everything in a big pile and hope to sort it out at the end of the year. (Some people actually use a

Bright Idea
If you have not kept your tax returns, it is worth the investment to get copies of all that are available. To get a copy of your return, use Form 4506, Request for Copy or Transcript of Tax Form. If the IRS does not have your return, ask for a "literal transcript" of your account.

shoebox.) The shoebox approach is a useful method if you don't end up with a room full of them at the end of the year. If you have many records, you'll have to be more organized during the year.

You might try the "modified shoebox" approach. At the beginning of the year, take an envelope or file and mark it "Taxes 1999." Into that folder go all tax-related documents, *as you get them during the year.* That means you decide as you get a document whether to keep it and put it in the file. Use this test: "Is it possible that I might need this piece of paper at the end of the year for taxes?"

For example, you'll need your check register. Medical records, real estate tax bills, records of charitable deductions, possibly bank statements, receipts for other deductions—all of these can go into your modified shoebox. As you write checks during the year, note on the check and the check register what the payment is for and whether it may be deductible. Use some type of memory aide, like an asterisk, a check mark, or *"deduct"* to remind you at the end of the year that the checks for doctor visits or the contribution to the church are deductible. Do the same even with the more obvious ones like mortgage, real estate taxes, state income taxes, and unreimbursed business expenses. That's really all most of us need to do. Records won't be so voluminous or complex during the year that you will need to organize them any better than this. Then, at tax time, it's only a short step to separate your expenses to prepare your return.

Rule 2: Separate business from personal

Sole proprietors (unincorporated businesses) report their business income and expenses on Schedule C of their individual Form 1040s. For proprietors, an absolute, hard-and-fast rule is never to mix business and personal expenses. Use two checking accounts: one business, one personal. Many people will object, "But it's not required that I keep separate accounts." True, but you are 100 percent better off if you do. When you need personal money during the year, write a check from the business account to the personal account.

Cumbersome? Somewhat, but well worth the pain and suffering if the IRS ever questions your Schedule C deductions. Also, it saves monumental time and effort when tax return preparation time comes around. You'll be certain all your business expenses are in fact business-related and deductible on Schedule C. Of course, keep all business records for at least four years. For corporations and partnerships, the "separation" rule is usually less of a problem, because these entities have a separate legal existence, and therefore are required to maintain separate bank accounts and records.

Rule 3: The computer is your friend

Nowadays, excellent software is available for people to computerize their personal and business lives. There are programs for calendars, scheduling, tax return preparation, organizing records, filing—you name it. These programs can be a good discipline tool.

Probably the best advice for the 1990s is to keep your business and personal finances on computer, not on paper or by hand. And back up your data onto a disk, storing the disk off-site. Also, remember the computer adage, "Garbage in, garbage out." The data you enter must be complete and accurate for the computer to do any good. A printout that looks pretty is not necessarily accurate. Some people

Timesaver
Any good computer program for business records will feature "one entry" to generate a cash receipts and disbursements journal, general ledger, balance sheet, income statement, bank reconciliation, or other financial report.

sit at a computer every day to log in their business or personal expenses, receipts, and checks. Others do it on a weekly or monthly basis. But if you have the discipline, by all means go ahead and use that computer. At the end of the year, a click of the mouse generates your financial history and tax life.

In the new year—preparing for tax season

Now the year is over. It's January 2. You've recovered from New Year's parties (and you'll deduct the allowable expenses, of course). The faster you file your return, the faster you'll get that tax refund. Let's explore some easy steps on what to do if you don't use a computer. These guidelines apply whether you use a paid return preparer or prepare the return yourself. What should you do with the inch-thick pile of records you've been keeping all the past year?

A good rule is: Use the "envelope" method. Start out with about twenty empty envelopes for your personal return and your business return (Schedule C). Using last year's return as a guide, mark the backs of these envelopes with your tax categories, taken from the lines and categories you will use on the return itself. For example, one envelope could be marked "W-2 Income." Another could be marked "Form 1099 Income." On the deduction side, mark envelopes such as "medical," "taxes," "contributions," and so forth. Make sure that no paper is an orphan.

What about your checks and check registers? Separate these expenses for tax purposes by any method that works for you and is traceable. One method is to go through the check register and make a list of the check amounts for all deductible expenses. Then separate the items on that list into their respective envelopes. Tally them on a tape, then transfer the totals to your return. If you use a home computer, the software available today can quickly separate all of your deductible expenses. Tax return software practically does everything. All you do is enter the number and select an expense category.

A key rule is: *start early,* January 1 if you can. You'll have most of your tax records available even then because you've been filing them in the modified shoebox all year. Of course, you'll have to wait for your W-2, Form 1099, or Schedule K-1, but at least your other records will be in good shape and available. A tax-related record-keeping guide can be another big help. Many excellent guides are available in bookstores and office supply stores, or are included in software programs. Some focus on personal records, others on financial records, still others on tax records. Tax record guides will likely be more comprehensive than you need; they try to cover everyone's case. Don't be deterred. Instead, select the categories or organizational aids from those books that apply to you. You'll find that the same categories recur, year after year.

A word of hope: Keeping and organizing your tax records for a painless tax day is not heavy lifting. Once you get the hang of it, it's easy. You'll find yourself designing variations of a record-keeping program, personal hints that make record keeping and reporting easy for you. Customizing is the key. And once your methods are in place, they'll keep you tax-comfortable year after year.

This box suggests how long you might wish to retain tax-relevant records. There is no hard-and-fast rule, and opinions differ among practitioners. But you will generally find broad agreement on the following items:

HOW LONG YOU SHOULD KEEP RECORDS

1. Keep these records forever: tax returns (federal and state), all home purchase and improvement records, records of gifts (cash or noncash) by and to you, deeds, birth certificates, financial statements and business accounting records such as general journals, general ledgers, balance sheets, and cash receipts and disbursement journals.

2. Keep for seven years: cancelled checks, deductible expense records, receipts, contracts of employment and other contracts, other tax-related records such as Forms 1099 and W-2, and credit card statements.

3. Retain until sold, plus four years: stock certificates, brokerage statements reflecting sales of securities, and purchase and sale documents for any other large asset, such as home, land, and a car.

4. Keep for four years: all other tax-related documents.

If you keep these records in a well-organized system, you will greatly improve your ability to deal with the IRS successfully.

Just the facts

- Pay attention to detail. Try to make your return as accurate as possible, the first time.

- Never fail to take a deduction to which you are entitled.

- Consider hiring a professional to prepare your return, or to check it after you prepare it.

- Pay laser beam attention to keeping accurate records.

- Use a computer wherever possible to organize your records and prepare your tax returns.

GET THE SCOOP ON...
■ Don't play dead if you "lose" an audit ■
Preparing your appeals protest ■ The appeals
conference ■ The "injured" spouse

Appealing a Bad Audit Result

Tax audits and other tax investigations can often be frustrating or futile. By training, IRS agents see many issues in black-and-white terms. It's therefore reassuring to know there is an appeal you can file without having to go to court, where you may find some "gray."

This is the function of the Office of Appeals. Founded in 1925, this office exists for the sole purpose of settling your tax case, if possible. Its mission is to craft the right settlement based on *litigating hazard,* that is, the chance the IRS might lose in court. Appeals officers have the authority to concede issues, to sustain the case agent's findings, or to split issues. Only in rare cases involving issues of widespread impact and importance will the appeals officer lack discretion to seek a good settlement. This chapter guides you on this very important function of the Internal Revenue Service, a function that is becoming more encompassing every year.

Moneysaver
Even interest can sometimes be contested, such as in a long, drawn out audit that is prolonged by the IRS, not you. Now, the IRS has discretion to abate some interest where the delay results from "ministerial" or "managerial" errors. If you lose on this issue, you can appeal the loss to the U.S. Tax Court.

Where the cases come from

Each of the IRS's thirty-three districts has one Office of Appeals staffed by five to fifteen appeals officers. Sometimes there are satellite or branch offices. Six main types of cases filter up to the Office of Appeals.

The income tax audit

Chapter 9 discusses the income tax audit in detail. If you and the agent can't agree on every issue in your case, the agent writes a report on the unagreed issues and sends it to you. That report is known formally as a *thirty-day letter*. You have thirty days to agree, disagree, or do nothing. If you agree, you sign it, date it, and send it back. Doing nothing allows the IRS to conclude that the agent was correct and bill you accordingly. If you disagree, you appeal to the Office of Appeals simply by filing a "protest." Appeal rights apply to any item the revenue agent adjusts, whether tax or penalty.

File the protest within the thirty days or any extension you obtain before the thirty days run out. Ask for this extension from the same IRS office that issued the thirty-day letter, usually the revenue agent's office. Once you file the protest, the audit machinery grinds to a halt until your appeal is considered and resolved. That could be a minimum of two months, but appeals lasting a year or more are common. Of course, interest on your tax bill continues to accrue.

Employment tax investigations

These investigations fall into two categories: Trust Fund Recovery Penalty and employee-independent contractor cases. In a Trust Fund Recovery Penalty investigation, the revenue officer investigates who is responsible for a corporation's failure to pay its payroll taxes and recommends an assessment against the officers as a personal liability. Each officer has the right to appeal the recommendation to the Office of Appeals before the assessment can be made official.

In employee-independent contractor investigations, the revenue officer examines whether workers are "employees" or "independent contractors." Corporations don't withhold taxes for contractors; instead, they furnish 1099 forms at the end of the year. Quite often the IRS concludes these workers are employees, making the corporation liable for the workers' payroll taxes. The corporation has the right to protest such a finding to the Office of Appeals before the IRS assesses the tax.

Penalty appeals

A late return, an insufficient estimated tax payment, a late payment, and many other types of penalties are assessed directly by the IRS's seven regional Service Centers. You may contest these penalties at whatever level the IRS recommends or imposes them. If you get no relief, you can appeal the denial to the Office of Appeals.

Offers in compromise and refund claims

If your offer in compromise to settle a big back tax bill (see Chapter 11) is rejected, you may appeal the rejection to the Office of Appeals. And you may file a refund claim for taxes you overpaid in the past. If it's rejected, an appeal is handled by the Office of Appeals. Also, if you decide to sue the IRS in Tax Court (see Chapter 15), you can sometimes still get appeals office consideration. This can happen when the auditing agent proposes more taxes and you petition the Tax Court right away rather than first taking your case to appeals.

Unofficially...
In 1996, the Office of Appeals received 73,000 cases and closed 64,000. At that time, it had 49,000 cases pending. The overall chance of your obtaining a settlement at appeals is 50 percent. Those are encouraging odds, considering how easy and inexpensive it is to file an appeal.

Unofficially...
Bypassing an appeal by going directly to Tax Court results in the case being transferred back to appeals.

Collection cases

Finally, the Office of Appeals has been given a number of collection-type cases to review. Under the 1998 tax reform act, the Office of Appeals can now review a pre-levy protest, a notice of lien filing, and other proposed or completed collection actions.

Preparing your protest and your case

An appeal is made by preparing a protest. There's no official form; it's just a letter you send to the office that proposed your tax. The protest has seven parts. Of the seven parts, four are of the fill-in-the-blank variety: your name, other identifying information, the office that issued the letter, and the tax periods. The heart and soul of the protest are parts five, six, and seven. In these three sections, the task is to tell the appeals officer:

1. the findings with which you disagree (part five),
2. the facts (part six),
3. why the agent was wrong based on the law and the facts (part seven)

Keep part five brief. Here are examples of appropriate statements:

- "The revenue agent erred in disallowing my deduction of $1,000 for a wheelchair for my dependent aging mother."
- "The revenue agent erred in characterizing a loan from my Aunt Josephine as unreported income."

Number each such summary point so as to negate, point by point, the same items in the Revenue Agent's Report.

In the next part (six), tell all the facts underlying the issues you are protesting. You need not protest every issue; in fact, often people change their minds after reading the Revenue Agent's Report and decide not to protest certain issues (for instance, because they cannot document their claim). But as to the issues you wish to fight, recite all the facts in detail, and prepare to prove them.

State the facts logically and cogently. Avoid opinion and hyperbole. Assume the appeals officer knows nothing about your case but will learn quickly from a cogent presentation. (The officer will in fact have read the Revenue Agent's Report in advance.) So, begin at the beginning if that will make your factual statement complete and understandable.

Next, prove your facts. Most people believe they already did that at the agent's level, so they'll use the same proof at appeals. But be on the lookout for even more evidence. In fact, new evidence at the appeals level often provides the justification to settle your case. Appeals officers can and do consider evidence that would never make it past the front door of a courtroom—hearsay, third-party information, and anything else that appears to be relevant. In fact, the more third-party information you can bring to the table, the more credible your case.

Above all, include and rely on your own testimony. After all, you, the taxpayer, have the most intimate knowledge of the relevant facts. Whenever you can, put the evidence in writing, under oath. Of course, sometimes an agent or appeals officer objects to your statements of fact as "self-serving," meaning that they lack credibility because you are naturally biased in your own favor. Your statements under oath, however, are subject to penalties of perjury and are fully admissible in any court. They may, therefore, carry weight with the IRS.

Watch Out!
Some people claim that it is better to file a "bare-bones" protest, giving only enough detail to preserve their right to appeal the issues, but not enough to show all their cards. In general, however, taking a strong, well-supported stand right away has a better chance of achieving a good settlement.

Bright Idea
Some appeals officer will hesitate to change the result if your protest brings no new evidence to light. Your response should be that the agent was wrong in his recitation of the facts or conclusions from them. Appeals officers should not consider the Revenue Agent's Report to be presumptively correct.

Part seven is the statement of law. Here, your tax representative can write or help you write the section if she is familiar with the law. If you represent yourself, a statement of the law is still required, so consider performing your own legal research. Still, the process is very informal. You need not file a Supreme Court–style brief with citations to cases, rulings, and other authority (though solid research like this does add credibility). But you do have to say what the law is.

Bear in mind that the appeals officer is always well-versed in the law governing your issues. In fact, she will sometimes assist you in your research if you ask and indicate a willingness to do copying, legwork, and other tasks. When you have the law firmly in mind, write it in this section as best you can, and then apply the facts to those legal rules.

An example might be something like this:

My mother, Rose, is seventy-five years old, barely ambulatory, and lives with me. I am her sole support. I provide more than one-half of her support in terms of food, clothing, shelter, and other necessities. She has no income of her own. She is not married. Last year, she underwent total hip replacement surgery on the right side and needs a wheelchair to get around the house. Since I work for a living, she needs the wheelchair to feed herself and stay out of bed. Dr. Smith Jones prescribed a wheelchair for her last year, and I bought it. A letter from Dr. Jones and a copy of his prescription are enclosed. The wheelchair cost $2,000. Of that cost, I deducted $1,600 because of the 7.5 percent floor on medical expense deductions. However, the agent disallowed this deduction. The rule on medical expense deductions is that such an expense is deductible if medically necessary for a dependent's condition. Here, the facts show that the wheelchair was in fact medically necessary for my mother. Therefore, the agent's conclusion to the contrary was in error.

At the end of the protest, include the following statement above your signature: "Under the penalty of perjury, I have examined the foregoing statement of facts in the foregoing protest, together with all exhibits, statements, and other documents referenced therein, and to the best of my knowledge and belief, it is true, correct, and complete."

"Face-to-face" time—the appeals conference

Your next stop is the conference. The appeals officer normally sends a preliminary letter letting you know she has the case, will review it, and will call you for a conference. Sometimes these letters set a conference date, which you should confirm or change immediately (a phone call will do). To prepare for the conference, review your protest throughly. Also review the Revenue Agent's Report and all your files to have them firmly in mind. Keep looking for other evidence. In fact, appeals officers will give you ample opportunity to gather more evidence (even *after* the conference). Then, on the appointed day, you go to the Office of Appeals.

Appeals conferences are very informal. You go in, sit across the desk from her, and begin to talk about the case. No one records the conference. You may take notes, as will the appeals officer, where appropriate.

Your task is to convince the officer that the agent's mistake should result in a full or partial concession by the government. In theory, the appeals officer's role is to be neutral. She weighs the evidence for and against the revenue agent's position and tries to compromise based on the chances that the IRS might loss if the case is tried.

Moneysaver
If you are unsure about the facts, or what the agent had written up about a particular issue, ask the appeals officer. They are usually forthcoming with information and documents in their own file.

Many appeals officers try to act with neutrality; others unintentionally slide into defending the revenue agent against your attacks. This slippage is a danger and one major reason why your protest and demeanor at the conference should be unemotional, businesslike, and firm. Moreover, the appeals officer has heard it all before—all the facts, all the law, all the name-calling. This does not mean you should downplay the agent's mistakes. Hit them all. Showing how wrong the agent was, and how contrary to the facts, goes a long way toward obtaining a good result.

The appeals conference proceeds issue by issue until all issues have been covered. The appeals officer might indicate she is willing to concede some issues. On others, she may sustain the finding, deciding that the agent was right. On still others, she may need more information. It often helps to ask what additional facts she would need to accept your position. She may suggest evidence you might be able to gather, and, if so, she will give you ample opportunity. Then go assemble that evidence and send it to the appeals officer as quickly as possible. She will give you a deadline and reasonable extensions if you ask for them in advance.

The end of this process is the appeals officer's report. If all has gone well, she writes an "agreed report," formalizing the final settlement on all issues. She then sends it to you for signature. A tax bill or tax refund follows. If you can't agree on all issues, try to agree on most. "Unagreed" issues are written up in a *ninety-day letter*. This is the formal letter the law requires the IRS to send you before it assesses your tax. You then have two choices. If you do nothing, the bill soon arrives. To forestall that bill, you may file a petition in the United States Tax Court to contest the remaining unagreed items. Chapter 15 discusses this course of action.

The appeals process can be lengthy, but it's usually fairly simple to get through. Moreover, it's your one chance at reasonable expense to get a better result than you obtained from the revenue agent. There's little harm in trying and much to be gained.

The injured spouse

The "injured spouse" concept has nothing to do with "innocent spouse" status discussed in Chapter 8. It's a fancy name for a spouse who did not receive his or her fair share of a joint refund. These cases arise often in the aftermath of a divorce or separation. One spouse has two-thirds of the income and has paid two-thirds of the taxes through payroll withholding, but does not receive two-thirds of the refund. In fact, the injured spouse may receive nothing. So, the IRS devised a form to file by which you can receive your proportionate share. Form 8375 and its detailed instructions explain how to file your claim.

Basically, you are entitled to get back your share of a joint refund, based on your proportionate share of the tax you and your spouse paid together. You can file an injured spouse claim at any time before the IRS issues a refund.

Just the facts

- Be fully aware of your right to appeal adverse audit results.

- Prepare your appeal logically and according to the IRS's forms.

- Prepare for your appeal, and be businesslike in your presentation and relations to the appeals officer.

- Familiarize yourself with Form 8375 and how your can claim injured spouse status.

Tel:_____

Date:_____

Internal Revenue Service Collection Division

500 N. Capitol Street, N.W.

Room 3207

Washington, D.C. 20221

Att: Ms. Jones

Re: Penny Pencil, 000-00-0000; Wonder Widgets, Inc., EIN 00-0000000

Dear Ms. Jones:

    PROTEST

Protest is hereby made of the proposed assessment of Trust Fund Recovery Penalty with respect to Penny Pencil. The following information is submitted in support of this protest.

1.   Name, Address, Social Security No.

    Penny Pencil

    1 Main Street

    Anytown, USA 11111

    SSN: 000-00-0000

2.   Conference.

A conference relating to this protest is hereby requested.

3.   Date and Number of Letter.

Letter dated July 26, 1995; Letter 1153(DO)(Rev. 3-93)

4   Tax Periods.

3rd quarter 1993; 4th quarter 1993; 1st quarter 1994

5.   Findings Disagreed With.

The revenue officer erred in determining that Penny Pencil was a person responsible for the failure of Wonder Widgets, Inc., to collect, account for, and pay over the withholding and Social Security/Medicare taxes of the employees of Wonder Widgets, Inc., for the above periods, and that Penny Pencil willfully failed to ensure that these amounts were paid over.

6.   Statement of Facts.

[Here state all facts to support your case.]

7. Statement of Law.

The Trust Fund Recovery Penalty may be imposed under IRC 6672 only if two separate requirements are fulfilled. First, the person must be under a duty to "collect, truthfully account for, and pay over" the withheld taxes, that is, he or she must be a "responsible person." IRC 6672 imposes liability only upon the person or persons who are actually responsible for an employer's failure to withhold and pay the government, that is, the person who is under the duty to perform the act, and not necessarily the individual who is nominally charged with disbursement of the funds. White v. United States, 372 F.2d 513 (Ct. Cl. 1967); Turner v. United States, 423 F.2d 448 (9th Cir. 1970).

The second element, willfulness, requires that the responsible person shall have intentionally, deliberately, voluntarily, or knowingly failed to pay over the withheld taxes. White v. United States, supra. Mere negligence in failing to ascertain facts regarding the tax delinquency is insufficient to constitute willfulness under IRC 6672. Bauer v. United States, 543 F.2d 142 (Ct. Cl. 1976).

Under these standards, I am neither responsible nor willful for the following reasons. [State additional grounds.] In view of these cases, I should not be deemed a responsible person. By contrast, the evidence in this case shows that others may have been the responsible persons. Also, I had no knowledge that the taxes were unpaid until the time period when the business closed.

For the foregoing reasons, the proposed assessment of the Trust Fund Recovery Penalty against me should not be sustained.

Under the penalties of perjury, I have examined the foregoing statement of facts in the foregoing protest, together with all schedules, exhibits, and attachments, and to the best of my knowledge it is true, correct, and complete.

Sincerely yours,

Penny Pencil

Bright Idea
It's usually best to file an injured spouse claim with the tax return itself, or soon afterward. Sometimes you can get back money from years past if the IRS has not issued the refund. But once the refund has been issued, you can only get it back from the other spouse.

Your Options—and You Do Have Them

PART IV

GET THE SCOOP ON...
How the IRS views your offer ▪ The downside of
making an offer ▪ The nitty-gritty of making an
acceptable offer ▪ Appealing a rejected offer

"Let's Make a Deal"— Offers in Compromise

T his chapter describes what is probably the single most effective way anyone can nullify a big tax bill—the offer in compromise. It is no surprise that the IRS is willing to compromise on back taxes. About 10-20 million Americans owe as much as $200 billion in back taxes. And that number does not include the underground economy, where billions more flow unnoticed and untaxed.

Every few years, Congress hauls the IRS Commissioner before one of its committees to fry the agency for not collecting the billions it has on the books. The IRS dutifully recognizes, publicly, that it will never collect all of that money, but says that it's "doing the best it can." (Even with increased collections, the dollars it collects this year are often replaced by fresh accounts receivable next year.)

For decades, the agency had the statutory authority to settle any tax debt for less than full payment, but the authority was seldom used. In February 1992, this offer in compromise program was taken out of deep-freeze and became a genuine alternative for settling tax debts. In short, the IRS got serious about cleaning up its accounts receivable and advertised a new willingness to accept less than 100 cents on the dollar.

The 1998 tax act contains a provision that is somewhat offer-friendly, but it will make little additional difference unless the Commissioner truly elevates the importance of offers. Still, even today, the program is not the Filene's Basement of tax collection. The IRS's goal is to give you a fresh start by accepting an offer, but only after it has squeezed out the last dollar it expects to be able to get from you now or in the near future. If that's 90 percent of what you owe, so be it. If that's 10 percent, so be it.

There is reason for hope, however: nationwide, in fiscal 1996 the IRS received about 57,000 offers and accepted about half of them. Astoundingly, the average accepted offer was thirteen cents on the dollar.

This chapter will analyze how the compromise program works and how you can make a successful offer. As you read this chapter, bear in mind that you do not always need professional tax help such as that of a lawyer, accountant, or enrolled agent. Many taxpayers successfully make their own offers. But tax professionals often make the difference between success and failure and can help you reduce your offer amount by thousands of dollars.

> 66
> The purpose of the [offer] investigations is to determine whether the amount offered reasonably reflects collection potential.
> —IRS Manual 57(10[12].1)
> 99

How the IRS thinks about offers

To understand the rejuvenated offer program, we should look at it from the point of view of the IRS. The IRS generally has three years from the time you file a tax return to assess a tax, and ten years to collect the assessment. (The ten-year collection statute can be extended in many ways, however. For example, the act of making an offer extends it for the offer period plus one year. The government can also sue to extend the ten-year period for collection, although it rarely does so.)

The IRS could choose to hound you for ten years—levy your bank accounts, file notices of lien, sell your property, levy your wages—but the agency knows people cannot live that way. It is also politically unacceptable, and in any event, the IRS is just not that efficient in keeping constant pressure on you.

Rather than endure that slow agony (for both sides), if you can't pay the full amount in the ten year period, the agency is better off taking what it can get now and forgetting the rest. In this sense, the IRS is like any other creditor with good business judgment.

When the IRS looks at your finances to evaluate how much you should offer, it focuses on two main sources of value or payment: your current assets and your future income potential (the money you might expect to pay the IRS in the future, using a five-year rule). Logically, those two baskets of assets are all anyone has to offer. An acceptable offer must equal or exceed the total of these two baskets of assets.

Still, even meeting these financial tests does not guarantee that your offer will be accepted. The IRS also looks at your age, health, employment history, and any other factors that might bear on whether it can expect to collect more in the future. Is the tax liability fresh, giving the IRS up to ten years? Are you young, with greater potential earning capacity, even if the IRS can't exactly pinpoint your future success? If so, your offer may be rejected even if it

Watch Out!
When determining how much you should pay, the IRS also considers other sources of payment. Examples would include the Trust Fund Recovery Penalty and assets beyond the reach of the IRS in which the taxpayer has an interest, such as, tenancy-by-the-entireties property or foreign real estate.

Moneysaver
Be sure to list your current assets at "forced sale" value, not "current market" value designated in Form 433-A. "Forced sale" value is typically 80 percent of fair market value, according to the Internal Revenue Manual. "Quick sale" value, which is less than that of forced sale, may also be used.

meets the numerical minimum identified above. But it is still worth a try, because of the sizeable tax break you might get with an accepted offer.

Current assets

You must offer an amount at least equal to the equity in your current assets. A full explanation of this appears below, but here is an example. Let's say Tom Taxpayer owns a car worth $10,000, with a first lien of $6,000. In theory, the IRS could seize the car, sell it, pay the $6,000 first lien and apply the difference of $4,000 toward Tom's back taxes. But the sale would never yield $10,000. As a rule of thumb, the IRS would net only $2,000. The forced sale value of a $10,000 car might well be only $8,000. Consequently, after paying off the first lien of $6,000, only $2,000 would be left for Tom's taxes. So, for offer purposes, the "equity" is $2,000.

Similar reasoning applies to other assets, with varying discounts. Assets that are very difficult to sell at full value, such as household goods and furniture, are subject to deep discounts. Liquid assets such as bank accounts merit no discount at all.

Future income potential

The second source of equity is your future earning power. Here, so the theory goes, the IRS asks hypothetically, "If Tom paid us a fixed amount of money per month from his salary and other earnings stream, how much could we collect over the remainder of the ten years we normally have to collect?" Some tax debts have only a few years left for collection, while others have more. So the IRS uses a five-year average. Then it calculates a one-time, lump-sum payment amount that represents the present value of what it could hope to collect over five years.

For example, Tom Taxpayer makes an offer in compromise on a $10,000 tax bill. Looking to the future, he can afford to pay the IRS $100 per month after paying his necessary living expenses. Over five years (sixty months), he would pay $6,000. Instead of putting Tom on a payment plan for sixty months, Tom could offer a discounted lump sum, now, that would equal the present value of that series of sixty $100 payments. The IRS has a formula for calculating present value; in this case, it is $4,857. So, for this part of Tom's offer, he must offer to pay a lump sum of $4,857.

Putting it all together

The equity in Tom's car for offer purposes is $2,000. The present value of his future earning potential is $4,857. Adding up the two baskets, Tom must make an offer of at least $6,857.

Apply the same logic to all other assets you own, add them up, and you have your offer amount.

This financial formula might sound simple, but in practice there is plenty of room for maneuvering, negotiation, and slippage. And the IRS, like any other smart creditor, doesn't always take the first offer that comes along. Remember, the agency's goal is to find every dollar it can. Moreover, if it is prepared to give up more than 80 percent of its claim, it wants to be sure there is no more to be collected.

How bankruptcy affects offers

As we discuss in Chapter 13, you can often use the bankruptcy laws to discharge some, or even all, of your back taxes. It's a complex subject: some taxes are dischargeable; others are not. Some are dischargeable if certain time frames are adhered to

Unofficially...
Probably the most famous successful offer in compromise was made by country singer Willie Nelson, who offered $17 million to satisfy a $34 million tax debt.

Bright Idea
Legally, you can file for bankruptcy to discharge some taxes, then file an offer in compromise to discharge the rest. This takes guts: the IRS is helpless to fight a bankrupcty discharge; the offer may seem like adding insult to injury. But in theory the IRS evaluates post-bankruptcy offers on their own merits.

and others are not. And there are exceptions to all the bankruptcy rules. The IRS knows that everyone has the right to file for bankruptcy, but this threat is rarely a factor in convincing the agency to take an offer.

In theory, if you are actually threatening to file for a bankruptcy that would discharge taxes, the offer examiner is supposed to take this threat into account when negotiating the proper offer amount. In the real world, examiners rarely pay attention to the threat of bankruptcy in making a "calculated business decision." If you actually file for bankruptcy to discharge some or all of your taxes, they rarely care. They simply ship the case to a different office for the processing of the IRS's bankruptcy claim.

Consequently, offers during bankruptcy are not favored, but are allowable and should not be ruled out. It all depends on the type of bankruptcy and the type of tax involved.

Look before you leap

The idea of making an offer and paying the IRS far less than your current tax bill sounds good—so what's the catch? Actually, there are at least eight "catches." Some you might be able to live with; others may be too onerous.

1. **Statute of limitations on collection**. The act of making an offer suspends the IRS's ten-year statute of limitations on collection for the time the offer is pending, plus one year. So if your offer is rejected, you've accomplished nothing, while adding a year plus the offer time to the IRS's already-long collection period.

2. **Timing and results vary around the country**. An offer can be processed in as few as sixty days in

some districts; in others, it can take as long as a year. Also, some districts have higher acceptance rates than others. The range is from 15 percent to 75 percent, raising the question of whether it might be wise to move. Naturally, the generosity of offer examiners (or revenue officers, in districts where they oversee the offers) also varies widely. Some are lenient, some strict, depending on the district rules and their own personalities. The official IRS offer guidelines restrain this variability, however.

The best course is to ask the revenue officer with whom you are dealing whether an offer is possible, or likely, and whether he or she will help. If the answer is, "Forget it. Not in this century," you have your answer. The party line you will likely hear is, "Well, every taxpayer has the right to file an offer." Don't settle for that—you already know that. Ask the Revenue Officer whether he or she really believes there is a chance to make a successful offer in *your* particular case.

Incidentally, the IRS officially states that it will should make a real effort to work with you to find a mutually beneficial offer. As the official IRS manual (IRM 5710[10].1.) states: "Rejection of an offer solely based on narrow asset and income evaluations should be avoided. The Service should attempt to negotiate offer agreements which are in the best interest of all parties. Included in determining the government's interests are the costs of collection." But don't hold your breath.

3. **You've shown your cards.** To make a successful offer in compromise, you must disclose your

Timesaver
Ask the revenue officer or offer examiner whether she will agree to a "pre-offer review," a quick look at your preliminary financial papers to see if you're in the ballpark for a successful offer. This review can save you hours of time and much agony.

Unofficially...
Do revenue offi-
cers invite an
offer just to get
you to open up
about your
assets, then
lower the boom
on you? Possibly,
but such cases
must surely be
extremely rare.
Their oath, train-
ing, and personal
integrity would
normally dis-
suade them from
such a course.

finances completely and truthfully. If your offer
fails, look what you've voluntarily revealed: your
entire financial picture. Now agents can go out
and collect to their hearts' content. So, by making an offer, you take a real chance that the IRS
will use the information against you if the offer
is rejected. But revenue officers can get all the
information anyway, either by asking you directly or using their summons (subpoena) power to
drag you into their office to complete an interview about your finances. So they really have no
need to use the offer program as a subterfuge to
discover your assets.

4. **The IRS keeps refunds and credits.** If the IRS
   owes you a refund or you have a tax credit due
   from a past year, the IRS keeps these as a condition to accepting any offer. So do not count on
   making an offer using a $5,000 refund from last
   year's taxes. The IRS figures it's got that money
   anyway; you need to offer more.

5. **Five-year compliance.** You must agree to be a
   model tax citizen for five years after the offer is
   accepted. That means filing your returns on
   time and paying your taxes, including estimated
   taxes, on time. If you don't, the Service can
   revoke the offer, keep the money you've paid,
   and collect the rest of what you originally owed.
   Of course, this condition does not mean that
   after five years you're free to default again. But
   the Service reasons that if you are a reformed
   taxaholic for five years, you have a reasonable
   chance of remaining on track.

6. **Collateral agreement.** You may have to sign a
   "collateral agreement." This is a side agreement,
   not something to do with collateral on your tax

debt. This collateral agreement binds you to pay more money in the future if you strike it rich. The IRS reasons that it can accept an offer for the most money it can expect to get right now, but if your income suddenly *and unexpectedly* goes way up, the Service wants a piece of it. These collateral agreements are not common practice, but a few offer examiners demand them. When used, most last for five years and take only certain percentages (usually up to 45 percent) of your net income above your current level.

7. **Bankruptcy impact.** Making an offer can also disarm one of your main weapons against taxes—bankruptcy. One of the many rules for discharging taxes in bankruptcy is the requirement to file the bankruptcy petition more than 240 days after the IRS bills you. Making an offer in compromise during that 240-day period suspends that rule for the time the offer is pending, plus thirty days. Filing bankruptcy also suspends the IRS's ten-year period of limitations on collection for the entire bankruptcy, plus six months. If you are thinking about making an offer, it is critical to get accurate legal advice about if and when to use the bankruptcy alternative.

8. **Public record.** An accepted offer becomes public record. That means your wife, husband, partner, neighbor, local newspaper, and so on, can find it and publish it. Every once in a while one sees a newspaper feature about prominent citizens who compromised their taxes.

The good news about offers

So much for the bad news. There is good news, too.

1. **It's easy to do.** The paperwork for an offer is relatively easy. You need only a few forms. These are well-designed, understandable, and easy to complete.

2. **Collection is suspended.** When you make an offer, the IRS suspends its collection efforts (except for installment payments you are already making) while the offer is being considered. This informal policy became law in 1998. And even if the offer is rejected, collection does not resume right away. The IRS waits to see if you will appeal the rejection, holding off while the appeal is being considered. This gives much-welcome peace of mind to many taxpayers. And, while there are some slip-ups, generally the IRS lives up to its word about suspending collection.

3. **An accepted offer wipes out the debt.** This is the best news of all. The threat of the IRS sword hanging over your head, affecting your job, your marriage, credit, livelihood, and other important things, is totally relieved by an accepted offer. The debt is reduced to the offer amount, which you then pay. The IRS releases the lien and forgets about you. Moreover, the amount of an acceptable offer can be very little. As noted above, nationally, on average, it is thirteen cents on the dollar—a terrific deal in anyone's book.

Making an acceptable offer

The process is straightforward: get the forms, fill them out, mail them in, and when the IRS contacts you, answer its questions. Work with the offer examiner to see if your original offer is acceptable or if you can negotiate another amount. Try in every possible way to reach an agreement. If you can't and the offer is rejected, consider appealing the rejection. You can also withdraw an offer at any time before it is accepted or rejected.

You need at least two forms: Form 656 ("Offer in Compromise") and Form 433-A ("Collection Information Statement for Individuals"). If you own all or part of a business, you also need a financial statement for that business, Form 433-B.

The offer is made on Form 656. This is a two-page form, prepared with two originals, both for the IRS. It is actually one of the easiest of all IRS forms to understand and fill out. Complete all parts that apply except for the offer amount. You will not know this until you complete your financial statements.

Items 1-4 require identifying information and are self-explanatory.

In **Item 5**, fill in all the periods for which you owe taxes, such as: income taxes for 1994 and 1995). This means everything—even taxes that you may owe but for which you have not yet been billed. It's in your interest to be complete anyway, because the offer is a contract. If you do not list a tax debt, the IRS hasn't compromised it. It can still collect. Nor is the IRS "scared off" by how much you owe or for which tax periods. You may be making a $10,000 offer on a $100,000 liability, but in theory, if the IRS concludes that this is all you can pay, it should not matter whether you owed $100,000 or $1,000,000. So list every tax period for which you owe or may owe taxes, assessed or not. The IRS checks its computer records anyway and will make you refile the offer if you have omitted any tax.

Timesaver
You can obtain Form 656, Form 433-A, and many other IRS forms from the IRS website.

Bright Idea
Starting in 1997,
the IRS is
required to send
you an annual
reminder of the
taxes you owe.
Use that
reminder as a
guide, or simply
attach it to your
offer and write:
"See attached
IRS Form" in
Item 5.

If you don't know exactly how much you owe, or for what periods, call the IRS at (800)829-1040. IRS representatives are always pleased to remind you of how much you owe.

If your case is already being handled "in the field," that is, by a living, breathing revenue officer at the local IRS office, you may be sure that she will tell you exactly what you owe. In fact, the revenue officers and other collection personnel are required to help you make your offer, if you ask.

Item 6 of the form asks whether you are offering to compromise because you don't owe the taxes (doubt as to liability) or because you can't pay them (doubt as to collectibility). Logically and legally, these are the only two ways in which a tax can be compromised. Liability offers are rare and collectibility offers common. So in almost every case, check the box marked "doubt as to collectibility."

Item 7 asks when you want to pay. People typically ask for thirty to ninety days after the offer is accepted. This means that from the time you make the offer, you may have as long as one year to come up with the money: one to two months for the IRS to log the offer in and assign it to an agent, two to six months to negotiate the offer, another one to two months to process the acceptance, and two to four months to pay after acceptance.

Then sign the offer in the bottom right corner box (**line 8**) and date your signature. The offer is officially made only when the IRS signs its part of the form (lower left). Also, the Service will enter your offer on its computer system, so you'll have a firm "offer made" date. That could become important when you calculate how long the collection statute of limitations has to run.

Filling out the collection statement: Form 433-A

Now comes the heart of the offer process—filling out your personal financial statement.

Page 1 (sections I and II) asks for personal and employment information (**lines 1 through 12**). The IRS will check its computers to see whether you are current in your tax payments and filing requirements. It makes no sense to discuss your past defaults if you can't even keep current. And if you can't agree to stop the tax bleeding now, the IRS reasons, there is no point in settling the past by an offer. Inevitably, you will be back again.

Sections III, IV, and V are the heart of this form, the places where your offer sinks or swims. List all assets at their "forced sale value," not their current market value. The discounts this rule allows are crucial; the IRS wants you to offer only the equity it could theoretically get by forcibly selling your assets.

Section III calls for your bank accounts, including savings and loans, credit unions, IRAs and retirement plans, certificates of deposit, and similar items. Consider each of these separately and differently when you calculate the equity in them for offer purposes.

- **Checking accounts.** This one seems easy. After all, we all spend everything we make, so if you're a normal American, you'll have a checkbook balance of zero or close to it. But that is not the way the IRS thinks. It goes by "average daily collected balance," the average amount the bank shows in your checking account. The average daily balance reflects the checks that have cleared into your account minus the checks you have written that have "cleared"

> " Asset values are generally subject to market forces and interpretation. Therefore, a flexible negotiation position should be taken when negotiating an offer.
> —IRM 57(10[10].2) "

(been paid). The average daily balance is higher than your checkbook balance. The IRS reasons that if it seized your bank account, it would get that collected balance, not your checkbook balance. So list what the IRS could get anyway—the average daily balance. If your checkbook reads "$100" but your bank balance is "$1,000," list $1,000 for this asset in your offer calculation. Offer examiners will typically ask for three to six months of bank statements (from all banks), from which they will figure the average daily balance.

Calculating this figure for the examiner adds credibility to your financial statement. Just indicate in the "balance" column that you have figured the average daily balance.

Hint: The more homework, substantiation, backup, and analysis you do on these forms, the more credible is your offer. This also means less work for the offer examiner and increases the chances of acceptance.

- **Savings and loans, credit unions.** These types of accounts are usually less active than your checking account, but the same principle applies. List the average collected balance in these accounts.

- **Certificate of deposit.** Here list the face amount minus early withdrawal or other bank fees, and minus any federal and state taxes that would be due if you withdrew the money.

- **IRAs, Keoghs, and 401(k)s.** State and offer the face amount, minus the premature withdrawal penalty and minus the federal and state taxes inherent in this asset. For example, your retirement plan has $10,000. The penalty for early withdrawal is $1,000. The federal and state taxes that will be due on withdraw total $3,000, for an overall total of $4,000. Include $6,000 ($10,000 minus $4,000) for this asset. Add up the balance column in the lower right-hand corner, and you are done with that page.

A pension or profit-sharing plan has no equity for offer purposes if you are required by your employer to contribute and you can't tap the plan until retirement. In a voluntary plan, your "equity" is the gross amount minus the employer's contributions.

Page 2, line 14 asks for your charge cards and lines of credit. In most cases, that's charge cards only, but if you also have an unsecured line of credit, list it here. A secured line of credit such as a home equity loan goes on **line 28 (section IV)** or on **line 50 (section V).**

Once you list all credit cards and lines of credit, add the four columns marked "Monthly Payment," "Credit Limit," "Amount Owed," and "Credit Available," as shown on the form. The key item is the Monthly Payment column. The offer examiner looks at this and says, "I see you are paying $533 per month to VISA, MasterCard, and Discover. That is money you could be paying to us, and, after all, we are ahead of those credit card companies because we are a secured creditor (we have a lien on file)." The examiner might allow some payments for necessary living expenses, calculated in section V. Otherwise, the IRS sees those charge card payments as available for the "future income potential" calculation.

Examiners also reason that you might be able to work out a deal with the card companies to pay less, or to stretch out the payments. Even if you can't, the

Watch Out!
You can't "randomly" pick a low-balance three-month period. Doing that makes the statement false and potentially prosecutable. Besides, the agent will request the most recent available three–six months of statements anyway.

IRS reasons, "Well, you tried your best to work something out with VISA, but were unsuccessful. Too bad, but that doesn't mean we have to roll over and give you an offer just because VISA was tough with you."

Often people have "credit available" on their charge cards. A big worry, usually justified, is that offer examiners will ask you to borrow up to the hilt immediately, pay that amount down on your past taxes, and then talk about an offer. Try to resist this unless it's clearly in your best interest. Instead, suggest borrowing the credit available as a down payment on the offer, rather than to reduce the tax you are trying to compromise. If the offer fails, the IRS must send back your down payment. But it won't return pre-offer money you've paid on your past-due taxes.

Line 15 asks about safe deposit boxes. The IRS can inspect these boxes with your permission, but it rarely does so. After all, if you are so far in debt that you have to make an offer, you've probably used all the money in that safe-deposit box anyway. Still, you must describe the location, box number, and contents.

Line 16 asks about your real property. This is the place to list your home and the type of ownership, but not its value. State something like this: "Personal residence-single-family home, owned as tenants by the entirety." The right-hand column asks for the address.

Line 17 calls for life insurance. For offer purposes, the IRS is interested only in policies with cash or loan value, not term policies. Still, list all policies. (After all, one day term policies will ripen into real proceeds. If you still owe taxes, the IRS can make a claim against your estate if the estate receives the proceeds.)

List the loan value of each policy. For example, a $10,000 policy may have $1,000 of loan value. Include $1,000 for this asset in your offer amount.

Line 18 asks you to list securities, including stocks, bonds, mutual funds, money-market funds, government securities, and others. You can easily find the value of publicly traded stocks from newspapers, brokers, or on-line services (as of a certain date). The form expects you to list and offer the net equity in those stocks, that is, their market value minus any sales fees or other charges. If the value declines substantially between the time of the offer and its acceptance, bring that to the IRS's attention and ask for a reduction in the offer amount.

Stocks that are not publicly traded pose a very different and troublesome problem. Stock in a closely held corporation such as a family business normally has a limited market, or no market at all. Tight rules restrict its sale; the net worth of the company may be zero or negative if you owe back taxes. Sometimes, the balance sheet will show a positive number for "retained earnings" (generally the business's accumulated profit from its start). Some offer examiners calculate the value of this stock at the amount of retained earnings multiplied by your ownership percentage.

If you own all or part of such a business, you are in any case required to complete Form 433-B ("Collection Information Statement for Businesses"), so the IRS can evaluate your small business from that financial statement, too.

For example, Wonder Widget, Inc., has been in business eight years. It made money in the first three years and lost money in the last five. At the end of the eighth year, when the offer is made, it has

Bright Idea
Do a little trading. If the offer examiner insists that you borrow to the max, counter that the extra monthly payments you will be forced to make are an allowable expense for future income potential calculations. The same reasoning applies if the offer examiner requests that you take out a home equity loan or other loan.

Timesaver
Assemble three years of all available financial data about the closely held corporation, such as tax returns and financial statements. Then consider having an independent expert render an opinion on the market value of the stock. This may avoid drawn-out argument with the IRS agent.

an accumulated profit of $100,000. Willy Wonder owns 40 percent of the stock. The IRS may require Willy to include $40,000 ($100,000 times 40 percent) in his offer for his interest in Wonder Widget. This may not reflect the true forced sale value of Willie's stock.

When a business has zero or negative retained earnings, you may think that nothing should be offered for the stock. But the IRS's guidelines usually require you to offer something for small business stock. The Internal Revenue Manual takes into account such factors as the net worth of the business's assets, its record of earnings, dividend policy, current financial condition, future prospects, and value as a going concern. But if you can show you have a truly minimal interest in the business, no control over its affairs, and your stock can't be liquidated, the IRS considers your stock to have no value.

If you own an unincorporated business (a sole proprietorship) or a partnership, list the assets elsewhere on this form or on Form 433-B, the business collection statement.

Line 19 asks for information about court proceedings, bankruptcy, asset transfers, repossessions, and anticipated increases in income. It also asks whether you have a source of income from a trust, estate, or profit-sharing plan. If you check "yes" for any of these, explain in the Additional Information or Comments box on page 4 or on a continuation page.

Section IV (page 3) summarizes the information you have just given and adds more detail. Remember that for offer purposes the column marked "Current Market Value" does not mean "fair market value between a willing buyer and seller." It means "forced sale value."

Line 20 (cash) means the dollars in your pocket when you sign the form. **Lines 21 and 22** are carryovers from lines 13 and 18. **Line 23** carries over the cash value of insurance from line 17. **Line 24** asks about your vehicles. As a rule of thumb, the liquidation value of a car, truck, van, or similar asset is at least 20 percent less than fair market value. Take this discount on the form itself, listing the net number.

For example, Tina Taxpayer owns a car worth $10,000. For offer purposes, its current market value is $8,000. If the car has body damage, rust, broken glass, and so on, the discount may be even deeper. If the car loan is $3,000, Tina would have to offer $5,000 for this car.

The form also asks for the lienholder, the date the asset was pledged, and the payoff date.

Line 25 deals with real property. You may discount the fair market value of your home by 20 to 25 percent as a general rule, more if the local real estate market is weak. If you own other real property, such as rental property, you may discount that as well. Note the level of discount you are taking and your reasoning. Then list all secured debts against the property, including the date pledged and the payoff date. List the monthly payment in the appropriate column.

How much should you offer for these real estate assets? If you have borrowed against them to the maximum, and they have no equity after you have taken the 20 percent (or more) discount, then offer nothing. But if they have equity after this analysis, something must be offered. If you own the home or rental property by yourself (not jointly with anyone else), the equity for offer purposes is simply the debt minus the (discounted) fair market value.

Moneysaver
Be sure to include all arrearages, such as late fees, accrued, unpaid taxes, and interest on all of these fines. Check your area's Master Plan to see if an overriding government plan for your area or environmental regulations affect market value.

Unofficially...
Usually, you don't need a formal real estate appraisal, though if you have a recent one, that may help. Try using comparables or a statement of value (in letter form) from a knowledgeable real estate agent.

What if you own jointly with others? If Tom Taxpayer and his wife, Tina, own as tenants by the entirety and both owe taxes, the equity is equal to forced sale value minus the secured debt. If only Tom owes taxes, the offer guidelines require some amount even though the IRS legally cannot sell the property. Unfair? Possibly, and a violation of the spirit of the offer guidelines. After all, if the idea is to offer only what the IRS could forcibly collect, then Tom should offer zero for a home owned with his wife as tenants by the entirety where only he owes taxes. But the IRS guidelines still require something. The amount is usually between 20 percent and 50 percent of the net equity.

For example, Tom and Tina's house is worth $100,000. The mortgage is $20,000. Only Tom owes taxes. Tom discounts the market value to $80,000, making the total equity for offer purposes $60,000 ($80,000 discounted value minus $20,000 debt). Of that $60,000 of potential equity, Tom must offer somewhere between $12,000 and $30,000 (20 percent and 50 percent).

The lower figure applies if Tina paid the mortgage over many years and the higher applies if Tom paid it.

What about other properties, such as rentals? Here again, the rules allow a discount from fair market value to arrive at current market value for offer purposes. Subtract the debt on the property. Then figure your share of the net equity, and that is the offer amount for that asset.

Line 26 calls for "other assets." This includes household goods, rings, jewelry, art, and anything else of value. It is also the place to list your interest in a partnership, whether general or limited. If you are doing business as a partnership, also complete Form 433-B, "Collection Information Statement for Businesses."

Line 27 transposes the bank revolving credit figure from line 14.

Line 28 asks for other liabilities. List every other debt you owe (except the federal taxes, which go on **line 29**) . Some of it may be secured, some unsecured. But the IRS wants to know about it all. It may not allow any payments on these debts as "necessary" living expenses, but list all debts anyway.

Monthly income and expense. Are you having fun yet? The fun continues in **section V**, "Monthly Income and Expense Analysis." This section determines the future income potential portion of the offer. The IRS reasons that if you can afford to pay, say, $100 a month after allowing for these expenses, that's $6,000 in its pocket over five years. Instead of that dragged-out solution, it will take the present value of that stream of payments in a lump sum immediately.

The 1998 tax reform act now requires that the IRS develop national and local "allowances," a law that codifies prior practice. Still, the whole idea is to be more flexible in offers and to take the "facts and circumstances" of you, the individual taxpayer, into account, rather than to apply even "local" standards rigidly. One example might be a real estate agent who "needs" a high-priced car, or frequent changes of expensive suits, to impress clients and where such spending is normal in the trade. A disallowable expense would be a physician who "needs" a second home and boat in Florida to "chill out" from a grueling work schedule.

Moneysaver
As a rule of thumb, you must offer $5,000 for every $100 of net positive income per month. So it is to your advantage to argue for every expense dollar as being "necessary." What the IRS considers necessary and what you consider necessary can be quite different.

In all events, the new law requires that the tax-payer's expenses not be denied as "necessary" where that would leave him without "adequate means to provide for basic living expenses."

Bear in mind that offer examiners in every part of the country still follow formal and informal guidelines on how much of each expense is "necessary" for living. The IRS has also developed national and regional guidelines for three major expense categories.

Basically, the left side of the page asks for all sources of money and the right side for necessary living expenses. The difference between the two is the amount of disposable income that you could theoretically pay the IRS each month. It's that amount from which the IRS figures your future income potential.

Let's look at each item. As we do, you'll find a handy summary and fill-in chart on the following pages. Your expenses must meet two overall rules:

- They must be within the IRS's guidelines, and

- They must be necessary for health and welfare, or for the production of income.

National Standard Expenses

The first item is National Standard Expenses (**line 42**). National standard expenses are expenses for:

- Apparel and services (shoes, clothing, laundry, dry cleaning, and shoe repair)

- Food (all meals, home or away)

- Housekeeping supplies (postage, stationery, laundry and cleaning supplies, household products, cleansing and toilet tissue, paper towels and napkins, lawn and garden supplies, and miscellaneous household supplies)

■ Personal care products and services (including hair care, hair cuts, oral hygiene products, shaving needs, electric personal care products and repairs of these, and similar items)

■ Miscellaneous expenses

Add these up, and you have your National Standard Expenses. How much is "necessary" depends on your gross income and the number of people in your household. For example, a single person grossing less than $830 per month is allowed $315. A family of four grossing $5,830 per month or more is allowed $1,397. Households with more than four get more of an allowance. To find the amount you qualify for, consult the chart.

You can usually allocate the expenses within this category without much problem. For instance, if you spend a little more on clothing and a little less on food, that is OK, as long as the totals are within the overall limit.

Housing and utilities

The second big expense is housing and utilities (**line 43**). This includes almost everything you would associate with housing: the rent or mortgage payment, insurance, parking, necessary maintenance and repair, homeowner or condominium dues, and utilities. Utilities are gas, electricity, water, fuel, trash, and telephone, and similar items. Again, if you are within the government's limit, the amounts are usually accepted. Here, the IRS sets a local (by county), not national, limit, because these expenses vary so widely around the country. Call your local IRS office to find out what the limits are. An agent may even send you a list of them.

INCOME SOURCES—MONTHLY

Wages (self) _____

Wages (spouse) _____

Interest-Dividends _____

Net Business Income _____

Rental Income _____

Pension _____

Child Support _____

Alimony _____

Other _____

Total _____

NECESSARY LIVING EXPENSES—MONTHLY

National Standard Expenses

Clothing _____

Clothing Services _____

Food _____

Housekeeping Supplies _____

Personal Care Products and Services _____

Miscellaneous _____

Subtotal _____

Housing and Utilities

Rent or Mortgage (principal residence only) _____

Property Taxes _____

Homeowners or Renters Insurance _____

Parking _____

Necessary Maintenance and Repair _____

Homeowner Dues _____

Condominium Fees _____

Utilities _____

Gas _____

Water	_____
Fuel Oil	_____
Coal	_____
Bottled Gas	_____
Trash Collection	_____
Wood Fuel	_____
Other Fuel	_____
Septic Cleaning	_____
Telephone	_____
Electricity	_____
Other	_____
Subtotal	_____

Transportation

Lease or Purchase Payments	_____
Insurance	_____
Registration Fees	_____
Normal Maintenance	_____
Fuel	_____
Public Transportation	_____
Parking	_____
Tolls	_____
Subtotal	_____

Health Care

Health Insurance	_____
Medical Services (including co-pay)	_____
Prescription Drugs	_____
Medical Supplies	_____
Subtotal	_____

Unofficially...
The IRS Restructuring and Reform Act of 1998 now officially requires the IRS to develop monetary guidelines for offers. These guidelines are to allow "adequate means...for basic living expenses" based on national and local conditions.

Taxes

Income _____

FICA/Medicare _____

Past Due Taxes (incl. state) _____

Other Taxes _____

Subtotal _____

Court-Ordered Payments

Alimony _____

Child Support _____

Other _____

Subtotal _____

Child/Dependent Care

Elderly _____

Invalid _____

Handicapped _____

Babysitting _____

Day Care _____

Nursery _____

Preschool _____

Subtotal _____

Life Insurance

Subtotal _____

Secured or Legally Perfected Debts _____

Subtotal _____

Other Expenses

Accounting/Legal Fees _____

Charity _____

Other _____

Subtotal _____

GRAND TOTAL _____

For example, Tom and Tina have a first mortgage payment of $1,400 per month. This is at the high end of what the IRS will allow as "necessary" in their part of the country. They took out a second mortgage for a new wing, making their total monthly payments $2,500. Then Tom incurred a separate $50,000 tax liability. Even though the second mortgage is superior to the IRS's tax claim (because it was recorded before the lien arose), the IRS will allow only $1,400 per month. This limit is enforced even though in theory the IRS cannot legally sell the home or force the couple to move. The IRS reasons, "We may not be able to sell your home and force lower monthly mortgage payments with a smaller home, but we don't have to accept your offer, either."

Transportation

The third big expense item is transportation (**line 44**). Again, the IRS sets regional amounts for operating costs. Ownership costs are nationwide. This category includes car payments (either lease or purchase), insurance, maintenance, fuel, registration fees, inspection fees, parking fees, tolls, license fees, and public transportation. But, like anything else, if you spend money on transportation that does not produce income or ensure health and welfare, the expense is not "necessary." So you can have two cars as long as you meet this test and don't exceed the IRS standard.

Principal other expenses

After these three big expense categories, the IRS does not set national or local standards, but the expense still has to be necessary for health or welfare or for the production of income. Otherwise, it's a "conditional" expense and not normally allowable for offer purposes.

Health care expenses

Line 45 lists your health care expenses. This category includes health insurance, doctor and dentist visits, prescription drugs, and medical supplies (including eyeglasses and contact lenses). It also means special items such as guide dogs, and probably also includes stair chair lift and other medical devices necessary for health and welfare. The copay part of your medical bills is included here.

Taxes

Line 46 makes taxes a necessary expense. (What a relief!) Here, the IRS has in mind your current federal, state, and local tax payments (including FICA and Medicare). If you owe taxes to a state or local government for past periods and are paying them, these can also be "necessary," but you must work this out with the IRS.

Court-ordered payments

Next come court-ordered payments (**line 47**). These can certainly be necessary for the production of income, such as a judgment that a supplier has against you. They may be necessary for health and welfare, such as a suit by a doctor for past fees. Court-ordered payments also include alimony and child support. It is up to you to prove that the expense meets the "necessary" test.

Child and dependent care expenses

Child and dependent care expenses go on **line 48**. Day care and babysitting, nursery, and preschool expenses can be included where they meet the health and welfare or production of income tests. For instance, a mother who drops junior at day care so she can work would incur "necessary" day care or sitters' fees. But only "reasonable" amounts are allowed. The IRS knows children are costly, but it also warns that costs can vary greatly. The examiner will ask if there are alternatives to private tutors or one-on-one day care.

Life insurance

Line 49 lists your life insurance as a necessary expense. Only the premiums on term policies are deemed necessary (or the term component of a whole life policy). Some IRS districts restrict this to small policies only.

Debts and other expenses

Line 50 allows for secured or legally perfected debts as an expense. This means judgments other people have against you, or other secured debts such as secured lines of credit. Once again, the debt must meet the health, welfare, or production of income tests.

Finally, there are the "other expenses" (line 51) that life always throws your way, and this is where to list them.

How about education? For your children, the IRS seems to draw the line at private schools. It's unclear whether the "extras" many people pay, even in public schools, would be included, but you can certainly argue the extras are necessary for your health and welfare.

For handicapped children, expenses would normally be allowable, but prepare to show that no public school or other public alternatives are available.

How about adults? Education expenses are "necessary" if they help your production of income. Examples would be real estate courses for real estate brokers or continuing professional education courses.

Other allowances

Bright Idea
Court-ordered
payments that
predate the IRS
lien may have
priority over it.
If so, argue in
favor of these
being considered
a "necessary" liv-
ing expense.

What else might the IRS allow? Accounting and legal fees. (Did you think the IRS would forget the struggling tax professional trying to help you out of all this?) The IRS lets you pay your tax lawyer, accountant, or enrolled agent for representing you before the IRS. Other legal or accounting fees must meet the health and welfare or production of income tests.

Charitable contributions. The IRS does not consider these necessary unless they promote your health and welfare, or that of your family, or unless they are required for your job.

Other expenses. Do not bother calling certain expenses necessary since the IRS will disallow them almost automatically. For instance, in some districts, the IRS disallows all entertainment expenses. ("Go read a book.") It usually disallows college tuition payments, private school payments, and pet expenses.

That completes section V. Sign the agreement and date it. The total from line 30 (equity in asset column) plus the present value of your net monthly income (from **line 53**) will dictate the amount of your offer. That's where to start and, you hope, end.

Proving your finances

Would you like to gain instant and impressive credibility with the offer examiner? It's easy. Anticipate his or her request for proof of your financial statement, and supply it with the offer itself. Here are some guidelines on what to supply with your Form 433-A.

1. **Bank statements.** Last six months, for all accounts over which you have signature authority or control (business or personal).

2. **Investments.** Current statement, such as IRA account statement, brokerage statement, and so on.

3. **Credit card debt.** Last statement.

4. **Insurance.** Copy of the face of each policy of any kind (life, health, disability, and so on), plus statement of premium. Also include latest statement of cash value, if that applies.

5. **Home.** The deed, mortgage, evidence of recordation, monthly mortgage coupon, or other evidence of payment, and latest statement of equity. Also, if you have it, include a statement of the market value of the home, such as from the county land records or an appraisal.

6. **Other real estate.** The deed, the mortgage, and current statement of fair market value and amount owed. If you own real estate in a partnership, supply the same information.

7. **Cars.** Copy of title, latest statement of the amount of the lien, copy of payment coupon, copy of the "blue book" page on which your car is listed. (Fun fact: the *NADA Used Car Guide* or "blue book" actually has an orange cover).

8. **Household goods.** Make an informal list of your furniture, by room. Do not include every piece, but be sure to cover all the main items, including any artwork. Make an estimate of the value of each on a forced sale basis.

9. **Other debts.** Any documentation, such as promissory notes, for other debts you owe. If your uncle loaned you $10,000 and there is no note, see if you can get the check. If not, write up a statement for the uncle to sign that demonstrates that he loaned you the money, the date of that loan, and the terms of repayment.

Timesaver
Try to keep good records of all your professional bills, and write down the business, health, or welfare purpose of each.

Moneysaver
You need not engage an appraiser or some other expert to evaluate the value of household goods unless the IRS requests.

10. **Income items.** Three latest pay stubs for you and your spouse, and other evidence of income such as bank interest, brokerage statements, distributions from estates or trusts, and so on.

11. **National standard expenses.** These normally do not have to be proved, unless the IRS requests. Be prepared to prove any unusual items.

12. **Housing expenses.** Be prepared to prove utility bills, telephone bills, repair bills, and other housing type expenses, in addition to rent or mortgage payment. Sometimes, the offer examiner will not ask for proof if the amount you state on Form 433-A is within the IRS's guidelines.

13. **Transportation expenses.** Aside from showing title to the cars, be prepared to prove expenses, such as lease payments, repair bills, gas, and so on.

14. **Court-ordered payments or secured debts.** A copy of the court order, such as for alimony or child support order. Supply a copy of any judgments against you, and executions on those judgments, or security instruments you gave to others.

15. **Safe-deposit box.** Provide an inventory of the contents.

16. **Other.** Consider supplying three years of back-tax returns for yourself and your spouse.

If you own a business

If you own a business that you operate as a proprietor, partner, or corporation, complete and submit Form 433-B ("Collection Information Statement for Businesses"). For a sole proprietor, the IRS will simply look at net assets, which legally you own, and increase your offer by the equity in those assets, discounted for forced sale value. But if you are a partner or a shareholder in a corporation, legally you do not own those assets as an individual. The partnership or corporation owns them, and *it* does not owe taxes. (If it does, *see* below.)

The IRS usually respects the existence of the corporation or partnership, but still makes you offer something for your ownership interest in those entities because it considers you the true owner of assets in a family business even if, technically, you own only the stock. Also, it looks carefully at how much you are being paid and whether you are hiding gross income inside the corporation or partnership. This is important if you have many partners unrelated to you, or if your corporation or partnership documents restrict your authority to sell your shares or interest.

Offers for businesses

Corporations, partnerships, and sole proprietors that owe back business taxes, principally employment taxes, can also qualify for an offer. Here, the process is usually easier than with an individual who seeks to compromise income taxes. Paying is not easier, only making the offer. The same number of forms are involved, but there is normally less debate over which expenses are "necessary."

A "C" corporation commonly owes income or employment taxes. Partnerships and "S" corporations do not owe income taxes since their profits pass through to the owners individually. But these enterprises can owe payroll taxes. Also, an unincorporated proprietor can have employees and owe payroll taxes.

Watch Out!
The IRS can col-
lect delinquent
payroll taxes in
part from the
responsible offi-
cers (see Chapter
6) as well as
from the corpo-
ration. In such a
case, you should
expect the agent
to ask for per-
sonal financial
data from the
officers as well
as from the
business.

For all these business taxes, use Form 433-B,
"Collection Information Statement for Businesses."

The IRS looks at the business the same way it
looks at an individual: What is the business's maximum ability to pay? Businesses are different from
individuals in that their assets are directly involved
in production and the business may not be able to
borrow against or sell them. Moreover, they often
need a cash flow cushion, particularly if they have
seasonal ups and downs. Many times the IRS takes
this into account; other times you may need to argue
for it.

Form 433-B asks for typical introductory information: the owners, partners, officers, and major
shareholders. **Section I** then asks for the latest tax
return information, bank accounts, bank credit
available, safe-deposit boxes, real property owned,
life insurance, and accounts and notes receivable.
The IRS wants this information to see if the business
can liquidate assets to pay the taxes, or for future reference if the IRS decides to force a liquidation. List
all accounts and notes receivable, and in the "status"
column indicate whether they are collectible.

Section II of Form 433-B **(lines 16 through 27)**
summarizes the assets and liabilities of the company.
Line 16 ("Cash on Hand") is the amount of money in
the cash register. **Lines 17 through 20** carry over
information on bank accounts, receivables, life insurance loan value, and real property from section I.

Lines 21 through 24 require a list of all other
assets, including vehicles, machinery, and merchandise inventory. State the market value, the debt on
the asset, the equity in the asset, and the monthly
payment if there is one. As with offers for individuals, you may discount the market value to forced sale

value. Also, list the lienholder or noteholder and the dates the debts are due.

Section III, the "Income and Expense Analysis," is the most important part of this form. **Lines 28 through 32** require listing the gross receipts of the business from all sources. **Lines 34 through 44** call for the expenses.

The form also asks for a period of time covering the income and expenses. Many businesses choose one year. Others use six months. Pick a range in which income and expenses are typical, especially if you have a seasonal business. And try to choose a time period that ends within two to three months of the date you sign the statement.

If all of the income and expenses check out, the IRS totals them. The income minus the expenses is a net number, which the Service uses for the future income potential calculation.

Can the business afford it? Often it cannot, because of problems related to cash flow or seasonal fluctuations. You must argue these points to the offer examiner.

Proving your business expenses

Be prepared to prove your business expenses, as with offers for individuals. Normally, this is easy. You have your checkbook and your cancelled checks. But you should consider supplying other information to the offer examiner, such as:

1. **Inventory.** A detailed statement of your inventories, including date of purchase and liquidation value.

2. **Accounts receivable and notes receivable.** Copies of these, including an aging report (describing how old your receivables are) may be helpful to your offer.

Unofficially...
The IRS usually assumes that all business expenses are "necessary." But if an expense is personal, out it goes. For example, if the company pays for your personal Cadillac, the IRS may not see that expense as necessary.

Bright Idea
The rejection letter may not indicate which items were the basis for being turned down. Still, try to guess, and include those items in your appeal. The appeals officer will have the complete file and will know each ground on which the offer examiner rejected your offer.

3. **Machinery and equipment.** These are easily obtained from your depreciation schedule. Otherwise, make a list, including date or year of purchase, description of the item, and fair market value (including the debt on any equipment).

Appealing a rejected offer

You've negotiated. You've dug up and produced reams of supporting data. You've argued, cajoled, even begged. Still, the offer examiner wants $50,000, not the $10,000 you offered nor the $20,000 you could possibly pay if you robbed a bank. What happens then? You can either withdraw the offer or appeal the forthcoming rejection. Tell the offer examiner that you want to appeal, and she will be more than happy to accommodate you. You'll soon receive a rejection letter that gives you either thirty or sixty days to appeal. Those deadlines are hard and fast. If you miss them, you lose your appeal rights.

The rejection letter instructs you how to prepare a protest and where to send it.

A timely appeal is soon followed by a letter from the office of appeals telling you who is assigned to the case and letting you know if a conference date has been scheduled. To prepare for the appeal, assemble as much supporting data as you can, or review what you've already sent. Prepare to argue each point (or at least each point you can think of). It might help to call the appeals officer before the conference. Ask her exactly what items the offer examiner changed to reject the offer, then address those points.

Often months will have elapsed between the rejection and the appeals conference. Use that time to gather more data. For example, suppose you told the offer examiner that you were about to be downsized, that is, lose your job or take a cut in pay, but he did not believe you. By the time of the appeals conference, you may be on unemployment. Or suppose that your health insurance went up by $200 per month after the rejection. That is new evidence the appeals officer can consider. The worst the appeals officer can do is to sustain the rejection, so there is little downside to appealing a rejected offer. The only legal downside is that the ten-year statute of limitations on collecting your tax remains suspended. The upside is that collection may also be suspended.

Is there life after appeals?

If the appeals officer sustains the rejection, you are back to square one. The Collection Division regains a live account receivable it is required to try to collect. Sometimes you can then work out an installment agreement. Offer examiners will sometimes suggest that alternative in their rejection letter. But you are still back at the beginning.

On the other hand, the appeals officer could overturn the offer examiner's finding, or suggest some other figure for a compromise. If you agree, the appeals officer will write this up and send it forward for final review. Statistically, the chances of a reversal are small, but again it is often worth a try.

The bankruptcy option

What if you threaten the IRS with bankruptcy? In theory, the offer guidelines require bankruptcy to be considered and "negotiated" if some or all of your taxes can be discharged in a Chapter 7 or Chapter 11 liquidation.

Unofficially...
According to the official Internal, Revenue Manual: in a liquidating bankruptcy case it is "almost certain" the IRS will collect more through an offer. Still, don't expect that the agent will keel over when the word bankruptcy passes your lips.

In the real world, however, offer examiners are reluctant to take bankruptcy into consideration at all. This is unfortunate, but it is their attitude. They don't take these threats seriously enough. Actually, if you file for bankruptcy, offer examiners and revenue officers may be secretly relieved—it's a case off their inventory; they send it to another unit, the Special Procedures Function. So do not count on a bankruptcy threat to help your offer, even though it should.

The subtleties and permutations in taxpayers' offers are many and varied, as varied as people's personal and business affairs. No one chapter can address all of them, but every delinquent taxpayer owes it to himself or herself at least to consider making an offer to resolve—permanently—a nagging tax problem.

Just the facts

- Always consider an offer to solve your tax problems.

- Never look at an offer in isolation. Compare it with the other choices: doing nothing, installment agreement, and bankruptcy.

- Be prepared. Preview your offer with the IRS if possible, with your tax advisor if you have one.

- Assemble all your backup data and keep it up to date.

- Don't be afraid to appeal a rejected offer. Often taxpayers get a good deal.

- Be aware that suspending the collection statute of limitations is one price you pay for making an offer.

GET THE SCOOP ON...
Types of installment agreements ▪ When
to apply for one ▪ Tips on getting
the best deal ▪ Filling out the
required forms ▪ Revising the agreement ▪
Appealing denials up the chain and in court

The Installment Agreement

A big IRS bill can be unnerving at best, paralyzing at worst. Sometimes you see it coming, like a bill following a three-year audit. Other times, the IRS bill can be a total shock, leaving you with the terrifying question—"How am I ever going to pay this?" That's what the installment agreement is for. The IRS has long had the legal authority to allow past-due taxes to be paid in installments. With one exception, the installment agreement is not a legal right you can enforce, but the Service can and does grant these agreements frequently.

The installment concept seems salutary on the surface; the tax bill is too big to swallow all at once, so you pay in digestible chunks. And, in fact, most parts of an installment agreement are negotiable, such as the time period, the amount paid per month, and the date of payment. Its biggest advantage is to allow you breathing room to pay a bill you cannot pay in full right away. But it has drawbacks, too.

281

First, the effective interest rate of some installment agreements, when you include late-payment
penalties, is higher than 20 percent. The magic of
daily compounding increases this total. So if you can
possibly borrow the money to pay the IRS, even from
a high interest credit card, you may be better off.

Second, the IRS may file a Notice of Federal Tax
Lien while you are paying. That notice is like a mortgage on all your property, a legal charge or encumbrance to secure the tax debt. The lien ties up
almost everything you own until the debt is paid.

Third, the IRS sometimes asks you to "voluntarily" extend the period of limitations on collection as
the price for an installment agreement. The agent
may not insist on this extension if you can pay in a
relatively short time, such as three years. But if your
agreement stretches longer than that, especially past
the ten years the IRS normally has to collect, the IRS
may demand a waiver, or else refuse the installment
agreement.

The IRS's menu also includes the installment
agreement, but it's way down on the Service's list.
First on the list is always: Pay in full, and now! Sell
assets if you have to. Borrow money if you can. But
pay now, and in full. The IRS manual explicitly
emphasizes collecting the back taxes from "available
assets," a phrase that contemplates forced sales of
your valuable properties. Other methods such as
installment agreements are considered only if the
IRS cannot collect in full, quickly. So when you propose to pay with an installment agreement, bear in
mind it is not the IRS's first choice. In fact, the
default rate on installment agreements at one point
hovered around 80 percent. No wonder the agency
is reluctant to grant them.

Watch Out!
Sometimes the
waiver demanded
by the IRS can
last for five more
years, sometimes
ten. The IRS will
also file a Notice
of Federal Tax
Lien for such
long-term agree-
ments. So if your
choice from the
tax collection
"menu" is the
installment
agreement,
watch out for the
aftertaste.

The installment agreement menu

There are four main types of installment agreements. Ask for the one that is right for you.

- **A regular installment agreement**, nothing more or less than a monthly payment plan. Once the agreement is in place, the IRS sometimes even sends you a payment coupon each month; you send it back with a check.

- **A Direct Debit Installment Agreement**. Here, you give the IRS the authority to debit your bank account each month for the payment. (Don't play the bank float on this one!)

- **The Payroll Deduction** Installment Agreement. Here, the money is deducted directly from your paycheck, just like current taxes.

There is also a fourth option, the *name your own*, or *streamlined*, installment agreement. The IRS established this one in 1994 for people who owed less than $10,000. In 1998, Congress made this a legal right. But you can demand this type of installment agreement only if you meet these conditions:

- The tax (not including penalties, and other charges.) is no more than $10,000.

- You've filed all required tax returns for the past five years.

- You've paid all the taxes on those returns.

- You have no prior installment agreement for those five years.

- The IRS finds you can't pay in full now.

- You agree to pay in full within three years.

- You agree to be fully tax-compliant for the period of your installment agreement.

Unofficially...
The IRS granted about 2.6 million installment agreements in 1996, covering $12 billion in back taxes.

If you qualify, use Form 9265 and put down the amount you think you can pay per month. As long as you pay within thirty-six months and the other conditions are met, the IRS automatically accepts it.

Where to get an installment agreement

If you qualify for the "name your own" agreement, all you need is Form 9265. You can find this from an on-line computer service, the IRS's web site, a local IRS office, some libraries, or by dialing (800) TAX-FORM. Fill out the form, attach it to your tax return, and send it in. (Keep a copy!) That should be the end of the matter. The more complicated agreements, involving more than $10,000 or several years of taxes, usually find their way to the IRS's service centers or the Automated Collection System (ACS). Still more complex ones are referred to revenue officers "in the field."

Here's how the process generally works at any of these levels. The IRS computers catch up with you for past taxes by sending a number of letters. Starting in 1997, you will also get an annual update of your tax bill. Most people take the hint and respond to the letters. You can propose an installment agreement by return mail in this way.

At whatever level you discuss an installment agreement within the IRS, you will often be interviewed. This is known as the "TDA Interview," standing for *Taxpayer Delinquent Account Interview*. Remember that the IRS is after the most money in the shortest possible time. So the Automated Collection System representative, or the revenue officer, will demand full payment up front. That's step one.

Timesaver
The earlier you decide an installment agreement is for you, the better off you are. Jumping on the IRS notice averts later collection notices and possibly levies. It also positions you for an offer in compromise.

Failing that, in step two you will be quizzed on all of your assets and liabilities. If the agent sees that you can sell something quickly, such as a stock, bond, or savings account, he or she will demand that this be done. He may also demand that you liquidate a retirement account, despite the penalty for early withdrawal and the income tax you have to pay on it. He will look for sources of borrowing—credit cards, home equity loans, family loans, you name it. Often the agent will ask you to apply for one or two loans, and to send evidence that you have done so, even if you know you can't qualify and are sure to be rejected.

When all "quick money" sources are exhausted, the agent moves on to review your monthly income and expenses to arrive at an installment amount. An agent will ask questions in interview form to see how much you can pay. Figure on spending up to two hours on the telephone. Essentially, the agent goes through the same financial data, verbally, that she would have asked you to put in writing. This includes verifying your name, address, employment, family circumstances, where you bank, assets and liabilities, income, and expenses.

The agent first asks how much you earn from all sources, taxable or not. She then catalogs your necessary living expenses. Review the checklist in chapter 11 before responding so that you are prepared when the IRS calls. Often that IRS call scares people. As a result, they underestimate their living expenses. This mistake is as costly an error as if you overestimated them. Be accurate. That accuracy depends on thinking through your expenses, item by item, category by category, in advance of the IRS's call. Later, this chapter provides a guide to this process.

Moneysaver
The telephone interview carries inherent pressure to settle, or to avoid levies and liens by "giving in." Try to avoid this pressure by putting your finances in writing first. Then you are negotiating from a more solid foundation. Don't guess.

Bright Idea
You can always
ask the agent not
to file the notice
of lien. Be pre-
pared with a
good reason. Be
ready to file an
appeal if notice
of the lien is
filed. You may
also request
withdrawal of the
notice if you
enter into an
installment
agreement that
will pay the tax
debt in full.

At the end of the interview, the IRS adds up your "necessary" living expenses (according to its standards) and subtracts these from your pay and other income. If the result is a positive number, the agency will expect you to pay that amount or close to it.

For example, Tanya Taxpayer works at Churner Stockbroker as a salaried stockbroker. Her gross pay is $6,000 per month. She has necessary living expenses of $1,500 for taxes, $1,000 for rent, $1,000 for food, $1,000 for child care, and $1,000 for all other items. These total $5,500, so she has $500 left. The IRS will expect Tanya to pay $500 per month. Possibly it may shave that to $450 or $400 if it's near Christmas. The agent must also decide whether to file a Notice of Federal Tax Lien (Chapter 3 discusses this lien).

If you owe less than $5,000 or if you owe between $5,000 and $10,000, a lien is not required if you use the streamlined installment agreement. In all other cases, the IRS will almost always file a Notice of Federal Tax Lien. The actual rules for lien filing are more complex, but these may be your general guides.

Ignoring the Service's past-due notices is usually futile. Agents will begin calling either from the Service Center where you filed your returns or from the Automated Collection System if the case has been transferred to that function after the Service Center gives up. The representative goes through the same interview process described above. She enters the information on the computer screen and proposes an installment agreement based on your net monthly income. You can agree or disagree, and you can even appeal, but normally the figures will not change much.

The third way you can get an installment agreement is to delay, hide, or stall long enough to prompt "the field" into action. This means your case has merited the personal attention of a revenue officer of the Collection Division. Millions of people adopt this "head in the sand" attitude toward paying their past taxes. This only makes things worse; after all, when an ostrich sticks its head in the sand, remember which part of its anatomy is likely to be kicked.

Revenue officers have the same menu as the other collectors. They call, visit, or otherwise find you. They are out to get the taxes, so they also demand full payment, up-front. But they, too, recognize that you may not be able to pay in full right away. Certainly they will ask you to borrow from lines of credit or credit cards, refinance assets, or liquidate assets, before an installment agreement can be granted. In other words, they will try to get the most money in the shortest time and save the installment agreement for any balance.

Finally, you also ask for an installment agreement simply by walking into your local IRS office. The same interview process will occur, and often you get quick, one-stop service in this way. If you negotiate with the Automated Collection System representative, you can often obtain a short-term payment of sixty days or less. It's often in your best interest to look around everywhere for those dollars, because interest and penalties mount up very quickly.

Tips on negotiating the agreement

Keep the following seven tips in mind throughout the negotiating process.

Unofficially...
The 1998 tax reform act makes IRS collectors subject to fair debt collection practices that prohibit, among other actions, harassing calls, threats, calls at odd hours, and calls to the workplace.

Know your finances

Don't guess about your finances. The IRS agent, at whatever level, will usually try to keep you on the phone (or in an interview) to get as much personal and financial information as she can on the first contact. If you are nervous or unsure about information, say that you do not know, you need to verify, or you are unsure. Don't guess, and don't try to please the agent by stabbing at a number you think the agent might want to hear.

Most people know what they pay for rent or mortgage, but few know the figures for transportation, food, or medicine without looking at bills and receipts. Official policy allows this breathing room if you ask for it. In fact, it is perfectly acceptable to tell the agent (if true), "Please let me know all the categories of expense you want me to research. I will call you back with the exact figures, which I can't recall now." Then be certain you call back on or before the next deadline. Try to ask for a date far enough ahead that you know for sure you can have all the information. This leads us to

Meet all deadlines

If you cannot meet the deadlines, call the agent back anyway *before* the deadline and say you cannot meet the deadline. Then set another one. If your account is in ACS, you'll get a different agent each time you call, but all have access to the same computer screen and data bank. Each agent notes what you say every time you call. So the first agent notes that you promised to call back on November 1. The second agent sees that deadline, and checks whether you met it.

Appeal

Let's say that at the end of the interview the agent proposes $1,000 per month, a figure you just can't meet. You can afford only $200. You don't have to accept $1,000, at least not right away. You can appeal. Tell the agent you want to appeal to her supervisor. Ask what the process is and how long it takes. In the meantime, show good faith by sending in what you think you can afford. Often such appeals take several weeks. In the meantime, you have generated a track record of paying what you think you can afford.

Get credit

If you decide to borrow money against an asset, get credit for the repayments. Borrowing means your monthly expenses go up, which should reduce your installment agreement.

For example, you owe $15,000 in taxes. At the IRS's request, you borrow $10,000 against your home, leaving $5,000 for the installment agreement. The IRS wants you to pay $500 per month, but because of your new home equity loan, you can pay only $250. The IRS should give you credit for that new loan payment as an additional "necessary" living expense, and ask for only $250 per month. The same reasoning should apply if you borrow on your credit cards, even though the credit card debt is not "secured" as a home loan would be. But the Internal Revenue Manual is silent on this point.

Stay current

The agent always looks at your compliance and tax history before granting you an installment agreement. If you have defaulted once or more in the past, if you are behind on your current taxes, if your expenses have recently increased without justification or explanation, she may be reluctant to let you pay over time. So make every effort to stay current.

Unofficially... The good-faith pattern you develop when establishing a track record of payment can work in your favor when you try to negotiate a lower monthly payment.

Timesaver
Computer geeks:
You can get all
of these forms
(and many oth-
ers) on interac-
tive format from
a number of ven-
dors, or from the
IRS Website
(non-interac-
tive). We recom-
mend software
that will accom-
modate as much
text as possible,
as well as
generate
continuation
pages.

Ask for lien withdrawal

Ask the IRS to withdraw any Notice of Federal Tax Lien it has filed against you. Since the agency will be reluctant to do this, you need to have a solid business or personal reason for asking for the withdrawal. This withdrawal must be considered a long shot, but may be worth a try. In theory, you can ask the Office of Taxpayer Advocate to intervene for you to obtain this withdrawal, but you will probably be required to show substantial hardship. If the IRS agrees to the withdrawal, you may also write the agency, asking it to notify your credit reporting agencies, banks, and other creditors of the withdrawal of the notice.

Request nonfiling of Notice of Federal Tax Lien

If you believe the filing of a notice of lien will hurt your credit, or otherwise damage your finances, you can always request that one not be filed. The IRS has discretion here, though only if you owe more than $5,000 can you be relatively sure this discretion will not be exercised. But even in cases in which the lien appears "mandatory," it doesn't hurt to make the argument.

Filling out the Collection Information Statement

The heart of the installment agreement is the Collection Information Statement, Form 433-A for individuals and 433-B for businesses. Often agents now use the short form, Form 433-F.

Completing these forms is relatively easy as IRS forms go, but heed the old expression, "The devil is in the details." Remember also that you sign them under penalties of perjury.

Form 433-A, Sections I-III

Let's start with Form 433-A. Section I asks for employment information. Section II lists personal and tax information, including the adjusted gross income from your last-filed federal tax return.

Starting with Section III, the form gets serious.

Line 13

Line 13 calls for your bank accounts, including savings and loans, credit unions, IRAs, retirement plans, and certificates of deposit. List all, even if some are held jointly with your spouse or children. As long as you have the authority to withdraw from the account, it must be listed. Explain on page 4 if the account belongs to someone else under the law of your state. The "balance" column means the checkbook balance on your last statement. (If this were an offer in compromise, you would list the average daily collected balance. *See* Chapter 11.)

Revealing your accounts, of course, gives the IRS valuable information about assets it can then more easily seize. But experience shows that agents do not use this form as a subterfuge. They genuinely try to work out an installment agreement or other arrangement to pay or compromise your taxes. If all else fails, however, they can certainly use the information. Still, you're only making their job easier; they could get the financial information by other means anyway.

Line 14

Line 14 asks for your charge cards and lines of credit. This is the place to list all charge accounts, the monthly payments, the total amount owed, and available credit. Most of these types of cards are unsecured, meaning the card issuer has no security for the debt. The IRS gives credit for those components of your monthly payments that are for "necessary" living expenses.

Watch Out!
A recent amend-
ment to the
bankruptcy laws
provides that the
debt for money
you borrow on a
charge card to
pay taxes is not
dischargeable in
bankruptcy.

The general test for "necessary" living expenses is whether the payment is for your or your family's health and welfare or for the production of income. So most credit card payments will not qualify. But food is a necessary living expense (within the IRS's limits), so if you charge your groceries, that amount would qualify. You bear the burden of showing that a charge card payment is for a necessary expense. List the necessaries that you pay by plastic in part IV, discussed below.

The IRS will sometimes ask you to borrow against available credit before allowing you to pay the rest of the tax in installments. Many people have already maxed out their credit cards or other credit sources, but often there is some room for further borrowing. It is not pleasant, but you're no worse off by essentially exchanging one debt (the taxes) for another (the credit card debt). Which is easier to bear? In most cases, it's easier to deal with the credit card company than with the IRS. Credit card loans usually cost 18 to 20 percent, substantially more than the 8 percent the IRS typically charges these days for interest, but if you include the tax penalties as well, the effective IRS interest rate starts to climb.

Lines 15 and 16

Line 15 asks for the location and contents of your safe deposit boxes, the valuables in which the IRS may ask you to sell. It can also ask you to inventory the box. You can refuse, but the Service can get a court order to seize the box. This doesn't often happen, but the power is there. The agency might even want to if you refuse to say what's inside the box.

Line 16 discusses your real estate. This category includes your home, land, rental property, and other real property you own. It does not mean partnership interests that invest in real estate, nor any corporations. These go on a different line. On line 16, describe the real estate, such as in the following two examples. *Example 1:* "Single family home, 123 Main Street, Anytown, USA, owned as tenants by the entirety." *Example 2:* "Townhouse in Breezy Acres Subdivision, 3 floors, owned as joint tenant with my brother." Don't fill in the values or the mortgages here. These go in section V.

Lines 17 and 18

Line 17 asks about life insurance. The IRS considers only term-life premiums a necessary expense, and then only if the premium is not "excessive." Experience varies on what is excessive. In some districts, the IRS will allow the premiums on $500,000 of face value. In others, it can be as low as $10,000. If you have whole, universal, or some other investment-type policy, the extra premiums over a comparable term policy are not "necessary" in the IRS's view.

Line 18 asks for your securities, including stocks, bonds, mutual funds, money-market funds, and government securities. State what they are, how much you have, who owns them, where they are located, and their current value. Publicly traded stocks are easy enough. Call your broker or look in the paper. But stock in a small, closely held corporation like a family business is also a "security." Often such stock has no value, either because the company is not doing well (after all, that's why you owe back taxes) or because there is no market. Still, the form requires you to list some value, even if it's zero. Whatever value you list, be prepared to back it up.

Moneysaver
See Chapter 11
for the factors
the IRS reviews
on small business
stock. Also con-
sider asking an
expert for an
opinion (or, more
formally if neces-
sary, an
appraisal) of
your closely held
business

Line 19

On **Line 19,** the IRS wants to know about court proceedings, that is, whether you have been sued or are
suing anyone. If you are the plaintiff, your claim
may be valuable. For example, suppose you owe
$100,000 in taxes, and yesterday your lawyer filed
suit against Big Burger because you spilled their
scalding coffee on your lap. Your claim for $1 mil-
lion for pain and suffering, plus actual damages of
seventy-five cents for the coffee (hold the cream), is
a valuable asset. Check the "yes" box and explain the
details in the "Additional Information" section on
page 4.

The Service also wants to know about repossessions and bankruptcies. Do you anticipate getting a
raise? Check the "yes" box. Do you participate in a
trust, estate, or profit-sharing plan? The IRS wants to
know about that. All these are sources of collection
either now or at some time in the future. That completes section III.

Form 433A, Section IV

Section IV, "Assets and Liabilities", summarizes the
data you have given and adds a few more details.
Line 20, "Cash," means the actual greenbacks you
have in your pocket on the day you sign the statement.

Lines 21 and 22 carry forward the totals from
lines 13 and 18. **Line 23** asks for the cash or loan
value of insurance, a figure you carry over from line
17. **Line 24** calls for vehicles, including cars, trucks,
and anything else with wheels. List the current market value, the amount owed, and the equity (the difference between market value and amount owed),
as well as the monthly payment and data on the lien-

holders. The IRS wants this information for two reasons. On the one hand, it may ask you to borrow against your car. If it's a clunker, the Service may conclude the car is not worth the debt. On the other hand, it now knows what to look for if it wants to seize your car.

Line 25 sets out the numbers on your real property. List current market value, the amount you owe, and the equity.

This is the place to list your mortgage payments and the payments on your rental and commercial properties. Real estate is often the first place the Service looks when it asks you to borrow against assets. Still, the IRS knows borrowing is hard even when you have good credit. And many lenders run for cover when they find you owe taxes. Still, some lenders lend against solid assets, such as a home, despite the IRS lien.

The IRS agents who look at these statements are human, too. They have mortgages; they pay bills. They also know about things like loan-to-value ratios and second trusts. So don't be worried if line 25 seems to show a large "equity" in your home. In the real world, all of that equity may not be available to pay your taxes.

Line 26 asks for other assets. Here list jewelry, furniture, and anything else of value you own. Be realistic in your estimates, but remember that these assets have a value to you that is greater than to others on the open market. **Line 27** carries over bank revolving credit from line 14.

On **line 28**, list other debts you owe such as bank loans, judgments, notes, and charge accounts not otherwise stated. Note the monthly payments and the name of the lender. Listing the monthly pay-

Timesaver
In line 25, list the market value for installment agreements purposes, and forced sale value for offers in compromise. See Chapter 11.

Timesaver
Always ask the
agent for the
written local and
national guide-
lines on neces-
sary living
expenses. These
will always
include food,
clothing, hous-
ing, and trans-
portation. They
may also include
insurance, health
care, and some
other categories.

ment doesn't mean the IRS will allow the payment
as "necessary," but the agency wants to know about
it anyway. And if the expense is for health and welfare, or to produce income, it may well qualify as
"necessary."

Finally, list your delinquent federal taxes on **line
29**, and take the column totals on **line 30**.

That finishes section IV.

Form 433-A, Section V

This brings you to the heart of the installment agreement process, the "Monthly Income and Expense
Analysis" (section V). Remember that the agent will
start with your gross income and subtract the
expenses he thinks are "necessary" (and therefore
allowable for this purpose). The difference is what
he will expect you to pay, every month, until your
taxes are down to zero. So it is important to argue
for every possible allowable expense.

Lines 31 through 40 ask you to list all income,
including wages and salaries, interest and dividends,
rentals, pensions, child support, alimony, and
"other." This includes loans and gifts, even if nontaxable. List the gross amounts, without any deduction for taxes or anything else withheld from your
paycheck.

All expenses are classed as either necessary or
conditional. Necessary living expenses are always
allowable for installment agreements. "Conditional"
expenses are allowable if your tax debt can still be
paid in three years through the installment agreement.

IRS guidelines allow one year to eliminate the
"unnecessary" expenses. Also, an expense is "necessary" only if it promotes the health and welfare of
you and your family or if it is necessary for the production of income.

Lines 42 through 51 cover necessary living expenses. Your expenses for these categories are preapproved for allowance within certain limits. The IRS has established upper limits for three of these categories, depending on household income and size.

National Standard Expenses

The first is National Standard Expenses (line 42). National Standard Expenses are expenses for the following items:

- Apparel and services (shoes, clothing, laundry, dry cleaning, and shoe repair)

- Food (all meals, at home or away)

- Housekeeping supplies (postage, stationery, laundry and cleaning supplies, household products, cleansing and toilet tissue, paper towels and napkins, lawn and garden supplies, and miscellaneous household supplies)

- Personal care products and services (including hair care, hair cuts, oral hygiene products, shaving needs, electric personal care products and repairs of these, and similar items)

- Miscellaneous expenses

Add these up, and you have your National Standard Expenses. How much is allowable depends on your gross income and how many people are in your household. (It's based on Bureau of Labor Statistics numbers for 1992 through 1993.) For example, a single person grossing less than $830 per month is allowed $315 for these expenses. A family of four earning $5,830 per month or more is allowed $1,397.

People sometimes chafe at these limits; after all, how can the IRS tell you how much to spend for your family's food? Agents respond that they do not, that

Bright Idea
Consult your local
IRS office for the
government's lim-
its on housing
and utility
expenses. These
limits are set
locally because
expenses vary so
much around the
country.

you may spend as much as you like, but only certain amounts are "allowed" for purposes of calculating the monthly installment agreement. You can usually allocate the expenses within this category without much problem. For instance, if you spend a little more on clothing and a little less on food, that's OK, as long as the totals are within the overall limit.

Housing and utilities

The second big expense is housing and utilities (**line 43**). This includes almost everything associated with housing: rent or mortgage, insurance, parking, necessary maintenance and repair, homeowner or condominium dues, and utilities. Utilities include such items as gas, electricity, water, fuel, trash, and telephone. Again, if you are within the government's limits, the amounts should be accepted.

Transportation

The third big expense is transportation (**line 44**). This category includes car payments (lease or purchase), insurance, maintenance, fuel, registration fees, inspection fees, parking fees, tolls, license fees, and public transportation. But like anything else, if you are spending on transportation that does not produce income or ensure health and welfare, it's not a "necessary" expense. So you can own two cars as long as you meet this test and don't exceed the IRS standard. Within that limit, the IRS does not care how you spend the money.

Other expenses

After these three big expense categories, the IRS sets no national or, usually, local standards, but the expense still has to be necessary for health or welfare, or for the production of income. Otherwise, it's a "conditional" expense, allowable only if the IRS will get all its money within three years.

Line 45, health care expenses, is clearly a necessary item for everyone. This category includes health insurance, doctor and dentist visits, prescription drugs, and medical supplies (including eyeglasses and contact lenses). It also means special items such as guide dogs, and probably also includes stair chair lifts and other medical devices that are necessary for health and welfare. The copay part of your medical bills is also included here.

Line 46 makes taxes a necessary expense. Here, the IRS has in mind your current federal, state, and local tax payments (including FICA and Medicare). If you are paying back taxes to a state or local government, these can also be "necessary," but you must work out the amount with the IRS. Next come court-ordered payments (**line 47**). These can certainly be necessary for the production of income, for example a judgment a key supplier has against you. They may also be necessary for health and welfare, such as suit by a doctor for past fees. Court-ordered payments also include alimony and child support. It is up to you to prove the expense meets the "necessary" test. It always helps if the court-ordered payments are in place before the IRS files a notice of its tax lien.

Child and dependent care expenses go on **line 48**. The IRS is usually understanding about these. Day care, babysitting, nursery, and preschool expenses are certainly included, but they must meet the health and welfare or production of income tests. For instance, a father who drops junior off at day care so he can work would have "necessary" day care or sitters' fees, if they are "reasonable" in amount. The IRS knows children are costly, but also warns that these costs can vary greatly. An agent will often ask if there are alternatives to private tutors or one-on-one day care.

Unofficially...
A prior-filed judgment, lien, or garnishment often means that payment/debt has legal priority over the taxes. But if you are not currently paying on it, the agent will not allow it as "necessary" despite the priority.

Line 49 lists life insurance as a necessary expense. Only term policies are deemed necessary, and only for premiums the IRS does not consider excessive.

Line 50 allows an expense for "secured or legally perfected debts." This means judgments other people have against you, or other secured debts such as secured lines of credit. A secured charge card, or even a second mortgage, might fit here. Once again, the debt must meet the health, welfare, or production of income tests.

Finally, there are the "other expenses" (**line 51**) that life always throws your way, and here is where to list them. How about education? For your children, the IRS seems to draw the line at private schools. It's unclear whether the "extras" we all pay for schooling our children, even in public schools, are "necessary." You can certainly urge that these extras are necessary for your health and welfare, as well as that of the kids.

Adult education expenses are necessary if they help you produce income. Examples would be real estate courses for real estate brokers, or continuing professional education courses for others. Master's or doctorate program expenses to train you for a new profession or field would also seem to fit this test, but the IRS has not said so publicly. Expenses to care for handicapped children would normally be allowable, but be prepared to show that no public school or publicly available alternatives exist. What else might the IRS allow? It can permit "conditional" expenses if you will be able to pay in full within three years.

Accounting and legal fees. (Did you think the IRS would forget the poor, struggling tax professional trying to help you out of all this?) The IRS lets you pay your tax lawyer, accountant, or enrolled agent for representing you before the IRS. Other professional fees must meet the health and welfare or production of income tests.

Charitable contributions. The IRS sees these as unnecessary unless they promote your health and welfare or are required for your job.

Education. Private school and college tuition are viewed as not necessary. Possible exceptions include special schools for the handicapped.

Voluntary retirement payments. These are allowable if your taxes can be paid within three years.

Other. Almost any other expense can be considered conditional. These might include family debts, other unsecured debts, credit card payments above the minimums, life insurance premiums that have an investment component (for example, whole life or universal life), boats, second or third cars, and so on. That completes section V. You then sign and date the agreement (if the agent has asked for a signed agreement). Remember that the IRS can, in theory, still allow a conditional expense, as long as the numbers show you can pay the full tax within three years.

Make your financial statement the "quick and easy" one

Form 433-F is a simplified financial statement that is now routinely used by the Service Centers and other IRS personnel.

The first part calls for identifying information. Then, Box A asks for your accounts, including banks, S&Ls, brokerage accounts, and retirement accounts. Use a continuation sheet if necessary. Box B requests a listing of your real estate, including the value, equity, and monthly payment.

Bright Idea
Depending on your payment flexibility, if you can arrange for full payment (from your own funds or borrowing from friends) within three years, otherwise "unnecessary" expenses suddenly become "allowable."

Next, in Box C, come "other assets," including boats and RVs. Again, the liens are requested on these. Finally, in Box D come the credit cards.

Box E requests information on your gross pay, the deductions, net pay and "other income," the balance of which becomes your "available" income. The same is requested of your spouse. If only one spouse owes taxes, the IRS requests the information anyway. Then Box F lists your expenses. The IRS will fill in the National Standards line (normally allowing the maximum regardless of whether you put down a lower number). You should list all other expenses as the form requests.

Box G asks for your dependent information, and, most importantly, the amount you propose to pay each month. This is important. If it is possible for you to pay off your taxes within thirty six months, the IRS will look favorably on such a proposal, usually accepting it. If you can't, then list the amount you believe you can pay. This may or may not be in line with your "available income" minus your expenses.

Finally, sign and date the form. If you fill in this form in advance of any discussion with IRS personnel, you will always be better prepared and therefore better off in the end.

Revising the installment agreement

What if circumstances change? What if you default? If your income goes down or necessary expenses increase, call and write the IRS immediately. Ask for a lower installment agreement. Send whatever information the agent requests. If your income goes up or your expenses decline, you are not legally required to let the IRS know you can pay more. But you may want to. Paying more sometimes makes sense because of the high penalty and interest charges that accrue on your tax bill. In any event, the IRS has the right to review your agreement periodically, and often does.

The worst course is to default. Eighty percent of these agreements in fact default, with dire consequences. A default opens the door to full collection by the IRS, with its levy and seizure powers. True enough, you may reinstate a defaulted installment agreement at least once without much problem (at a cost of $24), but probably not more often than once. You get a small break on these defaults, courtesy of the 1996 Taxpayer Bill of Rights. The IRS must give you thirty days' warning before terminating or changing your installment agreement. The agency routinely did this even before the new law. In fact, the default notice invites you to reinstate the agreement.

If only one spouse owes taxes

It's quite common for only one of two spouses to owe taxes. If both list their income on Form 433-A as the IRS requires, it looks like the IRS is collecting from the spouse who does not owe taxes by making one earner pay part of the other's tax bill. Still, the Service requires listing "total household income" and expenses. The only exception occurs where you and your spouse handle and track expenses separately. Note that fact on Form 433-A and separate your income and expenses as best you can.

Installment agreements for businesses

Corporations, partnerships, and sole proprietors that owe back taxes (usually employment taxes) can also qualify for an installment agreement. The

Moneysaver
What if your installment amount will never pay the tax in full (within the statute of limitations)? The IRS may ask for a waiver. Such waivers are not routine but are now making a modest comeback. If the agent fails to request one, the unpaid tax debt will simply expire.

Bright Idea
If your tax bill results from an audit increase, one spouse may be eligible for the new innocent spouse, "separately calculated liability" law. See Chapter 8 for details.

process is usually much simpler than with an individual. The same number of forms must be completed, but there is less debate over which expenses are "necessary." A "C" corporation can owe income or payroll taxes. Partnerships and "S" corporations normally incur no income taxes since their profits pass through to the owners individually. But they can owe payroll taxes, as can an unincorporated proprietor. All these businesses must complete Form 433-B, the Collection Information Statement for Businesses.

The IRS looks at the business in the same way as it looks at an individual: what is the business's maximum ability to pay? But businesses in tax trouble are different from individuals in that they cannot always or easily sell assets to pay back taxes and still operate. Borrowing against business assets may also be hard. Moreover, a business often needs a cash flow cushion, especially when it has seasonal ups and downs. Many times, the IRS takes this into account; other times, you must argue long and hard for it.

Form 433-B asks for typical introductory information: the owners, partners, officers, and major shareholders. **Section I** then calls for the latest tax return information, bank accounts, bank credit available, safe-deposit boxes, real property, life insurance, and accounts and notes receivable. The IRS wants this information to see if the business can liquidate assets to pay the taxes, or for future reference if the IRS forces a liquidation. List the accounts and notes receivable, and in the "status" column indicate the extent to which they are collectible.

Section II of Form 433-B (lines 16 through 27) summarizes the assets and liabilities of the company. **Line 16** ("Cash on Hand") is simply the money in the cash register. **Lines 17 through 20** carry over information on bank accounts, receivables, life insurance, loan values, and real property from section I. **Lines 21 through 24** require the listing of all other assets, including vehicles, machinery, and merchandise inventory. List the market value, the debt, the equity, and the monthly payment. Also show the lienholder or noteholder, as well as the due dates for the debts.

Section III, the "Income and Expense Analysis," is the most important part of this form. **Lines 28 through 32** show the gross receipts of the business from all sources. **Lines 34 through 44** show all expenses. The IRS usually assumes that all business expenses are "necessary." But wave good-bye to personal expenses. For example, if the company pays for your personal Mercedes, that's not "necessary." The form also requires a time period for which the income and expenses are stated. Many businesses choose one year; others, six months. Select a range that is typical, especially if you have a seasonal business. And try to choose an ending date within two to three months before the date you sign the statement. If all of the income and expenses check out, the IRS totals them. The income minus the expenses is a net number that the Service will ask for every month.

Can the business afford it? Sometimes not, because of problems related to cash flow or seasonal fluctuations. Argue these points to the agent and ask for a lower amount for the installment agreement, possibly to be reconsidered when business picks up.

Watch Out!
The Service often pressures a business by investigating the officers and directors for their personal liability for payroll taxes. As a corporate officer, you may feel somewhat more motivated to find those past-due payroll taxes if the Service is reaching for your wallet at the same time.

Bright Idea
Comply with the terms of the installment agreement. As long as you do, the IRS will leave you alone. That in itself is worth a lot in terms of daily living and mental stability.

Rules of the road

Installment agreements can be like slow medieval torture, or they can be a real blessing. It depends on your particular circumstances, the total to be paid, and the amount of the monthly payment. The big advantage of such an agreement is the peace of mind it gives you. You know exactly how much you will have to pay, and when.

But whether you want an installment agreement or the IRS forces you into one, remember these rules:

- **Be prompt.** Don't miss deadlines. If you run up against a deadline, call and write the IRS in advance to request an extension. Give the IRS the data it wants on time.

- **Be truthful.** You are signing these financial statements under the penalties of perjury. You can go to jail for a false statement. You'll rarely get away with falsehoods anyway, since the IRS knows all the tricks. Be complete in the data you provide.

- **Don't take no for an answer.** Don't let one agent pressure you into an agreement you can't fulfill. Consider an appeal, or signing on for a short time, then appealing or asking for a reduced payment.

- **Request courtesy and respect.** And give the same to the agents you deal with. Try not to be intimidated by threats that the agency will immediately start collection if you don't agree to the number it wants.

- **Be patient.** These agreements can take weeks or months to negotiate, and years to pay.

- **Prepare for a tax lien filing.** If you owe more than $5,000 or you will take more than sixty days to pay in full, the IRS will likely file a Notice of Federal Tax Lien. Be prepared for this. If it will cause hardship, tell the agent why and ask for a delay. Under the 1996 Taxpayer Bill of Rights, you may request that the agent withdraw the notice of lien in exchange for an in-place installment agreement.

Just the facts

- Always look carefully at installment agreements as a way of paying your tax debt in full or in part.

- Work through the alternatives: doing nothing, offer in compromise, part payment followed by installment agreement, or bankruptcy.

- Be sure you know the effect on the statute of limitations of any choice you make; it can change with each choice.

- Be accurate with your expenses when negotiating an installment agreement.

- It's usually in your best interest to get the lowest possible monthly payment to avoid default. You can always "voluntarily" pay more.

- Don't hesitate to appeal an unfavorable decision on your installment agreement request.

GET THE SCOOP ON...
Myths, lies, and truths about taxes
in bankruptcy ▪ How a bankruptcy case works ▪
Discharging your taxes through Chapter 7 ▪
Managing your tax debt in Chapters 11 and 13

The Bankruptcy Alternative

Chapter 13

C an bankruptcy solve your tax problem? Yes, possibly. But there are more myths, errors, and misconceptions about managing taxes through bankruptcy than there are politicians making election-year promises to lower your taxes. Bankruptcy is a detailed and complex subject, one not for the fainthearted or the uncounseled. You need an experienced bankruptcy lawyer to advise you on whether, when, and how to file a bankruptcy petition, and no one chapter can hope to cover the subject entirely. Undaunted, this chapter will discuss one aspect of bankruptcy: whether it makes sense for you to consider bankruptcy as a way of handling all or part of your taxes.

Bankruptcy fiction and fable

Let's start by looking at the most common myths or misconceptions about taxes in bankruptcy.

1. "Taxes aren't normal debts. You can never discharge a tax in bankruptcy." This misconception centers on the bankruptcy "discharge," the

Watch Out!
While the IRS
can't seize assets
after you file for
bankruptcy
(without court
permission), it
can still audit a
return and send
a deficiency
notice.

technical term for legal relief of a debt through bankruptcy. Most normal debts are "dischargeable" by the simple act of filing a petition under Chapter 7, the liquidation chapter of the Bankruptcy Code. If this myth were true, there would be no need to learn about the relation between bankruptcy and tax debt, because the former would not affect the latter. In fact, however, taxpayers discharge millions of dollars of taxes in bankruptcy every year.

2. "I can always discharge my taxes in bankruptcy—just file and forget." Myth #1 states that taxes are **never** dischargeable; this myth states that taxes are always dischargeable. This too as false. The technical and detailed bankruptcy rules relating to taxes are monuments to poor writing and confusing syntax. Yes, some types of taxes are dischargeable in some cases; others never are. Even if a tax possibly qualifies for discharge, the timing and detail can trip you up.

3. "If I file for bankruptcy, I'll lose everything." There is an element of truth to this myth: some bankruptcies do require you (or a trustee) to sell your assets, but other types of bankruptcies assume precisely the reverse: they anticipate you will not sell but will rehabilitate yourself by negotiating your way out of burdensome debt, including tax debt. This protocol can be applied to tax debts. The myth is: "If I file for bankruptcy, the IRS will get everything, including my home and pension." Not so. In fact, in many cases, the IRS gets very little on its tax claim. Sometimes you can even save a pension or a home in the aftermath of a bankruptcy.

These are just some of the common misconceptions that surround taxes in bankruptcy. The good news is this: Bankruptcy is a powerful, effective instrument you can often use to manage an otherwise impossible tax collection problem. It always stops the IRS in its tracks for at least some period of time, giving you much-needed breathing room. It sometimes stops the IRS completely and forever.

The bad news is that you won't always be able to discharge your taxes. Moreover, regardless of what happens with your taxes, bankruptcy can also trigger other financial problems, and a bankruptcy on your credit record is like a scarlet letter B you wear for years (usually about seven years).

How bankruptcies work

Individuals and businesses normally file one of three types of bankruptcies: Chapter 7, Chapter 11, or Chapter 13. In a Chapter 7 case, you throw in the towel: it's a complete liquidation. A court-appointed trustee takes title to your assets, sells them, and pays the creditors with the proceeds. If you choose Chapter 7, you're cleaned out; but in return, you get a fresh start from your debts, paid or not. At least, that's what Chapter 7 is supposed to do. It doesn't *always* work out that way, especially for taxes.

Chapter 11 and Chapter 13 are the converse of Chapter 7. They are not liquidations but rehabilitations—or, in the language of the Bankruptcy Code, *reorganizations*. Both of these chapters assume that you intend to continue on in business (whether as a corporation, partnership, proprietor, or wage earner), that you want to compromise on some of your debts and stretch out others, but that you intend to pay something on your debts without liquidating all of your assets.

Unofficially...
More than 1 million personal bankruptcies were filed in 1997; the IRS had a tax claim in about one-third of these cases.

Bright Idea
While filing a bankruptcy petition puts the IRS's creditors' collection activities on hold, you have to let them know you have filed! The best way is a phone call to (800)829-1040. You (or your lawyer) can also alert the local IRS collection office, or the Office of Special Procedures.

No matter which chapter you use, when you file a petition in bankruptcy, the mere act of filing puts an immediate and automatic stop to all your creditors' collection efforts. That includes everyone from the phone company to credit card companies to the IRS. From the instant you file, the IRS and other creditors are forbidden from seizing assets, filing liens, making assessments, and taking most other creditor-type actions. They know this rule and obey it in most cases. If they don't, they can be—and are—held in contempt of court.

Special rules allow the IRS to perform a few tax-related actions even after a bankruptcy filing. For instance, it may mail a Notice of Deficiency (see Chapter 15), investigate some claims, and conduct some audits. But if you are really afraid for your assets and you fear the IRS is about to lower the boom, any bankruptcy filing will stop collection, at least for the pendency of the case. This "automatic stay" of creditors' attempts to collect is the strongest weapon you have as a taxpayer. In fact, it's usually the *only* legal weapon *you* have the power to exercise.

In other cases, when the IRS forbears from collecting against you, it's because the agency chose to forbear—its decision, not yours. So, filing for bankruptcy calls a big "time out" to the creditor versus debtor contest. You have breathing room, time to think, time to plan. When taxes are part of the bankruptcy filing, you also need to plan before you file, because the timing of bankruptcy as an instrument for handling your tax problem is absolutely critical.

Discharging taxes in bankruptcy

Only a few types of taxes are dischargeable under any circumstances, but two are big ones: federal and state income taxes. Also dischargeable are gross receipts taxes and certain excise taxes. Some taxes are never dischargeable, such as employment taxes, Trust Fund Recovery Penalty taxes (see Chapter 6), and others. To discharge a federal or state income tax, you must meet certain strict rules:

1. The bankruptcy petition must be filed more than three years after the due date of the tax return involved. For example, if you filed your return on April 15, 1996 (for 1995), you must file the bankruptcy petition on or after April 16, 1999. If you went on extension to file, measure the three years from the extended date—not the date you actually filed, but the true extended date. In one court case, for example, a taxpayer extended his filing date to October 15, 1990 (for 1989), and filed his bankruptcy petition on October 10, 1993, five days too soon. He consequently missed the three-year rule and could not get a discharge.

2. The second rule is: If your return was filed late, file the bankruptcy petition more than two years after you actually filed your return. Again, this rule is ironclad: either you meet it or you don't. If you are planning for this rule, it's usually wise to find out from the IRS when it received your return so you don't get into a dispute as to when you actually sent it.

3. File the bankruptcy petition more than 240 days after the IRS's assessment of the taxes you want to discharge. For example, suppose Nina Nopay files her 1995 tax return on April 15, 1996. She owes $10,000 on the return, which the IRS assesses against her on April 17, 1996. Nina must wait until December 16, 1996 (the 241st day after the assessment) to file her petition.

Watch Out!
Watch out for offers in compromise. If you file one, the 240-day time period is suspended while the offer is being considered, plus thirty days.

Unofficially...
The bankruptcy estate is an artificial entity, something like a trust in which you might put assets. When you file a Chapter 7 petition, it is created automatically.

Now, let's say she files on December 16 but the IRS audits her return on December 18, 1996, and finds she owes another $5,000. Nina's discharge won't extend to the new $5,000 bill.

4. You cannot have evaded your taxes. That means you can't have filed a fraudulent return or evaded the payment of the taxes.

5. You cannot discharge a tax that is "still assessable" when you file. For example, if your return is under examination and the IRS proposes more taxes, those taxes can't be discharged (see the "Nina Nopay" example, above).

But the taxes you reported on the return are dischargeable if you meet the other rules described above. Penalties and interest can also be dischargeable, though not always. A good rule of thumb is: A late-filing, late-payment, or negligence penalty (the most common penalties the IRS imposes) is dischargeable if the underlying tax is dischargeable. Even if this is not the case, the penalty is dischargeable if it relates to conduct that is more than three years old.

For example, in 1990, Thaddeus Thumbnose committed civil tax fraud by failing to include $100,000 in gross income on his tax return. He filed the return promptly on April 15, 1991. The IRS caught him in 1993 and assessed $30,000 in tax and a $22,500 civil fraud penalty (75 percent). Thaddeus filed for Chapter 7 (liquidating bankruptcy) on April 16, 1994. The taxes were not dischargeable because of the tax fraud, but the fraud penalty was dischargeable because Thaddeus committed the fraud more than three years before he filed his bankruptcy petition.

Getting the discharge from taxes

Here's how a discharge from taxes works. Let's say you have satisfied all the rules and have carefully planned for your Chapter 7 liquidating bankruptcy. You then file your Chapter 7 petition. A "bankruptcy estate" springs into being automatically when you file the petition. In a Chapter 7 case, by law everything you own (with a few exceptions) automatically becomes part of this bankruptcy estate. The non-exempt assets are not yours anymore; they belong to the estate.

A trustee is assigned to handle your case. The trustee's job is to sell any assets that might raise cash, distribute these to your creditors, and close the estate. The trustee may decide that some assets can't be sold for cash, or would not yield enough after paying off the pre-bankruptcy liens. The trustee will return ("abandon") such assets to you. The trustee might also abandon a home if it has no equity. (All states also have a homestead exemption that varies in amount.)

What about the taxes? The IRS is often at the top of the food chain in bankruptcies. It may get paid first, or it might be paid after other, prior secured creditors. But if there's not enough to go around, the unpaid taxes are discharged by law. If the IRS has filed a notice of lien, you still get the discharge of dischargeable taxes, but the lien remains attached to the assets in your bankruptcy estate. Usually, the bankruptcy court will not specifically rule that your taxes (or any debt) have been discharged. It will simply grant a "general discharge," a one-page document. That document is your legal "fresh start" as to any debt that was legally dischargeable, including taxes.

The IRS then decides, on its own, whether your particular taxes have in fact been discharged. The IRS office that handles bankruptcy cases is the "Special Procedures Section." When you file your case, this office gets the case file and looks over the assessments, the due dates of the returns, the liens on file, and the rules described above. If you meet all the rules, in almost every case the agent will note the file for discharge and close it. You will never hear from them again. Your account in the IRS computers will be adjusted to "zero" tax for each tax year involved.

Sometimes the IRS concludes that your taxes are not dischargeable, or the computer makes a mistake and continues to try to collect against you. Then you have to convince the agency that it made a computer mistake (if that is what it was), or that your taxes were in fact legally discharged. If worse comes to worst, you can always reopen your bankruptcy and ask the bankruptcy court to declare formally that your taxes have been discharged.

How Chapter 11 and Chapter 13 work

Since these are not liquidations but rehabilitations, you handle taxes a little differently. In both types of cases, you propose a "plan of reorganization." This is a written plan that tells the court how much you intend to pay all of your creditors. As with any type of bankruptcy, in Chapters 11 and 13 you file your petition and make a complete statement of assets and liabilities. Then, you propose a plan to pay your debts.

In such a plan, some debts are more "equal" than others. At the top of the heap in any bankruptcy are secured creditors.

These are creditors who have a valid, perfected lien against one or more of your assets. A good example would be the bank that loaned you money for your home mortgage. Another might be a receivables financier for a business. The IRS becomes a secured creditor in a bankruptcy whenever it files a Notice of Federal Tax Lien. As Chapter 3 explains, that Notice of Federal Tax Lien ties up all your property and rights to property, wherever located. As against real estate, the lien is valid if it is filed in the place required by state law, usually the county land records. When it is filed, all the equity in your property is tied up by this federal tax lien.

If the agency has not filed a notice of lien, the taxes are "unsecured." They may be "priority" taxes or "general unsecured" taxes, the cutoff being whether they are and whether they met the discharge rules described earlier in this chapter. Priority taxes must also be paid in full according to the plan, unless the IRS compromises them. General unsecured taxes have the same low standing as any other unsecured debt. You must propose a plan that will pay as much or more as would be received if the case were a Chapter 7 liquidation.

Chapter 13 plans are intended for wage earners and other persons with periodic income. Basically, you propose a plan to pay your priority taxes (and other debts) over three years according to the rules of the Bankruptcy Code. Courts can approve plans that stretch an additional two years. Once you are finished with your plan payments, that's it. You receive a discharge from all the debts that are "provided for" in the plan. In most cases, the tax debts are all provided for because the IRS has filed a proof of claim in your case. But that's not universally true. Sometimes it fails to file a proof of claim, often losing its claim because of this failure.

Chapter 13 plans are specifically geared toward

Unofficially...
Strictly speaking, secured creditors are not first in the pecking order of who gets paid. Before them, the lawyers draw their fee.

Moneysaver
Traditionally, some bankruptcy courts are pro-debtor, though don't count on any particular bias in your favor from the bankruptcy judge simply because you have come to her for help. Still, the bankruptcy courts are open and available to adjudicate your tax disputes in most cases.

paying your debts out of future income. Moreover, you can be very flexible in designing a Chapter 13 plan (or Chapter 11 plan). Payments must start "as soon as practicable" after confirmation of the plan, but nothing in the bankruptcy code says they have to be equal. So, debtors have designed plans that deferred some debts for awhile, and paid others that were in arrears. The most common example is a mortgage in arrears. Even tax debts can be deferred until later years this way. The IRS doesn't like it, and it often opposes these postponements, arguing that it should be paid equally and evenly along with everyone else. But the courts are lenient about approving Chapter 13 plans that defer some types of creditors, including the IRS.

What if things don't work out, and you lose your job or suffer other "hardship" during the years you had operated under your confirmed Chapter 13 plan? You can apply for a hardship discharge. The result? You get your discharge even though you have not paid for the full three to five years.

The bankruptcy laws can be important tools in other respects as well. Let's say you dispute a tax, such as an income tax or even the Trust Fund Recovery Penalty. The bankruptcy courts have wide discretion to try many types of tax cases. You don't have to go to Tax Court or federal district court if you think you can do as well or better in bankruptcy court.

To be eligible for Chapter 13, you must have regular income, unsecured debts of less than $250,000, and secured debts of less than $750,000. Wage earners, pensioners, sole proprietors, and other types of earners are eligible to file for Chapter 13. Chapter 13 plans are simpler than those in Chapter 11, and less expensive in terms of professional fees. They have other advantages over Chapters 7 and 11 that your bankruptcy attorney can review with you.

Putting these concepts into practice

Always seek professional help when planning for a bankruptcy. A bankruptcy attorney, especially one familiar with the tax rules, should plan your bankruptcy, file it, and advise you as it goes along. Preplanning is absolutely essential: the casebooks are littered with the financial corpses of people who thought they were getting a fresh start from their taxes by filing for bankruptcy, only to awaken the next day to tax liens and levies. But if you plan it well, a bankruptcy can be a satisfactory solution to your tax problems, either through discharge or reorganization.

Just the facts

- Be aware of the opportunities bankruptcies afford to manage your tax debts.

- Never file for bankruptcy without full evaluation of the effects on your taxes, your other debts, and your credit.

- Use Chapter 7 to discharge income taxes, and 11 or 13 to pay them over time.

GET THE SCOOP ON...
Count'em—four taxpayer bills of rights ▪ What's
useful and what's not ▪ The new "superman" of
taxes—the National Taxpayer Advocate ▪ IRS
emergency? File "911"

The Problem Resolution Program and the Taxpayer Bills of Rights

I f you've developed a headache from reading
how one-sided the balance of power is between
you and the IRS, you are not alone. In fact, in an
agency with so much legal power, it's almost
inevitable that there will be bureaucratic slip-ups,
red-tape snafus, and abuses of power: some merely
negligent, others occasionally deliberate.

The last decade has seen the mantle of secrecy
lifted from the IRS, and also from the abuses,
intended or not, that inevitably accompany the exercise of the IRS's wide-ranging authority. The result
has been numerous administrative changes and four
"Taxpayer Bills of Rights," though they go by various
names. There likely will be more.

The thrust of these statutes, and all of the administrative changes, has been to give you, the taxpayer,
a true ally within the IRS and to set clear, mandated,
enforceable standards by which the agency must

Chapter 14

321

operate. This chapter will guide you through these extraordinarily helpful ways of dealing with the IRS when all else seems to fail.

"Help!"—the Problem Resolution Program

In recent times, the Swedish word *ombudsman* has come into the English language. The ombudsman has a license to seek out and destroy bureaucratic red tape, snafus, and other incomprehensible messes wherever they existed in government agencies. Many private corporations now use ombudsmen, too. The federal and state governments have them aplenty.

The IRS has had an ombudsman for twenty years. It was even in the name—the Office of Ombudsman, changed in 1996 to the Office of Taxpayer Advocate. The National Ombudsman had charge of thirty-three suboffices, one in each of the IRS's districts around the country. (See appendix B for a list of them.) This local branch, formerly called the Problem Resolution Office (PRO) and now the Office of Taxpayer Advocate (OTA), exists for one purpose: to untangle the mess you are in because some part of the IRS has shut the steel trap of bureaucracy on you. The Office of Taxpayer Advocate's job description includes taking your side over the IRS's when the bureaucracy overwhelms you. If that means the IRS will get less money, so be it.

In 1988, Congress gave the old Problem Resolution Office a huge new club to subdue the bureaucracy: the Taxpayer Assistance Order. This part of the OTA's authority is so important that it can be viewed as a distinct service. That is, the OTA handles

- applications for taxpayer assistance orders,

- all other bureaucratic snafus.

In collection trouble? File "911"

When you have the IRS blues, when collection officers threaten your business, when you just can't pay but the revenue officer insists on it despite the hardship it will create, the District Taxpayer Advocate (DTA) can come to the rescue. DTAs have wide authority to intervene and stop all collection action when you file an *Application for a Taxpayer Assistance Order.*

This halt is usually short, but it gives you a chance to work things out with the Collection Division. The OTAs in fact grant some measure of relief in about 75 percent of all cases.

Relief from a too-harsh tax collector is spelled *Form 911.* Yes, it is true, they actually have Form 911, intentionally numbered to remind you of the emergency phone line, for situations of "significant hardship" in the collection of taxes. Form 911 is a one-page form in which you tell the IRS what hardship the collection officer is causing or threatening and the relief you want.

Under the 1998 changes, the law authorizes the DTA to intervene when it determines that you are about to suffer or are suffering a significant hardship as a result of the manner in which the Internal Revenue laws are being administered. For this purpose, the law defines *significant hardship* to include:

- An immediate threat of adverse action,

- A delay of more than thirty days in resolving taxpayer account problems,

- The incurring by the taxpayer of significant costs if relief is not granted (including professional fees), or

- Irreparable injury to, or a long-term adverse impact on, the taxpayer if relief is not granted.

Unofficially...
The 1998 IRS tax reform act changed the name "Problem Resolution Office" to the "Office of Taxpayer Advocate." The name change was deliberate, and part of a massive effort to make the IRS more user-friendly. In fiscal 1996 the OTA received more than 282,000 cases.

The Application for a Taxpayer Assistance Order is a legal remedy *you* can invoke, reserved for true collection emergencies where you've tried your best through the normal channels.

For example, Roger and Rosetta have been married for twenty-five years. For the last three years, Roger has been clinically depressed, in and out of hospitals, on and off medications. He also has terminal cancer. As a result, he did not file tax returns for those three years. The IRS filed substitute returns for each year and assessed the taxes. Then it levied on the couple's bank account for a much larger amount than they actually owed. They needed time while another branch of the service considered their request for abatement of tax and penalty. They filed Form 911, claiming undue hardship. The Problem Resolution Office moved to release the levy. But it also ensured that Roger and Rosetta filed tax returns of their own.

As a second example, suppose you have a restaurant that is behind on payroll taxes for six months. It's now summer, the slow season. You know you can catch up in the fall, but cash is even tighter now than usual. The revenue officer demands immediate payment and threatens to close your business or seize your bank accounts. Suppliers may get wind of this. Customers may flee, and the whole enterprise may come crashing down. You file Form 911, asking for a delay of three months on collection of the back taxes while you stay current on present taxes. The DTA has the authority to grant your request over the opposition of the Collection Division.

As a third example, suppose you owe $10,000 in back taxes on last year's return. The Automated Collection System representative calls you. She is abusive and threatening. She demands you stay on the phone, even after you ask for a time-out to consult a professional. She demands information from you upon penalty of immediate collection. After you hang up, you are nervous and shaky. You file Form 911. The DTA should again intervene to help get you courteous treatment and a reasonable time to respond.

The "hardship" the DTAs look for in this type of case must be "significant," a standard that leaves room for discretion. This means that they won't necessarily intervene simply because you are upset at the revenue officer—after all, her job is to get the money, not to make you feel good. But the revenue officer crosses the line if, for instance, she threatens to deprive you of the money you need for necessary living expenses, such as rent, utilities, and groceries.

Hardship may be undue if, without giving you a fair chance to pay, she threatens to file a Notice of Federal Tax Lien, if that would unnecessarily ruin your credit, cause a default on loans, or force a bankruptcy. The revenue officer also could cross the hardship line by threatening to levy your business or personal accounts, depriving you of the necessary cash flow to continue, in cases when you could easily pay in large installments.

The DTA officer will also look at every category of necessary living expenses to determine whether the collection action threatens those necessities. This includes food, clothing, housing, medical supplies, utilities, and even education. She will take notice if the collection action will threaten your job or business, if the action is imminent, even if you become "so overwhelmed" or overcome by the pressure from the revenue officer that you begin crying.

Watch Out!
An Application for a Taxpayer Assistance Order has only one drawback. It suspends the period of limitations on collection for the time the application is pending. Usually that suspension is very short, however, and well worth it, especially if you get the relief you want.

Timesaver
In your application for a TAO, you must invoke one or more of the four standards mentioned above. Show exactly how the threat of adverse action is immediate, or why you will suffer irreparable injury or other negative effects as a result of a levy or threatened seizure.

In theory, she is not supposed to "blame" you if you are the one whose intransigence or fault caused the problem. In practice, DTA officers are human beings; they take that into account.

How to file 911

You can get the form from any local IRS office, download it from the IRS's address on the Internet (see Chapter 17), or obtain a copy from many libraries. You can even call the local IRS office, whose representative will send or fax you a copy. Also, you may get the form by dialing (800)TAX-FORM.

Before you file Form 911, you are required to exhaust at least one level of review. So if the revenue officer was nasty to you or threatened to levy your business accounts, appeal to her immediate boss, the Group Manager. This is usually a waste of time; the boss will nearly always back up her revenue officer. In some IRS districts, you must make one more appeal, to the Branch Chief. All of this takes time, but it can be done by phone. Take notes on all the calls you make.

If hours count, call the Group Manager directly, or ask the revenue officer if she has pre-cleared the levy, lien, or other seizure action with her group manager (as the 1998 law requires). If so, you have "exhausted" your appeal responsibilities, and you can now go to the DTA. If the Group Manager is absent, ask for the Acting Group Manager. If that person is unavailable, immediately call the District Taxpayer Advocate and explain that the internal appeal was futile because everyone was absent or unavailable. That is usually enough to give jurisdiction. They will see you have tried to work it out, but the bureaucracy stood in the way.

Once the DTA will listen, the next step is to call, mail, or fax your Application for Taxpayer Assistance Order to the Office of Taxpayer Advocate.

Most of the form is self-explanatory. The most critical sections are Blocks 12 and 13, though all parts must be completed. Block 12 asks what the problem is. Be clear, concise, and detailed. State facts, not opinions. Tell what the revenue officer did or threatened to do. Start with a summary paragraph, such as, "The revenue officer is threatening to levy on my retirement account when I need this money·for the care of my elderly parents, who are otherwise without support." Then start a new paragraph. Begin at the beginning and tell what happened.

Your story need not be more than one typewritten page, though many good applications are longer. Sacrifice no detail, but do not ramble. This is not the place to state your candid opinion of the revenue officer or to editorialize about the tax system. Just state what she did or is threatening to do that you believe to be unduly harsh.

In Block 13, tell the Taxpayer Advocate precisely what relief you want. Do you want the Collection Division to stop collection forever? For a time? Do you want the revenue officer to release or withdraw a lien? To release a levy?

Do not be concerned about legalisms or fancy language. State in plain English what you want the DTA to do. If the DTA officer accepts the application, she immediately calls the revenue officer's Group Manager and tells her to stop everything. This halt-in-place is like a bolt of lightning: it strikes fast and hard, but it lasts for only a short time, usually no more than forty-eight hours. It gives you, the DTA, and the Collection Division time to work things out.

Bright Idea
You can file the TAO application by phone, but you're usually better off doing it in writing, so they have the full story.

Unofficially...
Under the 1998 tax reform act, a Taxpayer Assistance Order may require the IRS to release property that has been levied upon or to cease any action, or refrain from taking any action, relating to collection, bankruptcy, discovery of liability, or any other provision of law that the Office of Taxpayer Advocate may describe.

At this point, the Office of Taxpayer Advocate becomes a mediator. Experience shows that this mediation helps in many cases, though not all. In some IRS districts, the officers interpret "significant hardship" very narrowly, almost always taking the side of the revenue officer. So be careful to use this weapon sparingly. At the end of the process, with any luck you will have worked out a livable deal with the Collection Division. If not, there is nothing more the DTA can do for you, and you are on your own once again.

This Application for Taxpayer Assistance Order is a fantastic weapon at your command when it is truly merited. Everyone hopes that things never get that hot between you and the Collection Division, but it happens.

Other red-tape issues

The Office of Taxpayer Advocate also helps you slash red tape in every other area where bureaucracy threatens strangulation. By and large, the DTAs do this extremely well. The types of problems and snafus they encounter are dizzying in their variety. After all, the IRS is so big and complex that things can go wrong almost anywhere. And once a problem occurs, it's hard to fix. But the majority of these cases fall into several classes.

- The first is your **tax refund**. The IRS usually sends your refund within six weeks after you file your return, faster if you file electronically. But sometimes refunds are lost or delayed. Other times, when you file a separate claim for refund after your return has been filed, the claim can get lost. If you get no action after your second request, or thirty days pass, the DTA has jurisdiction to help.

■ Second, if you make any other **request for information** to the IRS and forty-five days pass without action, it's now a job for the DTA. Many
people do not realize they can ask for help in
virtually any procedural IRS matter after this
forty-five-day period. Often they make call after
frustrating call through normal channels, or
write letter after unanswered letter, getting
nowhere for months or years at a time.

■ Third, if you receive two collection notices from
the Automated Collection System, or **two other
notices** that you owe taxes from an IRS Service
Center, and you answer them but the Service
fails to respond to you, the DTA can take action.
It can stop the notices, conduct a "prayer session" with the collection agent who is harassing
you, and take other helpful action. Beyond
these examples, the DTA can help with a wide
variety of bureaucratic problems. These are too
varied to be described, so recall the basic rule:
When all else fails, call the Taxpayer Advocate.
In fact, call them before all else fails; they will
help you through the worst of IRS gridlock.

The Taxpayer Bills of Rights

A popular myth has pervaded the country for years:
People have few if any rights against the IRS. In fact,
you have plenty of rights. The myth persists because
the IRS's powers sometimes seem arbitrary and
overwhelming. Other times people may not appreciate the powers, legal rights, and procedures they
can exercise to defend themselves. Congress tried to
help in 1988 by passing the first Taxpayer Bill of
Rights, and three similar bills after that.

Unofficially...
The name "Tax-
payer Bill of
Rights" does a
disservice to the
real Bill of
Rights, the first
ten amendments
to the Constitu-
tion. The Taxpay-
er Bill of Rights
does not define
your relationship
to the federal
government or
the IRS.

That law had a few useful features (in particular,
the Taxpayer Assistance Order, described above). To
supplement the 1988 act, in 1996 Congress enacted
the second Taxpayer Bill of Rights. The 1997 Taxpayer Relief Act and the IRS Restructuring and
Reform Act of 1998 added further important rights
to the list of weapons you can use to protect yourself
against an overzealous IRS.

Let's review these "Bills of Rights" as a group.

When you are audited

You have four rights that apply to the IRS audit.

1. **Right to an explanation.** The IRS must explain
    its audit procedures and findings in simple,
    nontechnical language. This right applies to the
    taxes and penalties it proposes and to your audit
    and appeal rights. By and large, the Service suc-
    ceeds in this obligation. True enough, audit
    notices can sometimes be confusing. But gener-
    ally, the IRS's notices are now more clear, sim-
    ple, understandable, and complete than ever
    before.

2. **Right to interest abatement.** The Service can
    also abate interest if it unreasonably delays your
    case. Let's say the IRS concludes you owe $1,000
    after an audit. What if they don't send a bill for
    four months? For many years, the Service has
    been able to abate interest if it made such a
    "ministerial" error. With the 1996 Act, the
    Agency can also abate interest if it makes a
    "managerial" error, that is, if one of its agents or
    managers unreasonably delays a computation or
    a bill. On top of that, if the Service refuses your
    request for abatement, you can now take the
    IRS to court. Before the 1996 Act, no one could

judge the IRS but itself. But now, if your case is strong enough for interest abatement, you can ask the United States Tax Court for an independent ruling.

3. **Right to abate penalty and interest if you rely on the IRS.** The IRS is required to abate tax and penalty if you reasonably relied on advice from the IRS in preparing an item on your return. Of course, there are several catches. The advice has to be in writing (not verbal). The IRS agent has to have acted in his official capacity (informal advice doesn't count). And you must have given adequate and accurate information to the IRS about your transaction. If the tax and penalty are abated, the computers will automatically abate all of the associated interest.

4. **Right to tape record interview.** It's hard to believe anyone actually uses this right, and for the most part it's unnecessary and counterproductive. Congress put it in the law for that occasional audit where the revenue agent or tax auditor truly misunderstands your position or misquotes it (either deliberately or inadvertently). As a matter of strategy, it is normally unwise to record an interview with an IRS agent. Think how you would feel in a similar situation. Recording hardens attitudes, stiffens and formalizes communication, and therefore undermines your ability to get the best result. The IRS has no statistics on how many people ask to record interviews.

Bright Idea
Don't hesitate to take your case to the United States Tax Court. Its judges are very independent. They call cases as they see them.

Timesaver
Refer to IRS Pub-
lication No. 1,
"Your Rights as a
Taxpayer," for a
great deal of
information in a
succinct form. If
you follow its
advice and exer-
cise all your
rights, you will
rarely have an
IRS problem you
cannot solve.

When the IRS comes to collect your taxes

The next set of rights apply to the IRS's attempt to collect taxes from you.

Right to a clear explanation

The IRS must give you a clear and complete explanation of its enforcement procedures and your rights against them. Its vehicle is Publication No. 1 , "Your Rights as a Taxpayer." This is an excellent publication, clearly written, fair, and informative.

The explanation of rights in Publication No. 1 covers four topics:

1. Your rights and the IRS's duties in an audit,

2. Appeal rights within the IRS and to the courts,

3. Procedures for filing refund claims and taxpayer complaints,

4. The IRS's enforcement powers to collect a tax that is past due.

The publication explains the right to negotiate with the revenue officer, the availability of an appeal to her boss, the right to legal and accounting representation, the right to appeal within the IRS, and your right to contest some matters in court. The IRS sends this flyer with almost every collection notice, and if you read nothing else, you should read this publication.

Installment agreement

The IRS has explicit legal authority to let you pay your taxes in installments. With one exception, it's not a right—you cannot force the IRS to accept such an agreement—but at least the authority is now clearly part of the law. In fact, the Service enters into more than a million installment agreements every year.

The 1998 tax reform act contains a limited *right to demand an installment agreement*. The IRS is required to grant one if you owe no more than $10,000 and, in the preceding five years, you didn't fail to file a return or fail to pay a tax, or enter into another installment agreement. Also, you must agree to pay the full liability within three years and be tax compliant for the entire time. Chapter 12 tells you how and when to ask for one, and how to negotiate a livable payment plan.

The 1996 Taxpayer Bill of Rights requires the IRS to notify you thirty days before terminating your installment agreement. The agency had already come around to doing this anyway, but now the law requires it. The Service can end an installment agreement if you don't pay, if the information on which you based the agreement turns out to be wrong, or if you strike it rich and the IRS thinks you can pay more. Now, this thirty-day window gives you a chance to renegotiate.

Bright Idea
You can ask for an "independent" review of the termination of your installment agreement. So far, however, the Service has not established any review procedure.

Right to pre-levy thirty-day cooling-off period

By law, the IRS has to tell you in advance that it is about to seize your assets. Ten days used to be all the notice it had to give; now it's thirty days. That may not sound like a lot, but it can make a big difference if you are moving fast to convince the IRS to lift a wage or other levy.

The 1998 IRS reform act added an extremely important right: the **right to a pre-levy** hearing to determine whether the levy should be issued. All it takes is a letter to the agent and the Office of Appeals demanding the right to a hearing. In fact, IRS levy notices must now advise you of this right. You are entitled to one hearing for each tax period,

Unofficially...
The 1996 Taxpayer Bill of Rights shifted the burden to the IRS to show that its position in your case was "substantially justified." This provision will likely result in more awards to taxpayers of their attorneys' fees.

although the law encourages consolidation of such hearings. At the hearing, you may raise the following issues:

- Appropriate spousal defenses (such as "innocent spouse")
- Challenges to the appropriateness of collection actions
- Offers of collection alternatives, including posting a bond, substituting other assets, an installment agreement, or an offer in compromise
- Whether the tax liability is correct

Moreover, the IRS is required to withhold levy action while that hearing is pending, and, if you lose, you can ask the Tax Court to review the decision (if the underlying liability is in dispute). The hold on collection stays in place if the underlying tax liability is in dispute. Of course, this dispute must be in good faith.

Right to post-lien notice hearing
When the IRS files a Notice of Lien, you will now have a right, within thirty days after the filing, to request a hearing on the Notice of Lien. The hearing is similar to the pre-levy hearing. The remedies available include withdrawing the Notice of Lien.

When you sue the IRS
Six additional rights apply to lawsuits against the IRS.

Right to attorneys' fees and other costs
If you beat the IRS in court, you can sometimes win attorneys' fees, accountants' fees, and other costs and fees. Naturally, the IRS fights these attorneys' fee requests with all the resources at its disposal. So it's hard to win. However, experience shows that

courts award attorneys' fees in about one-third of cases that the taxpayer wins.

Right to sue for damages

If the IRS abuses its authority by publicly disclosing information about you it should not, failing to release a lien when it should, or otherwise not following the collection laws, you now can sue for damages. Most of these suits are thrown out, but a few succeed. To win, you have to show the IRS agent acted recklessly or intentionally, or negligently outside the law. Also, you can now recover your actual, direct economic damages, or $1,000,000, whichever is less (there is a $100,000 limit for negligence).

You normally have to bring your claim to the IRS first, and you must try to minimize your damages. If you sue, the limitations period is two years after the IRS's violation, whether you knew of it or not. These are high hurdles to jump, so it's no wonder most of these suits fail. Still, everyone needs to know of this right for the rare case where the IRS greatly oversteps its authority.

Right to representation

You have the right to ask a tax practitioner or other representative to do battle on your behalf with the IRS. It can be a lawyer, accountant, enrolled agent, enrolled actuary, or other type of representative. Chapter 2 discusses these IRS-qualified representatives in detail. People were aware of this right even before these recent laws, but sometimes the IRS worked around the representative. Either it ignored her or required the taxpayer personally to attend one or more meetings with the IRS agent. Now the agent can require that you attend an interview only by issuing an administrative summons.

Bright Idea
Some banks
understand this
twenty-one day
wait rule; others
do not. Call your
bank to be sure
it understands
how the levy is
supposed
to work.

This rejuvenated right to representation has made agents more respectful of taxpayer representatives, and the agents generally allow the full range of representation the law permits and encourages.

Right to twenty-one-day wait

Banks must wait twenty-one days after receiving an IRS levy before sending the money. They used to jump the gun all the time, often even before you knew a levy had been served. As a courtesy, many banks now notify you if an IRS levy or other garnishment or judgment is served, but the law does not require this. So when you learn of a bank levy, you have twenty-one days to try to get the levy released. This doesn't mean your account is useless, because, in theory, any money you deposit after the levy is served is not subject to it.

The IRS must also now send you simple, nontechnical explanations of how the levy works. The Service routinely does this. Its explanation is clear and concise.

Right to quick appeal for some property seizures

Sometimes the IRS will seize a business to stop the business from bleeding away payroll taxes or simply to collect the past-due taxes. If property is essential to your trade or business, the IRS must grant an accelerated appeal to determine whether the levy should be released.

It is hard to think of any business property as unessential, but that is the way the new rule reads. Appeals, even quick ones, are not often successful. Where they are, the IRS can extract major concessions or big payments in exchange for releasing the property. In other words, this provision of the taxpayer bill of rights does not give you quick relief; it just gives you a quick appeal. The only way you can force the IRS to give back your business property is by filing for bankruptcy. (See Chapter 13.)

In addition, the 1998 new law requires that the seizure of business assets must be pre-approved by the District Director or Assistant District Director, personally and in writing (except in cases of jeopardy). The official may not approve the levy unless he or she determines that the taxpayer's other assets subject to collection will be insufficient to pay the amount due.

Personal residences are even harder to seize. There must be a review, as described above. In addition, the IRS must now go to court to seek the approval of the United States District Judge or a magistrate before a residence may be seized.

Short of that, you can appeal threatened seizures by telephone right up the chain of command and at least get a quick answer. Sometimes the IRS's middle or upper management is more sympathetic to working out a deal than the agent who is intent on collecting the tax. So after you speak with the agent and his group manager, consider calling the branch chief, the division chief, or sometimes even the district director, the highest official in the district. You may even consider filing an Application for a Taxpayer Assistance Order. This right is a flanking movement around the chain of command and often works extremely well.

Right to review of liens
The IRS is supposed to release a lien against you if the lien has expired or the tax has been paid. In the past, the agency often delayed, but now you have a legal right to a quick release. The idea is to let you begin repairing your credit as quickly as possible.

Timesaver
Form 9423, "Collection Appeal Request," and Publication 1660, "Collection Appeal Rights for Liens, Levies, and Seizures," are intended to guide you through this process.

You can't use this new law to "unpay" your taxes, only to finish the lien release process if the IRS has balked for some bureaucratic reason. This new right to review the lien simply forces the IRS to file the release. You can sue for damages in federal court if the IRS fails to release a lien when it should.

What type of damages? Let's say you're on the verge of a big business deal, but closure depends on a lien release. If the deal falls through because the IRS delayed, you might have recoverable damages.

Additional rights in the 1996 Act

In 1996, the IRS supplemented the Taxpayer Bill of Rights by administrative action in a number of areas. The most important of these is the right to appeal liens, levies, and seizures before the IRS makes them, within the IRS to the Office of Appeals. This can mean the IRS will stop collecting, at least during the appeal.

Nationally, most of these appeals are rejected, but give it a try if you feel the revenue officer has gone beyond his or her authority.

- **"But my ex promised to pay!"** How many times do we hear that one spouse of a broken marriage has fled to parts unknown, leaving the other in the gunsight of the Collection Division? The revenue officer may be sympathetic, but he or she still must get the money from whatever source is available. Often your protests go unheeded. The 1996 reform act changed this situation—but only a little. You may ask the IRS what efforts it has made to collect from your ex, and how much. That can be very helpful when you press the right to payment in divorce court as well.

■ **Withdrawing a public notice of lien.** Filing a Notice of Federal Tax Lien used to be a permanent, irrevocable act, even if the revenue officer acknowledged that it was wrong. That Notice of Federal Tax Lien also had a tendency to frighten lenders and buyers away from your real estate. True enough, with much pushing and shoving, you might have been able to discharge property from the lien, or subordinate the lien (see Chapter 3), but you could not remove the lien unless you paid in full. Now you can. You must convince the IRS that the withdrawal of the lien will facilitate collection or would be in the best interests of you (the taxpayer) and the IRS. You may also try to persuade the IRS that the lien should be removed because you have entered into an installment agreement.

■ **Trust fund taxes.** When a corporation fails to pay its employment taxes, the IRS can go after its officers as well as the corporation. (See Chapter 6.) The 1996 Taxpayer Bill of Rights makes no change in that rule, but does give a few more protections. You can ask the IRS to tell you what it has done to recover the taxes from other officers. Also, you can now sue those other officers in federal court for "contribution." The 1998 reform law expanded these rights by allowing you to sue the government without having to deal with the Collection Division: all collection actions are stopped while your appeal works its way through the courts. Also, the 1996 Act protects volunteer, unpaid members of the boards of directors of tax-exempt organizations, but only if they did not participate in the day-to-day financial operations of the organization and did not know of that charity's failure to pay the taxes.

(Nearly) useless provisions enacted in 1998

As important as many of these changes are in giving you some measure of protection against the IRS, some of them are virtually worthless, despite their impressive names.

- **IRS Oversight Board.** Don't count on this new creature to help you. While the original idea was to have an outside board to ride herd on an overreaching IRS, the law just didn't turn out that way. Instead, the new Oversight Board will have wide-ranging but quite diluted authority to help the IRS manage itself on a *national* level. This new Board has no chain of command authority to help you in your particular case.

- **Reversal of the burden of proof.** In certain cases, the IRS will now be required to bear the burden of proof. But those cases will be narrowly defined. In fact, to achieve a reversal of the normal burden of proof, which is on the taxpayer, you will now have to prove that you were entitled to a deduction in the first place, and that you followed all the required rules and regulations. If you do that, courts generally grant a reversal of the burden of proof anyway, so the provision is useless. Moreover, it may be counterproductive, because it may force the IRS to be more intrusive in its requests for information in order to avoid the threat of just such a burden reversal.

- **Right to confidentiality.** The 1998 Act enacts a so-called "Accountant/Client Privilege." This was advertised as being important to keep your discussions with your non-attorney representa-

tive confidential. However, in practice it will
also be far more narrow than advertised. That's
because the attorney/client privilege is itself a
narrow privilege and does not cover most items.
For example, nothing that goes on a tax return
is confidential. And once disclosed on a return,
it's unlikely that the underlying backup data
would also be confidential. So don't count on
this one for help.

Just the facts

- Become familiar with the Taxpayer Assistance
  Order and be ready to use it when necessary.

- Get to know your Office of Taxpayer Advocate if
  you have any problem that lasts more than thirty days.

- You have many new rights to hold the IRS in
  check—be familiar with them.

- Don't be afraid to appeal within the IRS any
  threatened seizure action.

Going To Court

GET THE SCOOP ON...
"Take 'em to court"—The United States
Tax Court ▪ Getting your case to
court ▪ Prepare, prepare, prepare
▪ Getting the judge to listen—and hear
▪ Appeals of IRS denials of interest abatement

PART V

Handling Your Case in Tax Court

Have you ever pictured yourself as a giant-killer in the courtroom? Have you ever thought, "Wait 'til I get those IRS so-and-so's in court. I'll slash them from ear to ear"? Lots of people have this vision. For about 20,000 people each year, it's no fantasy—they sue the IRS in the U.S. Tax Court to contest a proposed tax bill. Tax court litigation is a perilous, sometimes high-stakes contest. And if there is one thing to remember, it's this: Do not try this on your own if you can help it. Find a competent lawyer or other qualified representative to help with your case in Tax Court. If you absolutely must act as your own lawyer, this chapter may help you emerge with your skin intact (well, mostly intact).

Since the IRS consistently wins 70 to 80 percent of cases that are not settled, it's hard enough for Tax Court petitioners to win even when they are represented; it's harder still when they go it alone. The procedures, the standards of proof, the rules of evidence, and other factors always stand in the way.

345

The Tax Court rules make available a "small case" procedure for matters involving less than $50,000 in controversy for any one tax year. These are usually handled by taxpayers themselves. The rules and procedures in "S" cases are similar to those of regular cases, but here, you get a break. The judges operate more informally; the process of trial preparation and trial itself is less cumbersome. Still, the chances of winning are no greater. You don't have to elect this small-case track, but it's available if you want it. Since all the Tax Court rules still apply, the trial phases described below are still important, but the judges conduct proceedings quite informally.

What is the United States Tax Court?

Our nation has many different court systems. Every state has at least one trial-level court in each county or city, sometimes more than one. States also have courts of appeal to at least one intermediate level, and then a state supreme court.

The federal government also has a court system, separate from but parallel to the state system. The federal district courts try cases in ninety-six districts, one or more for each state. Appeals go to the United States Courts of Appeals, thirteen in total (one or more for groupings of states, territories, and commonwealths; one for the District of Columbia; and one for a special federal circuit). Appeals from the courts of appeals are made to the United States Supreme Court.

After 1913, when the permanent federal income tax was enacted, it became clear that tax disputes should not be funneled routinely to these court systems. Litigation was very expensive, and the judges tended to be unfamiliar with the intricacies of tax law. So, in 1924, the IRS created a board within itself, called the Board of Tax Appeals, to which you could bring a tax dispute you could not resolve with the agents or the Office of Appeals. The idea was to channel disputes to an expert neutral panel that heard nothing but tax cases. If you wanted to sue in federal district court, you could still do so. But you had to pay the whole tax in advance. Most people didn't have the money, so the Board of Tax Appeals was the place to contest their proposed tax bill without first paying.

In 1969, Congress made this Board of Tax Appeals a separate, freestanding court, the United States Tax Court. Today, this court resolves more than 20,000 cases a year. An additional 20,000 new cases are filed each year.

The Court's headquarters is in Washington, D.C., but the judges travel all around the country, holding two-week sessions in many major cities. This makes it very convenient for people to file their cases in Tax Court; trial time is almost a judicial "house call." The "S" cases are handled by Special Trial Judges. Procedures are informal. Rules of evidence are relaxed. Everyone bends over backward to let you tell your story without too much lawyering or legalese getting in the way. Roughly 10,000 "S" cases are filed each year, heard by nineteen special trial judges, all appointed by the Chief Judge of the Tax Court.

What cases can you bring to Tax Court?

Most Tax Court cases are income tax appeals, that is, cases in which the IRS says you owe more per-

Unofficially...
Thousands of people try their own cases in Tax Court. They are called pro se petitioners, from the Latin phrase meaning "by yourself." In fact, fully one-half of all Tax Court cases are handled by non-lawyers, the tax-payers them-selves, or in rare cases certain nonlawyer representatives.

Moneysaver
Try to settle your case "at appeals." Appeals officers have wide authority and discretion to settle cases based on the possibility that the IRS may lose in court. They can split issues, trade issues, and generally compromise cases.

sonal taxes. Recently, however, the court has acquired jurisdiction over a number of other types of cases. Among these are:

- Certain cases where a tax refund is available
- Employment tax cases to determine whether workers are "employees" or "independent contractors"
- Appeals of IRS denials of interest abatement
- Appeals from the IRS's intent to levy

This chapter will focus on the income tax case—still the most common.

Getting your case to Tax Court

In most cases, the road to the United States Tax Court starts with an audit. Any type of audit will do. If you can't agree with the revenue agent on all issues, he or she writes a report called a *Revenue Agent's Report* and slaps on a cover letter called a "thirty-day letter." This letter states that you can appeal the revenue agent's proposed findings within thirty days. If you appeal, the case is transferred to the Office of Appeals, where appeals officers review it with an eye toward settlement.

If you can't agree at that level, the IRS issues a Notice of Deficiency, or, informally, the *ninety-day letter.* By law, the IRS must send you this letter (by certified mail) when it formally proposes a deficiency in your tax that was not resolved at the audit level or appeals. Attached to the Notice of Deficiency are schedules setting out in detail taxes, penalties, and interest the IRS proposes. You'll be familiar with all the issues because you worked with them at the audit or appeals level. You then have ninety days from the date stamped on the notice to file a petition in the United States Tax Court (150 days if the notice is addressed outside the United States). People sometimes call this ninety-day letter the "ticket to Tax Court."

The heart of the statutory Notice of Deficiency is a table of adjustments. Let's say the table identifies two issues, making this a "two-issue case." For example, the IRS proposes to increase your income by $5,000 for the tax year 1994 because you received a $5,000 loan from your rich and very nice Uncle Gaston. You told the IRS that it was a loan, but you had no evidence such as an IOU, a promissory note, or Uncle Gaston's check marked "loan." The second issue may be a "deduction" issue. Here, the IRS proposes to disallow your medical expense deduction for $2,000 because you couldn't prove to the agent's satisfaction that the lift you installed in your home was medically necessary for your aging, dependent mother. The rest of the table goes on to make the tax and penalty (sometimes interest) calculations that result from these changes.

These are just two examples. Sometimes deficiency notices are very thick, with dozens of issues. Most of the time they are confined to about five or fewer issues. But they all have the same pattern.

Representing yourself in Tax Court

Anyone can represent himself in Tax Court. In most cases, it's wiser to have someone represent you, but thousands of people choose the *pro se* alternative either because they want to or because financially they have no other choice. If you want someone to represent you, that person must be specially admitted to practice before the Tax Court. Lawyers get almost automatic admission. Anyone else must pass a rigorous examination the Tax Court administers once a year. Not many pass, so your choice is usually between yourself and a lawyer.

Timesaver
It's a good idea
to make contact
with the IRS's
lawyer early in
the case to
establish a line
of open commu-
nication. This
prevents any
damaging sur-
prises later on as
the two of you
prepare for trial.

On the other side are the IRS's lawyers. Every IRS district has a legal arm called the Office of District Counsel. That office employs from one to thirty-five lawyers, depending on the size of the district. Offices are located in all major cities. The IRS's lawyers handle many types of matters, including representing the IRS in the United States Tax Court.

So, if you try your own case, you're going up against experienced lawyers who work with the tax code and Tax Court rules every day and understand them thoroughly. They probably forget more tax procedure between breakfast and lunch than most *pro se* petitioners will ever know.

Still, all is not lost. Remember that you have only one case to try; they have dozens. Also, the Tax Court judges look to the IRS to bend over backward in your favor, especially in "S" cases. Often IRS lawyers will give you a bit of help with your case, trying to go the extra mile and telling you what you need to do before you get to court. Knowing *pro se* petitioners are unfamiliar with Tax Court procedures, the judges encourage this. Judges are also somewhat more lenient with you, expecting more from government lawyers who are supposed to know their business inside out.

Despite these courtesies, however, remember that you, the taxpayer, bear the burden of proof in most cases. This means the IRS lawyer can sit back and do nothing, coolly watching you struggle to prove your case. If you don't, the IRS wins without lifting a legal finger. All in all, you do not have a level playing field. While you may be David and the IRS Goliath, you're not at all guaranteed to win every fight or hit the mark with your first stone.

Trying your Tax Court case

Think of a tax court case as encompassing seven main phases. The time line for normal cases is six months to a year, so you'll have plenty of time for each phase. Each main phase also has subdivisions. The phases are these:

1. Petition

2. Discovery

3. Preparation for trial

4. Pre-trial order and memorandum

5. Calendar call

6. Trial

7. Decision

Phase 1—get your foot in the door

To get started, file a "petition" within ninety days of the date on your Notice of Deficiency (150 days if the notice is addressed outside the United States). If you miss this deadline, the Tax Court lacks jurisdiction of your case and it will be quickly dismissed. A dismissal means you have lost your right to contest the proposed taxes in the Tax Court, and the IRS will soon issue a bill. This ninety-day deadline is as strict a deadline as exists in all of recorded history. It doesn't mean three months, nor ninety-one days, nor ninety days and one hour. It means ninety days. Sometimes people actually receive their statutory notice forty-five or more days into this period. That makes no difference. It's ninety days from the date stamped on the statutory notice. In fact, even if you *never* receive this notice, the ninety-day deadline holds as long as the IRS sent it to your last known address.

Moneysaver
Some people ensure that the IRS has their correct address by writing to the agency. That's okay, but you can also ensure that you get the Notice of Deficiency by verifying your address at the audit and appeals levels. Good agents do that anyway.

The safest way to ensure that you meet the ninety-day deadline is to send your petition by certified or registered mail, return receipt requested. A special law says "mailing is filing" if you do it this way. Since you have proof of mailing, you can prove you filed your petition on time. Private delivery services such as Federal Express and DHL now also qualify as "approved" filing services, as may others in the future. You can send your petition on the ninetieth day by personal messenger or carrier pigeon, but if it arrives on the ninety-first day, you are out of luck. However, if you mail your petition on the eighty-ninth day by certified or registered mail, it can arrive a year later and still be considered "on time."

Don't despair if you're miles away from the court on the ninetieth day. You can mail your petition, and, as long as it's timely mailed by certified or registered mail, return receipt requested, it's "timely." The safest way is still to use the U.S. mail.

The tax court provides sample petitions, such as those for regular Tax Court cases and for the informal "S" case, to make sure everyone knows what to say. They are easy to follow. You need no formal language, and the court interprets them liberally. Just be sure to include all the issues and facts.

The heart of the petition are paragraphs four and five. In paragraph four, state which items the IRS got wrong. Usually you can take these straight from the Notice of Deficiency. You do not have to contest every issue, only the ones where you feel the IRS erred.

Paragraph five of the petition requires you to state all the facts on which you base your case. Here, it is wise to proceed issue by issue, with a headline for each issue. The recitation of facts need not be lengthy. In fact, it's best to be short, sharp, and to the point. Above all, be clear. This is your first chance to convince the judge. The clearer your story, the more credibility you have as the case proceeds.

After you file the petition (and four copies) and pay a $60 filing fee, the clerk of court sends copies to the IRS. Court rules require the IRS to respond within sixty days. If the IRS thinks your case should be dismissed, it will make a motion to dismiss it. But if you have pleaded correctly and on time, the IRS answers your allegations. Usually the answer is a point-by-point admission or denial of your facts, with a request at the end for the court to sustain the Notice of Deficiency. That ends Phase 1. You've told the IRS, "Let's fight." The IRS has said, "Okay. Let's fight." Now you move on to Phase 2.

Phase 2—what's up their sleeve: "Discovery"

It's now time to gather your stones and sharpen your arrows. This is the *discovery* phase. Here, ask yourself, "If this case goes to trial, what facts must I prove, and how do I prove them by admissible evidence?" You therefore need to know the legal standards for each issue, and to assemble all the facts, witnesses, and documents to meet those legal standards. In our example, the burden is on you to prove that the $5,000 Uncle Gaston gave you was a loan, not omitted gross income. If you can't prove it was a loan or gift, the law says it's taxable as unreported income. If you are not sure of the legal tests and standards you must meet, seek help. Ask your accountant, lawyer, or anyone else who knows the law. You can even ask the IRS's lawyer, hoping she is willing to educate you on the applicable tests or standards.

Bright Idea
If you don't contest an issue, you have conceded it. So if there is any doubt in your mind, put the issue in contest. You can always drop it later.

Watch Out!
The pre-trial order, standard in every case, warns that "continuances" (postponements of your trial) are granted only in exceptional circumstances. You'd better not say "I'm not ready" on trial day unless you have a very good reason.

Next, assemble your proof. Recall two key words: *witnesses* and *documents*. You need people to testify for you. You also need any documents you can find that support your case. Your main witness is probably yourself, but try to convince Uncle Gaston to testify that he intended to have you pay back the money. You may bring your aging mother and her doctor to court to say that she is disabled and needs a stair lift in your narrow three-floor apartment.

Also, look for documents. Paper is probably the most important single source of proof. Examples might include medical reports, notes, minutes, and just about anything else that supports your case. None of this should surprise you. You have handled this case at the audit level and possibly in the Office of Appeals. During that time, the revenue agent and the appeals officer have asked you for the same documents and witness statements you are now required to produce in court. Still, always look for more in this second phase of the case.

The IRS is also in its second phase. Upon request, you must give the IRS lawyer any evidence she does not already have, a process called *informal discovery*. She also must give you anything in the government's files that helps or hurts your case. This process can go on for several months, but it's best to conduct all informal discovery and evidence-gathering as quickly as possible. That trial date creeps up on you, and before you know it, it's tomorrow.

Finally, informal discovery exposes the weaknesses in your case. The sooner you know these, the better. If one witness is unavailable, maybe you can find another. If a document is missing, it may take time to get a replacement. You won't get much sympathy from the judge if you start asking for bank documents the day before trial, or complain that Dr. Smith wasn't available but Dr. Jones might be, except you can't find her. The best attitude is to treat your case as if it were going to trial next week. Then you, rather than the IRS, will be in control.

In this phase, the court's procedures also strongly emphasize the "stipulation of facts." You are required to agree with the IRS on as many facts as the two sides possibly can, and to put those stipulated facts in writing. Examples would include stipulating to the Notice of Deficiency, the tax returns, background facts about you and your deductions, and any other facts that all agree are true.

Phase 2 is also the time you or the IRS may make motions to the court. People make motions for a number of reasons. These include asking for extensions of time for some deadlines, motions to compel answers to formal discovery, requests for admission of facts, consolidating trials, and many other procedural matters. The Tax Court rules spell out the types of allowable motions. The function of these motions is to get the case in shape, procedurally, for development and for trial, so that nothing stands in the way when trial time comes.

Either side also can file a *dispositive motion*. This is a motion the granting of which decides ("disposes of") the case completely one way or another without a trial. One example of a dispositive motion is a motion to dismiss where the petition is filed late. Another is if your case is so good that the material facts and the law are all on your side. Then there is no need for a trial, so you may decide to file a *motion for summary judgment*. Few Tax Court cases fit this category, but they are not unheard of. Again, the Tax Court rules spell out what motions the court can consider.

Watch Out!
Don't make a
frivolous motion.
The Court can
impose sanctions
that can damage
your case or cost
you a fine.
Always discuss
your proposed
motion with the
IRS's lawyer in
advance.

Phase 3—prepare, prepare, prepare

In this phase, prepare your witnesses, facts, and documents for a logical presentation to the court. Some of this can be done in Phase 2 as well. There is no magic formula for preparing your case for trial. Whatever is logical and whatever works is, by definition, the way to do it. Some people "have it all in their heads." Others will map their case, issue by issue, on paper. On the left side of the page, they list the issue and the elements of proof needed to satisfy their contentions. On the right side, they list the witnesses and documents that prove each element, and what they expect those witnesses and documents to prove. Telephone your witnesses to inform them they might be called for trial. Advise them of the Court's subpoena procedures. Use the Court's subpoena power when necessary.

It is critical to interview adverse witnesses as well (you have a right to take their deposition). This avoids surprise at trial, usually a fatal error. Study the IRS's documents, which its lawyer has sent to you through informal or formal discovery.

Preparing a case for trial in the Tax Court can be complicated even for simple issues. As with everything else in such a court, the wise litigant gets help from a trial lawyer, even if he intends to try the case by himself. "S" cases tend to be less complex in this phase. Often there are only one or two witnesses, or only a few documents, which the judge will be lenient about admitting into evidence.

Phase 4—pre-trial order and memorandum

At some time three to six months after the IRS answers your petition, the Tax Court judges and clerks get together to schedule calendar calls and trials. They gather all the cases to be tried in your city and list them on a huge calendar. Sometimes these calendars include 200 to 300 cases. The Court finalizes the calendar, and the clerk publishes it. You know this is happening because you'll get a notice of calendar call about three to six months after the IRS answers your case, together with a standard pre-trial order. The notice tells you when your case will be called for trial, usually three to six months after the first notice is issued. So again, you'll have plenty of time. If you have been taking a long vacation, treat this notice as a wake-up call. The judges rarely allow postponements of your case from the calendar call. Be ready.

The pre-trial order also requires you to file a pre-trial memorandum. This fill-in memorandum tells the court all about your case. Include your witnesses, documents, and anything else you need to bring to the Court's attention. In fact, you can use the pre-trial memorandum as a checklist to test your case for readiness. Of course, the IRS must reveal its case to you as well. The judges take these pre-trial memoranda seriously. Many a sad taxpayer has found this by failing to file one, only to have the case dismissed as a result. Other times the judge punishes you, such as by excluding certain key evidence, even if she does not dismiss the case. So begin to write the pre-trial memorandum as soon as you get the notice. By their nature, the items in the memorandum also gently nudge you to continue preparation for trial; they tell you what the Court expects to see when the case is called.

At some point in Phase 4 or earlier, you can also ask the judge to hold a pre-trial conference. This conference can help narrow the issues, encourage a stipulation of facts, or simplify the presentation of

Bright Idea
Your demeanor should always show respect for the Judge and the IRS attorney. Address all remarks to the Judge, and use "Your Honor."

evidence. It may also resolve issues of the burden of proof and otherwise help to ready the case for trial or possible disposition without trial. Pre-trial conferences are not required, but either side can ask for one. If the judge agrees, she will usually set it during the calendar call. Phase 4 is also the time to continue conferring informally with the IRS's lawyer. Discuss such matters as the stipulation of facts, discovery, evidence (including, particularly, documents), and settlement. At the calendar call, the judge will ask about these and many other aspects of the case.

Phase 5—"call the case for trial!"

On the appointed day, everyone comes to court for the calendar call. By now, the 200 to 300 cases originally on the calendar have been whittled down to a manageable load. The rest have been dismissed or settled and have been marked off the calendar. The judge proceeds to "call the calendar." In open court, the clerk recites the number of the case and the petitioner's name. When yours is called, you are expected to stand at a central lectern and tell the judge whether you are ready for trial.

If you have not settled the case, be ready to try it or give the judge a very good reason why not. The same expectations hold for the IRS. Quite often cases don't need to be tried, or they are close to settlement and the parties just need a little more time or effort. The Tax Court judges understand this; they always help if settlement prospects are real.

When your case is called, the IRS lawyer might say, "Your honor, this case is for trial. We could not settle it despite our best efforts. We anticipate the trial will last one day." Then the judge will turn to you. You might say something like, "Your honor, I agree. But I think the case will last two days, not one." The judge asks many other questions, all with a view toward efficiency: there are many cases to try; the judge wants to schedule them as efficiently as possible. So the judge might say, "Your trial date is two days from now, for two days." Or the judge might ask you to wait until the end of the calendar so she can schedule other cases for trial. Sometimes the judge will schedule a special trial date outside the usual two-week window, a procedure typically reserved for more complex cases. Some cases take only an hour or two, especially if they are one-issue or simple cases. "S" cases tend to be tried quickly, often in less than a few hours.

It all depends on the number of issues, their complexity, the number of witnesses, and your estimate and that of the IRS on how long the trial will take. The calendar call usually lasts two to three hours if it's a long calendar. At the end, the judge has whittled down the calendar even further, ideally to a list of cases that can be tried within the two-week period of the calendar call. Once you have been scheduled, you are free to go. You then reappear for trial on the appointed day and hour.

Phase 6—the trial: time to fight

Now comes the actual fighting. Here's where you stand up, tell the judge what you intend to prove, and then prove it. You call witnesses (including yourself). You ask that documents be admitted into evidence. If you've done your homework, you have worked out the admissibility of most documents before trial by agreement with the IRS. If not, you must prove the admissibility of any documents you want the judge to consider.

Watch Out!
In pro se cases, the judges are usually lenient on admitting contested documents. But don't count on it. Pro se petitioners, untrained in the rules of evidence, are at a great disadvantage. This is a key reason not to try your own case if you can possibly avoid it.

After you present witnesses and move for the admission of documents, your part of the case is over. Then the IRS presents its case. Then you can rebut, as can the IRS, until both sides have nothing left to say. The judge then decides the issues, either in open court or after calling for post-trial briefs from both sides. In *pro se* or "S" cases, post-trial briefs are not the norm, but the judge can ask you to research the issues if your position is not completely clear. Also, the IRS usually files a brief. Since judges are trained to read briefs, you could be at a disadvantage if you don't file one.

Still, a bad brief is worse than no brief at all. If the judge knows your position and your evidence, she may not ask for a brief but simply announce that the case is ready for decision and that you will be notified when the decision is made.

Phase 7—decision
The judge is required to decide your case, but there is no formal deadline. It could be weeks, months, or sometimes years. *Pro se* cases are usually decided quickly, either right there in court or soon after in a written opinion. The fight is then over. You have either won, lost, or come out somewhere in between on each of the issues. The judge then enters a one-page "decision," the formal end of the case. You can appeal an adverse decision, but such appeals are rarely successful. Again, consult professional help before considering any such appeal.

Other traps and rules
These seven phases of a Tax Court case are the bare bones of what you need to know. Many questions will arise. How do you subpoena witnesses? Is arbitration or mediation available? Can you take depositions? In

fact, the Tax Court's thick book of rules, running to 174 pages and over 250 rules, governs all its proceedings. Buy a copy from the clerk of the court. It will answer most of your questions, and the clerk is often available for others. The clerk won't try your case for you, but is often willing to be helpful on procedural matters.

Above all, when you handle a case in Tax Court, recall the words of a famous Tax Court judge, who said: "[T]he trial of a case is a human process and...judges, as well as litigants, are human beings with all the concomitant attributes, both good and bad." In short, judges bring their own lifelong experiences and wisdom to the trial of any case. If you present your case to address the common sense and human aspects as well as the legalities, you will have done the best you can.

Just the facts

- In Tax Court, use a lawyer if you can.

- Prepare your petition and your evidence thoroughly.

- Try to work cooperatively with the IRS's lawyer.

- Be ready for trial as soon as possible, but settle if you can.

GET THE SCOOP ON...
Strike back by "suing the feds"
▪ Cases you'd love to file ▪ Defending
when the empire strikes back
▪ Statutes of limitations

Suing or Getting Sued by the IRS

Some people think you can always sue the government over taxes; others believe you never can. The answer lies in between. In colonial times, people used self-help to resolve tax disputes with the government, such as dumping tea into Boston Harbor when they didn't like the King's tax. These days, we take our tax disputes to court. But even an accessible court system is not open to tax suits whenever the mood strikes us. You may sue the government over taxes (or anything else) only when Congress gives you permission, a concept called "sovereign immunity." The prohibition of sovereign immunity dates back to medieval England, when you could not sue the king (the "sovereign") without his consent because "the king can do no wrong."

Nowadays, Congress has granted permission to sue the federal government in a wide variety of cases, including several types of tax cases. But your case must fit within the bounds of that permission, strictly construed, or the court will dismiss it. Thousands of tax cases are filed every year on behalf of individuals, corporations, and partnerships. Of those not dismissed, the government wins many, but taxpayers also win a healthy percentage. Many are also settled short of trial.

This chapter will help you keep a close eye on your rights to sue over taxes.

Bright Idea
A wise litigant uses a lawyer to sue the government over taxes. Lawsuits of any type are rarely successful when handled on your own; in tax cases, representing yourself is even more perilous.

Cases people bring

The following are the twelve most common types of tax suits people bring against the IRS.

Suit for tax refund

If you've overpaid your tax, filed a timely claim for a tax refund with the IRS, and the claim has been denied (or six months elapse without action), you can sue the United States for a tax refund.

A tax refund suit may be filed in one of two federal courts. The first is federal district court, usually the one where you live or where you filed your tax return. It joins all other suits over which the federal courts have jurisdiction, including cases involving securities, environmental litigation, criminal cases, and civil rights, among others.

The other forum is the United States Court of Federal Claims, located in Washington, D.C. This is a special court that handles tax cases and a few other types of claims. In a tax refund suit, you, the taxpayer who overpaid your taxes, are the plaintiff. Until 1995, the courts routinely dismissed cases in which someone other than the taxpayer tried to sue. Then the Supreme Court carved an exception to this rule, allowing an ex-wife who paid her ex-husband's tax (so she could sell their house) to sue the government. These types of nontaxpayer refund suits are rare, though its likely we'll see more of them in the future.

You may base a tax refund suit on just about any provision of the entire Internal Revenue Code. It could be a disallowed deduction or an IRS assessment that is barred by the statute of limitations. It might be a bank deposit the IRS concluded was unreported income, or a penalty abatement claim. Your case can be based on any events that, you contend, caused an overpayment of the proper amount of your taxes. For most tax refund suits to proceed, you must have first paid the full amount of the taxes, penalties, and interest. Other requirements are to file a timely claim for refund with the IRS and wait six months, or wait for the IRS to disallow the claim.

Consider undertaking this type of refund claim or suit only with the help of a qualified professional. Many a valid claim has been lost through violations of the technical rules governing refunds.

Civil damages for unauthorized disclosure

Congress takes the sanctity of tax returns and tax information very seriously. After Watergate, it passed a law strictly limiting the IRS's authority to make tax information public. Of course, the confidentiality law has dozens of exemptions—so many, in fact, that in fiscal 1997, the IRS made over 3 million *permitted* disclosures of tax information.

In general, IRS employees scrupulously observe this law. If they don't, the government can be sued for unauthorized disclosure. Every once in a while a case like this is filed. Most fail, but there are some spectacular examples of real messes caused by overzealous IRS employees.

Here's one true story. Roland was a professional. The IRS audited his tax returns and found a $100,000 error in his records. The Criminal Investi-

Moneysaver
The general rule is that your refund claim must be filed within the later of: (1) three years of the due date of your tax return and (2) two years from the date you paid the tax you now want back.

Unofficially...
Not many suits are filed for civil damages for failure to release a tax lien. One reason is that it is sometimes hard to prove the extent of your actual damages. But the right of action is there. The IRS, aware of it, usually releases liens quickly.

gation Division was called in. The special agent sent a circular letter to hundreds of Roland's clients, informing them that Roland was being investigated by the Criminal Investigation Division and asking for information about the fees they had paid to Roland. Before the agent sent the letters, he had not reviewed the law forbidding unnecessary disclosures, nor, had he asked the approval of his chief.

The clients were furious. "*Our* pro, under criminal investigation? How could that be?" Many deserted Roland's practice. The fact that the Criminal Investigation Division was involved and had made unauthorized, unnecessary disclosures meant that the government had to answer in damages. Cases like these are rare, but the 1998 IRS reform act made them somewhat easier to win.

Civil damages for failure to release a tax lien

For many years, people complained bitterly to Congress that the IRS was slow to release tax liens even after the tax had been paid. Suffering a tax lien was hard enough in the first place; it ruined credit and sabotaged the sale of property. So Congress passed a law requiring the IRS to release a lien within thirty days after a request if the tax was paid or was no longer legally collectible. If the Service fails to release the lien and the failure causes damages, you may sue the government to recover.

For example, Albert and Jeanne, husband and wife, made a terrible mistake. They invested in a tax shelter to earn a big tax break. Of course, in the 1970s the IRS declared World War III on tax shelters. Albert and Jeanne's case went to Tax Court, with a neutral result: no tax was due, nor any refund payable. In other words, all their hard work earned them nothing and lost them nothing. But that didn't dissuade the IRS, which proceeded to make big assessments against them for six more years. On top of that, the revenue officer filed a notice of tax lien, seized their home, and put it up for sale.

Albert and Jeanne's accountant asked the revenue officer to stop. Even an appeals officer got into the action, instructing the revenue officer to stop, but he sold their home for $8,600 at auction. Albert and Jeanne were unhappy. They sued because the revenue officer had failed to remove the tax lien when it had been filed in error. "That's right," said the court. Now the IRS had to answer in damages.

Civil damages for unauthorized collection actions

This type of suit has been authorized since 1989. You have the right to sue in federal court for damages when an IRS employee negligently, recklessly, or intentionally violates the tax laws, usually in connection with collecting taxes assessed against you. Once again, many procedural roadblocks stand between you and a suit like this. These include filing your claim first with the IRS (or else the court may reduce your damage award), mitigating your damages, and suing within two years after the violation occurs. As usual, the burden is on you to prove damages, which are limited anyway to the lower of actual damages and $1,000,000.

But suppose there are multiple violations. That happened in one case, where a court found the IRS had made eighty-four separate illegal disclosures. For example, remember Albert and Jeanne? Their suit included a count for unauthorized collection action. The IRS tried to defend itself by claiming that only the "assessment" was incorrect, not the subsequent "collection." "Too cute," said the Court. Such a narrow interpretation of the law would thwart Congress's intent to have the IRS answer for its unauthorized actions. So, again, the IRS had to pay.

Suit to contest a summons

You can sue the government to contest the enforce-ability of an IRS summons. The IRS has always had broad authority to look into your tax affairs. For this reason, it's rare to find an IRS summons that exceeds the Service's authority. But an occasional summons may do so, for example, by requesting attorney-client privileged information or information clearly irrelevant to the tax investigation. Possibly the summons is overbroad, or procedurally its issuance may harbor other defects. The law gives you the right to have a federal judge review the legality of that summons.

The constitutional tort

Timesaver
Carefully weigh your options before devoting a lot of time to a Bivens action. There are many defenses to Bivens suits, and very few ever proceed to trial, much less result in a taxpayer victory.

There is a type of suit that is not authorized by any statute but by the Constitution itself. It's called a *Bivens* action, named after the 1967 Supreme Court case that established this right. In a Bivens-type case, you sue individual IRS agents on the ground that they have personally violated your constitutional rights and must answer personally in damages.

For example, Harry promoted tax shelters, many of them whether they made any economic sense or not. Of course, the IRS said they did not and sued him for an injunction to stop this activity. They also assessed taxes against him. Harry protested long and hard because the IRS filed notices of federal lien and levied on his many bank accounts. One of Harry's allegations was that by suing him, filing notices of lien, and levying, the IRS had unconstitutionally interfered with his freedom of speech, liberty, and property rights. Specifically, it abrogated his right to engage in a chosen profession. He claimed the IRS issued the levies and liens only to punish him for criticizing the IRS. "That's enough," said the Court, "for the lawsuit to survive." Of course, Harry would have to prove his allegations, but if the agent did as Harry claimed, the agent would not be immune from the suit.

Suit for wrongful levy

Sometimes an IRS seizure injures the property rights of third parties who have claims superior to that of the IRS. An example would be the IRS's seizure and sale of a tax delinquent's truck on which a bank holds the first lien. The law calls such a levy "wrongful" because it takes property subject to a better claim. You, the delinquent taxpayer, can never sue for wrongful levy. But a third party with a superior lien or claim can sue and often win. The claimant files this suit in federal district court and tries to prove its superior claim to the property the IRS seized.

Here are two examples from the case files.

In case one, Big Bank made a number of loans to Carl, who signed a promissory note pledging his deposits as security. What Carl knew, but the bank didn't, was that Carl also owed federal taxes. So the IRS naturally filed notices of federal tax lien and levied on Carl's bank deposits. The bank dutifully sent the money to the IRS and then sued for "wrongful levy." The bank said it had a perfected security interest in the accounts, an interest that arose before the IRS's liens and was therefore superior to it. By taking the money, the bank argued, the IRS destroyed the bank's superior interest. "That's right," said the court. The levy was wrongful.

Moneysaver
File your wrongful levy suit immediately. The filing deadline is a mere nine months after the IRS seizes the property (sometimes extendable to twelve months). As many people unfortunately discover, the court must dismiss any case filed after this short deadline.

Daniel and David had a similar story. Daniel bought a car on a promissory note, listing the car as security. He never made any payments, but instead sold the car to David. Meanwhile, the IRS filed a notice of lien and seized the car. That levy was wrongful because Daniel never had an ownership interest in the car at the time the notice of lien was filed; he had already sold it. The IRS also wrongfully levies when it seizes a bank account that in fact belongs to a nondelinquent taxpayer. This happens often in parent-child situations where only the parent owes taxes. If the parent can prove the money really belongs to the child, was held in trust for the child, or represented money someone else had contributed, to that extent the levy is wrongful and should be remedied.

Suits for surplus proceeds

The IRS often seizes and sells property that belongs to both a delinquent taxpayer and someone else. One example might be a friend who has loaned you money secured by your home, but only after the IRS filed a notice of lien against you for taxes. Another example might be a piece of land you own as joint tenant with a friend. The nondelinquent owner is entitled to his share if the IRS sells the property. The law gives that owner the right to sue the government to claim that share. It's not always necessary to sue; usually rights are fairly clear and the IRS honors them. But since tax life is not perfect and disputes do arise, it's nice to know a *suit for surplus proceeds* is available. Even where rights are clear, there can often be a dispute about interest and penalties on taxes. These take the same priority as the underlying tax claim.

Suit for substituted sale proceeds

Sometimes you may need to sell real or personal property, but the IRS and others have claims against it. You've got a hot buyer, so you need to discharge the federal tax lien quickly to give clear title. You can enter into an agreement with the IRS to sell the property free of the tax lien. The IRS's lien and all other claims then attach to the proceeds. If everyone cannot agree on who is entitled to the proceeds, anyone who claims them can sue the United States to enforce the claim.

Suits to adjudicate rights to property

The government gets involved as a defendant in a variety of state and federal court lawsuits in which people fight over entitlement to property. One such case is called an *interpleader* suit. The basic idea is this: If a third party is holding money or property that you and the IRS are fighting over, that third party should have to pay it once—to either you or the IRS, but not to both. The stakeholder's remedy is to sue you and the IRS, throw the money into court, get out of the lawsuit, and let you and the IRS fight it out.

People file interpleader suits in all kinds of cases.

- A common example comes from the construction industry. Suppose a general contractor owes money to a subcontractor, who owes it to plumbers, and electricians. The subcontractor also owes payroll taxes to the government. The general contractor does not know whom to pay, so it sues everybody: the IRS, the subcontractor, the plumbers and the electricians, and throws the money into court. The claimants then fight it out. The entity with the superior legal claim will win. And, despite the conventional wisdom, the IRS does not always win.

Bright Idea
Don't hesitate to
assert your legal
claim against a
debtor who also
owes the IRS.
Quite often, par-
ticularly in con-
struction cases
and other cases
involving real
estate, the IRS
does not have
the superior
claim to being
paid. It's all
determined by a
combination
of state and
federal law.

- A second type of property case is a suit for *quiet title* to property. When real estate such as land, a building, or a home is sold, sometimes the chain of title is ambiguous. Other times, the IRS has filed a notice of lien, which itself puts a "cloud on title." The buyer needs to be absolutely certain he got what he paid for. So the buyer, a title insurance company, or any of the parties can sue the government in state court for quiet title to the property.

- A third example is a suit to partition property. A property owner may wish to divide his property, but an IRS tax lien stands in the way. The government may be sued to participate as a defendant in that type of case.

- A fourth type of property suit is a condemnation suit where the IRS has a federal tax lien on file.

- Finally, the government may be named as a defendant in a suit to foreclose a mortgage or other lien on property. This includes both real property and personal property, because the federal tax lien attaches to everything the taxpayer owns, real and personal.

These five types of cases make it relatively easy and convenient to sort out everyone's priorities and property rights. This goal would be impossible if the government's lien could stand on the sidelines, creating uncertainty for everyone else.

Declaratory judgment

A "declaratory judgment" case is a lawsuit in which the court declares the rights and legal relations of the parties. This suit requests no damages, injunction, or other relief. The law prohibits anyone from suing the government for a declaratory judgment over taxes, with one exception. You can sue to declare that a charity or private foundation is tax exempt. Again, you must exhaust the remedies within the IRS before filing such a suit, and certain time limits govern, but the suit is available if all else fails.

Suit to contest jeopardy levy or assessment

Among the most devastating of IRS weapons is the jeopardy or termination assessment. This type of assessment, followed immediately by a seizure of property (cash, bank accounts, cars, drugs, and anything else lying around), can come so swiftly that you have little if any time to react. That's the whole idea. Though giving the IRS immediate levy powers, Congress did not want to leave people without a remedy. So it enacted a law that allows you to sue the government to contest a jeopardy or termination assessment, but only after it has been made.

It's not a full-scale trial, but a quick look by a federal court to rule whether the making of the assessment was reasonable and the amount assessed was appropriate. From start to finish, the whole case normally takes less than forty days. In most circumstances, neither side can appeal. The government wins most of these cases, but taxpayers win a few. This type of suit is at least somewhat of a check on the government's jeopardy assessment practices.

That's it. That's the list of common tax suits that may be brought against the government. Any attempt to sue outside the allowed types of cases will be dismissed. In fact, Congress has passed several laws explicitly stating that you cannot bring certain types of lawsuits. For example, you cannot sue the government for an injunction against collection action. This would include suing the IRS when it levies on assets, files a notice of lien, or takes most other collection actions.

Unofficially...
The only injunc-
tion available
against the col-
lection of taxes
is the automatic
injunction of a
petition in
bankruptcy.

People normally think of suing the government only as a last resort, usually a wise attitude. Tax litigation can be expensive. Moreover, several types of cases that are available require that you go to the IRS for relief first. Lawsuits over taxes can be viewed as the top section of a tax claim pyramid; only a few claims eventually rise to the summit. If you have a tax claim or dispute, you need to understand and evaluate your right to sue, even if it may never be used. Your lawyer should be in a position to discuss this "menu choice" along with other alternatives.

Deadlines when you want money from the IRS

When you seek money from the IRS, either through a refund, a credit, or a lawsuit, pay attention to the hard-and-fast deadlines that apply to your case.

Claims for credit or refund

You must file a refund or credit claim within three years from the date you file your return, or two years from the date you pay, whichever is later. If the government owes you a refund on your original return, there is no need to worry. The return is the claim for refund. But if you file an amended return later, claiming a refund, you must do so within three years. For this purpose, returns filed early (before April 15) are considered filed on the due date. Late returns are considered filed on the date you mail the return.

Now, let's say you pay a tax three years after you file your return, but you really do not owe it. Can you get it back? Yes. You have another two years from the date of payment to file a claim for refund.

Suits against the government

People sue the government over taxes all the time. For example, about 20,000 people file tax court petitions each year. Thousands of others file suits in federal district court or in the United States Court of Federal Claims. Certain deadlines apply, or else your suit will be thrown out of court.

Tax Court

You must file suit in the United States Tax Court to contest the IRS's formal Notice of Deficiency within ninety days from the date stamped on the notice. That's not three months; it's ninety days, counting from the day after the date on the notice. Sometimes people get the notice well into the ninety-day period; some receive it after the ninety days have run. Some people never get the notice even though it was mailed. In these disasters, the issue is always whether the IRS mailed the notice to your "last known address." If so, you're out of luck if you file your Tax Court case too late.

Federal district court

People also sue the government in the federal district courts. The deadlines there depend on what kind of suit you file. The shortest is for a suit to contest a jeopardy assessment. That deadline is thirty days after the IRS sends you the notice of jeopardy determination. The next deadline is nine months. This applies when the IRS has levied or seized property that really belongs to a nondelinquent taxpayer with a claim superior to that of the IRS. For example, if the IRS seizes a car and you have a first lien on it, it has "wrongfully levied" the car. But you have only nine months to sue, sometimes extendable to twelve.

Unofficially...
The law does
allow exceptions
from these harsh
deadlines, but
not often
and only in
narrow cases.

The next deadline is two years, which applies to suits for refund of taxes. Thousands of these suits are filed every year. They must be filed within two years of the date the IRS disallows your claim for refund.

Other deadlines

Other deadlines pervade the tax laws. Some are formal, others informal. Many are obscure and relate to very few taxpayers. But the common thread is that all are strictly construed, either against the government or against the taxpayer.

Defending suits by the government

The IRS collects most taxes through its administrative enforcement powers—assessment, liens, levies, and other weapons. But sometimes, the IRS resorts to the courts when its agency powers don't get the job done. In such cases, the government sues you, the taxpayer, rather than the reverse. The IRS's litigating arms are part of the Department of Justice, specifically, the Tax Division, and the United States Attorneys' offices.

Just as you may go to court only as a last resort, so too the IRS normally goes to court only when all else fails.

You'll certainly know when the government has sued you. A complaint will be filed. The United States Marshal will serve you with a copy. In these types of suits, help from a lawyer is critical, particularly a tax lawyer experienced in tax litigation. Don't try to go it alone; defending these suits is complicated and expensive. Few nonlawyers are familiar with the rules governing federal court litigation. Few others have enough skill with these rules to make informed decisions on how to defend against IRS suits. Moreover, federal district courts are reluctant to help with procedure and substance if you represent yourself.

So if you face a suit by the government to collect your taxes or otherwise enforce the tax laws, it's almost mandatory to get help from a lawyer. This section provides an opening acquaintance with the types of suits people may have to defend from time to time. Congress has authorized the government to file eight main types of cases relating to taxes.

Suit to reduce a tax assessment to judgment

Despite the IRS's firepower in collecting taxes, sometimes people manage to dodge the bullet. For instance, some try to outwait the tax collection period, normally ten years after assessment. But just when you thought you were home free, the IRS drags out a little-known weapon to prolong the agony for at least another ten. It asks the Justice Department to file a federal lawsuit against you to reduce the tax assessment to a judgment.

Usually, the Department of Justice files suit close to the ten-year deadline. Also, the Service often chooses high-dollar or high-profile cases; it will not sue on every assessment that otherwise would lapse. But think how you would feel if, on the last or next-to-last day before the ten-year collection period expires, the Justice Department files suit against you. It could ruin your whole decade.

If the government wins, it has a court judgment on which it can collect. That judgment also gives the IRS some extra authority to put assets up for sale because it does so through the arm of the United States Marshal's Office and the Federal District Courts. The tax lien is also extended for however long state law provides for these types of judgment liens, often ten years or more.

Watch Out!
This Department of Justice suit will allege liability for taxes, penalties, and interest accrued through the date the suit is filed. Other federal laws then kick in to give the Justice Department interest on the judgment it obtains in such a suit. This compounding is onerous, but perfectly legal.

The legal issue in a suit to reduce an assessment to judgment is always whether you owe the tax. The court presumes the IRS's assessment is correct. You have the burden of showing it's not. That's a hard burden to bear, one you would have gladly shouldered in the previous ten years if you had had adequate proof. Still, a few people shoulder that burden and win.

For example, in one case, Oscar owed taxes dating back to 1981. The government made timely assessments of these taxes in 1984, and sued him in 1994, within the ten-year time limit. Oscar's defense: "I don't owe the taxes because you didn't give me credit for many deductions." Fortunately for Oscar, he actually had the proof. Granted, he had to dig it out from among trash bags full of records, but he found it, proved his case, and eliminated the assessments.

Suit to enforce a lien or to subject property to the payment of tax

The Justice Department can sue to foreclose the federal tax lien on specific property such as your house, business equipment, or any other property subject to the federal tax lien. The Justice Department often combines one count to reduce the tax assessment to judgment with another to foreclose the federal tax lien (if it knows of property you own). The government's assessment and lien are again presumed valid and enforceable absent your proof to the contrary.

If the government wins, it asks the court to appoint a United States Marshal to sell your property. In difficult cases involving many items of property or hidden assets, it may ask the court to appoint a receiver to take charge of the property and sell it over time. This happens often with homes the IRS wants to sell, where a nondelinquent third party such as a spouse or a co-owner claims legal interest in the property.

Getting a federal court involved means that everyone will be forced to have his or her claim resolved in one case, once and for all.

For example, Lance and Lisa owned farmland. Since they also owed taxes, the government sued them to reduce the assessment to judgment and to foreclose the federal tax lien on their farm. Lance and Lisa had no real defense against the tax bill, but they said the government should not be allowed to sell because they each had a "homestead" interest that state law granted to them. This type of state law could not stop the IRS, ruled the court, because federal law allowing a tax sale was superior to any state exemptions. So they lost their farm in a foreclosure sale. Owning a home as "tenants by the entirety" also did not help, since Lance and Lisa jointly owed federal taxes. But if only one had owed taxes, the government would not have been able to sell their farm.

Suit for erroneous refund

If the government sends you a refund and later figures out that you really owed the tax, it can sue you within two years of the payment to recapture the erroneous refund. This type of case might arise where you filed an amended return to get a refund, but the IRS later adjusted your return (such as after an audit). A variation of this scenario occurs where you get a refund out of the blue. You know you are not entitled to it, but you got it because the computer skipped a beat and issued you a lottery-size refund. Should you keep it, hoping the IRS will miss

Bright Idea
If you receive
from the govern-
ment a refund
check that you
know has been
sent to you erro-
neously, send the
check back to the
IRS with a cover
letter explaining
the circum-
stances. Keeping
the money
is fraud.

the two-year deadline for filing an erroneous refund suit? No! The government can sue you simply for taking money that doesn't belong to you, a fraudulent act.

Suit to enforce an IRS levy

If the IRS serves a tax levy on you, common sense and the law dictate that you have to surrender the taxpayer's money or property that you possess. For example, an employer served with a levy pays a delinquent taxpayer's wages to the IRS, not the taxpayer. A bank drains the taxpayer's account for the IRS. If you owe the taxpayer money and the IRS levies on you, you pay the IRS, not the taxpayer. When someone refuses, the IRS can sue for the amount not surrendered, plus a 50 percent penalty.

Banks suffer headaches over this rule, because they can't possibly police all the business loans they make. All of a sudden, when one of their borrowers gets into tax trouble, the first thing they see is a levy on the borrower's account. The bank desperately wants to call the loan and offset the borrower's bank deposits against the loan, but legally it cannot. It's too late after the levy hits. Many banks have suffered the wrong end of a suit for failure to honor a levy when they've taken the borrower's money and applied it against the loan instead of sending it to the IRS.

Suit to enforce estate taxes

The government has special authority to sue to collect estate taxes. Such suits are rare because the estate typically will pay the applicable tax, or the IRS collects it administratively by seizures and sales. But failing that, the government can sue to subject the decedent's property to sale by court order.

State law suits

The federal government has the same rights as any other creditor to sue under state laws. One of the most important of these is the right to rescind a fraudulent transfer of property, a cause of action in every state. With the IRS hot on their heels, many taxpayers make the mistake of transferring property. They make a "gift" of a car, house, pension, bank accounts, jewelry, or anything else of value.

It's perfectly fine for someone to buy these things from you, even if it's a close friend or relative, but it's not OK simply to transfer them without any payment to avoid taxes, or to sell them after the tax lien attaches. Also, if you shed assets or put them in someone else's name, becoming insolvent as a result, that too is a badge of a "fraudulent transfer" that the IRS can undo by suing you. It happens all the time, and the courts take a dim view of such fraudulent transfers.

For example, in one such case, the government sued William and Zack, his son. Apparently, William hadn't filed a few federal tax returns, so the government began investigating him. This is a good time, thought William, to transfer my country inn with its land to my son, Zack. And I can still run the place. Thereafter, William was indicted and convicted for willful failure to file tax returns. The government then sued him and his son to get the inn. William had transferred the property by gift (that is, without fair consideration) to a blood relative, with intent to hinder or defraud the IRS. The transfer was fraudulent. So the government's tax lien attached to the property, which was sold for taxes.

Watch Out!
In some cases of fraudulent asset transfer, the government can sue not only you but also your transferees, imposing liability on them for the value of the property you transferred.

Suit against third-party lenders of wages

When a bank makes a business loan to a shaky employer, sometimes it stipulates that the loan be used to pay wages. The bank figures that if workers' wages are assured, the project will go to completion. For example, sometimes general contractors designate subcontractor payments to go directly to workers. But even these stipulations don't ensure that the wages will be paid; the borrower sometimes defaults on payroll taxes. Under these circumstances, the government can sue the bank or general contractor for the money that was designated to pay wages. These types of suits are not that common these days, but they are still filed from time to time.

Suit to enforce an IRS summons

Most IRS summonses are self-enforcing. If you, the summoned person, take no action to contest it, the summons is presumed valid. The government can then haul you into court for contempt if you don't surrender the records. But not all summonses are self-enforcing. For the exceptions, the government must sue to enforce the summons. All it takes is a quick trip to federal court, where the government asks the judge to issue an order to you. The order says, "Appear in court to show cause" why the summons should not be enforced. On the hearing date, if you or the summoned person fails to respond or cannot mount a substantial defense, the judge will order the summons enforced, with the penalty of contempt or criminal prosecution if the summoned person fails to obey.

These are the main lawsuits that the government can file against delinquent taxpayers and third parties. It files thousands of them every year, in every federal district. Defending them is hazardous and expensive, but if you think you have a defense, the best course is to let a lawyer experienced in tax matters evaluate the case and advise you.

Just the facts

- If you think the IRS has "done you wrong," see an attorney.

- Congress has granted the right to sue in a wide variety of cases, more every year.

- Don't be afraid to take on the IRS in federal court.

- Pay close attention to all procedural hurdles before filing any type of tax case against the government, including statutes of limitation.

- Be aware of cases the government can bring against you over taxes.

- Pay close attention to the statutes of limitation that govern these cases.

Everyday IRS Issues

GET THE SCOOP ON...
Make the IRS give you information ▪ FOIA,
phones, and free information ▪ The IRS
leaps into cyberspace ▪ A website anyone
can love ▪ Make them give you money

PART VI

Turning the Tables: Getting Information and Money from the IRS

Sometimes it seems that the information flow between you and the IRS is one-way: it asks, you tell; it demands, you produce. In fact, the IRS is a gold mine of information you can get—about yourself, about corporations in which you have some ownership, and much else. You are probably entitled to learn 90 percent or more of the information that the IRS has about you.

The IRS is also a source of money—money you can bet back or even earn. This chapter tells you how to turn the tables on the IRS by getting both information and money from the IRS.

Big Brother does watch you

The Service maintains vast databases and stockpiles of electronic and paper records. As a general rule, very little of this mountain of data is publicly avail-

Watch Out!
In 1996, these permitted disclosures of tax returns occurred more than 4 billion times. In most cases, it was the IRS sending information about taxpayers to the state governments.

able—that is, yours or anyone's for the asking. Tax returns and return information are exempt from disclosure except to people who have a legal right or need to know, that is, a legal interest recognized by the law. This "Don't ask me—I won't tell" policy came into the law in the aftermath of Watergate. Although tax returns are confidential, however, the IRS is permitted to make over 20 types of disclosure—for example, to the Justice Department, to interested persons, and to Congress.

A *legal interest* means that the information is about you, a client of yours, or a partnership, corporation, or other business entity in which you have an interest, such as by ownership, directorship, or corporate office.

Knowing how to get these data can be useful or even vital in many ways. You may need to know when the statute of limitations on collection against you expires, or when your deadline runs out for filing a refund claim. You may need a back tax return, or to learn how much someone in your family paid to the IRS in withholding taxes, and when. You may need third-party information such as 1099 or W-2 forms, or other income information. The list of potential needs is lengthy.

When the Service investigates you, you can usually find reams of information helpful for your case that the IRS is not legally entitled to withhold.

Method 1: call the agency

There is a tremendous amount of information about you available with a simple telephone call to the toll-free number, (800)829-1040. All you need is a telephone and your Social Security number or employer identification number. The IRS will quiz you on certain other identifying data, such as address or (possibly) telephone number to make sure you are not an imposter. But once satisfied, the agent can tell you many things, using a computerized search mechanism that retrieves much of your tax history with the push of a button.

For example, the agent can tell you when the IRS received your most recent return or returns from several prior years, how much you earned, and your itemized deductions. The computer knows your withholding. It knows whether the IRS added penalties and interest, how much, and when; whether adjustments were made to your taxes by audit or otherwise; and how much you owe as of a recent date.

The agent can tell whether and when the Service filed a tax lien against you, whether levies were issued, when you filed an offer in compromise, and many other details of your account. The IRS Restructuring and Reform Act of 1998 codified a number of important and helpful access items. For example, the IRS must now place specific phone numbers and identifying numbers on pieces of correspondence. That way, you have a living, breathing person to call. Additionally, the Service must make telephone contact available in Spanish and must publish, in local telephone directories, the phone numbers for the IRS district offices in the area. Before this change, an agent's number was not listed, and taxpayers were bounced all around the country by dialing an 800 number. Now, you will have the option of "staying local."

To get a copy of a tax return you must use Form 4506, pay a $12 fee for each return, and wait six to eight weeks.

Unofficially...
In fiscal 1996, the Service issued 88 million refunds, including 85 million individual income tax refunds, for a total of over $131 billion (over $106 billion for individual income taxes).

Timesaver
You can request
by phone a
plain-English
transcript of your
entire account
for any tax year,
a process that
usually takes
about fifteen
days. If you want
only information
on your income,
useful for credit
or other financial
reasons, request
Letter 1722.

Method 2: ask the agent

If your return is audited or a Collection Division agent is assigned to your case, use this opportunity to ask for information. Within limits, the agent will accommodate you. Among the things you can ask for are tax account information (such as the information you can get by telephone described above), case history sheets, and affidavits and other statements (sometimes from third parties, with the names deleted). You may also request tax returns, other witness statements, and many other types of documents.

Even the Criminal Investigation Division (CID), secretive as it is, discloses some information as long as the investigation is not undermined. For example, CID agents often tell you the specific transactions they are examining for criminal purposes and by how much they think you have evaded your taxes. You can also ask these agents to provide a copy of the sections of the Internal Revenue manual that apply to your case. The manual itself is a huge, multi-thousand-page book divided into major subparts according to IRS function—for example, "Examination," "Collection," and "Criminal Investigation."

Why is it so big? In part, because it tells agents in great detail how to audit, investigate, and collect. The agents will not give you the whole collection or examination section of that manual, but they might point you to a reading room where the manual can be found. Except for the section on the Criminal Investigation Division, the book is public record, available at all principal IRS offices around the country and many satellite offices, and on the Internet.

Method 3: find and analyze the tax rules

Analyzing the tax rules is a daunting task for any-one, but for those so motivated, it can be useful. Generally, you will be searching three sources for these tax rules:

- libraries,

- the IRS itself,

- sources available electronically, such as through the Internet.

Square one in beginning any such search is the *Internal Revenue Code*. This Code can be found in all law libraries, many public libraries, in Fedworld on the Internet, and through commercial publishing companies that specialize in legal products. The code is complicated, intricate, and obscurely written, but we're all stuck with it. It is still the basic source of authority for all tax law.

Of course, no law Congress passes would be complete without *regulations*. The regulations that interpret the Internal Revenue Code are three times the length of the code itself. These are also available from the same sources.

1. The *Internal Revenue Bulletin* is a weekly IRS publication that covers many topics. Among other things, the bulletin publishes notices, announcements (for example, "The interest rates for the next quarter will be 8 percent" or "Hurricane Andrew victims will have longer to file their returns"), and interpretations of the Internal Revenue Code known as *Revenue Rulings and Revenue Procedures*. This bulletin is available from law libraries, commercial tax publishing services, and the Internet.

Bright Idea
Make frequent use of the IRS's website, www.irs.ustreas.gov. It is among the best on the Internet, and is updated daily. The IRS is constantly adding information, much of it able to be downloaded.

Timesaver
Getting a tax form is easy. Just call (800)TAX-FORM and ask for it. Expect to receive it within fourteen days. You can also access all publications and forms through Fedworld on the Internet.

2. IRS *Publications.* The Service has long maintained a publications program that attempts to explain discreet segments of the tax law in plain English. For the most part, it succeeds. IRS publications are well written, thorough, and useful.

3. *Teletax.* The IRS has about 150 tax topics on its Teletax system. Each is a three- to five-minute recording on a tax topic. You simply call and listen. Examples of topics covered include "Filing Your Payroll Tax Returns" and "Mortgage Interest Deductions." To access Teletax, call (800)829-4477.

4. *Private-Letter Rulings, Technical Advice.* Sometimes you are thinking about a business or personal transaction that you hope will have favorable tax treatment, but you are not sure. Or, you are fairly sure but you want the IRS's stamp of approval in advance. That's what the "private letter ruling" is for. In many, but not all, areas of tax law, the IRS will officially rule, in advance, on the tax effect of your proposed transaction. It could be a business merger, the sale of some property, the sale of assets, or other business or personal transaction. When issued, private letter rulings become public record, though names and other identifying data are deleted. You can find these rulings from commercial publishers in the tax field, from the IRS itself, or through Fedworld on the Internet. They are not precedent; you can't cite them in court even if they favor your case, but they tell you what the IRS is thinking and often help you plan.

5. *Technical advice* is given during a tax audit when you and the agent cannot agree on a particular-

ly complex or unsettled tax question. It's usually an important tax question, so either you or the agent can ask a special IRS office for "technical advice" on how the issue should be resolved. The IRS then publishes the technical advice in a memorandum available through the Internal Revenue Bulletin, commercial publishers, and the Internet. Again, the names are deleted.

6. *The Office of Appeals.* If your tax return is audited but you and the agent cannot agree on all issues, you may appeal within the IRS to the Office of Appeals. Chapter 10 discusses the function of the appeals office in more detail. This office is another good source of information about you and your case. Simply ask the appeals officer for information in the file, and he will give it to you. For example, he might show you portions of the revenue agent's files, her notes, transmittal letters, letters from third parties, and much other information the revenue agent did not feel free to reveal.

Method 4: the Freedom of Information Act and the Privacy Act

Congress passed these two acts twenty years ago in reaction to Watergate. Both have proved extremely useful for people who want tax information from the IRS. (Of course, these acts apply government-wide to the entire executive branch.) People make so many requests under both acts that most agencies, including the IRS, have special offices devoted exclusively for them, plus reams of regulations on how requests must be made and what can be disclosed.

Unofficially...
The appeals officer is not required to reveal all the information in your file, but often he will, just to get the case moving.

Watch Out!
You can request
information that
is already part of
your record with
the IRS, but you
may not ask the
IRS to perform
research. You'll
have to handle
any investigation
of this kind on
your own.

The Freedom of Information Act (FOIA) aims to make government records widely available, with a number of important exemptions. Through it, you can get such things as your own tax file, transmittal letters, and third-party statements (with names and other identifying data blocked out). The act permits some limited access to the revenue officer's or revenue agent's history sheets, narratives, and other notes of your case, sometimes the agent's legal analysis, and third-party statements such as those of other witnesses.

All of this can be extremely useful in any tax case. For instance, such information is often critical in defending against the Trust Fund Recovery Penalty, discussed in Chapter 6. Through the Freedom of Information Act, you also can obtain some staff manuals, statements about the agency's operations, and descriptions of its organization and addresses. Of course, much of this information is available elsewhere, but it is certainly accessible through the FOIA.

To make a request under the Freedom of Information Act or the Privacy Act, write to the disclosure officer in your IRS district. A list of the thirty-three Internal Revenue districts and their addresses is contained in Appendix B. Your letter requesting information should ask for a "record," that is, something that already exists on paper or electronically.

Describe as clearly and specifically as possible what you are asking for. Include your name, address, and telephone number. You may wish to limit the copying and search fees the IRS can incur without your prior approval. For example,

"You are authorized to incur $250 of research and copying fees without my prior authorization. Costs in excess of this amount should be discussed with me in advance at the telephone number listed above."

But even the FOIA won't get you everything. Important exemptions include classified documents, Criminal Investigation Division files, internal personnel rules and practices, confidential business information, and all information about third parties. That's why the names and identifying data of third parties, such as other officers in a corporation and third-party witnesses, are deleted from some records you get. But often you can guess enough to fill in the blanks. Even if you can't, it's better to know what the third-party affidavit states even if you don't know who gave it.

The Privacy Act overlaps the coverage of the FOIA in many respects. People often make requests under both statutes just to be sure they have covered everything. But the Privacy Act was intended for a different purpose: to enable you to learn what the agency has on record about you and to correct any errors. So, under the Privacy Act, the IRS must allow you to see and copy its records about you and to change or amend them if they are incorrect.

To make a request under the Privacy Act, write a letter (see below) to the district Disclosure Officer stating that the request is made under the Privacy Act. Include your name, address, signature, and telephone number, and a description of the records as specifically as possible. Sometimes people simply ask for "all records pertaining to or relevant to the undersigned."

The Agency has a fee structure for copying, but does not charge for search time. Like the FOIA, the Privacy Act contains exemptions, such as for classified information and investigatory materials. Once you obtain your Privacy Act information, you can ask to amend it. To do this, send a letter stating that it is a request to amend a record under the Privacy Act of 1974. Identify the specific record or information, state the reasons why the information is not accurate, relevant, timely, or complete, and why (with supporting documentation or evidence). Finally, correct the information by stating what you believe should be included. The IRS acknowledges your request under either the FOIA or the Privacy Act (or both), usually within ten to sixty days, and responds with the information or requests an extension. If the Service withholds information, it so advises you, citing the specific statutory exemption on which it relies.

With all of these tools at your disposal, information gathering should be a two-way street. The IRS expects that you will ask for information; it is geared up to respond.

Pages 397-398 show you a letter you could write.

The IRS in the electronic age

The Internal Revenue Service has both feet planted firmly in cyberspace. So swift are the electronic changes the Service is making that by the time you read this chapter, mant details will have changed. Thousands of additional documents, publications,

Tel:_____
Date:_____

Director
Baltimore District
Internal Revenue Service
P.O. Box 1018
Baltimore, Maryland 21203
Re: Freedom of Information Act Request
         Wonder Widgits, Inc.
         EIN 00-0000000
Ladies/Gentlemen:
Pursuant to the Freedom of Information Act, 5 U.S.C. Section 552, as amended, I hereby request copies of the following records of the Internal Revenue Service:

    1. All original documents and files created or maintained by any person or division of the Internal Revenue Service or any other agency or department of the United States government that relate to the tax liability of Wonder Widgits, Inc., EIN 00-0000000, and/or relating to the Trust Fund Recovery Penalty assessment that is proposed against Penny Pencil, SSN 000-00-0000.

    2. All documents relating to the above request, including but not limited to the following: IRS forms 4180, 433, 433-A, 433-B, 2848, 2973, 2275 (Collection Support Unit check sheet), Requests for Quick or Prompt Assessment (Form 2859), Trust Fund Recovery Penalty file transmittal, Form 4183 (Trust Fund Recovery Penalty Data), forms 941, 1120 or 1120S, Internal Revenue Service Memoranda, Appeals Transmittal Memoranda and supporting statements, routing slips, correspondence, transcripts of account, correspondence from the

Bright Idea
Getting information from the agency in the ways described here can never hurt your case, and often it can spell the difference between failure and success.

Internal Revenue Service to any person, case history sheets, revenue officer notes, bank account statements, canceled checks, bank signature cards, bank corporate resolutions, affidavits, declarations, corporate minutes, any documents pertaining to Wonder Widgets, Inc., copies of notices of federal tax lien (IRS Form 668), and all other papers, documents, forms, letters, or documents of whatever description located in the Trust Fund Recovery Penalty file of the Internal Revenue Service with respect to the above-named individual.

The Internal Revenue Service is authorized to charge me for searching the records, for making deletions from them, and for making the requested copies, up to $250 in charges without further authorization. If the total charges are estimated to exceed that amount, please provide me with an estimate of the charges and seek further authorization from me.

If it is determined that any requested record or portion thereof will not be disclosed, please provide the nonexempt records and the nonexempt portions of the remaining records. If any requested record or a portion thereof is not disclosed, please also provide an index and a detailed description of each record or portion thereof not disclosed, and a statement describing the statutory basis for not disclosing each record or portion thereof.

Please address the requested material to me at the address set forth above. If you have any questions concerning this request, please contact me by telephone at the number set forth above.

Sincerely yours,

Penny Pencil

and forms will be on the government's World Wide Web site. Millions more people will file electronically. Those who are computer savvy will find much happiness here.

Electronic filing and payment options

Included in this electronic explosion are ways to file your returns and pay your taxes.

Unofficially...
In 1998, before the filing date, the IRS's website had over 340 million hits, for information of all kinds, including forms and publications.

IRS ELECTRONIC ADDRESSES		
1.	Internet: fed world.gov.FTP-ftp.fed world.gov.	
2.	World Wide Web Home Page: http://www.irs.ustreas.gov/prod/	
3.	a)	Internal Revenue Information System (IRIS) is on FedWorld's bulletin board or the IRS Home Page on the World Wide Web.
	b) By modem:	
	(i)	set modem parity at "none," data bits to 8, stop bit to 1;
	(ii)	dial (703)321-8020;
	(iii)	enter "guest."

EZ Telefile

Since 1992, the IRS has experimented with paperless filing of Form 1040EZ by telephone. For 1994, almost 700,000 people in ten states filed by phone. The Service expected twenty-three million people with gross incomes of less than $50,000 would be eligible to file this way for 1995. Starting in 1996 (for 1995), people who want to file by telephone need do nothing. The IRS notifies you, by letter/packet, that you might be eligible. The packet will include detailed directions, a personal identification number (PIN) that serves as a "signature," and all necessary worksheets. Only those who are so notified will

Watch Out!
Although the paperless filing phone call is expected to take about ten minutes, in actual experience, this program got off to a rocky start. The future is brighter, however.

be eligible. An IRS fact sheet gives the following additional requirements:

- you are single with no dependents
- you have taxable income of less than $50,000
- you filed a tax return in some prior year
- you have W-2 forms for all wages and taxable scholarships or fellowships, but not more than five W-2s
- you have taxable interest income of $400 or less
- you have no income from unemployment compensation
- you owe no employment taxes on wages paid to a household worker
- you are at the same address as last year.

The instructions guide you through entering the information, and the IRS automatically computes the tax and the refund. In theory, you may expect to receive the refund within three weeks, or to be notified of any balance due.

IRS tax facts

This service allows callers to receive instructions and other materials faxed back to them. The number is (703) 368-9694. Over 140 forms and instructions, and 147 tax information topics, are available.

Electronic refunds

Starting in 1996, most people have refunds directly deposited into a bank account. You need not file electronically to take advantage of this program. In the past, only those who filed electronically or used Form 1040PC could obtain this direct deposit. To get your refund by direct deposit, fill out Form 8888, Direct Deposit of Refund, and attach it to your tax return. Long form and short form filers will be eligible.

Form 1040PC

Millions now take advantage of this form of electronic filing. You buy the Form 1040PC software from a commercial vendor (most have it), install it, and then answer the questions. Form 1040PC is electronically sent to the IRS via your modem. This package shortens your form to include only the lines you answer; blank lines and "zero" lines are excluded. You can also have your refund deposited directly this way. If you owe tax, the software prints a voucher for the balance due.

Other electronic filing

Since 1989, when electronic filing became available, the IRS has seen a huge increase in its use, from about one million to about thirteen million in 1994. The IRS now also accepts electronic filing for non-individual returns such as fiduciary, partnership, and employee plan returns. Even quarterly payroll tax returns (forms 941) are now electronically fileable. The Telefile Program for forms 941 is up and running in most states.

Unlike telephone filing, electronic return filing is available only through providers, called Electronic Return Originators. These providers include tax preparation services, accountants, financial planners, and others. They apply to the IRS for a special identifying number and for the software that allows the provider to transmit returns electronically to the IRS. You can find these providers by canvassing the Yellow Pages or newspapers, or by asking your tax preparer or other financial adviser. The IRS's Home Page on the World Wide Web also has a list of On-Line Filing Program companies.

Unofficially...
Beginning in
1999, you can
pay taxes by
credit card! (Is
this a great
country or
what?) So far,
Mastercard and
American Express
have signed on.
Details will fol-
low from the
IRS. Check the
Internal Revenue
Bulletin or the
IRS's website.

According to the IRS, Electronic Return Originators must not have a foreign address, and must
take corrective action within twenty-four hours of
receiving acknowledgment that a return has been
rejected. Electronic filing and tax assistance are also
available for the VITA (Volunteer Income Tax Assistance) and TCE (Tax Counseling for the Elderly)
programs.

Internet filing

Don't want to use an Electronic Return Originator?
You can file via the Internet or by using your home
PC and modem to call a toll-free number. By the
year 2001, the IRS expects eighty million electronic
returns to be filed this way. The returns will be
received by FedWorld, a site the Department of
Commerce manages through its National Technical
Information Service. There is no fee for this electronic filing.

Filing on-line starts with a return you prepare
electronically on your own personal computer. You
then transmit this return to an on-line service or
transmitter. This service converts your data to the
IRS's format and transmits the information to the
IRS. The IRS then notifies you whether the return
has been accepted. The program had growing pains
in 1996.

Paying electronically

You can now pay electronically, too. The Service has
a program called TAX LINK available to businesses
to make payroll and estimated-tax payments. Many
large companies use it, but it's available to anyone.
Electronic paying is now mandatory for companies
with more than $50,000 in annual payroll.

Telephone help

You can call a toll-free number, (800)829-1040, for tax help anytime. Almost twenty million people make one or more calls during each filing season. You can ask any question, ranging from tax advice to account information. Naturally, these call sites get quite busy during filing season, so be patient. The earlier in filing season you call, the more likely you are to get through and to get the correct answer. According to the IRS, its accuracy rate in answering questions is about 90 percent.

Teletax

This is a prerecorded announcement service that gives you information on about 150 tax topics, and always growing. You need a push-button phone to call (800) 829-4477. Nearly 7 million people used this service in 1995.

The Internet

The IRS has a Web site and plenty of other presence on the Internet. Its World Wide Web address is http://www.irs.ustreas.gov. The IRS uses FedWorld as its Internet home, available at fed world.gov. The IRS updates its site on FedWorld daily. The Home Page lists these subpages:

- **Tax Stats:** Tax tables, Earned Income Tax Credit tables, and rate schedules. This sets the stage for a second phase later on—a full database application where a taxpayer can input adjusted gross income and marital status to get the correct tax.

- **Tax Info For You:** Hypertext versions of publications 334 and 17. Users can move from one section to a reference with a click of the mouse.

Bright Idea
The electronic versions of IRS forms are sometimes issued before the paper forms are available. Use the IRS website when you need information now.

■ "Tax Trails" is an interactive program that leads you through basic tax questions and answers. The Home Page also contains the following options:

■ **Electronic Services:** This topic leads to electronic filing options and other items on the Internet.

■ **Taxpayer Help** and Education: In this section, the IRS has listed summaries of 150 tax topics and frequently asked questions.

■ **Tax Info for Business:** Access to business information, forms, and publications.

■ **Tax Regs in English:** Plain-English summaries of tax regulations, and a library of the actual regulations.

■ **IRS Newsstand:** This contains a full library of tax news and press releases, as well as all Teletax topics.

■ **Forms and Pubs:** Electronic versions of IRS forms.

■ **What's Hot:** The newest options, items, publications, rules, and laws.

■ Meet the Commissioner

■ Comments and Help

■ Site Tree

Within the FedWorld on the Internet you will find the Internal Revenue Information System (IRIS). You can also find this service on the IRS's Home Page in the World Wide Web. The IRIS main menu options are shown in the box on page 405.

You may download forms and publications from IRIS. This requires a personal computer, a modem, and a printer.

IRIS MAIN MENU OPTIONS	
A	About IRIS at FedWorld
B	Tax Forms and Publications
C	Individual Income Tax Information
D	Business Tax Information
E	Tax Information for the Media
F	IRS Regulations and Plain Language Summaries
G	Goodbye
H	Help
I	Dear IRIS

Timesaver
Use the IRS CD-ROM for searching, viewing, and printing tax forms and publications at any time. The CD-ROM is set up for Windows 3.1 or higher, or through Macintosh System 7.5 using Adobe's Acrobat Exchange—LE Software.

Fax

In 1996, the IRS began a pilot program called "Fax on Demand." With this service, taxpayers can call from their fax machines and get tax information they need fast; a one-page menu of items is available.

Tax forms

There are now three ways to get tax forms, all in addition to walking down to your local IRS office. You can use (800)TAX-FORM, Monday through Friday during regular hours. You may also have most tax forms faxed to you at any time from the National Technical Information Service, maintained by the Department of Commerce. Use the voice portion of your fax machine and dial (703)487-4160. Finally, the IRS has issued a CD-ROM with more than six hundred tax forms and publications. This is available at $46 through the Superintendent of Documents of the Government Printing Office.

In the future, you will be able to get virtually any

Unofficially...
Strangely
enough, the
"amended return"
is not a creature
of any IRS
statute. In other
words, no law
directly permits
you to file an
amended return.
Nonetheless, the
agency has a
form for it and
it's so much a
feature of tax life
as to be taken
for granted.

IRS item that is public record. This includes all regulations, proposed regulations, possibly even the Internal Revenue manual. Cases, notices, announcements, and other items that interpret the tax law are already available electronically from other sources on the Internet, such as law libraries. The IRS is also exploring the use of paperless imaging, which will let you keep "paper" records electronically. For an agency that handles more than two billion pieces of paper each year, this may be the biggest blessing of all. From here on, the user must browse and click. The potential for information availability is unlimited.

Turning the tables: make the IRS give you money

Because the IRS is so aggressive about keeping the money it collects, many people believe the expression, "Once gone, always gone." There is truth in that expression, but it's helpful to know the exceptions. In fact, you can get money back from the IRS in at least four ways.

Claim for refund

By far the most common way people get money back from the IRS is by filing a claim for refund. Your tax return automatically functions as such a claim when you end up with a credit due to you (an "overpayment") on the return. You need only send in the return (or file it electronically), and your refund will follow absent any unusual circumstances.

You also may file a claim for income tax refund using Form 1040X, the Amended Return. This must be filed within the later of three years from the date you filed the original return or two years from the date you paid the tax.

Thousands of forms 1040X are filed every year. For other types of taxes, such as excise, employment, and penalty, use Form 843, Claim for Refund. The procedures and deadlines are the same. Fill out the return, send it in, and wait. Every claim for refund is reviewed at least once, sometimes at two or three levels, for accuracy and legality. If all is correct, a refund request is processed and the money comes your way.

Refund claims come in all shapes and sizes. Here are just some examples of actions or events that might result in a refund:

- Your business suffers an operating loss. The tax laws allow you to offset that loss against your future or past income (your choice), starting three years back. If you elect the latter course, a refund commonly results. If you carry the loss forward, you may get a refund in a future year.

- You forgot about a deduction, or you reported income that wasn't taxable. Either type of event can result in a refund if you amend a past return to claim the deduction or exclude the income.

- A husband and wife filed jointly and were due a refund, but the next year they divorced. If one spouse's income and tax payments were disproportionately larger than the other's, that spouse can claim a refund under the "injured spouse" principle. Chapter 10 discusses this in more detail.

- Your tax return is audited. You've been so meticulous and scrupulous that the agent finds nothing wrong, but actually spots a deduction you didn't take. That agent is duty-bound to give you that deduction and the resulting refund.

Watch Out!
Always seek professional help in filing a carry-back claim. It is too complex to be done by the average layperson. Besides, engaging a professional makes it less likely you will miss the statute of limitations on these elections.

Bright Idea
Be aware that under the 1996 Taxpayer Bill of Rights, the IRS may now grant rewards in civil tax collection cases. Previously, only criminal cases could generate rewards.

■ You're an "innocent spouse." Signing a joint return means you guarantee to pay all the taxes on that return, including tax increases from audits. But sometimes one spouse is innocent and should not be held liable for the extra. Chapter 8 discusses this issue. Proving innocent spouse status can be difficult. But if you succeed, you may be entitled to a refund.

Rewards

Want real, deep-down satisfaction, reduce the federal deficit, and get paid to boot? Turn in a tax cheat. Yes, it's true, the IRS pays bounties to people who turn in delinquent taxpayers.

The reward is generally up to 10 percent of the amount the IRS eventually collects (excluding interest). But before you go rushing off to the telephone, bear in mind that the IRS has discretion as to how much and even whether it grants an award. Form 211 and Policy Statement P-4-86 explain this in more detail.

It's a bounty system: the amount of the reward is paid from the amount the IRS collects from the delinquent taxpayer, a true whistleblowers' reward in the right case. Granted, the IRS will take into account the value of the information, and the amount is what the IRS considers "adequate compensation" under the circumstances. Still, there are some numeric guidelines. These are generally 10 percent of the first $75,000 recovered, 5 percent of the next $25,000, and 1 percent of additional recovery. The total maximum award is usually not more than $100,000. There are other monetary guidelines that depend on the value of the information the informant supplies.

Attorneys' fees

In the last ten years, the door has opened, at least a little, to awards of attorneys' fees where you beat the IRS in court or settle favorably. Progress is slow but steady.

Generally, to earn such an award of attorneys' fees, if you win, the court must rule the IRS's position was not "substantially justified." The 1996 Taxpayer Bill of Rights shifted the burden of proof; now it's on the government to prove that its litigating position was "substantially justified" even though it lost the case. The law also allows for fees where someone besides a lawyer represents you before the Internal Revenue Service (without going to court), and you "substantially prevail." You must apply to the agency first, and fulfill a number of important procedural requirements.

Suits for damages

For several years, the law has authorized anyone who is injured by the IRS's collection activity to sue for damages. To earn such damages, you must show in general that the IRS acted illegally, and did so negligently, intentionally or recklessly. Moreover, you must prove the extent of your damages and give the IRS the opportunity to pay damages in advance of any lawsuit. See chapter 16.

These are the main ways in which you can obtain money back from the IRS. If they seem too few, that's intentional on the part of Congress. The revenue stream was intended to run one way—away from you and to the IRS. Still, these are good ways to reclaim some of your hard-earned funds.

Just the facts

- Don't hesitate to demand information from the IRS.

- Make good use of the IRS website and the ever-growing array of electronic filing, payment and information options.

- Be alert to refunds and other money you may be entitled to get back from the IRS.

Common Business and Personal Tax Traps

The American dream often includes owning a business or working for yourself. Millions make this dream a reality every year. But the American dream can turn into a nightmare over taxes. Even successful small businesses can trip over the many tax rules they must all obey, not to mention the dozens of nontax laws and rules. And, by neglect and inadvertence, a failing business can multiply its tax problems beyond rescue. This chapter alerts you to the most common IRS problems that businesses and individuals encounter, and shows how to avoid them.

Choosing your business form

When you start or take over a business, you get to choose the legal form in which you want to operate. You can be a sole proprietor (working for yourself only), a proprietor (you own the business and have employees), a partnership, or a corporation. "Limited liability" companies and "limited liability partner-

411

Watch Out!
Most American
business is small
business, not big
corporations.
Upwards of four
out of every five
jobs exist in
nonpublic corpo-
rations. Yet the
IRS estimates
that more than
30 percent of
income earned
by unincorporat-
ed business is
not correctly
reported.

ships" are now also becoming more common. There
is no one right answer for all cases, but the corporation and limited liability entities have a major advantage over the others: the owners are not personally
liable for the corporation's debts. So if the corporate
car is involved in an accident, or the LLC's machine
injures an employee, your personal assets are protected. Only the business's assets are at risk.

The proprietorship. This is the simplest form of
business organization. In fact, in 1992 some 15 million people formed proprietorships—more than 70
percent of all businesses. With a proprietorship, you
and your business are legally inseparable. You own it
all. You receive all the profits or suffer the losses.
This arrangement has the advantage of simplicity,
but there are disadvantages as well. The biggest is
unlimited liability—personal liability for all debts of
the business. And all debts means taxes, too. So, if
you have employees and fail to pay employment
taxes, you are personally liable for all the payroll
taxes, plus penalties, plus interest.

A partnership. This is formed when two or more
people unite for the purpose of sharing profits and
losses, without incorporating. Again, it's easy to
organize—in most states it requires no special forms
(limited partnerships usually require greater formalities). The profits are taxed to the partners individually in proportion to their ownership shares; the
partnership itself pays no tax. The partnership does
have a separate legal status and filing and reporting
requirements, however, and so is more cumbersome
to manage than a proprietorship. Also, the general
partners are totally exposed to personal liability for
the partnership's debts, and well as being liable to
each other for breaches of the duty of loyalty.

Limited liability companies are hybrid entities, created under state law, intended to give their owners the advantages of limited liability (like a corporation) and partnership tax treatment. For qualifying LLCs, individual owners are taxed as if the entities are partnerships. These are still relatively new legal entities; many people may not be familiar with them.

A corporation is the most formal type of business organization. Every state has laws permitting corporations to be formed and regulating their operation. Corporations are complex, with many formalities and forms to be completed each year. Regular corporations, called "C" corporations in the tax law, pay taxes on their profits. A special type of corporation, the "S" corporation, does not. Instead, like partnerships, "S" corporations flow profits through to the owners in proportion to their ownership shares. An "S" corporation is still a real state-authorized corporation, with limited liability; it has simply chosen to take advantage of the special status the federal tax laws allow for such companies.

The tax traps for small businesses
Though no form of business is immune from tax troubles, there are certain difficulties that create special problems for small businesses.

Employment taxes
No matter what form of business entity you choose, you will be subject to filing several different types of business and personal tax returns—federal, state, and sometimes local. The most common are employment tax returns. Every business entity files payroll tax returns, such as Forms 941 and 940, W-2, and W-3, if it has employees. Sole proprietors, partners, and corporate shareholders also file estimated-tax returns based on their anticipated profit in the business.

Unofficially...
Many issues relating to the operation of LLCs have yet to be worked out by legislation or litigation.

Businesses that lose money usually run into trouble over payroll taxes more than any other type of tax. Quite often, the owners or managers pay the employees' net wages, recording on the books the business tax liability for withholding, Social Security tax, Medicare, and state income tax. Then they fail to pay these taxes to the federal and state governments. Reasons for doing so vary. Often it's a matter of tight cash flow. Managers may figure that a big payment will come in the next week or next month, or that they can "work it out" with the IRS later. They have to keep the doors open, so employees and suppliers get paid, but the IRS doesn't come calling until later—weeks, months, sometimes years later.

The IRS sounds the payroll tax alarm more quickly these days, but there are still two to six weeks of delay, at a minimum, after its computers detect nondeposit of taxes or the company sends in a quarterly tax return without full payment. This failure to pay payroll taxes is a ticking time bomb. The corporation, as a separate legal entity, is of course always liable for the full amount of tax, penalties, and interest it fails to pay. But on top of this, the owners and managers who were in control of the company's finances are personally liable for a portion of those taxes, that is, the portion withheld from employees' paychecks. This liability is known as the *Trust Fund Recovery Penalty*. Chapter 6 discusses it in detail. This danger of personal liability is the single most important reason why you may wish to incorporate your business.

As a rule, the personal liability component of the corporation's tax bill is 67 percent to 75 percent of the total tax bill. The owners and managers are not personally liable for the penalties and interest.

So using a corporation has the major advantage of shielding the owners and managers from one-third of the total liability for payroll taxes if the business fails. To be sure, a corporation is saddled with more cumbersome paperwork. But many a proprietor and general partner have sadly wished in retrospect that they had simply incorporated their business.

Another very important practice tip is to keep up the corporate formalities. The corporation must act like one, and maintain its existence separate and apart from that of its owners. The shareholders and directors hold meetings and record minutes. They advertise, write checks, and make contracts in the corporate name. They file all required forms and returns. If not, the IRS, like any other creditor, can hold the owners personally liable for every ounce of tax the "corporation" owed because it wasn't really a corporation.

Maintaining these corporate formalities is like getting a dull headache once a year. It nags at you to pay attention and do something; that, however, is easily done. Yet thousands of corporations are lax to some extent in keeping up their corporate records. The owners are too busy keeping up with business to worry about "the paperwork." When a crisis hits, they wish they had.

Employee-independent contractor disputes

A major payroll problem some companies encounter arises from the practice of treating workers as *independent contractors* rather than employees. Ordinarily, a business must pay its employees' withheld payroll taxes, in addition to the employer's share of Social Security and Medicare. But it is not

Watch Out!
In states where the IRS has classified the limited liability company as a "partnership" for tax purposes, it may take the position that the LLC members are personally liable for the entire amount of payroll taxes that the LLC fails to pay, not merely the withheld parts.

Unofficially...
Certain workers
are classified by
law as "statutory
employees." This
means they are
not really
employees, but
the law treats
them as employ-
ees for the sake
of withholding
purposes. This
includes certain
insurance sales-
men, homework-
ers, traveling
salesmen, corpo-
rate officers, and
certain drivers.

required to pay these withholdings for workers who
are independent contractors. The problem arises
when the IRS thinks that a business had so much
control over such workers that they should have
been considered employees, not independent contractors.

If the IRS decides that your business has misclas-
sified its employees in this way, all of a sudden the
business will be liable for a huge amount of payroll
taxes, sometimes going back years. For thirty years,
the IRS has conducted a nationwide running battle
with the business community over this issue. The
courts have ruled in dozens of cases involving nurs-
es, drywall installers, insurance agents, teachers,
doctors, and other worker classes. Even Congress
gets into the fight from time to time, usually granting some measure of relief to businesses that are
stuck with these types of investigations.

It continues to be a nagging problem. The easiest way to solve it is to give in: treat all your workers
as employees, subject to withholding. But many businesses cannot do this and remain competitive, if
competitors refuse to go along. Others decline to do
so simply in order to cut down on expenses and
increase their profits. Such businesses run the risk
of an IRS investigation.

If you define certain workers as independent
contractors, there are several steps you can take to
reduce the odds that the IRS will challenge you.

1. **Use a written contract** that explicitly addresses
   the factors the IRS considers in deciding
   whether your workers are independent contractors or employees. Then, be sure your business
   practices conform to the contract. Among the
   most important factors to address is the degree

of control you exert over the workers' methods, including your instructions and training. The IRS also looks at whether the workers are free to work for others, whether they furnish their own tools, how they are supervised and paid, where the work is done, who pays the expenses, and who bears the risk of loss.

2. **Collect information** as you go along about how your competitors treat their workers. If, for example, a substantial portion of your industry consistently treats workers as independent contractors, keep a record of this fact. It may help if you are investigated.

3. **Be consistent from day one** in your treatment of workers as independent contractors. You will have at least a few real employees, so your payroll tax returns will reflect the withholdings from the true employees' wages. Exclude independent contractors from those returns; instead issue Forms 1099.

4. Find a way to ensure that the independent contractors have **paid their income** and self-employment taxes. In the real world, this is easier said than done. But if you can conveniently police their tax behavior, the IRS should give you credit for each worker whose taxes have been paid, even if that worker ends up being your "employee." One way is to ask them. Another is to have them complete Form 4667 each year.

Keeping business records

These days, there is no excuse for keeping sloppy or incomplete business records. Even small start-up businesses can and need to keep their accounting and other records by computer. Luckily, hardware

Bright Idea
Use Form 4667 in each case involving an independent contractor. This is a form that, when signed by the worker, certifies that the worker has paid the relevant taxes on his own return.

and software are so inexpensive, so readily available, and so easy for bookkeepers and executives to use, that record keeping should be smooth and easy.

The biggest advantage of computerizing business records is that you enter data only once. From that entry you generate accurate income and expense reports, profit and loss statements, balance sheets, and any other reports you might need. You avoid losing track of legal deductions and avert problems with unreported income. Tax software will keep you abreast of all deductions, including depreciation. Software is also available to remind you about tax-sensitive dates such as deadlines for paying payroll taxes and filing. The computer will catch any arithmetic mistake as well.

Another big advantage of computerization is that it enables you to separate various accounts. For example, businesses and their owners should be separate, even if the owner is an unincorporated proprietor. With a computer system, this is easy to do. Every month, quarter, or year, print a hard copy of your financial statements. Keep a back-up disk of all your data off-site and maintain the integrity of your business's computer systems by having an accountant who can verify your work.

The IRS Education Program

The IRS publishes a number of excellent guides to help you start your business. Publication 583, "Taxpayers Starting a Business," contains a detailed analysis of the records that are required, a suggested record system, comments on bookkeeping and record-keeping systems, and explanations of accounting methods. The IRS also publishes a small business education kit, Publication 1466, an eight-part, six-inch-thick presentation of the following aspects of starting a business:

1. Business assets

2. Business use of the home

3. Employment taxes

4. Excise taxes

5. Starting a business/record keeping

6. Schedules C and ES and Form 1040-ES

7. Self-employed retirement plans

8. The small business as a partnership

9. Tip reporting and allocation rules

10. "S" corporation/"C" corporation

This publication is a gold mine of information about small businesses and is particularly helpful when the owner may not have previous experience. Finally, the IRS covers a vast amount of information on the small business on its Web site.

Divorce and separation

With half of all marriages ending in divorce and many divorcing couples owing back taxes, it's no wonder the IRS is the "third partner" in many divorces. Divorce taxation is a field of study in itself. Divorce lawyers routinely plan for tax issues in their cases and take advantage of the breaks the Internal Revenue Code gives divorcing couples. Many of the items that people bargain over in a divorce have tax implications: who gets the house, who gets the insurance and retirement accounts, or how much alimony and child support are to be paid. The Internal Revenue Code has rules covering each of these issues.

Timesaver
With so much help available from the IRS and from commercial publishers, including computer hardware and software makers, starting a business these days is relatively easy. Of course, it's up to you to make the sales and serve the customers. But at least compliance with the IRS has been made easier.

Unofficially...
Under the 1998
IRS reform act,
substantial relief
may be available
to "innocent"
spouses, or
spouses who
want to elect
separate treat-
ment. Chapter 8
discusses these
items. The effect
of this election
is to make each
spouse liable for
the taxes on his
or her own
income only.

But while those helpful rules may smooth the way toward understanding the tax results of property transfers resulting from divorce and separation, they have no effect on what happens when taxes have to be collected. For instance, special rules allow couples to allocate alimony and child support so that these items are deductible by one spouse and reportable as gross income by the other. The Code also allows very liberal transfers of property, such as homes or retirement accounts, without any current tax. But these rules do not bind the Collection Division when it goes out to collect delinquent taxes. Divorcing couples, and unfortunately sometimes their professional advisers, often overlook many tax traps in the often rocky road to a divorce or separation.

How the problem arises

Most tax collection problems in divorce can be traced to one basic fact: When you and your spouse sign a joint federal income tax return, you are each "jointly and severally liable" for the taxes on that return. By your signatures each of you agrees to pay the entire tax due. This means that the IRS can collect the whole amount from either one, or some from one and some from the other. This is true even if one spouse earned no income and the other earned it all.

There is another major factor that causes tax collection problems after a divorce or separation. While the spouses are bound by clauses in a divorce or separation agreement that allocate the tax liability between them, the IRS is not. These two principles play themselves out in a number of very common situations.

"But he promised to pay"

John and Jane's divorce decree makes John liable to pay the taxes on their past returns and any taxes that might become due if the IRS audits those returns. Two years after the divorce comes the dreaded audit. The result is a $10,000 bill. Jane waves the divorce decree in the IRS's face, but the agent scoffs. "You signed the joint return; you get to pay the extra tax." This agent would be entirely within his or her rights to demand payment from Jane unless she is an "innocent spouse" (see Chapter 8). This scenario and its many permutations are common in the world of divorce and separation. You can beg and plead all you want, but the IRS still has the right to come after either spouse.

To make matters worse, the more irresponsible spouse has moved away, leaving the wage-earning, responsible spouse exposed to the tender mercies of the Collection Division. Sometimes, agents take pity and try to locate the wandering spouse, but until the 1996 Taxpayer Bill of Rights, there was no such legal requirement. Now, agents must tell you generally of their efforts to collect from the other spouse if you ask.

Property transfers

A key part of many divorces is the transfer of assets such as bank accounts, retirement accounts, insurance policies, and the big one, the "marital home." Generally, the tax laws allow these to be transferred tax-deferred, that is, deferring the tax as the built-in profit. That profit makes these assets even more exposed to the Collection Division's outstretched hand. And if any asset has to be sold or if the IRS sells it, there is often a huge tax to be paid, on top of other fees.

Unofficially...
Although agents must inform you "generally" of any actions they've taken to collect from the irresponsible spouse, the law doesn't specify what "generally" means. Moreover, agents will always go for the easiest dollars first—no matter who has them.

For example, Tarzan and Jane divorce. Jane receives the couple's 1,000 shares of Megaplex Corporation, worth $50,000. The shares were purchased for $10,000. There is no tax on the transfer of these shares to Jane in the divorce (because a special law so provides), as there would be in a normal "exchange." After the divorce, the IRS comes after Jane for taxes on the joint return, even though Tarzan was the only wage-earner. The IRS seizes the stock to cover the taxes on Tarzan's income, sells the stock for $50,000, and goes away satisfied. So Jane not only loses her stock, but also, because of the IRS's forced sale, she is now liable for the tax on $40,000 "profit" the stock generated.

Sometimes a divorce gives the more exposed spouse other valuable assets the IRS may want to seize. For example, suppose Jane got the marital tree house from Tarzan in the divorce. Since the divorce gave Jane sole title, the house is no longer protected by the "tenancy by the entireties" rules of most states. Such laws normally protect a home owned by a married couple from the clutches of creditors, including the IRS, where only one spouse owes taxes. So, in addition to having to pay Tarzan's taxes, Jane would also have to pay these taxes using the equity in her only asset, the tree house.

Negotiating with the Collection Division after a divorce

Even if you are the "innocent" victim after a divorce, there are still steps you can take to help your collection situation. First, go to the source. Find your ex-spouse and demand that he or she live up to the divorce decree. And let the IRS know you have done this. Though this is sometimes easier said than done, most states have laws allowing a spouse to haul the delinquent party into court for contempt if he or she violates a divorce decree or property settlement agreement. A clause in Jane's divorce decree requiring Tarzan to pay the back taxes won't bind the IRS, but it will bind Tarzan on pain of contempt of court if Jane enforces it—a potent threat. If you exercise it, the IRS will often hold off and allow some time to straighten things out with your ex-spouse.

Even if that does not work, all is not lost. Granted, you are in the position of trying to convince the Collection Division that you can't pay, or can't pay much, but here your divorce decree can help. Sometimes the decree requires you to pay money to your ex-spouse, such as for maintenance, child support, or other "health and welfare" expenses. So when you fill out the IRS's financial statement (Form 433-A or 433-F—see Chapters 11 and 12), cite the divorce decree as authority that those hefty payments have collection priority over the claim of the IRS.

If the payments are ordered by a court and are reasonable in amount, the IRS should allow them as "necessary living expenses" ahead of its claim. If so, the amount you have to pay to the IRS might well be reduced. You also can try to negotiate an offer in compromise (Chapter 11 discusses this technique). The general idea is: With all your expenses and payments under the divorce decree, you will never be able to pay the full tax bill. So the IRS should be willing to take a reduced amount.

Bright Idea

You can ask the IRS for a statement regarding whether it has tried to collect from your ex, and how much it has collected. While that's all the IRS has to do, the information may be useful in trying to pursue the ex, as you may learn of assets or other helpful facts.

Protecting yourself and anticipating problems

Most of these problems can be avoided by some careful planning. When you review a divorce or separation agreement, think in "what if?" terms. What if the spouse who promises to pay the taxes does not? What if you can no longer find him or her? By asking these questions in advance and assuring yourself of reasonable answers, you go a long way toward protecting yourself, your family, and your assets from the "third partner" lurking outside the divorce court, the IRS.

Just the facts

- When you run a small business, pay more attention than you think you need to pay to keeping good, careful, computerized records.

- Choose the right business form—don't get caught by the personal liability tax trap.

- Think through your employment tax issues thoroughly.

- In a divorce or separation case, anticipate the audit and collection problems that accompany most divorces.

Glossary

accuracy-related penalty A 20 percent penalty added to the basic tax due, usually after an audit.

agreed case A case in which the taxpayer and the IRS agree on all proposed adjustments, positive or negative, and thereby avoid the case going to court.

Appeals Short for *Office of Appeals*. The office established within the IRS to attempt to settle income tax audit disputes on the basis of litigating hazards. The office also handles appeals in certain collection cases.

assessment The formal recording of the taxpayer's tax liability on the assessment rolls of the IRS.

attorney/client privilege A privilege against disclosure of confidential communications between an attorney and client, for the purpose of obtaining legal advice.

audit The formal examination of a taxpayer's income tax return for accuracy.

audit reconsideration An administrative procedure whereby a taxpayer may have the IRS reconsider the results of a prior audit, available in certain limited circumstances.

Automated Collection System A computerized collection system set up by the IRS to generate liens and levies automatically. ACS also has personnel at call sites to assist the IRS in collection activities.

balance-due return A return filed by a taxpayer that shows a balance due.

bank deposits method An indirect method of proving the taxpayer's reportable income by using the amounts deposited into bank accounts.

bankruptcy A legal procedure under which a taxpayer may seek to discharge or reschedule debts, including certain taxes.

Business Master File A central record within the IRS that tracks separate files for each business that has an employer identification number. See *Individual Master File*.

calendar call The start of a two-week Tax Court session in which the assigned judge calls the calendar of cases not yet settled.

"C" corporation Any state corporation that has not elected to be an "S" corporation. Generally, "C" corporations pay taxes on their profits, with the remainder taxed to shareholders when paid as dividends.

Circular 230 The formal set of rules promulgated by the IRS that govern the conduct of practitioners before the IRS on behalf of taxpayers.

Claim for Refund A formal request for the return of money, filed by a taxpayer with the IRS.

Collateral Agreement A side agreement as part of some offers in compromise whereby the taxpayer promises to pay certain percentages of his after-tax income over a specified period of years.

Collection Appeal Request An informal appeal of a revenue officer's proposed collection action, made to the Office of Appeals.

Collection Information Statement for Businesses Form 433-B, a four-page form stating the business's assets and liabilities, and containing an income statement.

Collection Information Statement for Individuals Form 433-A, a four-page statement of an individual's assets, liabilities, and income and expenses, on a monthly basis.

conditional expenses Used in connection with collection information statements, these are expenses that are higher than "necessary," but may be allowed if the tax liability can be paid within three years.

contribution A defense by some responsible persons in trust fund recovery penalty cases whereby they assert that another person was also responsible and should "contribute" to the payment.

correspondence audit An audit in which the taxpayer corresponds with the IRS but does not normally speak with an agent, either by phone or face-to-face.

court-ordered payments In connection with collection information statements, these are payments ordered by a court that may have priority over the federal tax lien and therefore may be allowable as "necessary" expenses.

Currently Not Collectible Accounts Delinquent tax accounts that the IRS has determined may not be collected efficiently at the present time, but for which the statute of limitations has not yet expired.

Direct Debit Installment Agreement A type of installment agreement in which the monthly amount is directly debited from the taxpayer's bank account.

discovery The formal process used by the United States Tax Court and other courts whereby the taxpayer and the IRS "discover" the facts and legal theories of the other side's case.

Discriminant Information Function (DIF) The scoring system used to identify tax returns for further examination and possible audit.

electronic return originators Firms and organizations specifically authorized by the IRS to transmit tax returns electronically to the Service.

enrolled actuary An actuary who is specifically authorized to practice before the Internal Revenue Service.

enrolled agents Usually a non-attorney or non-CPA, an enrolled agent is an agent of the taxpayer who has passed an exam and is specifically authorized to practice before the Internal Revenue Service on behalf of taxpayers.

Examination Division The functional division of the IRS that audits tax returns.

Fedworld The Website of the United States Department of Commerce that is authorized to receive tax returns.

field audit The most intensive type of IRS audit, conducted by a field agent at the taxpayer's premises or business.

Final Notice (of Intent to Levy) The legally required notice that preceeds a levy by a minimum of thirty days.

fraudulent conveyance The act of a taxpayer's transferring property to a nontaxpayer in fraud of creditors, with or without adequate consideration, for the purpose of avoiding or evading taxes.

Freedom of Information Act A 1974 statute permitting a citizen to request copies of the government's files pertaining to that citizen.

independent contractor A type of worker who is not an "employee" for purposes of the withholding and social security tax laws.

Information Document Request (IDR) A written request for specifically designated items, usually given by an auditor to a taxpayer or his representative, requesting production of such items on a specific date.

injured spouse One spouse who was due a portion of a refund from a joint return but has not received it.

innocent spouse A spouse who has fulfilled the five requirements of establishing innocent spouse status set forth in the Internal Revenue Code, the result of which is to be relieved of all taxes, penalties, and interest on a joint return.

installment agreement An agreement between the taxpayer and the IRS to pay back taxes, penalties and interest in monthly installments.

Internal Revenue Bulletin A weekly publication of the IRS giving extremely current information, such as interest rates and certain legal interpretations; and publishing revenue rulings, notices, announcements, and so forth.

Internal Revenue Code Title 26 of the United States Code, the basic statute by which the Internal Revenue Service operates.

jeopardy assessment/levy An immediate assessment and seizure of assets, without the otherwise-required statutory waiting periods, where the IRS has determined that collection of the taxes is in jeopardy.

levy The act of seizing a taxpayer's assets, either by service of a Notice of Levy with respect to liquid assets or the placing of a Notice of Seizure on physical assets.

lien An encumbrance on the taxpayer's property. The federal tax lien encumbers all property and rights to property belonging to the taxpayer or in which the taxpayer has an interest.

Market Segment Specialization Program A series of detailed audit guides on specific industries, published by the Internal Revenue Service to guide its agents in the conduct of audits of particular industries.

National Standard Expenses A set of expenses determined by the IRS to be "necessary" for food, clothing, personal care products and miscellaneous expenses in connection with a collection information statement.

necessary living expense An expense determined by the IRS to be necessary, for purposes of a collection information statement.

Ninety-day Letter The formal "Notice of Deficiency," required by statute before the IRS may assess a deficiency; also, the notice that is required in order for the taxpayer to challenge the proposed assessment in the United States Tax Court.

No change report The result of an audit, that proposes no changes in the taxpayer's returns.

nonfiler A person who has failed to file one or more federal income tax returns beyond any possible extension date.

non-wage levy An IRS seizure of assets excluding wages and other periodic payments.

Notice of Deficiency See *Ninety-day Letter.*

notice of federal tax lien The formal recordation of the federal tax lien in the land or court records of the county where real estate is located, or the county where the taxpayer resides.

notice of sale A required notice before the IRS may sell a taxpayer's property.

offer in compromise A settlement of the taxpayer's liability for less than the full amount owed, based on consideration that the taxpayer may never be able to pay the full amount within the statute of limitations on collection.

office audit An audit of a tax return that takes place in the office of the IRS agent.

Office of Appeals See *Appeals.*

Office of Taxpayer Advocate The former Problem Resolution Office, an office designated within the IRS to assist taxpayers in unsnarling "red tape" and in avoiding significant hardship in collection activities.

payroll deduction installment agreement A type of installment agreement whereby the agreed amount is deducted directly from the taxpayer's payroll and paid to the IRS.

petition The formal pleading that begins a case in the United States Tax Court.

Problem Resolution Office See *Office of Taxpayer Advocate.*

protest A letter of disagreement with the proposed result of an IRS audit. Protests are filed with the Office of Appeals.

Revenue agent An IRS officer whose job is to audit federal income tax and other returns.

revenue agent's report A report written by a revenue agent proposing changes in a taxpayer's return, either increasing or decreasing tax, or leaving tax unchanged.

S Corporation A corporation that has elected to be taxed as an S corporation under the Internal Revenue Code, generally relieving the corporation of federal taxation.

sovereign immunity The doctrine that holds that the United States government may not be sued without its consent.

Special Procedures Section The office within the Collection Division of the IRS that handles special collection cases and bankruptcy cases, as well as federal tax lien issues.

statute of limitations A time limit for audit or collection, or for filing various claims by the taxpayer.

Substitute for Return An administrative procedure under which the IRS files papers enabling it to assess a liability for an unfiled return, which papers do not formally constitute a "tax return."

Taxpayer Assistance Order An internal injunction granted by the Office of Taxpayer Advocate against the Collection Division or other office within the IRS specifically forbidding it from taking certain action or requiring it to take certain action, all on behalf of the taxpayer.

Taxpayer Compliance Measurement Program A type of audit in which the IRS intensively examines individual or business returns, generally used for research purposes.

Taxpayer delinquent account An account for a specific tax period sent to a local IRS office for collection of a delinquency.

Trust Fund Recovery Penalty A personal assessment against "responsible persons" of corporations for the trust fund portion of employment taxes not paid over to the IRS.

United States Tax Court A court established under Article I of the Constitution to hear and resolve tax cases, predominantly cases involving income tax.

voluntary payment rule A rule under which a taxpayer may designate the type of liability, and the tax period, to which a specific payment must be applied.

wage levy A levy directly on the wages or other remuneration of the taxpayer.

Resource Guide

Here are Web sites, telephone numbers, and addresses of IRS Problems Reso;ution Offices and other useful numbers

The IRS Web site is:

www.irs.ustreas.gov

The Nationwide General IRS Number is:

(800) 829-1040

Service Center Problem Resolution Offices

Correspondence and facsimile transmissions should be addressed to:

Problem Resolution Office
Internal Revenue Service

with the appropriate address from the following list.
Street addresses are provided in case you wish to
send correspondence by courier. FAX numbers are
also listed in case you prefer to send information by
facsimile transmission.

Andover Service Center
310 Lowell Street (Stop 120)
Andover, MA 05501
FAX: (978) 474-5640

Atlanta Service Center
P.O. Box 48-549 (Stop 29A)
Doraville, GA 30362

or

4800 Buford Highway (Stop 29-A)
Chamblee, GA 30341
FAX: (770) 455-2527

Austin Compliance Center
3651 Interregional Hwy. (Stop 1005 AUSC)
Austin, TX 78741
FAX: (512) 460-1930

or

Austin Service Center
P.O. Box 934 (Stop 1005)
Austin, TX 78767

Bookhaven Service Center
P.O. Box 960 (Stop 102)
Holtsville, NY 11742

or

1040 Waverly Avenue (Stop 102)
Holtsville, NY 11742
FAX: (516) 447-4879

Cincinnati Service Center
P.O. Box 12267 (Stop 11)
Covington, KY 41012
FAX: (606) 292-5405

Fresno Service Center
P.O. Box 12161 (Stop 1)
Fresno, CA 93776

or

5045 East Butler Avenue (Stop 1)
Fresno, CA 93888
FAX: (209) 456-5272

Kansas City Service Center
P.O. Box 24551 (Stop 1005)
Kansas City, MO 64131
FAX: (816) 823-1932

Memphis Service Center
5333 Getwell Road (Stop 13)
Memphis, TN 38118
FAX: (901) 546-2181

Ogden Service Center
P.O. Box 9941 (Stop 1005)
Ogden, UT 84409

or

1160 W. 1200 South Street (Stop 1005)
Ogden, UT 84201
FAX: (801) 620-6319

Philadelphia Service Center
P.O. Box 16053, DP 111
Philadelphia, PA 19114
FAX: (215) 516-2677

District Problem Resolution Offices

Correspondence and facsimile transmissions
should be addressed to:

Problem Resolution Office
Internal Revenue Service

with the appropriate address from the following list.

ALABAMA
801 Tom Martin Drive
Rm-268-PR
Birmingham, AL 35211
(205) 912-5631
FAX: (205) 912-5632

ALASKA
949 East 36th Ave. (Stop A-405)
Anchorage, AK 99508
(907) 271-6877
FAX: (907) 271-6824

ARIZONA
210 E. Earll Dr. (Stop 1005 PX)
Phoenix, AZ 85012
(602) 207-8240
FAX: (602) 207-8250

ARKANSAS
700 West Capital St. (Stop 1005 LIT)
Little Rock, AR 72201
(501) 324-6144
FAX: (501) 324-5183

CALIFORNIA
Laguna Niguel District
P.O. Box 30207
Laguna Niguel, CA 92607

or

24000 Avila Rd., Rm 3362
Laguna Niguel, CA 92677
(714) 360-2175
FAX: (714) 360-2463

Los Angeles District
300 N. Los Angeles St.
Room 5206 (Stop LA 1005)
Los Angeles, CA 90012
(213) 894-6954
FAX: (213) 894-6365

Sacramento District
P.O. Box 2900 (Stop SA 5043)
Sacramento, CA 95812

or

4330 Watt Ave.
North Highlands, CA 95660
(916) 974-5007
FAX: (916) 974-5902

San Francisco District
1301 Clay St., Suite 1540 S
Oakland, CA 94612
(510) 637-2703
FAX: (510) 637-2715

San Jose District
P.O. Box 100 (Stop MS0004)
San Jose, CA 95103

or

55 S. Market Street, Room 900
San Jose, CA 95113
(408) 494-8210
FAX: (408) 494-8065

COLORADO
600 17th St. (Stop 1005)
Denver, CO 80202
(303) 446-1012
FAX: (303) 446-1011

CONNECTICUT
135 High St. (Stop 219)
Hartford, CT 06103
(860) 240-4179
FAX: (860) 240-4023

DELAWARE
409 Silverside Rd.
Wilmington, DE 19809
(302) 791-4511
FAX: (302) 791-4511

DISTRICT OF COLUMBIA
P.O. Box 1553, Room 620A
Baltimore, MD 21203

or

31 Hopkins Plaza, Room 620A
Baltimore, MD 21201
(410) 962-2082
FAX: (410) 962-9340

FLORIDA
Ft. Lauderdale District
P.O. Box 17167
Plantation, FL 3318

or

One North University Dr.
Room A-312
Plantation, FL 33324
(954) 423-7677
FAX: (954) 423-7685

Jacksonville District
400 West Bay Street, Suite 35045
Jacksonville, FL 32202
(904) 232-3440
FAX: (904) 232-2266

GEORGIA
P.O. Box 1065 (Stop 202-D)
Room 1520
Atlanta, GA 30370

or

401 West Peachtree Street, N.W.
Summit Bldg., Room 1520
(Stop 202-D)
Atlanta, GA 30365
(404) 331-5232
FAX: (404) 730-3438

HAWAII
300 Ala Moana Blvd.
Box 50089 H-405
Honolulu, HI 96850
(808) 541-1158
FAX: (808) 541-3379

IDAHO
550 West Fort Street
Box 041
Boise, ID 83724
(208) 334-1324
FAX: (208) 334-9663

ILLINOIS
Chicago District
230 S. Dearborn Street
Room 3214 (Stop 1005-CHI)
Chicago, IL 60604
(312) 886-9183
FAX: (312) 886-1564

Springfield District
320 West Washington Street
(Stop 1005 SPD)
Springfield, IL 62701
(217) 527-6382
FAX: (217) 527-6332

INDIANA
P.O. Box 44687 (Stop 11)
Indianapolis, IN 46244

or

575 N. Pennsylvania Street
(Stop 11)
Indianapolis, IN 46204
(317) 226-6332
FAX: (317) 226-6222

IOWA
210 Walnut Street (Stop 1005 DSM)
Des Moines, IA 50309
(515) 284-4780
FAX: (515) 284-6645

KANSAS
271 W. 3rd Street, North
(Stop 1005 WIC)
Wichita, KS 67202
(316) 352-7506
FAX: (316) 352-7212

KENTUCKY
600 Dr. MLK Jr. Pl.
Federal Bldg., Room 363
Louisville, KY 40202
(502) 582-6030
FAX: (502) 582-6463

LOUISIANA
600 South Maestri Place
(Stop 12)
New Orleans, LA 70130
(504) 558-3001
FAX: (504) 558-3250

MAINE
68 Sewall Street, Rm. 311-PRP
Augusta, ME 04330
(207) 622-8528
FAX: (207) 622-8458

MARYLAND
P.O. Box 1553
Room 620A
Baltimore, MD 21203

or

31 Hopkins Plaza
Room 620A
Baltimore, MD 21201
(410) 962-2082
FAX: (410) 962-9340

MASSACHUSETTS
JFK P.O. Box 9112
Boston, MA 02203
(617) 565-1857
FAX: (617) 565-4959

MICHIGAN
P.O. Box 330500 (Stop 7)
Detroit, MI 48232

or

McNamara Federal Bldg.
477 Michigan Avenue, Rm. 2429
Detroit, MI 48226
(313) 628-3670
FAX: (313) 226-3502

MINNESOTA
316 N. Robert Street
Stop 1005 STP
St. Paul, MN 55101
(612) 290-3628
FAX: (612) 290-4236

MISSISSIPPI
100 W Capitol Street
(Stop 31)
Jackson, MS 39269
(601) 965-4800
FAX: (601) 965-5251

MISSOURI
P.O. Box 66776 (Stop 1005 STL)
St. Louis, MO 63166

or

Robert A. Young Bldg.
1222 Spruce Street
(Stop 1005 STL)
St. Louis, MO 63103
(314) 539-6770
FAX: (314) 539-2362

MONTANA
Federal Building
301 S. Park (Stop 1005 HEL)
Helena, MT 59626
(406) 441-1022
FAX: (406) 441-1035

NEBRASKA
106 S. 15th Street (Stop 1005 OMA)
Omaha, NE 68102
(402) 221-4181
FAX: (402) 221-3051

NEVADA
4750 W. Oakey Blvd.
Room 303
Las Vegas, NV 89102
(702) 455-1241
FAX: (702) 455-1216

NEW HAMPSHIRE
P.O. Box 720
Portsmouth, NH 03802

or

Federal Office Bldg.
80 Daniel Street
Portsmouth, NH 03801
(603) 433-0571
FAX: (603) 433-0739

NEW JERSEY
P.O. Box 1143
Newark, NJ 07102

or

970 Broad Street
Newark, NJ 07102
(973) 645-6698
FAX: (973) 645-3323

NEW MEXICO
5338 Montgomery Blvd., N.E.
(Stop 1005 ALB)
Albuquerque, NM 87109
(505) 837-5505
FAX: (505) 837-5519

NEW YORK
Albany District
Leo O'Brien Federal Bldg.
Room 617
Clinton Ave. & N. Pearl Street
Albany, NY 12207
(518) 431-4435
FX: (518) 431-4490

Brooklyn District
G.P.O. Box R
Brooklyn, NY 11202

or

10 Metro Tech Center
625 Fulton Street
Brooklyn, NY 11201
(718) 488-2080
FAX: (718) 488-3100

Buffalo District
P.O. Box 500
Niagara Square Station
Buffalo, NY 14201

or

111 West Huron Street
Thaddeus J. Dulski FOB
Buffalo, NY 14202
(716) 551-4574
FAX: (716) 551-5473

Manhattan District
P.O. Box 408
Church Street Station
New York, NY 10008

or

290 Broadway, 7th Floor
New York, NY 10007
(212) 436-1011
FAX: (212) 436-1900

NORTH CAROLINA
320 Federal Place
Room 125
Greensboro, NC 27401
(910) 378-2180
FAX: (910) 378-2495

NORTH DAKOTA
P.O. Box 8
Fargo, ND 58107

or

657 Second Avenue, N. (Stop 1005 FAR)
Fargo, ND 58102
(701) 239-5141
FAX: (701) 239-5104

OHIO
Cincinnati District
55 Main Street, Room 7010
Cincinnati, OH 45202
(513) 684-3094
FAX: (513) 684-6417

Cleveland District
P.O. Box 99709
Cleveland, OH 44199

or

1240 E. Ninth St.
Cleveland, OH 44199
(216) 522-7134
FAX: (216) 522-2947

OKLAHOMA
55 N. Robinson
(Stop 1005 OKC)
Oklahoma City, OK 73102
(405) 297-4055
FAX: (405) 297-4056

OREGON
1220 S.W. 3rd Avenue
(Stop O-405)
Portland, OR 97204
(503) 326-2333
FAX: (503) 326-5453

PENNSYLVANIA
Philadelphia District
P.O. Box 12010
Philadelphia, PA 19106

or

600 Arch Street, Room 7214
Philadelphia, PA 19106
(215) 597-3377
FAX: (215) 597-7341

Pittsburg District
P.O. Box 705
Pittsburg, PA 15230

or

1000 Liberty Avenue
Room 1102
Pittsburg, PA 15222
(412) 395-5987
FAX: (412) 395-4769

RHODE ISLAND
380 Westminster St.
Providence, RI 02903
(401) 528-4492
FAX: (401) 528-4312

SOUTH CAROLINA
1835 Assembly Street
Room 571, MDP 03
Columbia, SC 29201
(803) 253-3029
FAX: (803) 253-3910

SOUTH DAKOTA
115 4th Avenue, S.E.
(Stop 1005 ABE)
Aberdeen, SD 57401
(605) 226-7248
FAX: (605) 226-7270

TENNESSEE
P.O. Box 1107 (Stop 22)
Nashville, TN 37202

or

801 Broadway (Stop 22)
Nashville, TN 37203
(615) 736-5219
FAX: (615) 736-7489

TEXAS
Austin District
300 E. 8th Street
(Stop 1005 AUS)
Austin, TX 78701
(512) 499-5875
FAX: (512) 499-5687

Dallas District
1100 Commerce Street
(Stop MC1005 DAL)
Dallas, TX 75242
(214) 767-1289
FAX: (214) 767-0040

Houston District
1919 Smith Street
(Stop 1005 HOU)
Houston, TX 77002
(713) 209-3660
FAX: (713) 209-3708

UTAH
50 South 200 East
(Stop 1005 SLC)
Salt Lake City, UT 84111
(801) 799-6958
FAX: (801) 779-6957

VERMONT
Courthouse Plaza
199 Main Street
Burlington, VT 05401
(802) 860-2008
FAX: (802) 860-2006

VIRGINIA
P.O. Box 10113
Room 5502
Richmond, VA 23240

or

400 N. 8th Street
Richmond, VA 23240
(804) 771-2643
FAX: (804) 771-2008

WASHINGTON
915 Second Avenue (Stop W-405)
Seattle, WA 98174
(206) 220-6037
FAX: (206) 220-6047

WEST VIRGINIA
P.O. Box 1040, Room 1004
Parkersburg, WV 26102

or

425 Juliana Street
Parkersburg, WV 26101
(304) 420-6616
FAX: (304) 420-6682

WISCONSIN
310 W. Wisconsin Avenue
Room M028 (Stop 1005 MIL)
Milwaukee, WI 53203
(414) 297-3046
FAX: (414) 297-3362

WYOMING
5353 Yellowstone Rd.
Rm. 206A
(Stop 1005 CHE)
Cheyenne, WY 82009
(307) 633-0800
FAX: (307) 633-0880

NATIONAL OFFICE
1111 Constitution Avenue, N.W.
Room 3107 C:PRP
Washington, D.C. 20224
(202) 622-6100
FAX: (202) 622-4318

Taxpayers residing overseas or in the U.S. territories
should write to:

Problem Resolution Office
Internal Revenue Service
Assistant Commissioner
(International)
P.O. Box 44817
L'Enfant Plaza Station
Washington, D.C. 20026-4817

or

950 L'Enfant Plaza, S.W.
Washington, D.C. 20224
(202) 874-1930
FAX: (202) 874-1782

Offer in Compromise resources

Exhibit 5300-45   Guide to Expenses

Exhibit 5300-46   Financial Analysis—
                       Expenses

Exhibit 5300-47   Q & A to Assist in
                       Financial Analysis

Exhibit 5300-48   Total Monthly National
                       Standard Expense

Exhibit 5300-49   Monthly NSE (detail)

Exhibit 5300-50   Housing and Utility
                       Allowances—By State,
                       County, Family Size

Exhibit 5300-51   Automobile Transportation
                       Expenses

IRS seizures

Exhibit 5600-25   Questions and Answers to
                       Assist in Property Seizures

Recommended Reading List

The following publications and forms are useful in the IRS audit and collection matters.

IRS publications

FORM	TITLE
1	Your Rights as a Taxpayer
5	Appeal Rights and Preparation of Protests for Unagreed Cases
15	Circular E, Employer's Tax Guide
334	Tax Guide for Small Business
487	How to Prepare Application Requesting the United States to Release its Right to Redeem Property Secured by a Federal Tax Lien
533	Self-Employment Tax

FORM	TITLE
538	Accounting Periods and Methods
552	Recordkeeping for Individuals
556	Examination of Returns, Appeal Rights, and Claims for Refund
583	Taxpayers Starting a Business
594	Understanding the Collection Process
733	Rewards for Information Provided by Individuals to the Internal Revenue Service
783	Certificate of Discharge of Property from Federal Tax Lien
784	Application for Certificate of Subordination of Federal Tax Lien
794	Favorable Determination Letter
908	Bankruptcy and Other Debt Cancellation
910	Guide to Free Tax Services
919	Is My Withholding Correct for 1994?
937	Employment Taxes
947	Practice Before the IRS and Power of Attorney
1024	Certificate of Nonattachment of Federal Tax Lien
1035	Extending the Tax Assessment Period

FORM	TITLE
1153	How to Prepare Application for Certificate of Subordination of Federal Estate Tax Lien Under Section 6325(d)(3) of the Internal Revenue Code
1192	Catalog of Reproducible Forms, Instructions, and Publications
1345	Handbook for Electronic Filers of Individual Income Tax Returns
1383	The Correspondence Process (Income Tax Accounts)
1415	Federal Tax Compliance Research: Individual Income Tax Cap Estimates for 1985, 1988, and 1992
1450	Request for Release of Federal Tax Lien
1494	Table for Figuring Amount Exempt from Levy on Wages, Salary, and Other Income
1554	Obligations of Participants in the Electronic Filing Program for Form 1040, U.S. Individual Income Tax Return
1586	Reasonable Cause Regulations and Requirements As They Apply to Missing and Incorrect TINs

Important Documents

Forms useful in IRS audit and collection matters:

FORM	TITLE
SS-4	Application for Employer Identification Number
SS-8	Determination of Employee Work Status for Purposes of Federal Employment Taxes and Income Tax Withholding
SS-10	Consent to Extend the Time to Assess Employment Taxes
23	Application for Enrollment to Practice Before the Internal Revenue Service
211	Application for Reward for Original Information

Appendix D

FORM	TITLE
433-A	Collection Information Statement for Individuals
433-B	Collection Information Statement for Businesses
433-B(SP)	Information de Cobro—Informe Personal para Negocios
433-D	Installment Agreement
433-F	Collection Information Statement
433-F(SP)	Declaration de Informacion Sobre Coleccion
656	Offer in Compromise
668-A(c)	Notice of Levy
668-B	Levy
668-C	Final Demand
668-D	Release of Levy/Release of Property from Levy
668-W(c) (DO)	Notice of Levy on Wages, Salary, and Other Income
668(Y)	Notice of Federal Tax Lien Under Internal Revenue Laws

FORM	TITLE
669-A	Certificate of Discharge of Property from Federal Tax Lien (Sec. 6325(b)(1))
669-B	Certificate of Discharge of Property from Federal Tax Lien (Sec. 6325(b)(2)(A))
669-C	Certificate of Discharge of Property from Federal Tax Lien (Sec. 6325(b)(2)(B))
669-D	Certificate of Subordination of Federal Tax Lien (Sec. 6325(d)(1))
669-E	Certificate of Subordination of Federal Tax Lien (Sec. 6325(d)(2))
669-F	Certificate of Subordination of Federal Estate Tax Lien (Sec. 6325(d)(3))
792	United States Certificate Discharging Property Subject to Estate Tax Lien
843	Claim for Refund and Request for Abatement
866	Agreement as to Final Determination of Tax Liability
870	Waiver of Restrictions on Assessment and Collection of Deficiency in Tax and Acceptance of Overassessment

FORM	TITLE
870-AD	Offer to Waive Restrictions on Assessment and Collection of Tax Deficiency to Accept Overassessment
870-E	Waiver of Restrictions on Assessment and Collection of Deficiency and Acceptance of Overassessment
872	Consent to Extend the Time to Assess Tax
872-A	Special Consent to Extend the Time to Assess Tax
872-A(C)	Special Consent to Extend the Time to Assess Tax
900	Tax Collection Waiver
906	Closing Agreement on Final Determination Covering Specific Matters
907	Agreement to Extend the Time to Bring Suit
911	Application for Taxpayer Assistance Order (ATAO) to Relieve Hardship
921	Consent to Extend the Time to Assess Income Tax
945	Annual Return of Withheld Federal Income Tax

FORM	TITLE
945-A	Annual Record of Federal Tax Liability
952	Consent to Extend Period of Limitation on Assessment of Income Taxes
1117	Income Tax Surety Bond
1127	Application for Extension of Time for Payment of Tax
1128	Application to Adopt, Change or Retain a Tax Year
1902-B	Report of Individual Income Tax Examination Changes
2039	Summons
2045	Transferee Agreement
2063	U.S. Departing Alien Income Tax Statement
2222	Sealed Bid for Purchase of Seized Property
2261	Collateral Agreement
2261-A	Collateral Agreement
2261-C	Collateral Agreement
2270	Demand to Exhibit Books and Records

FORM	TITLE
2297	Waiver of Statutory Notification of Claim Disallowance
2433	Notice of Seizure
2434-A	Notice of Sealed Bid Sale
2435	Certificate of Sale of Seized Property
2436	Seized Property Sale Report
2504	Agreement to Assessment and Collection of Additional Tax and Acceptance of Overassessment (Excise or Employment Tax)
2688	Application for Additional Extension of Time to File U.S. Individual Income Tax Return
2725	Document Receipt
2750	Waiver Extending Statutory Period for Assessment of Trust Fund Recovery Penalty
2751	Proposed Assessment of Trust Fund Recovery Penalty
2751-AD	Trust Fund Recovery Penalty—Offer of Agreement to Assessment and Collection
2769	Computation of Deposit Penalty

FORM	TITLE
2797	Referral Report for Potential Fraud Cases
2848	Power of Attorney and Declaration of Representative
3040	Authorization to Apply Offer in Compromise Deposit to Liability
3242	Request for Information from Employer
3363	Acceptance of Proposed Disallowance of Claim for Refund or Credit
3439	Statement of Annual Income (Individual)
3439-A	Statement of Annual Income (Corporation)
3610	Audit Statement
3623	Statement of Account
3911	Taxpayer Statement Regarding Refund
3913	Request for Refund Check Cancellation
4089	Notice of Deficiency-Waiver
4089-A	Notice of Deficiency Statement

FORM	TITLE
4180	Report of Interview with Individual Relative to Trust Fund Recovery Penalty or Personal Liability for Excise Tax
4183	Recommendation re Trust Fund Recovery Penalty Assessment
4219	Statement of Liability of Lender, Surety, or Other Person for Withholding Taxes
4417-A	Request for Federal Tax Deposit Coupon Books
4419	Application for Filing Information Returns Magnetically/Electronically
4422	Application for Certificate Discharging Property Subject to Estate Tax Lien
4490	Proof of Claim for Internal Revenue Taxes
4491-A	Proof of Claim for Internal Revenue Taxes (Bankruptcy Act Proceedings—Administrative Claims)
4506	Request for Copy or Transcript of Tax Form
4549-E	Income Tax Discrepancy Adjustments

FORM	TITLE
4571	Explanation for Filing Return Late or Paying Tax Late
4585	Minimum Bid Worksheet
4669	Statement of Payments Received
4670	Request for Relief from Payment of Income Tax Withholding
4700	Examination Workpapers
4789	Currency Transaction Report
4789-T	Currency Transaction Report
4822	Statement of Annual Estimated Personal and Family Expenses
4862	Statement of Income Tax Changes
4868	Application for Automatic Extension of Time to File U.S. Individual Income Tax Return
5318	Penalties for Failure to File Tax Return and Pay Tax
5495	Request for Discharge from Personal Liability Under Internal Revenue Code Section 6905

FORM	TITLE
6018	Consent to Proposed Adverse Action
6112	Prior Years' Tax Forms Order
6166	Certification of Filing a Tax Return
6338	Proof of Claim for Internal Revenue Taxes (Bankruptcy Code Cases)
6513	Extension of Time to File Not Allowed
6637	Summons—Collection Information Statement
6638	Summons—Income Tax Return
6711	Proposed changes to Income, Deductions, or Withholding
6735	Computation of Penalty (Internal Revenue Code 6651)
6754	Examination Classification Checksheet
6847	Consent for Internal Revenue Service to Release Tax Information
6863	Invoice and Authorization for Payment of Administrative Summons Expenses
6882	IDRS/Master File Information Request

FORM	TITLE
7018	Employer's Order Blank for Forms
8109-B	Federal Tax Deposit Coupon
8265	Form for Verifying Deposits That Were Not Made
8275	Disclosure Statement
8275-R	Regulation Disclosure Statement
8379	Injured Spouse Claim and Allocation
8453	U.S. Individual Income Tax Declaration for Electronic Filing
8599	Request for Missing Information Regarding Refund
8626	Agreement to Rescind Notice of Deficiency
8633	Application to Participate in the Electronic Filing Program
8821	Tax Information Authorization
8822	Change of Address
8888	Direct Deposit Refund
9041	Application for Electronical/Magnetic Media Filing of Business and Employee Benefit Plan Returns

FORM	TITLE
9325	General Information for Taxpayers Who File Returns Electronically
9325-A	Acknowledgment and General Information for Taxpayers Who File Returns Electronically
9358	Information About Your Tax Return
9465	Installment Agreement Request

Personal and Business Penalties

Personal penalties

1. Late filing of a tax return

- **How much**? 5% of amount due per month; 25% maximum

- **When does the IRS impose or recommend it?** When you file your return; during audit; after assessment of tax

- **When can you appeal it?** When you file your return; when the IRS bills you; during audit; after payment, in claim for refund; in bankruptcy

- **This penalty can be excused if you show:** "Reasonable cause" and no willful neglect

- **What form should you use?** Form 2751 or letter; Form 843; Bankruptcy

- **Where do you send an appeal?** Service Center; Office of Appeals; Bankruptcy Court; IRS Auditor; Federal Court

2. Late payment of a balance due

- **How much?** 0.5% per month of amount due, escalating to 1%; 25% maximum; not imposed where late filing is imposed

- **When does the IRS impose or recommend it?** When you file your return; after an additional assessment of tax

- **When can you appeal it?** When you file your return; when the IRS bills you; after payment, in claim for refund; in bankruptcy

- **This penalty can be excused if you show:** "Reasonable cause" and no willful neglect

- **What form should you use?** Form 2751 or letter; Form 843; bankruptcy

- **Where do you send an appeal?** Service Center; Office of Appeals; Bankruptcy Court; IRS Auditor; Federal Court

3. Fraudulent failure to file

- **How much?** 15% per month; 75% maximum

- **When does the IRS impose or recommend it?** When you file your return; during audit

- **When can you appeal it?** When you file return; when the IRS bills you; after payment, in claim for refund; in bankruptcy

- **This penalty can be excused if you show:** No intent to evade the filing requirement

- **What form should you use?** Form 2751 or letter; Form 843; Bankruptcy

- **Where do you send an appeal?** Service Center; Office of Appeals; Bankruptcy Court; IRS Auditor; Federal Court

4. Fraud

- **How much?** 75% of amount due to fraud

- **When does the IRS impose or recommend it?** When you file your return; during audit

- **When can you appeal it?** When you file your return; when the IRS bills you; during audit; after payment, in claim for refund; in bankruptcy

- **This penalty can be excused if you show:** No intent to evade tax; "reasonable cause"

- **What form should you use?** Form 2751 or letter; Form 843; Bankruptcy

- **Where do you send an appeal?** Service Center; Office of Appeals; Bankruptcy Court; IRS Auditor; Federal Court

5. Estimated tax penalty

- **How much?** Penalty rate × amount underpaid × period of underpayment

- **When does the IRS impose or recommend it?** During audit; when you file your return

- **When can you appeal it?** When you file your return; when the IRS bills you; during audit; after payment, in claim for refund; in bankruptcy

- **This penalty can be excused if you show:** Casualty, disaster, or unusual circumstances so that penalty is against equity and good conscience

- **What form should you use?** Form 2751 or letter; Form 843; Bankruptcy; Form 2210, 2210F

- **Where do you send an appeal?** Service Center; Office of Appeals; Bankruptcy Court; Federal Court; IRS Auditor

6. Bad-check penalty

- **How much?** 2% of the check; if check is under $750, lesser of $150 and amount of check

- **When does the IRS impose or recommend it?** When you bounce a check to the IRS

- **When can you appeal it?** When you send the check in; after payment, in claim for refund; in bankruptcy

- **This penalty can be excused if you show:** "Reasonable cause" and good-faith belief that check was good

- **What form should you use?** Form 2751 or letter; bankruptcy

- **Where do you send an appeal?** Service Center; Office of Appeals; Bankruptcy Court; Federal Court; IRS Agent

7. Negligence

- **How much?** 20% of additional tax due

- **When does the IRS impose or recommend it?** During audit

- **When can you appeal it?** During audit; at appeals; in claim for refund; in bankruptcy

- **This penalty can be excused if you show:** Good faith and "reasonable cause," or no intentional disregard of IRS rules or regulations; adequate disclosure of nonfrivolous position

- **What form should you use?** Protest; Form 843; Bankruptcy

- **Where do you send an appeal?** Office of Appeals; Bankruptcy Court; IRS Auditor; Federal Court

8. Substantial understatement of tax in your return

- **How much?** In general, 20% of the understatement of tax

- **When does the IRS impose or recommend it?** During audit

- **When can you appeal it?** During audit; at appeals; in claim for refund; in bankruptcy

- **This penalty can be excused if you show:** Good-faith and "reasonable cause," or no intentional disregard of IRS rules or regulations; disclosure of the nonfrivolous item on the return; substantial authority for your position

- **What form should you use?** Protest; Form 843; Letter; Bankruptcy

- **Where do you send an appeal?** Office of Appeals; Bankruptcy Court; IRS Auditor; Federal Court

Business penalties

1. Failure to deposit payroll taxes

- **How much?** Up to 15%

- **When does the IRS impose or recommend it?** When you make the deposit or file the quarterly return

- **When can you appeal it?** When you make the deposit or file the quarterly return; after payment, in claim for refund; in bankruptcy

- **This penalty can be excused if you show:** Reasonable cause and no willful neglect; ordinary business care and prudence

- **What form should you use?** Form 2751 or letter; Form 843

- **Where do you send an appeal?** Service Center; Office of Appeals; Federal Court; Bankruptcy Court

2. Trust Fund Recovery

See Chapter 6 for details.

The *Unofficial Guide*™ Reader Questionnaire

If you would like to express your opinion about dealing with the IRS or this guide, please complete this questionnaire and mail it to:

The *Unofficial Guide*™ Reader Questionnaire
Macmillan Lifestyle Group
1633 Broadway, Floor 7
New York, NY 10019-6785

Gender: ___ M   ___ F

Age: ___ Under 30   ___ 31–40   ___ 41–50
___ Over 50

Education: ___ High school   ___ College
___ Graduate/Professional

What is your occupation?

_____

How did you hear about this guide?
___ Friend or relative
___ Newspaper, magazine, or Internet
___ Radio or TV
___ Recommended at bookstore
___ Recommended by librarian
___ Picked it up on my own
___ Familiar with the *Unofficial Guide*™ travel series

Did you go to the bookstore specifically for a book on dealing with the IRS?   Yes ___   No ___

Have you used any other *Unofficial Guides*™?
Yes ___   No ___

If Yes, which ones?

_____
_____
_____

What other book(s) on dealing with the IRS have you purchased?

_____

_____

_____

Was this book:
___ more helpful than other(s)
___ less helpful than other(s)

Do you think this book was worth its price?
Yes ___ No ___

Did this book cover all topics related to dealing with the IRS adequately? Yes ___ No ___

Please explain your answer:

_____

_____

_____

Were there any specific sections in this book that were of particular help to you? Yes ___ No ___

Please explain your answer:

_____

_____

_____

On a scale of 1 to 10, with 10 being the best rating, how would you rate this guide? ___

What other titles would you like to see published in the _Unofficial Guide_™ series?

_____

_____

Are _Unofficial Guides_™ readily available in your area? Yes ___ No ___

Other comments:

_____

_____

_____

_____

Get the inside scoop...with the *Unofficial Guides*™!

The Unofficial Guide to Acing the Interview
    ISBN: 0-02-862924-8   Price: $15.95
The Unofficial Guide to Alternative Medicine
    ISBN: 0-02-862526-9   Price: $15.95
The Unofficial Guide to Buying or Leasing a Car
    ISBN: 0-02-862524-2   Price: $15.95
The Unofficial Guide to Buying a Home
    ISBN: 0-02-862461-0   Price: $15.95
The Unofficial Guide to Childcare
    ISBN: 0-02-862457-2   Price: $15.95
The Unofficial Guide to Cosmetic Surgery
    ISBN: 0-02-862522-6   Price: $15.95
The Unofficial Guide to Divorce
    ISBN: 0-02-862455-6   Price: $15.95
The Unofficial Guide to Earning What You Deserve
    ISBN: 0-02-862716-4   Price: $15.95
The Unofficial Guide to Hiring and Firing People
    ISBN: 0-02-862460-2   Price: $15.95
The Unofficial Guide to Hiring Contractors
    ISBN: 0-02-862523-4   Price: $15.95
The Unofficial Guide to Investing
    ISBN: 0-02-862458-0   Price: $15.95
The Unofficial Guide to Planning Your Wedding
    ISBN: 0-02-862459-9   Price: $15.95

All books in the *Unofficial Guide*™ series are available at your local bookseller, or by calling 1-800-428-5331.

About the Author

Robert G. Nath can tell you everything you need to know about dealing with the IRS. His views on IRS matters have been quoted in the national media. He is a practicing attorney with more than 20 years' experience in IRS-related matters, both with the Department of Justice and in private practice. He has written and taught widely on tax topics for lawyers, accountants, and the public. His views on IRS matters have been quoted in national media. Mr. Nath is a partner in the Fairfax, Virginia law firm of Odin, Feldman & Pittleman, P.C., outside of Washington, DC.